"[Patricia] Evangelista makes us feel the fear and grief that she felt as she chronicled what Duterte was doing to her country. But appealing to our emotions is only part of it; what makes this book so striking is that she wants us to think about what happened, too. She pays close attention to language, and not only because she is a writer. Language can be used to communicate, to deny, to threaten, to cajole. Duterte's language is coarse and degrading. Evangelista's is evocative and exacting." —*The New York Times*

"A powerful story of disillusionment . . . Evangelista seamlessly segues from her own life story into a riveting police procedural. . . . [Her] book is an extraordinary testament to half a decade of state-sanctioned terror. It's also a timely warning for the state of democracy." —*The Atlantic*

"It is a cliché to compare such writers to George Orwell or, more lately, with justice, Martha Gellhorn. But, if the shoe fits . . . [Evangelista] has written a journalistic masterpiece. She is a very rare talent." —*The New Yorker*

"One of the most harrowing and brave books published this year . . . [Evangelista is] unflinching in bearing witness to the thousands of dead killed under Duterte's reign of terror, which he claimed was largely focused on drug dealers and users, but which wreaked havoc on almost every part of Filipino society." —*Time*

"Evangelista has written an intense, emotional lamentation for the thousands of suspected drug pushers, users, and innocent victims—including children—extrajudicially executed by corrupt cops and vigilantes during the rule of Filipino president Rodrigo Duterte from 2016 to 2022." —*Foreign Affairs*

"A landmark work of investigative reporting by a writer of formidable courage . . . Patricia Evangelista's searing account is not only the definitive chronicle of a reign of terror in the Philippines, but a warning to the rest of the world about the true dangers of despotism—its nightmarish consequences and its terrible human cost."

—Patrick Radden Keefe, *New York Times* bestselling author of *Empire of Pain*

"Completely astounding, and beautifully written, *Some People Need Killing* is a priceless act of documentation. Patricia Evangelista's account of Rodrigo Duterte's so-called drug war, and the conditions that made his regime possible, is one of the bravest things I have ever seen committed to paper. As each devastating page shows, the horrors of this war will echo for years to come."

—Jia Tolentino, *New York Times* bestselling author of *Trick Mirror*

"Tragic, elegant, vital . . . Patricia Evangelista risked her life to tell this story."
—Tara Westover, *New York Times* bestselling author of *Educated*

"Patricia Evangelista exposes the evil in her country with perfect clarity fueled by profound rage, her voice at once utterly beautiful and terrifyingly vulnerable. In short, clear sentences packed with faithfully recorded details, she reveals the nature of unbridled cruelty with a relentless insightfulness that I have not encountered since the work of Hannah Arendt. This is an account of a dark chapter in the Philippines, an examination of how murder was conflated with salvation in a violent society. Ultimately, however, it transcends its ostensible subject and becomes a meditation on the disabling pathos of self-delusion, a study of manipulation and corruption as they occur in conflict after conflict across the world. Few of history's grimmest chapters have had the fortune to be narrated by such a withering, ironic, witty, devastatingly brilliant observer. You may think you are inured to shock, but this book is an exploding bomb that will damage you anew, making you wiser as it does so."

—Andrew Solomon, National Book Award–winning author of *Far and Away*

"In this haunting work of memoir and reportage, Patricia Evangelista both describes the origins of autocratic rule in the Philippines and explains its universal significance. The cynicism of voters, the opportunism of Filipino politicians, the appeal of brutality and violence to both groups—all of this will be familiar to readers, wherever they are from."

—Anne Applebaum, Pulitzer Prize–winning author of *Twilight of Democracy*

SOME PEOPLE NEED KILLING

A MEMOIR OF MURDER
IN MY COUNTRY

PATRICIA EVANGELISTA

RANDOM HOUSE

NEW YORK

Published in the United States by Random House, an imprint and division of
Penguin Random House LLC, New York.

RANDOM HOUSE and the HOUSE colophon are registered trademarks of
Penguin Random House LLC.

Originally published in hardcover in the United States by
Random House, an imprint and division of
Penguin Random House LLC, in 2023.

Library of Congress Cataloging-in-Publication Data
Names: Evangelista, Patricia, author.
Title: Some people need killing: a memoir of murder in my country /
by Patricia Evangelista. Other titles: Memoir of murder in my country
Description: First edition. | New York: Random House, 2023
Identifiers: LCCN 2023019108 (print) | LCCN 2023019109 (ebook) |
ISBN 9780593133149 (paperback) | ISBN 9780593133156 (ebook)
Subjects: LCSH: Duterte, Rodrigo Roa, 1945– | Extrajudicial executions—
Philippines. | Drug control—Philippines. | Drug dealers—Violence against—
Philippines. | Drug addicts—Violence against—Philippines. |
Police brutality—Philippines. | Vigilantes—Philippines. |
Philippines—Politics and government—21st century.
Classification: LCC DS686.616.D88 E93 2023 (print) |
LCC DS686.616.D88 (ebook) | DDC 364.409599—dc23/eng/20230603
LC record available at https://lccn.loc.gov/2023019108
LC ebook record available at https://lccn.loc.gov/2023019109

Printed in the United States of America on acid-free paper

randomhousebooks.com

2 4 6 8 9 7 5 3 1

Book design by Jo Anne Metsch

*This book is dedicated to the survivors of the drug war,
named and unnamed, who have chosen to bear witness.
Without their courage, this record would not exist.*

What I want to do is instill fear.

—MAYOR RODRIGO ROA DUTERTE

Contents

Prologue

Every day, for a period of a little more than seven months beginning in 2016, the *Philippine Daily Inquirer* maintained what it called the Kill List. It was a public record of the dead, fed by reports from correspondents across the country. The circumstances of death were brief. The entries were numbered and chronological. The locations were limited to towns, cities, and provinces, without the specificity of street addresses. Names were recorded when they were available, numbers were used when they were not.

The first "unidentified suspected drug pusher," for example, was killed on July 1, the first day of Rodrigo Duterte's administration, the same morning that Jimmy Reformado, fifth most wanted drug pusher in the city of Tiaong, was shot by "unknown hitmen." The next day, July 2, Victorio Abutal, the most wanted drug pusher in the town of Lucban, was "killed by unknown hitmen in front of his wife" an hour and ten minutes before the death of Marvin Cuadra, second most wanted, less than fourteen hours before the seventh most wanted, Constancio Forbes, was "killed at close range outside a lottery betting station." A day later, on July 3, Arnel Gapacaspan, the most wanted drug pusher of San Antonio, was killed "by unknown hitmen who barged into his house" at exactly the same time that Orlan Untalan, tenth most wanted in Dolores, was "found dead in a spillway, body laden with bullet holes."

"Unknown hitmen" was a common phrase, but it was the nature of their victims—suspected drug pusher, suspected drug dealer, at large on drug charges, on the local drug list, most wanted—that demonstrated that what was occurring was far from random. These were targeted killings, as President Duterte had promised, directed against "people who would threaten to destroy my country."

The methods were limited only by the killers' imaginations. There was the man "found dead after being abducted from his house." There were the three "found dead in a canal, blinded and hogtied." There was the man "shot in the head in his bedroom" and the man killed at seven in the morning "in front of his daughter's elementary school." The daily death toll sometimes rose to double digits, as it did on July 9, beginning at midnight with a suspected drug dealer's aide named Danilo Enopia Morsiquillo, who was shot as he slept beside his girlfriend. The twelve other deaths that day varied in means and disposition. One, a former overseas worker, was shot as he drove down the highway. Two were found strangled under cardboard boxes with signs calling them criminals. Three others were found dead with "gunshot wounds to the head and mouths covered with packing tape." The rest were drug suspects—"killed by unknown hitmen."

None of these deaths were officially at the hands of the police. If the government was to be believed, these killings had been committed by private citizens and members of drug cartels, some of whom used the war as a cover to silence possible informants.

The constancy and sheer velocity required its own nomenclature. They were drug-related deaths. They were illegal killings. They were targeted assassinations, salvagings, body dumps, drive-by shootings. They were "casualties in the Duterte administration's war on crime," or, as the news network ABS-CBN would put it, "those who perished." Even Philippine officials seemed unable to agree on the terminology. One senator called them "summary killings." The interior secretary called them "alleged vigilante-style killings of drug personalities."

There is language for this phenomenon. The term is "extrajudicial killings." It was the single phrase that became commonplace on the street and on television, so common that a Senate resolution called for sessions investigating "the recent rampant extrajudicial killings and summary executions of criminals." The repetition forced a shorthand—EJK. The press used it as a qualifier. The victims' families used it as a verb. The critics used it as an accusation.

From the beginning of the Duterte era, recording these deaths became my job. As a field correspondent for Rappler in Manila, I was one of the reporters covering the results of the president's pledge to destroy anyone—without charge or trial—whom he or the police or any of a number of vigilantes suspected of taking or selling drugs. The volume of Duterte's dead was at times overwhelming, as was covering the powerful in a country where the powerful refuse to be held to account.

I ran away halfway through the war.

At the time, I was investigating a series of killings in the capital. It was slow work. I hunted down witnesses. I culled official reports. I met men who detailed the precise manner in which they killed their own neighbors on orders from above, then sent interview requests to the police officers they accused. Rappler decided my presence in Manila was a security risk. I agreed. It was safer to assume that the self-interest preventing vigilantes from shooting me on sight was unlikely to hold. My editor delayed publication until my plane lifted off the tarmac.

All this was why I found myself crossing the Pacific in early October 2018. If the good people of the Logan Nonfiction Fellowship believed I could produce literature, I was happy to pretend I could. The residency was three months long at a wooded estate in upstate New York. It should have come as a relief, but years of covering a state-sanctioned massacre does odd things to the mind. I had learned to qualify every statement and to burn transcripts on my balcony. I had lain awake nights convinced that a misplaced comma could be grounds for criminal libel. For someone with my sort of obsessive imagination, the practical caution required of a drug war reporter morphed into an almost paralyzing paranoia. Nothing was certain. Everyone was lying. The man with the selfie stick was a spy for the cops, or a killer, or a fanatical supporter of the president likely to upload my photo of meeting a source on to Twitter.

The fact that I was occasionally correct fueled the lunacy. Many things were suspect: white vans, flashing lights, spam emails, men on motorcycles, automated credit card transactions, the waiter at the coffee shop, the hotel clerk asking for my billing address, a ringing phone, a dropped call, the doorbell. I read and reread my own stories, hunting for gaps, agonizing over sentence construction, convinced I had missed the error that would get a witness killed. By the time I stood at JFK airport, blank disembarkation form in hand, I couldn't trust my memory to write out my own name. I verified the spelling against my passport. I remember distinctly the compulsion to find a second source—and found it, in my birth certificate.

The Albany countryside was a pretty place, even if a pack of cigarettes did cost thirteen dollars a pop. It was cold. People were warm. There was chocolate mousse for dessert, sometimes berries. I spent most of the first weeks trying to disappear into a fog of *Star Trek* and Agatha Christie, but the residency required I make an honest attempt at producing a book proposal. I did. I wrote about who I was, and where I came from, and what it was like to stand over a corpse at two in the morning.

I signed with a publisher at the end of the residency, committing to a first-person account of the Philippine drug war. It happened fast. I didn't intend to lie. That promise of intimacy was a distant thing, discussed inside a glass-walled conference room one winter morning, thousands of miles away from the heavy heat of a Manila under the gun.

I went home. I began to write. The first draft was a carefully detailed 73,000 words describing the circumstances of every death, the crime scenes so many and so thick on the page that it wasn't possible to distinguish one corpse from the next. It was reportage, cold and precise. Nowhere did I say who I was, or where I came from, or what it was like to stand over a body at two in the morning.

Journalists are taught they are never the story. As it happened, the longer I was a journalist, the better it suited me to disappear behind the professional voice of an omniscient third person, belonging everywhere and nowhere, asking questions and answering none. Every conclusion I published was double-sourced, fact-checked, and hyperlinked. My name might have been below the headlines, but the stories I wrote belonged to other people in other places, families whose grief and pain were so massive that mine was irrelevant.

All this is true, but it is also true that I was afraid. My inability to hold myself to account was due not only to a misguided commitment to objectivity. It was a failure of nerve.

This is a book about the dead, and the people who are left behind. It is also a personal story, written in my own voice, as a citizen of a nation I cannot recognize as my own. The thousands who died were killed with the permission of my people. I am writing this book because I refuse to offer mine.

—*Manila, June 2023*

I

MEMORY

1

POSITIVE

My name is Lady Love, says the girl.

The girl is eleven years old. She is small for her age, all skinny brown legs and big dark eyes. Lady Love is the name she prints on the first line of school papers and uses nowhere else. It was her grandmother who named her. Everyone else calls her Love-Love. Ma did, when she sent Love-Love to the market. Get the children dressed, Love-Love. Don't bother me when I'm playing cards, Love-Love. Quit lecturing me, Love-Love.

Nobody calls her Lady, and only Dee ever called her Love. Just Love.

Love, he would say, give your Dee a hug.

Dee is short for Daddy. It embarrasses Love-Love sometimes, not the hug, because Dee gives good hugs, but that she calls him Dee. Only rich girls call their fathers Daddy. Pa should be good enough for a girl who lives in the slums of Manila. But there they are, Dee and Love, Love and Dee, walking down the street in the early evening, the small girl stretching up a scrawny arm to wrap around the tall man's waist.

Love-Love was supposed to be the third of eight children, but the oldest died of rabies and the second was rarely home. It fell to Love-Love to tell Ma to stop drinking and Dee to quit smoking. You're drunk again, she would tell Ma, and Ma would tell Love-Love to go away.

Love-Love worried they would get sick. She worried about rumors her father was using drugs. She worried about all of them living where they did, in a place where every other man could be a snitch for the cops.

Ma and Dee said everything was fine. Dee was getting his driver's license back. Ma made money giving manicures. They had already surrendered to the new government and promised they would never touch drugs again.

Let's move away, Love-Love told Dee, but Dee laughed it off.

Let's move away, she told Ma, but Ma said the little ones needed to go to school. We can go to school anywhere, Love-Love said.

Ma shook her head. They needed to save up first. Don't worry yourself, Ma said.

Love-Love worried, and she was right.

Love, said her father, one night in August.

Love, he said, just before the bullet slammed into his head.

I meet her at her aunt's. She is sitting on a battered armchair. I crouch in front of her and stick out my hand to shake hers. If nothing else, an interview is an exchange. Tell me your name, and I'll tell you mine.

My name is Pat, I tell Love-Love. I'm a reporter.

I was born in 1985, five months before a street revolution brought democracy back to the Philippines. That year it seemed every other middle-class mother had named her daughter Patricia. Evangelista, my surname, common in my country, derives from the Greek *euangelos*, "bringer of good news." It is an irony I am informed of often.

My job is to go to places where people die. I pack my bags, talk to the survivors, write my stories, then go home to wait for the next catastrophe. I don't wait very long.

I can tell you about those places. There have been many of them in the last decade. They are the coastal villages after typhoons, where babies were zipped into backpacks after the body bags ran out. They are the hillsides in the south, where journalists were buried alive in a layer cake of cars and corpses. They are the cornfields in rebel country and the tent cities outside blackened villages and the backrooms where mothers whispered about the children that desperation had forced them to abort.

It's handy to have a small vocabulary in my line of work. The names go first, then the casualty counts. Colors are good to get the description squared away. The hill is green. The sky is black. The backpack is purple, and so is the bruising on the woman's left cheek.

Small words are precise. They are exactly what they are and are faster to type when the battery is running down.

I like verbs best. They break stories down into logical movements, trigger to finger, knife to gut: *crouch, run, punch, drown, shoot, rip, burst, bomb.*

In the years since the election of His Excellency, President Rodrigo Roa Duterte, I have collected a new handful of words. They rotate, trade places, repeat in staccato.

Kill, for example. It's a word my president uses often. He said it at least 1,254 times in the first six months of his presidency, in a variety of contexts and against a range of enemies. He said it to four-year-old Boy Scouts, promising to kill people who got in the way of their future. He said it to overseas workers, telling them there were jobs to be had killing drug addicts at home. He told mayors accused of drug dealing to repent, resign, or die. He threatened to kill human rights activists if the drug problem worsened. He told cops he would give them medals for killing. He told journalists they could be legitimate targets of assassination.

"I'm not kidding," he said in a campaign rally in 2016. "When I become president, I'll tell the military, the police, that this is my order: find these people and kill them, period."

I know only a few dozen of the dead by name. It doesn't matter to the president. He has enough names for them all. They are addicts, pushers, users, dealers, monsters, madmen.

Love-Love can name two of them. They are Dee and Ma.

It was a blow that started it, on the wrong door, just down the hall. There was a commotion, fists on wood, tenants protesting, and door after slammed door, punctuated by a man's voice.

Negative, said the man. Negative, negative, negative.

It didn't take long for the man to reach Love-Love's door. Open it, shouted the man.

Inside, Love-Love crouched with her mother. It was three in the morning. Dee was fast asleep on his back, one of the toddlers tucked into his chest. The other children slept scattered around the room. The man kicked the door.

This, Love-Love thought, was how her parents would die.

Her mother opened the door, afraid the men outside would

punch through the window and kill them all in a hail of gunfire. Two men burst into the room. Both wore full masks, with holes for eyes and nose and mouth.

"Positive," one of them said, looming over Dee. Get up, he said.

Dee jerked awake. He tried to sit up, but there was a baby curled into his chest. He fell back again.

Love, he said, before one of the men shot him dead. The bullet burst out of Dee's right temple. Blood spattered over the baby.

"Dee!" Love-Love screamed.

The baby wailed. Ma wept. She thrust a handful of paper at the man who killed her husband. Here was proof, she sobbed, that they had mended their ways.

Ma fell to her knees. Love-Love dragged her mother up until she was on her feet. It was Love-Love who squeezed her body between the gunman and Ma. It was Love-Love who stood with the barrel of the gun just inches from her forehead. It was Love-Love, all big eyes and skinny brown legs, who cursed at the gunman and demanded he shoot her instead.

Kill me, she said, not my Ma.

The second gunman held back the first. Don't shoot, he said. She's only a child.

They left. It wasn't for long. When they returned, the first gunman turned back to Love-Love's mother and raised his gun.

"We are Duterte," he said, and emptied the magazine.

Ma died on her knees.

Love-Love cursed at the killers. You motherfuckers, she said. You already killed my Dee. Now you've shot my Ma.

The gunman swung the muzzle at Love-Love's face.

Shut up, he said, or we'll shoot you dead too.

When they left, Love-Love found the hole inside Ma's head.

The blood gushed through Love-Love's fingers. Dee lay where he fell. His eyes had rolled back. Love-Love wanted to hug him, but she was afraid. He did not look like her Dee.

"Dee," asked the girl called Love. "Are you leaving me, Dee?"

In 1945 the reporter Wilfred Burchett broke the story of a nuclear warhead exploding over the city of Hiroshima for the London *Daily Express*. He covered what he called "the most terrible and frightening desolation in four years of war." Burchett marched into Hiroshima carrying a pistol, a typewriter, and a Japanese phrasebook. "I write these facts as dispassionately as I can," wrote Burchett, "in the hope that they will act as a warning to the world."

Like Burchett, I am a reporter. Unlike him, I'm not a foreign correspondent. I spent the last decade flying into bombed-out cities, counting body bags, and reporting on the disasters, both natural and man-made, that continue to plague my own country. And then came the last six years of documenting the killings committed under the administration of President Rodrigo Duterte.

The fact that I'm a Filipino living in the Philippines means that for me, there's no going home from the field. There is no seven-day shooting schedule with a pre-booked flight and an option to extend; only more corpses, every day. I do not need a translator to tell me that the man screaming *putang ina* over his brother's body means "motherfucker" instead of "son of a bitch." I understand why coffins sit in living rooms for weeks at a time, and I'm ready to refuse, with all manner of excuses, when I am offered a sandwich at a wake by a widow so desperately poor she cannot afford the twenty-dollar formaldehyde injection necessary to preserve a rotting body.

There were corpses every night at the height of the killings. Seven, twelve, twenty-six, the brutality reduced to a paragraph, sometimes only a sentence each. The language failed as the body count rose. There are no synonyms for *blood* or *bleed*. The blood doesn't gush by the time I walk into a crime scene. It doesn't burble or spurt. It sits in pools under doorways or, as in the case of the jeepney barker shot in front of a 7-Eleven, streams out of the mouth in rivulets.

Dead is a good word for a journalist in the age of Duterte. Dead doesn't negotiate, requires little verification. Dead is a sure thing, has bones, skin, and flesh, can be touched and seen and photographed and blurred for broadcast. Dead, whether it's 44 or 58 or 27,000 or 1, is dead.

I record these facts as honestly as I can, but I am not dispassionate as I set them down. That I am Filipino also means I understand guilt, in the complicated way only a Catholic raised in the colonized Philippines knows guilt. I know why a father kneels to wash away his son's blood while muttering apologies into the linoleum. I know he believes himself responsible for failing to stop the four bullets that burst through his thirty-year-old son's body: forehead, chest, and narrow shoulders, in a manner he sees as the sign of the cross—in the name of the Father, and of the Son, and of the Holy Spirit, amen. I know all this because I am my father's daughter and understand that while my survival is a privilege, my own father prays too.

President Duterte said kill the addicts, and the addicts died. He said kill the mayors, and the mayors died. He said kill the lawyers, and the lawyers died. Sometimes the dead weren't drug dealers or corrupt mayors or human rights lawyers. Sometimes they were children, but they were killed anyway, and the president said they were collateral damage.

I saw many young girls in the first months of the war, and not all of them survived to tell their stories. In the same week that Love-Love's parents were killed, a five-year-old girl named Danica Mae was shot with a bullet meant for her grandfather.

I spoke to him inside a cramped cement room where the face of Jesus Christ looked benignly down from a wall calendar. His name was Maximo, and he didn't attend his granddaughter's funeral. His family told him to keep away. His daughters promised they would take video on their phones. Wait for it on Facebook, they said. Wait for the funeral video, we'll make sure you can watch. He understood why he shouldn't go, and why his family had taken him straight from the hospital to a house far from where he had lived most of his married life. The men in masks could come back to the house and finish the job. Nobody would go to visit his Danica Mae. He wanted Danica surrounded by her mourners. She deserved it, and so much more.

Maximo had supported the Duterte candidacy. He still wore the red-and-blue baller band with the president's name stamped in white. Maximo had voted for Duterte because Duterte was a strong man. It didn't matter that Maximo had used drugs himself. Maybe Danica would have died even without Duterte in the palace, or maybe she wouldn't have. All he knew was that there had been many deaths, some of them men on the same list where his name had been found. The list called him a drug dealer.

"Let them come and kill me if they can," he said. "I leave it to God. God knows who the sinners are, and who is telling the truth."

So he waited alone, a big man with a hard, heavy belly and red-rimmed eyes. He cried a little, prayed a little, cleaned what bullet wounds he could reach. He called Danica's parents and told them to lean over her coffin and whisper that her grandpa loved her.

He told them to say he stayed away for her.

Until the year President Duterte was elected, I considered myself the most practical sort of cynic. I understood that terrible things happen to good people. I took a morbid pride in the fact that I belonged to that special breed of correspondent for whom it was possible to stand over a corpse and note that the body in the water was probably female, that there were remains of breasts under the faded yellow shirt, despite the fact the face above the shirt was missing skin and flesh.

If my journalism had a moral hierarchy, uppermost was that the loss of a life was the worst of all things, to be avoided at all possible instances. The concept wasn't revolutionary. I was raised a citizen of the oldest democracy in Southeast Asia, and I believed, as I thought most of my generation did, in free speech and human rights and the duty to hold my government accountable. I believed in democracy in 2009, when I reported on the murders of thirty-two journalists. I believed in it in 2013, when I covered the bombardment of Zamboanga City. I believed in it in 2015, after government arrogance sent forty-four unsuspecting policemen into a cornfield to die at the hands of rebels. I believed in democracy much the same way I believed in short sentences and small words.

Democracy, like *murder,* is a simple word. I saw it as a general good opposed to a general wrong. By democracy, I did not mean the elected administration. The government, every government, failed often, was complicit often, was by and large incompetent, hypocritical, and out of touch. The democracy I believed in was the nation, a community of millions who saw brutality as an aberration to be condemned as often and as vigorously as necessity demanded.

I still believed in democracy when I began counting President Duterte's dead. I didn't understand that the democracy my journalism depended on was particular only to myself and a minority of others. Elsewhere in the country, people died, starved, or were widowed or orphaned or ignored. In the world as imagined by Rodrigo Duterte, that nation was a crowd of idiots and innocents, set on by crooks and thugs. His nation was the badlands, where the peace was broken, no citizen was safe, and every addict was armed and willing to kill.

Duterte had your back, and he said the struggle ended here, today. Fuck the bleeding hearts. To hell with the bureaucracy. There would be no forgiveness, there would be no second chances, the line would be drawn, and on one side he would stand with a loaded gun. The law might be optional, the thugs might be at the helm, but Duterte was a man who said what he meant and meant what he said, who might give you a warning and then count one, two, three.

This was the Republic of the Philippines that Rodrigo Duterte promised to save. Give him six months, and there would be an end to crime and corruption. Give him six months, and there would be an end to drugs.

He was applauded, celebrated, and in the end, inaugurated.

"Hitler massacred three million Jews," he said. "Now there are three million drug addicts. I'd be happy to slaughter them."

In December, five months into the war, another little girl saw her father die. Her name was Christine, and she was fourteen.

One day, she said, the cops came looking for Pa. They found

her mother instead. The cops called Christine's mother an addict. She was eight months pregnant. They took her away in a white van. When Pa came home, everyone told him to run. The police, said his neighbors, would kill him if they found him.

Pa came home anyway, months later, late in the night. He said he missed the children. He cooked spaghetti. He sang songs. He fed the little ones by hand. He gave Christine half his cup of coffee. He told them all that he loved them and that it would be a while until he came back again.

They heard shouting from outside the house. Three guns appeared at the window, the barrels bright in the sunlight. The door burst open. Five policemen ran into the house. They had Pa kneel on the armchair and shoved his face into the back cushion. He clutched at his ID. He said he was clean.

Please, he said, please arrest me instead. I have so many children.

The police told the children to get out. Christine wrapped her arms around Pa. One of the policemen threw her against the wall.

Get out, he said.

Only Christine didn't get out, at least not fast enough. She was there when the policeman shot her father, through the back of the head, through the chest, shot him at such close range that the next day her little brother stuck his finger through the hole in the sofa and dug out the bullet.

The police said Pa had fought back. They said he was a drug dealer. They said they had killed Pa in self-defense.

It was a long time after Pa died before Christine spoke again. Her first word was *sorry*. She said sorry to her grandmother and sorry to her siblings. She said sorry because she had let go of Pa on the morning he was killed. Had she held on harder, had she hugged him tighter, Pa would be alive.

·　　　·　　　·

My news organization, Rappler, has a funny name. My bosses made it up, from *rap,* for "discuss," and *ripple.* They explained it on the day I was recruited on the third floor of a building along a street that flooded in the summertime. It had almost been Rippler, they said, and it would have stayed Rippler if someone hadn't pointed out that it sounded like *nipple.* I laughed then. For the first few months, I prefaced every field interview by a repetition of the company name to confused sources who were used to the call signs of broadcast television—"Raffler, you say? Rapper? Rapeler?" Rappler, I would say. Ra*ppl*er. Yes, you can find us on YouTube. No, I don't work for YouTube. Eventually I would resign myself to saying the name quickly, then offering to tag their teenage nephews with a Facebook link.

I joined Rappler in the late summer of 2011. I was twenty-six years old, and while I did not believe, as Rappler did, that social media would make the world a better place, I did believe that journalism might make some headway if we tried hard enough. Rappler believed it could produce the new correspondent for the digital age, a one-woman news crew who could take photos, roll video, ask questions, live-tweet developments, file text stories, and beat the competition, all while producing an on-camera report with nothing more than an internet dongle and an iPhone on a tripod. The experiment was bound for failure, at least for me. I was the reporter who got lost on the way to the office and took half an hour to compose a single sentence. I could, as this is an exercise in memory, write about arguments over word counts and editing software and the color orange they chose for the logo. I could write about the afternoon the editors finally bought a couch after discovering one too many reporters sleeping under desks. I could write about the day I made a future Nobel Peace

Prize laureate cry in frustration. It was my fault, but I still say she started it.

Those stories are all true, but what is also true is that Rappler sent me to many places where the ordinary ended with a body on the ground. Ask me for a story about Rappler, and I'll tell you that every story about Rappler is also a story about the people who told us theirs. I'm a trauma reporter. People like me work in the uneasy space between what is and what should be. My stories offered no solutions, no proposed salvation. I did not traffic in hope. Sometimes, if we were lucky, a reader would pay for a coffin, or a new salon chair for a barber out in Guiuan who had lost his barbershop to a storm.

Every story began with the ordinary because it underscored what happened next. The blue sky before the flood of corpses. The kiss goodbye before the barrage of bullets. Once after Super Typhoon Haiyan reduced Tacloban to rubble, I sat behind a camera in front of a man who asked if I could broadcast a message to his son. I focused the lens, pressed the record button. Please come home, Edgardo said, because Papa is making spaghetti for Christmas dinner. His son was gone, likely drowned, but Edgardo tried to reach out anyway because maybe the ordinary would bring his son home.

I wrote about terrible things that happened because those things shouldn't have happened and shouldn't happen again. Then one day the man who would be president promised the deaths of his own citizens. The terrible became ordinary, to thundering applause.

Night after night the gunshots echoed through the slums. Those stories also began with the ordinary. I woke up, said someone's lover, and he wasn't beside me. I was taking a bath, said someone's mother, when I heard the shouting. I was at home, said someone's daughter, when the cop kicked in the door and shot my father. I wrote down what I could, and while there were many who mourned, there were also many who read about the dead and said more should die.

Rappler was barely four years old when President Duterte was elected. There were very few of us, but we did what we could to report on corruption and abuses of power, along with the war on drugs. President Duterte gave Rappler another name. He called us fake news. He said we were paid hacks. We were charged with tax evasion and cyberlibel and ownership violations. Rappler's license to operate was revoked. It remains under appeal. Our reporters were banned from covering the president. We were threatened daily on social media. Because we were women, the threats included rape.

I published many stories, every one of them built around a corpse who had once had a name, even if all I had to go on was "Unidentified Body No. 4." I wrote that five-year-old Danica was shot before she got to wear her new pink raincoat. I wrote that Jhaylord was his mother's favorite, and that Angel had been carrying a Barbie doll on the night she was killed. I layered detail over detail, all of it, the color of the shoe, the tenor of the scream, the fact the dead man was wearing red-and-white bikini briefs when they stripped his body on the street.

"I'd like to be frank with you," said the president. "Are they humans? What is your definition of a human being?"

Here is Danica Mae Garcia, Maximo's granddaughter.

Here is Constantino de Juan, Christine's Pa.

Here are Love-Love's Dee and Ma.

Here is the man who killed them.

"We are Duterte," said the gunman in the mask.

I was born in the year democracy returned to the Philippines. I am here to report its death.

2

THE SURVIVING MAJORITY

In the story my grandfather told, the first of the white men arrived on a fleet of five warships led by the *Trinidad*.

It was 1521. The flotilla had survived more than a year of misadventure and mutiny. The *Trinidad*'s captain, a bearded adventurer by the name of Ferdinand Magellan, saw a wooded island stretching across the horizon. The men of the *Trinidad* dropped to their knees, praised the Lord, and having run out of rum, proceeded to get well and thoroughly drunk on Bireley's orange soda and Siu Hoc Tong rice wine.

Magellan dropped anchor. He hailed a boatload of passing natives.

"To show that his heart was in the right place," said my grandfather, "Magellan had his steward bring him some red caps, looking glasses, combs, bells, and the sixteenth-century equivalent of what we now refer to as the zoot suit. These Magellan gave to the native chieftain, saying, 'You won't find these in any

Sears, Roebuck catalog. They're the very latest in what the well-dressed headhunter will wear, take them with the king's and my compliments, and have you got any spare gold bars kicking around?'"

When I say my grandfather told Magellan's story, I don't mean to me, but to the people who might have purchased a book distributed by the Philippine Book Company, written by Mario P. Chanco in 1951. "The Fredding of Ferdinand Magellan" was one of a handful of folktales he had published while plying his trade as a newspaperman. My grandfather, so wrote one of his friends fondly, "indulged far too often in frivolous asides and irreverent remarks, especially as to Serious Writing."

And so his imagined Magellan sailed farther into the archipelago that would later become the Philippine Islands. He met other natives, traded his cargo for gold and spices, until he came upon the ferocious chief of the island of Mactan, Lapulapu. Lapulapu refused to pay tribute to Magellan or swear loyalty to the Spanish king.

"Naturally," my grandfather explained, "this made Magellan unhappy, for was he not propagating his monarch's goodwill and blessings for the enlightenment and benefit of infidels the world over? What did it matter if the said goodwill was offered at the point of a musket? Didn't it amount to the same thing?"

The conquistadors waded onto shore after a "terrific barrage on the beaches." They were met by the spear-carrying men of Mactan, who "swooped down on them like avenging demons." Magellan fell dead to a sharpened bamboo stake. His men sailed away, a broken band with only two ships of the grand flotilla surviving.

"As for Magellan," concluded my grandfather, "he remained where the Mactan islands got him. And the moral of this tale is: next time you ask for anything, say please."

.   .   .

No reader will mistake my grandfather for a historian, but his version of the time the Spanish conquistadors first sailed into the Philippines does bear a nodding acquaintance with the truth. Lapulapu of Mactan, whose warriors fired poisoned arrows into Ferdinand Magellan, delayed the Spanish invasion of the Philippines by almost half a century. Another attempt at claiming territory, by Ruy López de Villalobos, failed in 1544. Villalobos's only success was leaving behind a name for the islands whose people had driven him out—Las Islas Filipinas, in honor of the future king, Philip the Second of Spain.

Only in 1565, with the arrival of Miguel López de Legazpi, did the islands finally fall subject to the Spanish Empire. For decades afterward, Spanish galleons unloaded soldiers and governors and tonsured friars. My people were taught to kneel before the Catholic God and suffer before his earthly envoys, but the Spanish soon discovered their new colony in the southeast was unwilling to suffer years of rape and rosaries. There were secret societies and armed revolts, quiet insurgencies and public executions. Near the end, the Spanish attempted both force and conciliation, executing a writer here, exiling a revolutionary leader there.

By the late nineteenth century, it wasn't only the Philippines rebelling against Mother Spain. Mexico, Puerto Rico, and Cuba were also in revolt, just as Theodore Roosevelt, assistant secretary of the U.S. Navy, was agitating to expand the American frontier. In 1898 the United States declared war on Spain to protect its interests in Cuba. Hostilities spread to the edges of the waning Spanish Empire.

Here was America's manifest destiny writ large. A 125,000-strong volunteer army marched into Santiago de Cuba.

Roosevelt's Rough Riders thundered through Las Guásimas and San Juan Hill. An armada carrying the United States' Asiatic Squadron was dispatched to the capital of Spain's foothold in Asia—Manila.

We did not win the war against Spain, because America claimed victory for itself.

The Battle of Manila Bay was a rout. Spanish ships sank. The rest were captured. America's casualties were negligible.

So it was that Commodore George Dewey held the sea, but Filipinos fought on land, liberating city after city at the cost of thousands of lives. It was the tail end of years of native armed revolution. General Emilio Aguinaldo, returning from exile in Hong Kong, told his men to assemble in numbers wherever they saw the American flag fly. Americans, he said, "for the sake of humanity and the lamentations of so many persecuted people," had extended "their protecting mantle to our beloved country."

The Filipino armed militia formed an alliance with the United States. General Aguinaldo declared independence. Spain refused to raise the white flag to Filipinos, and America was happy to accommodate. The United States and Spain brokered a secret deal to keep Filipinos at bay and fought a choreographed battle. The Spanish flag came down. The American flag flew up. Filipino troops ringed Manila, barred from entering by their own allies.

Four months later, President McKinley demanded that Filipinos "recognize the military occupation and authority of the United States." The treaty, signed in Paris, between the United States of America and the Kingdom of Spain, thus accounted for the sale of an entire colony at the cut-rate price of $20 million.

Rudyard Kipling, across the sea in England, wrote encouragement to the gentlemen of the new American Empire to "take up the White Man's burden."

> Go, bind your sons to exile
>> To serve your captives' need;
> To wait, in heavy harness,
>> On fluttered folk and wild—
> Your new-caught sullen peoples,
>> Half devil and half child.

The half-devil, half-child citizens of the short-lived Philippine Republic demanded the freedom promised by the sons of liberty. America answered with an iron fist. Insurgents were massacred. Towns were razed. William Howard Taft might have called Filipinos America's "little brown brothers," but soldiers on the ground sang a different song as they marched. There were occasional defections to the Filipino cause, but the African American soldiers who switched sides were executed for their principles.

So began the reign of the new American Empire, purchased by a white president of the new world from a white king of the old world.

We were Spain, and for forty-eight years after that, we were America.

My grandfather was born in 1922, twenty-four years into the American occupation. He was the great-great-grandson of a Chinese tradesman named San Chang Co, who had sailed into Manila in the mid-nineteenth century and settled down with a Filipino wife. By the time my grandfather was born to a university bureaucrat and a department store heiress, the surname had evolved into Chanco. San Chang Co's descendants were born the English-speaking subjects of the United States of America.

Mario Chanco was the sixth of seven children. They lived on San Antonio Street, in a sprawling home with heavy furniture and walls of bookshelves. Much of the family wealth went toward the education of the younger generation. They learned Spanish at home, English in school, and Filipino everywhere else.

When my grandfather was twelve, the 73rd U.S. Congress signed the Tydings-McDuffie Act, a federal law directing the Philippines' transition to independence. The Philippines turned from colony to commonwealth with the promise of sovereignty within ten years.

The Second World War interrupted both my grandfather's schooling and the last years of the Philippine Commonwealth. My great-grandfather lost his job at the university after the Japanese discovered that my grandfather's older brother, a West Point–educated army colonel, was blowing up bridges to slow the advancing Japanese. Some of the family hunkered down in the capital, selling off what was left of their land and moonlighting as ticket sellers for underground boxing matches. Others dispersed.

The family survived. Many others did not, with over a hundred thousand people killed. An "atrocity report," filed on February 15, 1945, by a U.S. Army major in Manila illustrated the barbarity of the last months of the occupation. The major and his men had discovered eight decomposing bodies abandoned inside a suburban Manila home. Five of the adults, including two women, had been executed with their hands tied behind their backs. A baby had been bayoneted. Further investigation of the immediate neighborhood "led to an interview with a Filipino, one Mario Chanco, a neighbor of the deceased," whom the report described as a newspaperman.

"We watched [the Japanese] enter the house," my grandfather told the Americans. "Shortly after, we heard five shots. The rest I do not know because along with other witnesses, I fled the vicinity."

By then, the Japanese were in retreat. My grandfather's brother survived the Bataan Death March and returned to fight with the guerrillas, becoming commander of the 91st Engineer Battalion of the U.S. Army in the Far East.

In the immediate aftermath of Japan's surrender, the United States of America ended its "high mission" of what it called "benevolent assimilation." After nearly four hundred years of colonial rule, the Philippine Republic was declared a free nation, with a constitution described as "a faithful copy of the U.S. Constitution"—"a textbook example of liberal democracy." By then, America had discovered that global hegemony did not require the costly maintenance of an entire archipelago of inconvenient not-quite-citizens, particularly if a nation was willing to offer preferential trade and military bases.

My grandfather was twenty-four years old the year the United States relinquished its colonial possession. He refused to return to university, devoting himself to journalism instead. He wrote of Philippine-American economic relations and Studebaker-sponsored radio musical hours and noted the influx of "brand-new automobiles, the latest fashions in men's and ladies' wear, a dozen shades of lipstick, and colorful fabrics of all varieties." He hosted a radio show where he acquired the nickname Mao after his facetious questioning of politicians in a pidgin Chinese accent. He began operating a community paper and wrote fiction on the side. As a city hall reporter, he collected acquaintances from government offices, including "a trim young miss with an intriguing smile." His writing style—which I am forced to admit involved the reckless deployment of adverbs—was described as "deceptively light" and "disgracefully humorous." He was a founding member of the National Press Club and the first host of *Meet the Press,* where "his wit and tongue-in-cheek side comments kept politicians' pomposity at a minimum." His byline jumped from paper to paper, magazine to magazine, wandering across *The Philippines Herald, This Week,* the *Sunday Times, Literary Song-Movie, Women's Magazine,* until he was promoted to reporter at large for the *Manila Daily Bulletin.*

He was, according to all who remember him, a generally pleasant man. "He was always cheerful and earnest, never tragic, petulant, or cross-eyed as Humorists are supposed to be," wrote historian Carmen Guerrero Nakpil. "He was kind to what stray cats there were in the back alleys of Manila's newspaper row, tender-hearted with good-looking young women, and respectful to editors. He went to Paco church regularly, editing for his parish a vaguely religious, semi-Rotarian publication called the *Paco Town Crier.* He dressed in the imaginative fashion then forced upon the post-liberation Filipino male. He was also an enterprising young man, eager to get ahead, always fiddling with daring little publishing projects."

In 1955 he was named the country's Most Outstanding Young Man in Journalism. He accepted a Fulbright fellowship in the United States. He published a digest called *The Orient.* The "trim young miss" he met on the city hall beat became the mother of his four children, referred to forevermore in his columns as the Beautiful Wife, capitals included.

"Chanco, more than any other newsman around, most closely resembles the public conception—thanks to Hollywood—of what a newspaperman is like," wrote Felix Bautista for the *Sunday Times Magazine.* "He is bubbly, effervescent, incurably extroverted. He always has the snappy comeback, the sparkling repartee, and he has the average newsman's flair for the wisecrack and the excruciating pun. His hands, when they are not banging away at a typewriter, are either gladhanding people in a hearty hail-fellow-well-met gesture, or are pointing the accusing finger at something, usually shenanigans in government."

For the next few decades, he pecked out what he laughingly called "my deathless prose" for four hours every morning on his IBM Selectric typewriter. He opened a full-scale printing press, making it possible to produce his own supply of notebooks, of a size designed to fit the back pocket of his worn trousers. He smoked Rothmans after meals and Dunhills when he ran out, but he regularly kept a pack of Marlboro Reds open for when he wrote, flicking off ash every which way whenever the ashtray was out of reach. He raised his children, my mother his eldest, in a manner she remembered as largely comfortable. It was due, I am told, to the enterprise of the Beautiful Wife, a registered nurse, who was the axis of my grandfather's rapidly turning world. The Beautiful Wife invested in land, ran a range of businesses, and hosted the parade of friends my grandfather brought home. They were a mix of journalists and politicians and environmentalists, including a former war correspondent named Benigno Aquino, Jr.

In 1965 a senator who claimed to be "the most decorated war hero in the Philippines" was elected its tenth president. His name was Ferdinand Edralin Marcos. He was neither decorated nor a war hero, but his story took years to unravel. At the end of the two terms allowed by the Constitution, in 1972, Marcos announced he was declaring martial law on the pretext of widespread violence and the Communist threat. He promulgated a new constitution and effectively made himself president for life, while systematically silencing critics and the free press.

The conjugal dictatorship of Ferdinand and Imelda Marcos lasted fourteen years, with the cheerful support of the United States. Imelda danced with President Ronald Reagan and acquired several thousand pairs of size eight-and-a-half stiletto heels, along with the entirety of a Sotheby's auction, including the brownstone housing the collection. The martial law period, as we called it, was rife with corruption, patronage, and political repression. It would result in an estimated five to ten billion dollars stolen from the national treasury, the imprisonment of 70,000, the torture of 34,000, and the extrajudicial murders of 3,240 activists. It is likely there were more.

At the time, so family legend goes, my grandfather was jailed along with dozens of political prisoners. My mother's cousin, my uncle Boo, then a twenty-two-year-old reporter, saw all his friends arrested and promptly quit journalism: "I got away from being arrested, and I'm going to offer myself on a silver platter? No way."

Martial law ended, on paper at least, in 1981, after international pressure on the Marcos regime. Very little changed. In its aftermath, Vice President George H. W. Bush raised a toast to Marcos: "We love your adherence to democratic principle."

That adherence failed again two years later after the return of one of the country's leading opposition voices. Benigno Aquino, Jr., called Ninoy, had been a war correspondent before he was elected governor and later the Philippines' youngest senator. He was included in the first wave of martial law arrests and spent seven years in detention. In 1980 he was allowed to leave the country for the United States for a heart bypass operation on the promise he would end his crusade against the Marcos administration.

It was a promise he did not keep. He had spent three years lecturing at Harvard and ramping up international support for the opposition when he decided to come home. The Filipino, he said in one of his last speeches, was worth dying for.

In the early morning of August 21, 1983, he put on the same white suit he wore on his flight to exile and boarded China Airlines 811 carrying false papers. He was surrounded by a pack of journalists as the plane cruised to Manila. "You have to be very ready with your hand camera," he had told reporters the day before, "because this action can happen very fast. In a matter of three, four minutes, it could be all over and I may not be able to talk to you again."

A crowd of thousands waited at the Manila International Airport. Yellow ribbons had been tied around trees. It was in reference to a Tony Orlando song about a prisoner on his way home. *A hundred yellow ribbons round the ole oak tree; I'm comin' home. Tie a ribbon 'round the ole oak tree.*

A military boarding party appeared as the plane taxied into its gate. Aquino was escorted into the jetway leading to the terminal. All other passengers were asked to remain in their seats, even as reporters tried to argue their way past the soldiers. Gunshots rang out. A young woman, watching from one of the plane's windows, began screaming. Many years later, she testified before the Philippine Sandiganbayan and the U.S. Congress: "Your honor, even if I'm the worst person in the whole world, nothing will change that it was a soldier who shot Ninoy."

Ninoy Aquino, a limp figure in white, the bright hope of the Philippine opposition, bled into the tarmac before he could deliver the speech he had so carefully prepared in Boston—"I return from exile and to an uncertain future with only determination and faith to offer."

At least four million people braved the monsoon rains to march beside the coffin carrying his shattered body. They held

placards and signs—YOU ARE NOT ALONE. The procession lasted
eleven hours. The assassination was, for many, the final insult
after years of brutal human rights violations.

In the year I was born, two years after the assassination, international pressure forced Ferdinand Marcos to announce he was
holding presidential elections. His challenger was Ninoy Aquino's widow, a soft-spoken housewife who wore big glasses and
yellow dresses.

Her name, Corazon, means "heart." The country called her
Cory.

The campaign for the presidency lasted forty-five days. On
February 7, 1986, eighty-five thousand precincts opened at
seven in the morning. The cheating was blatant, committed
before international monitors, the Philippine press corps, and
more than a thousand foreign correspondents. At least eighty
people were killed across the country. Volunteers were beaten.
Armed men burst into polling precincts with guns and grenades. In Antique province, an assassin pumped twenty-four
bullets into the body of Aquino campaign director Evelio Javier
just beyond the capitol steps. In Manila, a sniper's bullet pierced
a sign carried by a twenty-three-year-old protester. The sign
read MARCOS CONCEDE. The protester died with a bullet in the
chest.

Cory Aquino led in an independent count, but the National
Assembly proclaimed Marcos's fourth term as president of the
Philippines. At least thirty young computer programmers tallying
the votes walked out. The government, they said, was manipu-
lating the numbers.

The Catholic Church, in unprecedented fashion, released a
statement condemning the elections as fraudulent. Foreign heads

of state held back their congratulations. President Reagan, at first claiming there was fraud on both sides, gave in to pressure from his own government and the American press, denouncing "widespread fraud and violence perpetrated largely by the ruling party." There were rumblings of a coup.

In the third week of February 1986, Secretary of Defense Juan Ponce Enrile and Armed Forces Vice Chief of Staff Fidel Ramos defected with a small band of rebel soldiers. They barricaded themselves inside the police and military headquarters. The underground radio station, Radio Veritas, operated by a woman and two teenage boys, broadcast an appeal from the archbishop of Manila: Protect the rebels.

"The full moon rose last night on a Philippines blown inside out by an act of rebellion," wrote Phil Bronstein for the *San Francisco Chronicle*. "At the gates of two of Manila's military camps, the people are guarding the soldiers."

Every country has its fairy tales. For many of my generation, the myth of the modern Philippines begins with Circumferential Road 4. The highway was one of six planned by the U.S. Army Corps of Engineers in the 1930s, designed to connect six cities before ending at Taft Avenue along Manila Bay. The Americans called it Highway 54. It was completed one year before 43,000 soldiers of the Imperial Japanese Army landed on the shores of the new Commonwealth of the Philippines.

In the late 1950s, after the war, a joint committee proposed a new name for what had become the capital's main thoroughfare. They called it Epifanio de los Santos Avenue, for a journalist and scholar who had championed Philippine independence from Spain. By the time Marcos called for snap elections in late 1985, the highway had a shorthand: Edsa.

I was in second grade when I first heard the story, sitting in a history class in my rumpled blue-and-white uniform, watching my teacher draw two parallel chalk lines on the board.

Edsa, Mrs. Chua said, this is Edsa.

She drew two small boxes on each line. Here, she said, were Camp Crame and Camp Aguinaldo, facing each other across Edsa. She colored in everything else with chalk.

All of these are people, she said.

I did not know what Edsa was at eight years old, so understand that my first conception of Epifanio de los Santos Avenue was not of a road but of a battlefield.

Think of a highway, five lanes on each side, in the early light of a Sunday morning. Think of it crowded, kilometer after kilometer, with a moving mass of men and women. They sweated through white T-shirts tucked into jeans. They carried crucifixes and boom boxes and sandwiches and umbrellas. They wore baseball caps and Christian Dior boaters and sweaty ponytails and grimy straw hats. The chalk drawing came alive before my mind's eye. Here were the makeshift fortifications: the pine tree, the storm drains, the broken lamppost, the sandbags donated by a nearby concrete factory, the telephone pole carried on the shoulders of men in belted slacks. Here was the human phalanx that snapped like a cordon around Camp Crame: grim-faced nuns, grandfathers bent over transistor radios, middle-aged matrons and fresh-faced girls with handfuls of flowers. Here was God's army, led by a young priest in jeans and boots on the front lines, the hem of his white cassock clutched in one fist as he roared in defiance at loyalist soldiers, *Are you going to shoot fellow Filipinos?*

Ferdinand Marcos sent the army. Troops on six tanks, eight jeeps, and thirteen trucks carrying grenade launchers and machine guns barreled down Edsa, their target the gates of Camp Crame.

My people saw the tanks. They did not run.

They stood with arms outstretched, palms pressed against the hot metal, knuckles tensed, pushing as engines rumbled and tailpipes billowed black exhaust. Some of them were crying. Some were swearing. A few dropped to their knees to pray. They held the line.

At noon on the morning of February 25, 1986, Ferdinand Marcos stepped out onto the balcony of Malacañang Palace and took his oath as president. His wife wore a white dress and sang a love song to a crowd of loyalists. That night, the Marcos family boarded a helicopter bound for the Clark airfield.

The headline flashed from wire to wire: MARCOS FLEES.

The revolution ended with the inauguration of Corazon Aquino. The Marcos family fled to Hawaii, granted asylum by President Reagan.

The world took notice. "It is a story that cannot be told too often," wrote *Asiaweek,* "and no matter how it ends this time, it is a lesson in the dynamics and wonder of democratic political leadership." French writer Nesta Comber called it a "moment worthy of ancient Greece." The Associated Press compared Corazon Aquino to Joan of Arc. CBS called it the closest the twentieth century had come to the storming of the Bastille. "We Americans like to think we taught the Filipinos democracy," anchor Bob Simon reported from his New York set. "Well tonight, they are teaching the world."

It could, said Harvard's Center for International Affairs, inspire nonviolent struggles elsewhere. "Which country will be the next to follow their example?"

In the aftermath of the Edsa Revolution, Thai protesters filled the streets of Bangkok. Another man stood before another tank at Tiananmen Square. The Berlin Wall fell, with Germany thanking the Philippines for showing them the way.

Once upon a time, we were heroes.

I tell this story not as a record of history but to explain the role the Edsa Revolution played in my understanding of who I was. Edsa was not my revolution, but it gave me a story grander than the dragon-slayers of my fairy tales. It was one part myth, two parts magic, peopled by giants, all thunder and power and bright yellow hope. It was that woman—smiling, kindly eyed Corazon Aquino—who stayed in my mind's eye at the ringing of the morning bell when the national anthem crackled through the school loudspeaker. The brave wore yellow in my imagination. Here was our manifest destiny writ large—land of the morning, pearl of the East, cradle of the brave, whose people pushed back the guns of a dictator with no more than a prayer and a song.

And as with most stories, the ending depends on who does the telling.

In 1986, during the tense days just before the snap elections, the Marcos motorcades were out in full force with paraphernalia paid for by the ruling party. Aquino traveled from city to city. Her supporters collected coins in mason jars. Old men stood on the roadside waving yellow banana leaves. On January 28, a full-page advertisement was published in the *Bulletin Today*. It was a manifesto in support of the Marcos ticket, written by the Coalition of Writers and Artists for Freedom and Democracy.

The manifesto ran nine paragraphs and began by saying "a nation founded by writers and artists cannot be insensitive to what men of thought and imagination in its midst have to say." The men of thought and imagination justified their support for the dictatorship with an eleven-point agenda for culture that the Marcos administration promised to finance. It included the creation of a Ministry of Culture, a publication fund for books, the establishment of an honor society "for the country's intellectuals," support for the "development of the native genius in arts and letters," an endowment for "the purchase of meritorious artwork," housing for "deserving but homeless writers and artists," and a variety of other endeavors for the encouragement of artistic talent.

The 130 signatories included journalists, filmmakers, poets, and actors. It was a failed campaign attempt, by and large, and was swept away with the confetti of the Edsa Revolution that took place a month later. When it was referred to at all, it was called the COWARD Manifesto—a name that a poet had coined from the organization's acronym. The signatories were alternately called traitors, cowards, and collaborators.

I came across the manifesto in my early thirties, well into my career as a journalist. A picture had been posted on social media. I read the names of the first twenty-one petitioners and stopped at the twenty-second.

It read Mario Chanco.

According to some accounts, the manifesto was circulated only among those who were known to support the administration or who had financial ties to power brokers. The signatures, I was told, were strictly voluntary.

The publication of the manifesto caused no small amount of "anger, dismay, and anxiety." According to an account written by Reuel Molina Aguila, members of the writers' group Galian sa Arte at Tula released an urgent statement calling on "fellow writers to even more tightly link their writing with the struggles of the Filipino nation." The *Philippine Daily Inquirer* quoted a warning from poet Ramon Villegas—"In autocratic states and in so-called democratic societies, it has been frequently proven that the state's patronage of the arts serves to advance the interests of the state and not those of the people." Another column denounced the signatories for "turning out black propaganda against the Opposition and singing hosannas to the Marcos regime."

It did not fit the narrative I knew.

My grandfather was sixty-three years old when the manifesto was released. He had been friends with Ninoy Aquino before martial law. He was rumored to have been Ninoy's ghostwriter, and one contemporary described him as Ninoy's publicist. The old Mercedes-Benz that sat for years in the family driveway had once belonged to the assassinated senator, although nobody knew if my grandfather had convinced Ninoy to sell or if Ninoy had unloaded it on my car-mad grandfather.

Here too was what I thought was an undisputed fact: my grandfather was one of many journalists who were rounded up and sent to the stockades.

"That's what I thought when I was young," my uncle Louie, my mother's brother, told me.

"That's what I was told," I said.

The truth, he explained, was more prosaic. My grandfather had been jailed for an outstanding debt to the government after a rice exportation deal went sour. He was certainly in the stockade with prominent political prisoners, but his incarceration had nothing to do with his journalism. While the case was decided in Mario Chanco's favor by the Supreme Court many years later, my uncle said the experience may have colored my grandfather's approach to the Marcos dictatorship.

I sat with my mother one day, out in her garden, under the blooming pink bougainvillea.

"Why would his name be on the manifesto?" I asked her.

"I don't know why," she said. "But I know he was very much for Imelda and Ferdy."

I am told that my grandmother, the Beautiful Wife, was in awe of Imelda Marcos, the provincial beauty queen whom historians later called the Iron Butterfly. My grandmother, a girl from the provinces who worked her way to Manila, saw in Imelda an ideal.

"Her favorite book was *Gone with the Wind*," my mother said. "She read it from cover to cover, three times, four times, five times. Because she was in awe of Scarlett. And the novel *Hawaii*? She was the same. In her mind, she immortalized the two. Nyuk Tsin, of *Hawaii*, and Scarlett. She so idolized them, and she pulled my dad and the whole family up herself because of that. She worked hard."

"And grandfather?"

"His support of Marcos was cynical," my mother told me. "But he was cynical of everybody."

I knew none of this for nearly thirty years. My grandfather considered politicians friends and found no ethical dilemma in occasionally serving as their public relations man. He shared a typewriter with Ninoy and sent bushels of fresh tomatoes to Marcos, a gift that resulted in a personal phone call of thanks from President Marcos himself. "By no stretch of imagination could you consider your grandfather a crusading journalist," my uncle Boo told me. Boo was also a reporter, and had trained under my grandfather. He said it was likely that my grandfather consented to the manifesto. Once, when Boo had published a particularly sharp column, my grandfather had called with advice. "You have to have a lot of friends," my grandfather told Boo. "But don't make too many enemies."

In an eyewitness history of the Edsa Revolution, a protester wrote of a bread delivery man who had taken to handing out breakfast buns outside Camp Crame. The man refused all payment. It was, he said, "the only help I can give my country." My grandfather noted the same phenomenon. In a column for the *Evening Post,* he wrote of how on the morning of the Edsa protests, bread deliveries had arrived late to his front door.

The bakers, said my grandfather, had headed off to the streets—"gone off with the hordes of shopkeepers, students, priests, workers, seminarians, and I think even middle-level bankers, accountants and barefoot vendors." Those among my grandfather's friends who had marched off to Edsa called to invite him. He refused.

"And when I demurred, pleading vertigo, anorexia, and semi-circular lumbago, to accompany them on their adventure, they were shocked, they couldn't believe their ears," he wrote. "History was in the making, they said, adding: 'and you're going to sleep it off?' I argued I belonged to the committed majority: the majority that's committed to survival. I said I'd spent all my life, through World War II, Central Luzon, during the Huk campaigns and a bit of Vietnam thrown in, trying to avoid the bullet that had my name on it. . . . What right did they have, I demanded belligerently, to turn myself into something I knew I wasn't?"

I cannot report with any accuracy what my grandfather thought of the dictatorship that killed thousands of his countrymen. His columns are long gone, and so are his notebooks. It may be that he was coerced into signing the manifesto. He might not have known his signature had been included at all. Likely he thought his support would please the friends I'm told he very much cherished and perhaps believed, genuinely, in the value of the Marcos contribution to art and literature.

It is also possible that he was afraid.

I did not live through the dictatorship, but his survival and the privilege of my education and upbringing are the result of choices he made.

Here is what I know. Once upon a time, we were heroes.

3

MASCOT FOR HOPE

My mother said my sisters were pretty. I never met them. Something troublesome about my parents' genes made any female babies unlikely to survive. They were born pale and sweet and quiet, living a few short months before their lungs gave out. I came along years later. My father told me the reason I survived infancy was because the family stormed the heavens. That was what he called it. Everyone hoped for a boy, hoped as hard as they could, all the way to the morning my mother discovered her water had broken.

It felt funny, my mother said in the car. My father could do nothing, only drive faster. The story goes that in the hospital, the doctor looked down between my mother's legs and laughed. The baby was in a hurry, he said, pocketing his pipe. That the doctor shook my tiny waving hand hello may have been more family myth than hard fact, but only later, when I was brought out red-faced and kicking, did my father think maybe the baby would live.

"We prayed for you," my grandmother told me as she sat at the kitchen table pasting church donation envelopes. She was my father's mother, half-Spanish and thoroughly Catholic. "We prayed and prayed, and then there you were."

I was a gift, I was told, the answer to a prayer delivered via cesarean section. It was the transactional nature of the religion I was born into. The rules were simple. You knelt, and magic happened. You believed, and miracles appeared. And if suffering through the ritual of seven churches and the fourteen stations of the cross didn't pay off, it would someday, unless you were a sinner, and of course all of us were.

We found many reasons to pray when I was growing up. We lived in a suburb of Quezon City, the largest city in the sprawling capital region of Metro Manila. For half the year, it was a pretty place, with a chapel in the park and pink bougainvillea curling around electric lines. In June, storm season, the waters rose up the sloping street to where my father stood guard under a dripping umbrella. He knew, through some complicated mental calculus, the exact moment it was necessary to evacuate all of us to the higher ground of my grandfather's house. We would go home the next day, to find the dogs shivering atop the piano and my father muddy and victorious.

It could have been worse, he would say.

It's because I prayed, my mother would answer.

I grew up the youngest of three in a family on the slow slide into genteel poverty. My father was an insurance executive who had given up his job to help run my mother's garment manufacturing business. The economy struggled in the early 1990s. Rolling blackouts hit the factory. Debts piled up. We were comfortable enough never to have to worry about the next meal, but never so comfortable that the next quarter's school tuition was a sure thing.

Many of us, the children of middle-class Manila, were fed on Catholic guilt and raised under the bright sun of the American dream. We went to church. We went to school. We recited the rosary every night and ate no meat on Good Friday. We hung tinsel on plastic Christmas trees, studied John Steinbeck, memorized the beatitudes, and measured our skirts a polite three inches below the knees. Money was tight, but there were books. When my mother's girlhood collection ran out, she sent me to my grandfather and his numbered bookshelves. I lived for most of my adolescence on rafts floating down the Mississippi, inside little houses on prairies, and around wood fires in the New England and Chicago and London of my imagination. I was Meg Murry. I was Jo March. I was Scout and Mowgli and Anne Shirley and Lyra Silvertongue and for one glorious summer Sherlock Holmes, with my father playing my indulgent Watson. My country may have thrown off the shackles of imperialism, but I was a volunteer colony of one.

My childhood may have revolved around books, but I had no compulsion to write stories of my own. I did not want to be a writer. I wanted to be written about. The single overriding goal of my childhood was to become a heroine. How I was to achieve this was irrelevant, as I was certain it was a function of destiny. Most children believe they are special. Not all of them are born miracles.

The Edsa Revolution, which would also come to be known as the People Power Revolution, had its sequel in 2001 when I was sixteen. The president, a mustached former action movie

hero, was Joseph Estrada. His administration was known for midnight cabinet meetings, drunken poker games, and a contempt
for the old guard that he would later prove to be his undoing. A
little more than two years into his term, he became the center of
a scandal involving illegal gambling payoffs. The political elite of
church and business, among them former president Corazon
Aquino, called for Estrada's resignation. He was tried for plunder
and for violating the Constitution in televised impeachment sessions. In one hearing, prosecutors introduced an envelope containing evidence allegedly proving his guilt. There was a vote. A
slim majority of senators decided to suppress the contents. State
prosecutors resigned. The capital exploded in revolt. The same
archbishop who led the 1986 revolution—his name was Cardinal
Sin—announced that the president had "lost the moral authority
to govern." Estrada's supporters, most of them from the impoverished classes, were dispersed by the police. The armed forces
threw in their lot with the opposition.

Three days after the interrupted impeachment hearings, Vice
President Gloria Macapagal-Arroyo was sworn in as the country's fourteenth president. She was a member of the political establishment and had won the vice presidency after plastering the
streets with posters featuring herself in a royal blue suit gazing
soulfully into a red rose. Her father was a former president who
in 1965 had lost reelection to Ferdinand Marcos. Estrada, while
expressing "strong and serious doubts about the legality and
constitutionality of her proclamation as president," evacuated
Malacañang Palace by boat. He resigned.

The protests were called Edsa Dos. I did not attend. My parents thought sixteen was too young to join the protests. Unlike
the revolution of 1986, the bloodless coup did not receive a
roundly celebratory international response. The event was further diminished by what is remembered as Edsa Tres, a string of

demonstrations protesting Estrada's arrest. The United States was one of the first governments to recognize President Arroyo's legitimacy, but critics inside and outside the Philippines were not shy about calling the event mob rule. It was, after all, a revolution by the Manila elite.

I went to college at the University of the Philippines with some vague notion of pursuing a career in law. The main campus in Diliman, where students had once thrown Molotov cocktails at soldiers during martial law, was where my grandfather and mother had been educated. It was also where, far more relevant to my situation, tuition was subsidized by the state. I joined the debate team. Debate had structure, logic, and drama, and having no personal causes of my own, it lent me an air of passionate defense for issues I knew very little about.

In my sophomore year, we hosted a national tournament. It included, for the first time, a public speaking contest. The winner would represent the country at the annual International Public Speaking Competition in the United Kingdom. I did not intend to compete, had assumed public speaking was a juvenile enterprise on a par with declamation recitals. Certainly it had none of the aggressive wrangling for points involved in competitive collegiate debate. My name appeared on the sign-up sheet anyway, courtesy of my beady-eyed club president, the result of my inability to contribute anything by way of organizing the tournament. Do it, she said, and I did.

The speeches were extemporaneous. The topic was innocuous. Discuss, for five minutes, "A Borderless World." It was a proposition I understood. I had witnessed the exodus of friends and family to the mysterious place we all called "the States" and could, with very little effort, cast myself as the wistful young girl left behind. "When I was little," I said, "I wanted what many Filipino children all over the country wanted. I wanted to be blond, blue-eyed, and white. I thought, if I just wished hard enough, and was good enough, I'd wake up on Christmas morning with snow outside my window and freckles across my nose."

In the weeks after I won, I wrote and rewrote my speech, on the advice of kindly literature professors who refined my case for global brotherhood while throwing in the occasional Shakespeare reference. I flew to the United Kingdom as the sole Philippine delegate. We could not afford to send a second.

There were fifty-nine competitors in London that year. We represented the thirty-seven countries of the English-Speaking Union. It is possible to believe I won the world championship because I was brilliant and delightful, but that would not be strictly true. It mattered where I was and to whom I spoke.

On a late afternoon in May, I stood on a stage before an audience gathered by the British crown and spoke about the Filipino diaspora and the promise of multicultural cooperation. "We are the forty thousand skilled nurses who support the UK's National Health Service," I said with a practiced smile. "We are the quarter of a million seafarers manning most of the world's commercial ships. We are your software engineers in Ireland, your construction workers in the Middle East, your doctors and caregivers in North America, and your musical artists in London's West End." That many of those laborers had been forced into contracts abroad for the sake of starving families at home was a fact I glossed over. The world I described was open and borderless, there for the taking for anyone who wanted it. During those five minutes in Trafalgar Square, I was the proud Filipino speaking the language of the West, offering a happy resolution to the brutal colonial past that my imperial masters had been pleased to forget.

Newspaper coverage included the fact that eighteen-year-old

Ms. Evangelista, world champion, "received a salver, a certificate, a dictionary and an encyclopedia."

Many things happened in the aftermath. The Duke of Edinburgh shook my hand in Buckingham Palace. Retired president Corazon Aquino had me over for iced tea and cake. I stood atop an Independence Day float with the boxer Manny Pacquiao. I gave television interviews that my mother replayed in front of hapless dinner guests. Random grandfathers shook my hand. One man stopped me at a mall to tell me I was a national treasure. The burst of attention landed me television work, including a morning show, a travelogue, a debate program, and an unfortunate series on good morals with an evangelical pastor. I was photographed advertising high-speed internet and yellow tea. I wore thrift-shop suit jackets at a half-dozen commencements and held forth on the glorious untapped potential of Filipino youth. Photocopied programs listed me by rote as the designated inspirational performance, and while I was unaware that my quest for heroism would include reciting my speech to a roomful of fast-food executives, I understood the character I had been assigned: mascot for hope, in a country desperate for good news.

Had I had any sort of capacity for natural charm, I might have parlayed my fifteen minutes of fame into a career on camera, but I had nothing more than an awkward adolescent bravado. The trouble with winning a public speaking competition was that the public wanted to hear me speak, and it was assumed, incorrectly, that I had something of import to say. In fact, I was an indifferent scholar. I was not a good Catholic girl. I was alternately too loud and too quiet, swore too much, argued too often, did not photograph well, and could not pretend, no matter how hard I tried, that I was interesting.

I did try. I was, after all, a working student with rent to pay and appearances to keep up. I shopped at sales for the neon off-shoulder blouses I had convinced myself looked expensive on-screen. I delivered a lecture at a conservative Catholic school on the value of critical thought and suggested to a grinning teenage audience and their terrified teachers that a case could be made for legalizing abortion. In an attempt to appear cultured, I told one interviewer that Shakespeare was my favorite author instead of Nora Roberts, then went to an English class the next week to fail a *Hamlet* pop quiz. A full year into my television career, my long-suffering producers sent me the results of a survey conducted among viewers. Points for improvement included the note that Ms. Evangelista's nose flared unattractively when she spoke. My manager suggested rhinoplasty. "There's a buy-one-take-one deal; we can do it together."

President Arroyo promised a reformist administration. While all presidents after Marcos were restricted to single terms, the odd path leading to President Arroyo's elevation allowed her to stand for president in 2004. She captured the presidency in an election rife with rumors of cheating and violence. It did not take long to discover that maintaining her grip on power required her to placate both the military and the United States. "I am determined to build a strong republic," she thundered. Her war became the war on terror.

By then, the Cold War–era antisubversion laws had been repealed. Years of internal purges had reduced the armed wing of the Communist Party of the Philippines, the New People's Army (NPA), to a fraction of its original numbers. President Arroyo supported the United States' designation of the NPA as a foreign terrorist organization. Her praise of military power began a free-for-all against suspected Communists, armed or otherwise.

None of this was relevant in my corner of the capital. I believed in Edsa. I believed in the rule of law. I did not think, when I thought about it at all, that my government was in the business of torture and murder.

I stayed on camera long enough to pay for school, then got a job as a production assistant at ANC, the English language news channel of broadcasting giant ABS-CBN. In between coffee runs and script editing, I wrote a column for the opinion section of the newspaper of record, the *Philippine Daily Inquirer*. It was made clear to me that I was offered the job for no other reason than that the rest of the columnists were more than a decade older. The paper needed younger writers, and I was available. "Your grammar is sound," my editor told me by way of polite reassurance. Every week I churned out a thousand words about sunny beaches and high heels and singing competitions with Pollyanna enthusiasm and an excess of adverbs. I knew my place. I had no expertise, no causes, and certainly no academic cushion to pad my metaphorical armchair.

Sometime during all this, in 2006, my twenty-first year, I learned a lesson about words.

In the Philippines, English is one of two official languages. The other is Filipino, also known as Tagalog, spoken in and around the capital region. English was the medium of instruction when I grew up, and it remains the language of law, government, and medicine. While the Philippines is listed among the largest English-speaking nations, individual levels of fluency depend on education and upbringing. In a country where more than a hundred languages are spoken, a command of English, much like pale skin, is a signifier of privilege.

That privilege meant that I could pass every English-language class without learning the technical intricacies of grammar. While I could not, without looking it up, distinguish an appositive phrase from a subordinate clause, I could say with a smug certainty that I could tell the difference between a good sentence and a bad one. When I say I learned about words at the age of twenty-one, I mean a particular kind of word.

Consider this sentence: "She speaks English." The word *speaks* here is a transitive verb. The act transitions to an object. *She* is not spoken. English is. Every transitive verb is always followed by the object it affects.

Consider then another sentence: "She speaks loudly." Here the verb *speaks* is intransitive. The thought is complete without an object. The fact that she speaks is sufficient. There is no specifying the language, no explaining the context, and it is irrelevant whether she speaks the truth or speaks Klingon. The point is that she speaks, an act in and of itself. *I am writing this sentence* uses a transitive verb. *I am writing* does not.

To judge the transitivity of a verb, it is necessary to see its environment. While most verbs can shift from transitive to intransitive from sentence to sentence, some verbs cannot. She arrived, he sneezed, it fell, we sat, they laughed, you fainted. Each sentence ends with a full stop, intransitive. The subject is the object. You fainted. You were not fainted.

Die, for example, is an intransitive verb. So is *disappear.*

Once upon a time, the word *disappear* was solely an intransitive verb. The dinosaurs disappeared. The clouds disappeared. Voldemort disappeared, as Hagrid told the young Harry Potter, even if it took seven books to explain why. A disappearance is a near-magical event in the English language, accompanied by a grammatical puff of literary smoke. You disappear around a corner, into a car, down a flight of steps, and nobody asks how or why. The lady vanishes, the audience applauds.

In the 1970s the Spanish word *desaparecer*, "to disappear," became a transitive verb. Between 1976 and 1981, an estimated 13,000 to 30,000 political dissidents vanished during the military junta led by Jorge Rafael Videla, the dictator of Argentina. Videla was later tried for crimes against humanity. He was sentenced to life in prison for the murder and torture of political opponents. Charges included, among many others, the systematic kidnapping of children. At the time it was happening, the repressive atmosphere meant that little could categorically be said about the manner in which dissidents were abducted. Those who were lost were called *desaparecidos*—the disappeared.

In the Philippines, the word came into use during the Marcos dictatorship, after thousands of activists were snatched from streets and safehouses. Many of them were never seen again.

The *Oxford English Dictionary* has the following updated definition: "To disappear, transitive: to abduct or arrest (a person), esp. for political reasons, and subsequently to kill or detain as a prisoner, without making his or her fate known."

In 2006 two young women, both students from my university, disappeared from a small farming village north of the capital. Sherlyn Cadapan and Karen Empeño were community organizers in their twenties. There were rumors they were Communists, had been abducted by soldiers, maybe killed. That did not fit the narrative I knew. As far as I was concerned, *disappear* was an intransitive verb, and the report was left-wing propaganda. It seemed necessary to find out just how wrong the story was.

I went to court to watch the hearings. I met the families. I read the affidavits. I put on a nice skirt to interview the bemedaled general whom his victims called "the Butcher." I looked for witnesses. One of them was a teenage boy. Another was an escaped detainee whom I slipped into my apartment late one summer night to interview. They told me about burnings and shootings and beatings and months hunched inside cells so cramped that one woman went mad while sitting in her own shit.

Somewhere between the depositions and the reams of reports produced by independent commissions, I discovered that I believed the survivors. It took years in the field before I could be certain of my phrasing. Karen Empeño and Sherlyn Cadapan did not disappear. They were disappeared, the accountability so direct it could be reduced to a subject and a transitive verb: *The military disappeared the women.* They were abducted early one morning, bound and blindfolded as they were dragged through the wild grass by armed men. One of the students was pregnant. One of them was raped with pieces of wood. Many of the abuses were committed inside military camps, places where soldiers made detainees drink their own piss. Some of them escaped. The women did not.

I went to many places after that. To sprawling haciendas owned by the Cojuangco family, where farmers demanding land reform were massacred. To a mall food court, where the son of a newspaperman was snatched one afternoon. To a small room in a house where a father told me about the nine-year-old daughter shot by a military raiding party. She was listed in official reports as a Communist killed in action.

It began as one column but became two, three, and then dozens more, until I found myself unable to write about anything other than the dead and the lost. Someone sent a funeral bouquet. Someone else sent a death threat. Well-meaning mentors expressed concern for my safety. The concern only drove me to ever more recklessness, but the truth was that I was at very little risk. The Philippines is one of the most dangerous places in the world for journalists, but the threat, in my mind at least, was out in the provinces, where private armies and local officials operated with impunity. I was working for the largest television network and the highest circulated broadsheet in Manila. I also assumed, correctly as it turned out, that the assassination of a onetime national treasure would be more trouble than it was worth.

I did, however, receive many letters. I read each one. The activists had it coming. The Communists were terrorists. Leftists were masters of propaganda. The first few times I wrote back. I said, with considerable righteous naïveté, that no person deserved abduction and torture, Communist or otherwise. It was a truth I thought was self-evident. I thought the problem was that the public didn't know, because if it did, it would rise up in the same roiling mass that had protested the atrocities of the 1970s and '80s.

I was wrong, of course. People knew, but by then the disappeared were no longer people.

It was in 2009, just a year before the national elections that would replace President Arroyo, that I saw my first corpse. I was down south, on the island of Mindanao.

Mindanao had been one of the last regions to fall to colonial rule. Large swaths of the population held fast to their Muslim identity even as Christian settlers flooded in to amass large tracts of land. The name is thought to have been derived from the ethnic group Maguindanao, "the people of the flood plain," whose territory spread over southwestern Mindanao during the Spanish colonial period.

Mindanao's many provinces include the modern sultanate of Maguindanao, east of Iranun Bay. During martial law, President Ferdinand Marcos appointed a politician named Andal Ampatuan, Sr., as mayor of one of the provincial municipalities. After the Edsa Revolution, Corazon Aquino replaced Ampatuan Sr. with another clan member, also an Ampatuan. In subsequent elections, members of the Ampatuan clan rotated in and out of local office until Ampatuan Sr. captured the governorship in 1998. For decades, the national government maintained an amicable relationship with the Ampatuans, sending arms and support to the province as Maguindanao played watchdog against rebels. In 2004 President Arroyo was the beneficiary of that intimate relationship: the Ampatuan stronghold delivered a landslide victory crucial to the tight race for her second term.

In 2009 a rival clan, the Mangudadatus, declared their intent to challenge the Ampatuans for the gubernatorial seat. Their decision would prove explosive. On November 23, less than six months before the national elections, candidate Esmael "Toto" Mangudadatu sent his wife to file his certificate of candidacy. She was not the only woman present. Mangudadatu had sent many of his closest supporters, including his elderly aunt, his sister, and a pair of female lawyers in a convoy of four vans that would drive through a remote section of the province to the office of the Commission on Elections. Mangudadatu would later say the choice of whom to send was deliberate, as Moro culture held sacred the protection of women. Local journalists followed, intent on documenting the event. It was understood that their presence was a bulwark against violent attack.

They packed into a Mitsubishi L-300 owned by news network UNTV, a black SsangYong wagon driven by a DZRH radio reporter, and four Toyota Grandia vans. Somewhere on the road to Sharif Aguak, two other cars swung into the convoy—a hospital-bound Toyota Vios carrying five government employees and a light blue Toyota Tamaraw FX driven by a forty-one-year-old senior government statistician on his way to work after a weekend with his wife and daughters.

All of them died.

They were murdered in the morning, ambushed on the side of a hill by men carrying high-powered machine guns. A mass grave had already been prepared. Thirty-two of the fifty-eight dead were journalists and staff, the highest toll of murdered media workers killed in a single day anywhere in the world.

The news hit the capital. Two days later I flew south and joined a pack of journalists traveling to the crime scene. We believed there was safety in numbers.

Soldiers stopped us at a military checkpoint. They were young, trucked out of their bases to stand guard along the highways.

We told them we were journalists.

They shook their heads. Be careful, one of them said.

It was then that I understood that there was no safety in numbers, least of all for journalists.

We were quiet in the van.

I spent most of that day looking down, counting bodies, snapping pictures, measuring the distance between one corpse and another, noting the color and pattern of the muddied kerchiefs trampled on the ground. I saw a corpse fall from the teeth of a backhoe. The stench boiled low and thick. Newspapers, laid over the broken bodies, fluttered in the breeze.

The military commander said recovering the bodies was like cutting through a birthday cake: a layer of soil, a body, a red Vios, more soil, then the bodies again, bloating bigger and bigger the deeper they dug. The circle of tape couldn't contain the crime scene, as more and more bodies were found, so many that I could drop to my knees over a pile of banana leaves to photograph the body beneath. There, just under the bright green leaves, fat flies circling, a man's palm lay open to the sun with a scuffed silver watch still ticking away on his wrist. I looked up once and saw photographer after photographer standing on the ridge of the hill, lenses flaring, silhouettes sharp against the noon sun. Some of them had missed joining the convoy by minutes, and still they stood watch, an honor guard for the dead. I still saw them in the decade after, the image burned into my mind's eye as I found myself wandering across other killing fields in other places—that long line of journalists standing witness over the corpses of their comrades. I wanted to stand with them.

Forensic pathologists would later say that some of the victims had been buried alive. Others had been abandoned after the killers ran. The excavation ended with the recovery of fifty-seven bodies.

Victim number fifty-eight was a newspaper photographer. His daughter clutched at my wrist when I got to my feet.

Please, she asked me, have you seen my father?

They found his teeth, his jacket, his press ID. That was all they found. His name was Reynaldo Momay. His friends had called him Bebot. It would take another year for his name to be added to the charges, and eleven more for the court to convict two dozen people, including an Ampatuan son, on fifty-seven counts of murder. They were sentenced to life without parole.

"The court is convinced that the prosecution was not able to sufficiently establish the death of Reynaldo Momay," said the decision.

On the day the verdict was read, I called his daughter. Her name is Reynafe. Her father had kissed her goodbye on the fore-head before he left for the convoy. She is grateful the killers are in jail. She is glad for the verdict. She is aware that the sentence would be the same whether there were fifty-seven or fifty-eight dead, but it still matters, because Reynafe's father is dead, and his death should be on the record.

. . .

Corazon Aquino died the year of the massacre in Maguindanao. She was seventy-six years old. Millions wept on the day she was buried. In the wake of national mourning, her only son ran for the presidency. It was as close to a coronation as democratic Philippines had seen. Benigno "Noynoy" Aquino III, a senator with a middling legislative record, wore his mother's yellow as he won. The queen was dead, long live the king.

Noynoy Aquino was elected in an outpouring of empathy from a public who grieved the loss of his mother. Son of saints and heroes, floating on a cloud of confetti, President Aquino was a moral man, at least, according to President Aquino.

On June 30, 2010, he stood before a yellow-clad crowd at the Quirino Grandstand and swore his oath before the Filipino people. "I will not be able to face my parents, and you who brought me here, if I do not fulfill the promises I made," he said. "My parents sought nothing less, died for nothing less than democracy and peace. I am blessed by this legacy. I shall carry the torch forward."

The presidency of Benigno Aquino III took its first hit nearly two months into office. A dismissed police officer climbed onto a bus packed with Hong Kong tourists and waved an M16. The standoff ended with eight hostages dead and accusations of government incompetence. In the aftermath, a smiling Aquino appeared on live television. He later explained that "in that particular instance," after the tragedy, "it was the absurdity" that had made him smile. It was, he said, "an effort to control" his emotions. Aquino, while saying he took responsibility for the botched negotiations, refused to apologize to the families of the victims.

One of the surviving hostages, a Hong Kong national, told the *South China Morning Post* that Aquino's attitude "only shows that he has no empathy."

That accusation would dog the president for the next six years.

By then I had been promoted to executive producer at ANC. The ABS-CBN newsroom, operating nationwide, was under the command of the former CNN journalist Maria Ressa. I produced a documentary series and had no aspirations of joining the on-camera talent. My boss, Glenda Gloria, was a veteran defense reporter who ran the cable network with military precision. It was Glenda who, on a day we were understaffed, first thrust me in front of a camera to report live from the court where the Ampatuans were being tried, and it was also Glenda who discovered, along with ANC's live viewing audience, precisely why I had stayed behind the camera.

"Joining us live is reporter Patricia Evangelista," the anchor said from the studio. "Tell us what just happened in court."

I remember explaining that the flooring of the courtroom was red-and-white tile, and that the Ampatuan son on trial had been sniffing a bottle of white flower ointment. I said that the families had been weeping. I said that the room was packed with widows and orphans. I did not report on any of the legal decisions made during the hearing, largely because I remembered none of them. I did note that the defendant was giggling, a fact that was irrelevant to the general public, but one that I had, for reasons I do not recall, decided was very important.

I made no more live reports after that.

A year into the Aquino term, Maria and Glenda left ABS-CBN to found a news start-up with two other journalists, Chay Hofileña and Beth Frondoso. It would be the first of its kind in the country, a social media news network for an online audience that was owned and operated by journalists. When they left, I followed. The start-up was called Rappler.

We were a small team, twenty people in all, with eleven reporters in their early twenties covering the national news. The fact that we were mostly women was not a function of affirmative action, as Philippine journalism is a largely female enterprise, with most of the major newsrooms run by women. I carved out a niche as a trauma reporter, although it was years before I understood what that meant.

On September 9, 2013, a group of over four hundred armed rebels from the Moro National Liberation Front took control of five coastal villages in Zamboanga City in Mindanao, using 150 civilians, including children, as human shields. The sky, one witness told me, rained blood.

"Was that not the skill demonstrated by our soldiers in Zamboanga?" President Aquino asked. "Of the one hundred and ninety-seven hostages there, they rescued one hundred and ninety-five, and the two dead were killed not because of the crossfire of rescue but because they were killed by escaping bad elements."

It was not strictly true. Thirteen of the dead were civilians. One of the hostages was a two-year-old baby named Eithan who died with a bullet in his skull. Eithan died in the crossfire, still a hostage, as his parents crouched over him in a sewer. Another 218 people would be dead one year later, many of them young children who had been forced to flee, dying from diarrhea and dehydration after the mortars stopped falling. Those deaths exceeded the total number of casualties killed in the crossfire during the twenty-one-day standoff.

"How should I have reacted?" President Aquino asked the media. "Tear out what's left of my hair and say, 'What should we do?' Would that have helped? When they presented the problem, should I have just sobbed over it? Should I have thrown a tantrum?"

For journalists, there are two seasons in the Philippines. Summer, and the drowning season. It begins in June, stretches to December, and staggers on to a rehabilitation period that continues past the moment the next typhoon hits the next province. In the time I worked for Rappler, it was a good year when we stayed inside the alphabet of typhoon names. Every year I counted bodies, interviewed survivors, and filed videos of families begging for aid. My grasp of geography, never strong, was marked by provincial death tolls. I knew localities by the number of dead and could recite them, year by year, at a time when I couldn't remember my own zip code.

On November 8, 2013, Super Typhoon Haiyan slammed into the Visayan Islands with storm surges reaching as high as twenty-four feet. The United Nations classified it as a level-three emergency, affecting over fourteen million, with 6,300 officially reported dead and an uncounted number missing. It was, at that time, the strongest recorded typhoon to make landfall anywhere in the world.

In Tacloban City, the survivors climbed down from trees to find bodies in backyards leaning on refrigerators, inside houses jammed in closets, in bathrooms and bedrooms and on the edges of the airport road wrapped in Rainbow Brite bedsheets. Container trucks floated in water with their drivers still clutching steering wheels. It was normal, for example, for a boy looking for his brother to ask for directions to the nearest pile of cadavers.

Out on the dark streets, I met a man named Ramil Navarro.

He was a handsome man, just past forty, his skin darkened by the sun, his hair a curly mop. An old gang tattoo tracked over his right arm. A fresh scar ran over his left. He wore rubber boots and a tattered pair of green shorts, the pair he wore every day for seventeen days. He was tough, and he was tall. It was his strength that nearly killed him when the storm came. Ramil was one of the few strong enough to fight the water. Drowning people clung to him, clutching at his hair, gripping his shoulders, clawing up his back, children, teenagers, a mother carrying a daughter, all clinging to Ramil while birds and turtles and snakes slithered up his chest.

He shoved them all away, abandoned them all in the water as he searched for his wife and daughter. He caught his wife just as she was going under. Only after the flood receded did he find his daughter in the wild grass. Her eleven-year-old arms were wrapped around a rock.

I asked Ramil if the families blamed him for letting their loved ones drown.

He said no, of course not. There was no one left to blame him. Most of the families were dead too.

President Aquino descended on Tacloban City to offer his people hope. The villages had been leveled. The airport security chief had lost his children and was walking shirtless on the streets. Body bags had run out.

"There were so many people outside," the president told the media, "I had to ask them why they felt they had to loiter around." Help would come from their local government, he told them. It would be better "if you all went home." Possibly he did not understand there were no homes to return to.

Those who could waited for the president at the temporary

command center. Officials reassured residents that clean water was available. They said there was order on the streets. The death toll, at that moment, was still at seventy-two. A resident raised his hand. He said no fewer than seven hundred corpses were piled nearby. He said the command center's kitchen was relying on rainwater to cook. He said there was looting and violence. He pointed to another man, a local hotel owner. "That man nearly got shot this morning," he said. "He's lucky he didn't get hit."

To which the president of the Republic of the Philippines replied, "You're still alive, aren't you?"

President Aquino was not incapable of emotion, particularly when cornered and criticized. He lashed out in indignation at his critics, claiming sympathy one moment, then dismissing its value the next, even going so far as to read out a Wikipedia definition of *empathy* to a mystified press. "I am not play-acting at being president," he said. "I perform my role as president."

Year after year the performance failed. Asked, for example, why he failed to appear at the wake of Jennifer Laude, who was murdered by a U.S. Marine, Aquino explained that a visit would have made him feel uncomfortable. "In general, I don't attend wakes of people I don't know," he said. On the morning the flag-wrapped coffins of dozens of dead policemen arrived at the Villamor Air Base, Aquino was not standing on the tarmac to salute the uniformed men killed in the line of duty. He was in the province of Laguna instead, praising Mitsubishi Philippines at a new manufacturing plant for standing by their "commitment to the Filipino people."

When he finally met with the families of the commandos killed by his own mismanagement, one widow said the president had included himself among the ranks of victims. "My father also died," Aquino reportedly said. "I know how you feel, so we're even now."

The president spoke often of his father's sacrifice and his mother's nobility. He walked the straight path, he said, the decent road, and he invited the nation to join him. He had integrity. He was virtuous. He was decent. By the standard set by many Filipino presidents, including his own mother, President Aquino's six years in Malacañang Palace were a success. His approach to foreign policy reaffirmed the Philippines' exclusive sovereign rights over the West Philippine Sea and contributed to the forming of the Paris Agreement. The economy was a billion dollars larger than it was when he was elected. Systems of accountability were set up for the military and police. The long-fought-for Reproductive Health Law was passed. The education budget doubled. K–12 education was established. A massive social welfare program claimed to have lifted seven million people from poverty.

But I am after all a trauma reporter, and my view of the palace is from the ground, inside the miserable tent cities stinking of piss and shit where fathers wait for their drowned daughters to come home. "You are my bosses," Aquino said of his people. If they were still alive, it should be enough.

It was in this context that word came from the south. Change was coming, and his name was Rodrigo Duterte.

4

THE RISE OF THE PUNISHER

Mindanao's favorite son will tell you his mother, Soling, was a Spanish mestiza, and his father was of Chinese descent. He will say his grandmother was of the southern Maranao, whose ancestral land curves around the blue waters of Lake Lanao.

"I am just the son of a migrant to Mindanao," he said. "I was born to a poor family. My mother was just a teacher."

Born poor, raised poor, lived poor, the chosen child of the south, an outsider from Davao City who spoke the language of the streets. He was no scholar, as he was happy to explain, scoffing at the Latin honors and Wharton degrees of the political rivals whom he accused of posturing elitism. Here was a man, by his own telling, who pulled himself up by his bootstraps and became a prosecutor, vice-mayor, mayor, congressman, then mayor again.

"I have no pretensions," he said.

"I am a small-town boy," he said.

"I am an ordinary Filipino," he said.

"I know the sentiment of the ordinary people. I can talk to them because that's where I come from."

For the duration of Rodrigo Duterte's public life, the Philippine press—which is only as free as it dares to be—would serve to both correct and enhance the myth of Duterte. The rest of the world would look on with a combination of awe, admiration, disgust, and alarm.

EXCERPT FROM A MAGAZINE PROFILE

The young "Rody," as Duterte was then known, was the son of a provincial governor on the southern Philippine island of Mindanao. Like many of the progeny of the Philippine political elite, he had enjoyed a privileged upbringing. He grew up surrounded by guns and bodyguards, flew his father's plane when he was in his hometown, and hung out with the sons of local notables in his Jesuit-run boys' school.

—*Sheila Coronel, "The Vigilante President,"*
Foreign Affairs, *August 12, 2019*

We all knew his story. He was a wild child, and he wanted everyone to know it.

He did not, so wrote his biographers, clap for bands at the Marrakech or order paninis at Aldevinco or join in the swinging dance parties that the children of Davao's upper class much preferred. The "good, clean fun" of his schoolmates was not his idea of a good time. He chose his own crowd, danced with bar girls at beerhouses, drank with his father's police bodyguards, joined a gang, bought guns, failed classes, went hunting, was stabbed, got transferred, was expelled, was whipped by his mother, was lectured by his father, and behaved much like a troubled son of privilege, which in fact he was.

He was born one of six, the son of a two-term governor and his schoolteacher wife who had left the Visayas for land-rich Mindanao. The Second World War had dealt a sharp blow to the family fortunes, but the Dutertes were connected by blood, marriage, and affiliation to powerful political clans. Young Rodrigo was raised in a house with a cook and a driver and an errand boy and a passel of bodyguards. He was "skinny and short and not handsome." He was "awkward and unattractive." He was "an ordinary and unspectacular student . . . who worked just to get a passing grade." He skipped school for months before the director of the Ateneo de Davao High School called the governor to ask where his son was.

He was eighteen when his father was reelected governor. He was twenty when his father was appointed to the national cabinet, chosen by President Ferdinand Marcos as secretary of the Department of General Services. When Vicente Duterte died of a heart attack after losing a congressional election, Rody went home for the funeral, wept at the casket, then returned to Manila to pursue a law degree.

Rody was brave, Rody was tough, Rody was fearless, so fearless, Rody said, that jail and violence did not trouble him. He was, he said, "used to shooting." It wasn't that he frequented target ranges, which he did, or that he had served in the army, which he hadn't, or that he was, as was a certain segment of the Philippine public, an enthusiastic collector of ranged weaponry. Rodrigo Duterte was used to shooting because he was used to shooting *people*. He was particular about the noun.

One of those people was Octavio Goco, Rody's fraternity brother at the Catholic law school where Rody was a senior. Their fraternity was called Lex Talionis. Every telling of the story describes Octavio as something of a bully, a young man who had needled Rody over his Visayan accent, who called Rody provincial, who had the gall to laugh at the governor's son who had come to Manila to learn to be a lawyer.

Octavio Goco was shot the year Rody turned twenty-seven. Three stories are told about how. The first story, one that the young Rody supposedly refused to tell despite advice, was that Octavio and Rody were playing with guns in the school hallway. At some point there was pushing, and shoving, then a gunshot. What happened was an accident, and there was no investigation.

The second story was that Rody, angry at Octavio's bullying, challenged him to a shoot-out. Octavio had a homemade revolver. Rody was armed with a .25 caliber. What happened was a duel, and Octavio's gun failed.

The third story was that Octavio had taunted Rody until Rody decided he had had enough. He lay in wait. He watched. In the hallway one day, Octavio instigated a scuffle. Rody howled that he would shoot Octavio if he got hit. He was hit in the nose, son of a bitch, so he shot, and bang, Octavio was on the ground. Rody jumped onto a boat and sailed to Davao with the police on his heels. What happened was an assault, and Rody had pulled the trigger.

All three stories ended the same way. Octavio Goco survived. Rody's Lex Talionis fraternity brothers rallied around him. A school prefect wanted him expelled, but the university decided it would be a pity to cut short a promising legal career. No charges were filed. Rody was banned from marching in graduation ceremonies. He told his mother that graduation rites had been suspended. He passed the bar in 1973 and was rewarded with a blue Volkswagen Beetle for his trouble.

Of the many versions of the story, the one that survives is the one Rody chose to tell, and has told, many times.

"I was about to graduate from San Beda when I shot a man," he said. "I waited for him. I said I'll put him in his place . . . bang!"

EXCERPT FROM A BIOGRAPHY OF
RODRIGO ROA DUTERTE

Soling Duterte knew that Rody wanted to be a fiscal (now called prosecutor). Sometime in 1976, she went to see Elias Lopez, her late husband's colleague in the NP [party] to ask if her son could be accommodated in the fiscal's office. . . . Elias told Soling that he will see what he can do. . . .

A few days after Soling's visit, August Tesoro, after playing a game of golf with Lopez, brought up the same request while they were having breakfast. "Lias, I pity the son of Tiring Duterte, I saw him in Agdao just notarizing papers. . . . Find a job for him at the fiscal's office."

After a month, the Minister of Justice Vicente Abad Santos visited Davao. Lopez, during their meeting, brought up Rody's wish to become a fiscal. . . . He handed the minister a paper proposing the creation of the position of Special Counsel for Military and Police Matters under Davao City Fiscal's Office. . . . In one of Lopez's trips to Manila soon after, he and Abad Santos presented the proposal to Marcos, which the latter signed. The justice minister then signed a separate paper appointing Atty. Rodrigo Duterte to the newly created post.

—*Earl Parreño,* Beyond Will and Power *(Lapulapu City, 2019)*

In 1983, just after the assassination of Ninoy Aquino, prayer vigils and street protests mushroomed across the country. In Davao City, an urban center of the island of Mindanao, the weekly mass actions were led by another widow in yellow.

Her name was Soledad Duterte. Her people called her Soling. Her Yellow Friday Movement was one of many pockets of dissent in the waning years of the Marcos dictatorship.

On the eve of Ferdinand Marcos's overthrow, Rodrigo Duterte woke his own children to lead them downtown to join the crowds cheering the fall of the dictator. "Remember this night," he told his children. "Do not ever forget."

Corazon Aquino's government began the work of restoration, which included the appointment of caretaker administrators across the country to fill the seats vacated by local government officials. The new officials were called officers-in-charge (OIC). Their mandates were to last only until new elections could be held in 1988. The seat for OIC vice-mayor of Davao City was offered to Soling Duterte, on the strength of her leadership during the protests. She was seventy years old.

"At the last minute," said the Interior Ministry, "Nanay Soling declined the post and suggested her son."

President Aquino approved of the substitution. Forty-one-year-old assistant city prosecutor Rodrigo Roa Duterte was appointed vice-mayor of Davao City. Soling Duterte's boy stepped firmly onto the shining yellow road of the Edsa mythology, on the side, he claimed, "of truth and justice." In two years, he would win the mayoralty of Davao, a city that had once lent itself to the grim prose of noir comic books. He would hold the seat for a total of twenty-two years.

"I am a child of destiny," he would later say. "I never wanted to be a mayor. If you believe in God, you believe in destiny." That destiny, or so he said, was the conclusion of a life fighting side by side with the people against the dictator. "I was with the people."

And so the saint baptized the son of another saint, and the man who would become the Punisher was born.

EXCERPT FROM A NEWSLETTER FROM THE
INSTITUTE OF CURRENT WORLD AFFAIRS

Until 1986, Davao City was considered a laboratory for the NPA's [New People's Army's] new strategy of urban operations. Davao's large slum area, Agdao, was run by a revolutionary government and nicknamed Nicaragdao after the Central American country. At the height of Communist Party power, NPA partisans, called "sparrows," carried out liquidations of police officers with impunity. There were an average of two to three killings a day, whether by the NPA, right-wing groups, or criminals. According to police records, in 1986, over 40 government and police officials were liquidated or died in encounters with the NPA.

—*Erik Guyot, "Alsa Masa: 'Freedom Fighters'*
or 'Death Squads'?," August 6, 1988

The Davao City that Rodrigo Duterte had been appointed to lead was, in 1989, described as "a sprawling expanse of urban slums racked by poverty, violence, vendettas and desperate crime." It was "murder city," the "crime capital," the stronghold of the Communist Party's New People's Army. "Davao City," wrote the *Sydney Morning Herald* in 1987, "concentrates every Philippines problem you can think of—a high birthrate, land shortage, absentee owners, prostitution and gambling rackets, corrupt police and military, and of course, the NPA whose avenging Marxist zeal not infrequently cloaks a penchant for unabashed thuggery."

Perhaps in no other area of Davao City was the Communist presence more visible than in Agdao. *The Christian Science Monitor* reported that the district was a place where "the Communist Party, not the government, raises taxes." Here a notorious local politician named Baby Aquino gathered together a paramilitary group to protect himself from the Communists—a failed proposition, as the politician was murdered in cold blood. Before his death, three of his men, in a much-repeated story, gunned down a suspected Communist, then raised their rifles in the air to shout "*Mag-alsa na ta!*"

Mag-alsa na ta. Let us rise.

The group became known as the Alsa Masa, "Masses Arise." There is some debate on who was responsible for its founding. One version names an Agdao native and former NPA guerrilla, Boy Ponsa Cagay. Another version names Lieutenant Colonel Franco Calida of the Metropolitan District Command (Metrodiscom). What is clear is that at some point, Alsa Masa began working for the Metrodiscom, and were considered members of the Civilian Home Defense Force. "In the fight between democracy and Communism there is no way to be neutral," Colonel Calida said in 1987. "Anybody who would not like to join Alsa Masa is a Communist."

Cagay drew up lists of suspected Communists. He demanded they surrender to the police. His judgment was enough to render anyone a target. Those who refused were considered enemies of Davao.

Asked by a documentary filmmaker how Alsa Masa persuaded suspects to surrender, Cagay said he sent word to their parents: "I tell the parents that they must surrender. Now, if they don't surrender, maybe, tomorrow they will die."

Alsa Masa operated "a system of checkpoints, armed patrols, taxation, propaganda, forced recruitment and summary justice that consciously mimics that of its Communist enemy." At its height, its membership was estimated at more than nine thousand in Davao City alone, including three thousand former NPA members, some of them assassins, who had surrendered.

Amnesty International noted that there was "strong evidence" that members of Alsa Masa had committed grave human rights abuses "with the knowledge or acquiescence of local military commanders." A U.S.-Philippine fact-finding mission in 1987 enumerated violations that included murder, harassment, forced enlistment, and threats from Calida himself. The group, said the New York–based Lawyers' Committee for Human Rights, was "notorious for its own lawless activities, including the liquidations of suspected rebels."

"I told you when we were discussing the peace initiatives that when they fail, as we feared they would . . . it becomes necessary to take out the sword of war," President Corazon Aquino told commanders of the Philippine Military Academy. "The answer to terrorism of the left and the right is not social and economic reform but police and military action."

The Communist insurgency in the Philippines was one of several "low-intensity wars" the United States chose to fight. Alsa Masa may have been the first and most notorious of the vigilantes, but they were by no means the only ones. By late 1987, the first year of Cory Aquino's administration, at least two hundred vigilante groups were thought to be operating in the country. They included another Davao group named Tadtad, literally "Chop-chop." Tadtad members posed with bloodied bolos and, once, with the head of a Communist guerrilla.

EXCERPT FROM A SPEECH BY
PRESIDENT CORAZON C. AQUINO

I am overjoyed to join you here [in Davao City] where the Alsa Masa was born. . . . You have succeeded in crushing the Communists, and we look up to you as the example in our fight against communism.

—*Corazon C. Aquino, Agdao, Davao City, October 1987*

A STATEMENT FROM THE U.S. STATE DEPARTMENT

As far as the citizens' groups are concerned, as I understand it, these are being organized within the framework of governmental authority. They aren't sort of free-floating vigilante groups, and President Aquino has supported this approach and we support what she's standing for there.

—*George Shultz, U.S. secretary of state, 1987*

EXCERPT FROM *THE NEW YORK TIMES*

Many military and Government leaders, including President Corazon C. Aquino and Gen. Fidel V. Ramos, the Chief of Staff, have endorsed the concept of anti-Communist vigilante groups, even as fears have grown that a new form of armed terror has taken root in this violent nation.

—*Seth Mydans, "Right-Wing Vigilantes Spreading in Philippines,"* The New York Times, *April 4, 1987*

And so after the miracle, the death squads wore yellow too.

In 1988, two years after he was appointed as OIC vice-mayor, Rodrigo Duterte ran for mayor of Davao City. He won. A newsletter from the Institute of Current World Affairs, published in the late 1980s, included an interview with the new mayor. Alsa Masa, Duterte said, had committed some abuses, but they were "isolated happenings." He emphasized the need to encourage Alsa Masa's continued momentum, even to subsidize Alsa Masa's fighters. "Without the support of the government," the mayor said, "the Alsa Masa would collapse."

The Communist presence in Davao City died down in the late 1980s. While there are competing narratives as to how exactly the city broke free of Communist control—including brutal purges within the Communist Party—Alsa Masa eventually disbanded, even as its methods remained.

Sometime during Mayor Duterte's second term, there was a sharp uptick in the murders of petty thieves, criminals, and suspected drug users. The manner of their deaths was reminiscent of Alsa Masa's methods.

FROM AN AFFIDAVIT
OF A DEATH SQUAD LEADER

In the beginning, we targeted and killed drug addicts, drug pushers, snatchers, holduppers, and other criminals. Later on, however, we were ordered by Mayor Duterte to go after and kill his personal and political enemies. We became like hired or contract killers who killed not only criminals but innocent people.

—*Police officer and self-described death squad leader,*
Makati City, February 19, 2017

There is a story told of how the new squad of killers found their name. The target was a known drug dealer. The squad leader, a retired police officer, had pulled in support troops from among the rebel returnees in Agdao. The plan required planting evidence ascribing credit for the kill to the New People's Army. The squad prepared a note—"Do not be like the scum of society"—signed, purportedly, by an NPA commander.

One of the squad members protested. It would be a chancy thing, he said, because the NPA would deny it. The mayor, deep in talks with the NPA, might be irritated. No one wanted to irritate the mayor. The note was scrapped, and a new one was written. It was the squad leader and the chief of the rebel returnees who decided on the group's name.

The house was surrounded. Bullets flew. Nobody shot back.

No guns were recovered. No drugs were confiscated. The only corpse they found was of a housemaid. They left the note anyway.

It was signed Davao Death Squad.

The regional police director described the squad as "mostly of former New People's Army partisans and some policemen." According to Human Rights Watch, most of the victims of death squad killings were alleged drug dealers, petty criminals, and street children, as well as the family members and friends of intended targets. "Their repertoire of warfare—drawn from both military counterinsurgency as well as communist guerilla methods and practice—was perfected during dictatorship and proved equally effective in democracy," wrote journalist Sheila Coronel.

There were many targets. A review of a single Davao newspaper's reporting showed at least eighty-four vigilante killings had occurred in the first three months of 2005. That year, the U.S. Mission in Manila reportedly filed a classified document describing the Davao Death Squad as "a vigilante group linked with Davao Mayor Rodrigo Duterte."

By 2007 Philip Alston, the UN Special Rapporteur on Extrajudicial, Summary or Arbitrary Executions, reported that the Davao Death Squad was responsible for up to five hundred deaths. The killings were preceded by warnings and were "carried out publicly and with methodical indifference."

Alston wrote that the mayor, "while repeatedly acknowledging that it was his 'full responsibility' that hundreds of murders committed on his watch remained unsolved . . . would perfunctorily deny the existence of a death squad." The mayor, said Alston, also insisted that his threats "were for public consumption and would have no effect on police conduct."

A STATEMENT FROM
THE MAYOR OF DAVAO CITY

I don't mind us being called the murder capital of the Philippines as long as those being killed are the bad guys. From day one, I said henceforth Davao [City] will be very, very dangerous for criminals. I've been telling criminals it's a place where you can die any time. If that's a cue for anybody, that's fine.

—*Rodrigo Duterte quoted in Alan Sipress,*
"In Philippine City, Public Safety Has a Dark Side,"
The Washington Post, *November 27, 2003*

EXCERPT FROM A REPORT TO THE
UN HUMAN RIGHTS COUNCIL

One fact points very strongly to the officially-sanctioned character of these killings: No one involved covers his face. The men who warn mothers that their children will be the next to die unless they make themselves scarce turn up on doorsteps undisguised. The men who gun down or, and this is becoming more common, knife children in the streets almost never cover their faces.

—*Philip Alston, Special Rapporteur on Extrajudicial,*
Summary or Arbitrary Executions, April 2008

EXCERPT FROM AN INTERVIEW
WITH CLARITA ALIA

When somebody informed me that Christopher had been stabbed, I was startled, shocked—I realized they had started killing my kids one by one. When I got to the market where the killing happened, I saw Christopher being held by his older brother, Arnold. I think that Arnold was probably the target as he is my oldest son. People at the market said that two men were following Arnold that morning, but then apparently lost him and targeted Christopher instead. Christopher suffered one fatal wound in the chest, and had some smaller wounds on his arms—apparently, he was trying to protect himself.

When the police arrived at the scene, they didn't try to find any witnesses, they just kept asking me, "What happened? Who killed your son?" I was hysterical, and kept telling them, "Why are you asking me? You are the policemen—ask witnesses around here!"

—*Clarita Alia, quoted in Human Rights Watch,*
"You Can Die Any Time": Death Squad
Killings in Mindanao, April 6, 2009

They killed Richard Alia first, as he stepped out for a drink. His mother told him to stay away from his gang, because she had heard the mayor speak on TV. The mayor had warned the parents of Davao City that if they had sons and daughters involved in crime, they should leave the city, or they would die.

Richard was already dead when his mother ran into the crime scene. He was eighteen years old. Christopher was next, three months later in the public market. He was seventeen.

Bobby's turn came three years later. He was fourteen. Police accused him of stealing a cell phone. He was arrested, then released, after he claimed torture at the hands of cops. The butcher knife that killed him came from behind.

The last was Fernando, the child Clarita had sent to school away from the city. He hid for three years, then came home to Davao. The death squad found him and told him he was next. Police arrested him for sniffing glue, then released him eventually. He survived the first murder attempt. He did not survive the second. He was stabbed on a bridge. He made it to the hospital. Doctors tried to revive him, but he was pronounced dead in hours. He was fifteen years old.

AN INTERVIEW WITH DAVAO MAYOR
RODRIGO DUTERTE

DDS is non-existent. It started during the NPA days; death squads were organized by the government. And it carried on after Martial Law and after the restoration of democracy by Cory, and it has really become a cliché. For every killing there is no identity of the killer or even of the victim. The easiest excuse would really be DDS.

—*Rodrigo Duterte, as quoted in*
Esquire Philippines, *March 2015*

In 2009, the Commission on Human Rights (CHR), the Philippines' primary human rights institution, announced a public inquiry into alleged summary executions in Davao City. The CHR, an independent government body created in the aftermath of the martial law atrocities, was led by a former election lawyer named Leila de Lima.

"We want to make people realize that [killing] is wrong, legally and morally," said de Lima. "Even assuming that these are criminal elements, it's wrong. It's completely wrong, morally and legally. Many of them are even minors."

De Lima was a former election lawyer who had been appointed to chair the commission by then-president Gloria Macapagal-Arroyo. She was later elected senator. During her term in the CHR, she spent two years investigating, among others, the murders and enforced disappearances of Communist activists.

The public hearings on the Davao Death Squad, held at the Royal Mandaya Hotel in Davao City, began on March 30, 2009. De Lima's first resource person was Davao City mayor Rodrigo Duterte.

"When I became mayor in 1988, Davaoeños know this, I made a statement, a very disturbing statement that I would make Davao City the most dangerous place for criminals," Mayor Duterte said. "It is my duty as mayor and I am responsible for the uplift of this community, for the lives, for the peace and order."

He said the deaths of minors were likely due to "rioting and retaliation." He emphasized that peace and order were a priority in his city, particularly against the major threats of drug trafficking and terrorism. "I do not go for small crimes," he said. He denied the possibility that any one group was responsible for the murders, insisting instead that if any public servants were involved, "they are doing it on their own."

The mayor said he believed in due process. He said his men shot only in self-defense. He denied the existence of a death squad—"No ma'am, there is none." And while he admitted there were "unexplained, unresolved" killings in Davao City, "if you mean summary killings in this sense that he is tied, a person is tied [up], or youth offenders, there is none because I have not seen one."

"You admit there are vigilante-style killings?" De Lima asked.

"I don't know about the reasons why," replied the mayor, "because I said I was not there or maybe it would be surmised that I'm only guessing."

"What is your view of vigilantes, sir?"

"Outside of the purview of the law, as simple as that."

"Who are the possible perpetrators?"

"Name, I really would not know. It could be a revenge."

Mayor Duterte claimed he had asked CHR regional director Alberto Sipaco, Jr., to investigate the killings. Sipaco was Duterte's fraternity brother from Lex Talionis—a Latin phrase meaning "the law of retribution," or, more simply, an eye for an eye. Sipaco was one of the founders of the fraternity's chapter at the Ateneo de Davao University. His co-founder was Rodrigo Duterte.

EXCERPT FROM A LEAKED
CABLE FROM U.S. AMBASSADOR
KRISTIE KENNEY

Commission on Human Rights Regional Director Alberto Sipaco (strictly protect) at a private meeting affirmed that Mayor Duterte knows about the killings and permits them. Recounting a conversation he once had with Duterte, who is his close friend and former fraternity brother, Sipaco said he pleaded with the Mayor to stop vigilante killings and support other methods to reduce crime, like rehabilitation programs for offenders. According to Sipaco, the Mayor responded, "I'm not done yet." Sipaco said he repeatedly attempted to reason with Duterte that the killings were unlawful and detrimental to society, but Duterte refused to broach the issue.

Sipaco expressed a sense of helplessness over the killings, as well as concern for his personal safety, but acknowledged that the CHR was taking its mission in Davao very seriously. On the margins of the public hearings, the CHR was working to locate witnesses, retrieve them in private unmarked cars, collect their testimony in undisclosed and protected locations, and seek their agreement to testify. These intense security measures were necessary to protect witnesses from the police, Sipaco said, who could seek to intimate or silence witnesses before they had a chance to appear in court.

> —*Ambassador Kristie Kenney, confidential cable to the*
> *secretary of state, via WikiLeaks, May 8, 2009*

EXCERPT FROM A DEPOSITION
BY WITNESS "JOSE"

QUESTION:

How many victims of summary execution were killed in your presence and buried by you and your co-[Anti-Crime Unit] members in the ground of the . . . compound?

ANSWER:

Thirteen male persons, your honor. They were all hogtied and blindfolded before they were killed.

> —*Witness using the pseudonym "Jose Basilio,"*
> *deposition, Manila, June 2009*

Jose worked in an office. The man who ran the office gave out lists. On the lists were names. When the office was efficient, the people on the list ended up dead.

In the story Jose told, most of the people who worked in the office were cops, and that wasn't an odd thing, because the office belonged to the Davao City Police. Jose was not a cop. He was a former NPA operative who had surrendered to the government. He was told that his new mission was peace and order in Davao City. He was given a gun, an allowance, and bonuses for every assignment. Some of the men got motorcycles. Other men got cars. One of the cops drove an Isuzu Fuego that had once belonged to Mayor Rodrigo Duterte.

On paper, Jose was a civilian auxiliary member of the Police

Anti-Crime Unit. In practice, his job was to bury the bodies. Sometimes he was asked to help in the killing, but he never held the knife. Mostly he pinned the men down.

That was what happened to Jovani, who was on the list because people thought he was a thief. Jose said he and eight other men snatched Jovani outside the market and took him to a quarry in a compound owned by a retired cop, Bienvenido Laud. The men blindfolded Jovani with a length of plastic packing tape. They trussed his arms behind him, and then his feet. One cop stabbed Jovani between the neck and shoulder, but Jovani gasped, so a second cop took the knife and brought it down on Jovani's chest, again and again, until Jovani went quiet and someone told Jose to pick up the body and go.

Not all the murders happened in the Laud quarry. Sometimes the teams went into homes and killed fellow cops. Sometimes there was collateral damage, because it was important to keep quiet, and that meant murdering witnesses too. Jovani was not the only man Jose buried. There were thirteen, and Jose watched them all die. He was one of the last who saw them alive, and the last who saw them dead, and all of it was why he remembered their names. There was Jovani, of course, Jose's first. There were Alex and Dondon, both alleged thieves. There were the suspected drug dealers, Tony and Bobong and Toto and Peping and Alvin, and then Jay, a teenager the cops said was a gang leader, and then Haron Lupon and Datu Ala and Alimudin Julkifli and Taib, who were supposed to be bombers and terrorists, although Jose didn't know very much about them.

The cops told Jose to be quiet, and he tried, but he couldn't sleep for many nights after the murders. He was afraid someone would make him go quiet too.

EXCERPT FROM A REPORT BY
HUMAN RIGHTS WATCH

Most members of the DDS [Davao Death Squad] fall into two main groups. According to several insiders, the older members, some of whom were recruited back in the early 2000s, were primarily former members of the so-called "sparrow units" of the NPA who surrendered to the government, as well as some former military and police personnel. . . . Other recruits are young men and boys, many of whom have no job and no place to live. They often have a criminal record, and were themselves at one time "on the list." Thus, for them the choice was between being a potential victim of the DDS, or joining the ranks.

—*Human Rights Watch,* "You Can Die Any Time":
Death Squad Killings in Mindanao, *April 6, 2009*

EXCERPT FROM A SWORN STATEMENT
BY WITNESS "RAMON"

I sat beside the target, who was also sitting down. Meanwhile my companions surrounded us, pretending to smoke. Suddenly two of them, Kulot among them, approached us and stabbed the victim. One of them stabbed him in the back while Kulot stabbed him from the front. While he was being stabbed, he was screaming "Mama." We left like nothing happened. My companions took off on motorcycles and I took the jeepney. I remember the store owner witnessed what happened, along with a couple that was also there.

—*Witness using the pseudonym "Ramon,"*
sworn affidavit, Davao City, July 4, 2009

Ramon was a paid informant. His job, he said, was to surveil targets. He reported to a different office, a satellite unit in the village of Agdao. The lists of targets changed every month. Most of them were drug addicts and thieves.

Every piece of information Ramon delivered was worth ₱500, what amounted to roughly ten dollars. Only once was he paid more, when the list included a thief named Marlon.

Marlon was Ramon's friend. For a thousand pesos, twice his usual rate, Ramon sent a tip that led operatives to the house where Marlon had been hiding.

Marlon was shot trying to jump out a window. It was "sad," said Ramon.

A STATEMENT FROM THE MAYOR OF DAVAO CITY

If you are doing an illegal activity in my city, if you are a criminal or part of a syndicate that preys on the innocent people of the city, for as long as I am the mayor, you are a legitimate target of assassination.

—*Davao City mayor Rodrigo Duterte to reporters, February 2009*

EXCERPT FROM A SWORN STATEMENT
BY WITNESS "CRISPIN"

I started my new job that Monday. After a week, I was given a list of the wanted men I was supposed to kill. The list had their names and addresses. It was handed to me and distributed to the rest of the squad members by our boss. Sometimes Mayor Duterte himself would come by our safehouse to hand out the list, after saying, "Here's the list of the bastards." I personally saw and spoke to Duterte several times. He would come by almost weekly to say hello.

—*Witness using the pseudonym "Crispin Salazar,"*
sworn affidavit, Quezon City, June 24, 2009

Crispin, a former NPA rebel, arrived at the mayor's home at nine on a Sunday morning. It was 1992. The job interview commenced. Would Crispin, asked the mayor, be inclined toward killing? Yes, certainly Crispin was.

The squad was made up of rebel returnees and people from other municipalities. All of them had been issued guns. All were given orders, sometimes by the office managers—called the Big Bosses—and sometimes by Mayor Duterte himself. The mayor gave Crispin a .375 revolver.

Crispin's first kill was a nineteen-year-old boy. Two shots, head and chest, done quickly enough that Crispin had time to report to his boss and pick up his check, all before the bank closed at four. Every kill was worth ₱15,000, at the time a little more than three hundred dollars. The checks had the mayor's name in front and his signature on the back. Crispin said he had counted a total of forty kills, including a uniformed cop and two women counting out drug money inside a motel room.

Crispin was a good employee. He had initiative. He was efficient. He was a one-man team, could run surveillance and plan operations and shoot a man cold, and he didn't need a driver for his getaway either. Sometimes he joined group operations, like the time an entire team had been assigned to neutralize a thief. The operation went wrong, and the target escaped. The mayor ran down the target himself. He emptied his entire magazine.

That was the day, Crispin said, when the cops learned to be afraid of the mayor.

EXCERPT FROM A COURT HEARING
WITH WITNESS "ERNESTO"

Judge: How were you able to remember [where the bodies were buried]? Were you present during the digging? Did you hide or did you do some digging yourself?

Witness: I helped carry the bodies, sir.

Judge: Around how many?

Witness: Six, sir.

Judge: Was there a mass grave dug?

Witness: There were three caves, most were small, one was big.

Lawyer: Actually they were man-made caves.

Judge: Who are these killers?

Lawyer: They're cops who got used to killing. It's not an extraordinary event for them.

Judge: What do they use to kill? Guns?

Witness: No, sir. Just knives.

Judge: They would stab them?

Lawyer: They didn't want to waste bullets.

> —*Witness using the pseudonym "Ernesto Avasola,"*
> *from stenographic notes, July 10, 2009*

The witness who called himself Ernesto was a hired hand at the Laud quarry. He helped bury six bodies, but he knew the names of only two. One was Pedro, and the other was Mario. They had been stabbed in the neck like chickens. Stabbed, not shot, because bullets were too expensive to waste. Ernesto said that all six were buried inside caves, two bodies to a cavern, in holes that he had hollowed as the dead men watched.

Ernesto had been at the quarry on the day the investigators from the Commission on Human Rights appeared with their first search warrant. He had heard that they had arrived from Manila. He wanted to tell them what he had seen. He led them far into the quarry, deep into the caves, all the way to a hollow where a single bone protruded from the dirt.

A Manila court issued a second warrant to cover the new area. Investigators found human remains: four skull fragments, a radius, part of a humerus, and an incomplete bone twenty-one centimeters long. Laud's lawyers contested the search. The Manila judge withdrew the warrant. The investigation stalled. The warrant was refiled.

Three years after the hearings in Davao City, the CHR released its official report. It said there was "a dearth of evidence to support a finding of direct complicity on the part of local police or government officials," but that the authorities' failure to conduct thorough investigations "could be construed as tolerance." Circumstantial evidence, said the CHR, "points to the existence of a Davao Death Squad and its responsibility for the killings."

FROM THE FINAL REPORT OF
THE COMMISSION ON HUMAN RIGHTS

While Mayor Rodrigo Duterte may claim that any government official involved with the so-called DDS would be doing so on his own, the fact remains that officials of the PNP [Philippine National Police] have noticed the volume and pattern of the killings, to which Mayor Duterte seems to have paid no attention or has chosen to ignore and not have investigated. . . . There was a systematic practice of extrajudicial killings, which can be attributed or attributable to a vigilante group or groups dubbed in the media as the Davao Death Squad.

—CHR Resolution, June 28, 2012

The Commission on Human Rights recommended a probe under the Office of the Ombudsman. That investigation was closed in 2014 with no categorical results, due, said the ombudsman, to a declaration by CHR regional director Alberto Sipaco, Jr.

According to Sipaco, his office had no proof that the death squad existed. Any allegations to the contrary remained "rumor and other gossips."

For five years, the search warrant for the Laud quarry made its circuitous way from judge to judge, until the Supreme Court ruled there was probable cause to search the area identified by the witness who called himself Ernesto. Despite the ruling, it remains unclear if the PNP conducted a search. The Coalition Against Summary Executions (CASE), based in Davao City, has put the number of deaths attributable to the Davao Death Squad at 1,424, committed between 1998 and 2015. Existing data "revealed a lull in the killings" when Duterte was elected to Congress, and "a noticeable spike" when he returned to another four terms as Davao City mayor.

It would be his last term. In 2016, the Davao Death Squad's purported leader was elected president of the Republic of the Philippines.

EXCERPT FROM AN EXCHANGE BETWEEN
WITNESS EDGARDO MATOBATO AND
SENATOR ALAN PETER CAYETANO

Senator Cayetano: Okay, sir. You said the DDS exists, am I right?

Witness: Yes, sir.

Senator Cayetano: What is the DDS?

Witness: Davao Death Squad, sir.

Senator Cayetano: So, not Diehard Duterte Supporter.

Witness: No, the DDS, sir, was a group formed by Duterte, not by ordinary people. Mayor Duterte created the DDS.

Senator Cayetano: So, Davao Death Squad.

Witness: Yes, Davao Death Squad.

Senator Cayetano: You're saying it exists.

Witness: It really does, sir.

—From the official transcript of the Senate inquiry
on extrajudicial killings, September 15, 2016

In the minutes before his face was beamed out to television stations the length and breadth of the archipelago, the witness sat, graying and unremarkable, on a padded green chair at the Session Hall of the Philippine Senate. It was September of 2016. The drug war had been raging for three months. Rodrigo Duterte had kept his promise of carnage. Opposition leaders watched the slaughter and registered their dissent. One of them was the chairperson of the Senate Committee on Justice and Human Rights, Leila de Lima, who in 2009 had investigated the Davao Death Squad as chairperson of the CHR.

"Perhaps," said Senator de Lima, "we can link what is happening now to what happened in Davao City in the 1990s until the present, and how the Philippines now mirrors the city of Davao under the two-decade rule of Mayor Duterte."

The witness stood, raised his right hand, and swore to tell the truth about the man who was president. The name he called himself was important, because it was his own. Edgardo, he said. Edgardo Matobato.

He was born on the outskirts of Davao, dropped out of school after first grade, and at eighteen watched NPA rebels behead his father. It was the reason Matobato joined the local civilian auxiliaries, and did his job so well that the mayor's driver invited him to join an elite unit inside Davao City.

"Our job, ma'am," he told Senator de Lima, "was to kill criminals such as drug pushers, rapists, snatchers. They were the sort of people we killed every day."

Matobato carried a Davao City ID that marked him a member of the city's Civil Security Unit. He could not read or write, so he sent his wife to open a bank account for the checks he received from the mayor. He was detailed to the Heinous Crimes Unit—"our office"—where Mayor Duterte would occasionally drop by with orders.

They were a small group, until 1993, when the office expanded. They then called themselves the Davao Death Squad.

Matobato didn't particularly like killing people, but neither did he hate it. It was a job. He had orders and targets. The orders came from cops, and if the cops said the targets needed to die, Matobato was happy to believe them, because they were cops, and cops made the decisions. Matobato had twisted a garrote around a man's neck and stood by as the dead man was stripped, dismembered, and buried in the quarry. There were no courts or judges. The investigations were for show, because the investigators always knew who the death squad members were.

The regular crew, the rebel returnees, dealt with the small fry—the gang members and petty thieves and the glue-sniffing teenagers who roamed the streets. Matobato was a veteran. His targets were the bigger fish: terrorists, drug dealers, the occasional political rival. The men of the death squad operated in the open. They kept a black van ready for abductions. They strafed mosques. They could, when so inclined, snatch a man in front of his office building, then shoot him three times, and it didn't matter that the man worked for the city government.

Every death squad cop carried two guns. The first would be for killing—head and chest, bang-bang—the second for evidence. A homemade .38 caliber, for example, abandoned in a puddle of blood beside a dead man's hand, provided an excellent basis for investigators to claim the victim had been killed in a firefight. "The cops would always have that gun in reserve," Matobato said. "Someone gets killed—he gets a gun."

Matobato left the business of planting evidence to the cops. His job was to sit pillion behind the driver and wait for the motorcycle to slow, then raise his gun to shoot. But those were the easy kills, when a body could be left on the street for the rubbernecking neighbors to see. The bodies that required disappearing were chopped to pieces for burial in the quarry or were dropped into the sea when the sea was convenient. The biggest haul was seven corpses on a single boat, bellies slit to reduce buoyancy, each corpse weighed down with concrete blocks, three blocks to a man. Once, Matobato saw a cop shove a bleeding man into a swamp. The target was alive long enough to see the crocodiles. He did not see them for long.

Matobato estimated that during the twenty-four years he worked as a hired killer, the Davao Death Squad killed at least a thousand in Davao City alone. He took personal credit for at least fifty. "Those were the ones I was ordered to kill. I don't remember their names, but I remember how many since I started killing."

Matobato called the man he worked for Charlie Mike. Charlie Mike sent orders to the team leaders of the death squad. Charlie Mike praised squad members for their service to the city. Charlie Mike approved of the targets and dropped by the squad's office to mete out orders personally.

Charlie Mike had a deputy, Police Chief Master Sergeant Arturo Lascañas, a man so close that Charlie Mike treated him like a brother.

Lascañas was the death squad's field boss. It was why Matobato knew, more than most, the daily business of running a squad of killers. If Lascañas was Charlie Mike's right hand, Matobato was Lascañas's. It was Arturo Lascañas who strangled the men Matobato held down, and it was Arturo Lascañas's watch that Matobato wore strapped around his wrist. The watch was a gift.

"Everyone reported to him, to Arturo Lascañas," Matobato said. "This was the most powerful cop in Davao, ma'am. Even generals bow to Arturo Lascañas."

Once, Matobato said, he heard Charlie Mike compliment Lascañas. "If you weren't around, Tur," Charlie Mike told Lascañas, "Davao City wouldn't be as peaceful."

Charlie Mike was a code name, Matobato said.

"It was Mayor Duterte," he said. "I worked in the city hall for almost twenty-four years. I've known him for a long time."

So had Arturo Lascañas, and he told a different story.

EXCERPT FROM AN EXCHANGE BETWEEN
WITNESS ARTURO LASCAÑAS AND
SENATOR LEILA DE LIMA

Senator de Lima: SPO3 Arthur Lascañas, what is the code name of Mayor Duterte?

Lascañas: Usually, Your Honor, it's CM.

Senator de Lima: CM represents? What does CM mean?

Lascañas: City mayor.

Senator de Lima: Are you sure? Why do you need to say CM when it just means city mayor?

Lascañas: No, often, Your Honor, it was the media. Their thing.

Senator de Lima: Mr. Matobato said CM meant Charlie Mike?

Lascañas: Yes, yes, Charlie Mike.

Senator de Lima: So it is.

Lascañas: But usually we know it means city mayor.

Senator de Lima: But you still use Charlie Mike. You just said so.

Lascañas: Personally, Your Honor, I don't—Mayor Rody is what he's usually called.

—*Police Chief Master Sergeant Arturo Lascañas, testimony to*
Senate of the Philippines, October 3, 2016

Edgar Matobato was a liar, according to Arturo Lascañas. "There is no Davao Death Squad, Your Honor," Lascañas told senators. He said Edgardo Matobato was lying when he said Lascañas was Mayor Duterte's right-hand man. He was lying when he said there was a death squad with orders to kill. He was lying, certainly, when he said he was witness to all the crimes Lascañas committed.

It was true, Lascañas admitted, that he occasionally worked with Matobato, but they were not in any way close friends. The fact that Matobato had slept in Lascañas's home, attended Lascañas's birthday, and wore Lascañas's watch proved nothing beyond Lascañas knowing Matobato in a casual, business-like fashion.

He, Arturo Lascañas, a cop who had never murdered, never tortured, and never bombed a single mosque in his life, was being made the villain of opposition propaganda designed to discredit the good man he once called his mayor.

And then at dawn one day, Arturo Lascañas saw Jesus.

EXCERPT FROM A PRESS CONFERENCE
BY FORMER POLICE MASTER SERGEANT
ARTURO LASCAÑAS

The Davao Death Squad is real. . . . I was one of those who started it. We implemented the personal instructions of Mayor Duterte to us. All of the killings we did in Davao

City, whether we buried or threw them out to sea. . . . I accept the consequences of my actions.

—*Retired Police Master Sergeant Arturo Lascañas, press conference,*
February 20, 2017

It started with his failing kidney. There he was, at the dialysis center of the Davao Doctors' Hospital, watching the other patients stagger in "like zombies." Lascañas could not accept his body's inexplicable collapse. He went home after each appointment to an empty condo. He told his family to leave him be, that he needed time to think.

It occurred to him, on the days when he could do nothing else but think, that the other patients were very possibly not killers. Suppose, he thought, he deserved the poison in his gut.

And then Lascañas had a dream. It was a bad dream. A demon appeared before him. Suddenly there was a bright light, and a child came to save him. He jerked awake and was afraid. "And that was when I embraced the name of Jesus Christ and promised that given another chance to live again, I will serve at his will."

He lived.

His act of contrition began with a confession before God and country. He listed murder after murder. He noted locations. He detailed the make and model of vehicles as well as the extent of financial payouts. He named the killers and the man who had ordered the murders.

It was the city mayor, Lascañas said.

A MEDIA INTERVIEW WITH
PRESIDENT RODRIGO DUTERTE

Reporter: Sir, Lascañas said that you were the one who created the DDS.

President Duterte: I need not do that. It wasn't necessary. I did not create an air force, I have an Air Force. I will not create a DDS, I had a police department.

—*Rodrigo Duterte, from a transcript filed by the Presidential*
Communications Operations Office, March 17, 2017

Despite the denial, Lascañas offered a detailed litany of the horrors he had committed on the mayor's orders. The mayor had ordered the bombing of mosques, in retaliation for the blasting of a Catholic church.

The mayor had ordered the murder of a journalist with a ₱3 million bounty. The bonus was another million: "I got the money from him, and I told him, 'Thank you.'"

The mayor had ordered the murder of Chinese drug dealers. There were eleven of them. "Finish them off," ordered the mayor. "Yes, sir," said Lascañas. He killed nine and handed off two to another shooter before both of them went home to celebrate the New Year. They split the half-million payout.

The mayor had ordered the murder of a kidnapping suspect. The squad stopped the suspect on the road and discovered he wasn't alone as he drove his van. His pregnant wife, father-in-law, young son, and two household helpers were also inside. They took everyone to the quarry.

Lascañas and the team leader, a colonel, left to report the developments to the mayor. The colonel suggested the entire family should be "erased." "Go ahead, just make it clean," said the mayor.

They drove back to the quarry. Lascañas suggested making an exception for the four-year-old boy. The suggestion was denied. Lascañas stood guard outside the shed and listened as six people were shot. They were stripped and buried in a single grave deep in the Laud quarry. The bounty was split across the squad. Wallets, bags, and a pair of children's shoes were burned.

Lascañas returned later to pour oil over the fresh soil.

In the list of his dead, Lascañas included two more alleged drug dealers. Their names were Cecilio and Fernando, and they shared more than his last name. "In my absolute loyalty to [the mayor's] campaign, I had my own two brothers killed."

"I submit myself to God," Lascañas said in testimony before the Philippine Senate. "I am satisfied."

A STATEMENT FROM PRESIDENTIAL CANDIDATE RODRIGO DUTERTE

Am I the death squad? True. That is true.

—*Rodrigo Duterte,* Gikan sa Masa, Para sa Masa,
May 24, 2015

5

DEFEND THE MAYOR

"Where I come from, most of the people were Duterte," a woman named Ann Valdez told me.

Where Ann came from was the seaside municipality of Baler, in the province of Aurora. The people she knew from Baler were not simply *for* Duterte. They *were* Duterte, the structure of the sentence direct, no prepositions involved. They were Duterte or they weren't, and most of them were.

For Ann, to be Duterte was to belong. Ann was Duterte. It was not a sudden thing. The decision had been twenty-five years in the making, since the day her mother discovered she was pregnant and decided she never wanted to see Ann's father again. Ann was raised by her grandparents on a farm in Aurora. Sometimes her mother visited. Mostly she didn't. All Ann wanted, as her classmates dreamed of becoming nurses or accountants, was to find her father. The father, she imagined, who looked like her, perhaps liked her, who scolded her when she came home late and hugged her whenever he told her he loved her.

She left for Manila at sixteen. She told her grandparents it was for college, but really it was because she heard a rumor her father was in the capital. She did not find him, could not, because her father was dead, had been shot in Ilocos while considering a run for mayor.

One day in 2015, Ann read about the mayor who was running for president. His name was Rodrigo Duterte. Duterte, who had cleaned up Davao City. Duterte, who said that under his watch, ordinary folk would be safe from harm. Duterte, who lived simply, so simply that pictures appeared of the mayor sleeping on an old bed draped with mosquito netting—"I thought it was so sweet."

It was easy to campaign for Duterte because where Ann was from, almost everyone was already Duterte. Ann was Duterte, because Ann, at the age of twenty-five, had finally found the man whose name she would carry with her own.

She called him Father, and called herself DDS.

For Ann, the DDS did not mean the Davao Death Squad. It meant Diehard Duterte Supporter.

The first time I heard the Duterte name was in 2011. I was twenty-five years old as well. The death squad investigations of the early aughts may have been news in the provincial press, but the story barely penetrated the capital. The pile of Davao City's bodies appeared as an occasional feature in national newsmagazines, if that. The massacre of journalists in Maguindanao in 2009 was my first reporting trip to the island of Mindanao. I was, at the time, a foreign correspondent in my own country, parachuting in, flying out, speaking none of the local dialects, and understanding little of the politics and historical injustices that made so many in Mindanao—and the rest of the country—contemptuous of imperial Manila. My comfortable ignorance did not withstand footage, aired nationwide, of an elected mayor punching a sheriff in Davao City.

In the aftermath of the Edsa Revolution, the writers of the Constitution, in a vain attempt to throttle warlord ambitions, restricted all local officials to a maximum of three consecutive electoral terms. Each ran roughly three years, limiting a mayor, or a governor, or a congressman, to less than a decade in office. This stricture was not proof against political ingenuity. Mayors stepped down, but not too far. The ballot often carried the same surnames in the next election. Sometimes the new candidates were wives, sometimes juniors or daughters, leading to photo captions, left to right, of Madame Mayor cutting a ribbon beside the former mayor at the groundbreaking of an elementary school.

Consider, for example, Rodrigo Duterte, nicknamed Rody, sometimes called Digong, sometimes Du30. He was appointed by President Corazon Aquino in his mother Soledad Duterte's place as officer-in-charge vice-mayor of Davao City. In the first election after the revolution, Soledad's son ran for mayor and won as mayor, and three years later he won again, then again three years after that, until the law said there was no more running left. Soledad's son ran anyway, all the way to the House of Representatives in Manila, whose chambers were so tedious that the new congressman sneaked out the side door to watch movies on days he was paid to make law. Three years later, when the clock reset, he went home to campaign again as mayor. He won once, twice, three times, and the third time he won with his daughter as vice-mayor at his side. It took another three years for Soledad's son to lead Rodrigo's daughter up the hall and into the mayor's office, to hold the mayor's post while the mayor called himself vice-mayor and bided his time until the next elections, when the vice-mayor turned mayor and the mayor vice-mayor, clocking in three decades of near-uninterrupted Duterte victories, mayor after Duterte mayor running and winning and running and winning, until Davao meant Duterte and Duterte meant Davao.

"I've been a prosecutor for ten years," Rodrigo Duterte once said to a crowd at the Manila Hotel. "I did trial work for eight years, and then I became mayor for twenty-three years in Davao. One term in Congress and another term—four years being the vice-mayor of my daughter. The one who, you know, punched the sheriff. That one."

The story of the mayor who punched the sheriff began with a riot. One summer afternoon in 2011, a city sheriff, armed with a court order, arrived at the village of Agdao to enforce the scheduled demolition of more than two hundred homes. The mayor had requested a two-hour postponement, a request the sheriff had refused. The residents were armed with slings and blades. One cop was hit by a dart. The mayor strode into the crowd, followed by cameras.

The mayor demanded to see the sheriff. The sheriff appeared; shoulders hunched inside a checkered shirt.

"Come here, sir," invited the mayor, and slugged the sheriff in the face.

The first punch caught the sheriff in the eye, so hard that the cameras registered the smack of knuckle against bone. The sheriff turned, tried to flee, curled into himself as blows landed on his back. The staccato of the next three punches was lost in the gleeful roar of the crowd. Someone clapped. Someone cheered. The sheriff was sent to the hospital.

The story broke into afternoon cable news. The evening broadcasts played the video on a loop. Mayor Sara Duterte, live on the phone with an ABS-CBN News Channel anchor, refused to apologize. The controversy remained in the papers for days due, in no small part, to the mayor's father, who raised a middle finger and announced that his daughter had done precisely what the situation called for. Vice-Mayor Rodrigo Duterte offered the hope that Sara would continue as she began. Were the situations reversed, had he been punched himself, he would have taken out his gun. "I'll shoot you," he said.

There was much consternation from human rights groups, and mixed reactions everywhere else. The Davao Death Squad, largely unknown to most of the country, became part of a narrative of southern violence and abuse of power. Columns were published. Pundits appeared on television. News reports from long-suffering provincial correspondents were finally aired in the first half of national newscasts.

"It's really the wrong kind of fame," Sara Duterte told me a year later, in 2012. We were in the function room of a Davao City hotel, minutes after the mayor had spoken at a local gathering of women leaders. The mayor sat at the edge of a chair, ramrod straight, a microphone clipped to the collar of a modest lavender blouse, her voice soft, the words careful, occasionally punctuated by a self-effacing laugh. "When you're a mayor you have to command, and you have to be authoritative. Usually they see it in males, that macho image, especially in Davao City when they're used to my father."

She is not close to her father, she said, particularly after his marriage with her mother broke up. Her father was rarely home, always at work, and that situation did not change after she was elected mayor. "Believe it or not, we never discuss work, because in the first place, we don't discuss anything else."

There is likely no clearer reading of the mayor from Davao than from his daughter herself. "He's known to be a very strong mayor, because of his type of personality, a personality he brought when he was working as a mayor. Whatever he wants—which is for the general welfare and greater good—he insists on, even though there's what is called collateral damage."

It can be argued that Sara Duterte, standing in the shantytown of Agdao among the desperate citizenry, was also in pursuit of the greater good. Here was the sheriff, the enemy who did not listen in spite of her warnings.

"I was so frustrated," she said. "I wasn't allowed to cry, because people would think, what sort of person is this, crying in front of people? I couldn't vent my anger."

She could not cry, so the sheriff was collateral damage. What happened was wrong, she said.

It was well done, said her father.

What might have been the first of the DDS Facebook pages came to life in the aftermath of the incident with the sheriff. "WE DEFEND OUR MAYOR," the first post from the Duterte Defense Squad screamed in capitals. Little was known of the group's members, beyond the single page with fifty-nine followers. Show those networks where we stand, they wrote.

The group was not, as may have been assumed, founded to defend Rodrigo Duterte—or only Rodrigo Duterte. Its objective, rather, was to "defend our mayor, because they defend us." It was not an error in grammar. *They*—plural, not singular— were the Mayors Duterte. The name allegedly scrawled by a pack of killers on a sheet of paper instantly became a defiant identity for the internet's generation of Duterte loyalists. The movement went national four years later, in 2015, when rumors of Rodrigo Duterte's presidential aspirations began circulating. They were, at the time, small groups with less than a hundred thousand followers, each carrying the DDS name. Digong Duterte Supporters. Duterte's Destiny's to Service to the Country. Digong Duterte

Swerte. Davsur Duterte Supporters. Digong Duterte Is the Solution. Duterte Got Doctors' Support. Its final permutation, one that would galvanize grassroots chapters across the country and in Filipino communities the world over, was Diehard Duterte Supporters.

By late October 2015, the phrase had become part of the daily lexicon. Their object was the same, with one crucial addition: Defend the mayor—and elect him president.

At fifteen minutes past noon on September 3, 2015, thirty-four-year-old dentist Dondon Chan posted on his Facebook page a picture of the smiling mayor. This, wrote Dondon, was "Sir Rody Duterte," a candidate who was "truly from the masses, for the masses!"

The post received a handful of comments. The mayor was "finger lickin' good" for the presidency. The mayor was smart. "All of us here" wanted him to run.

"Has he declared his candidacy?" asked a woman who described herself as "just a simple mom."

"No, not yet," Dondon replied. "But if he doesn't run, I can't think of anyone else to vote for."

"Everybody is praying for him to say yes!" she said.

"He said he would decide soon," replied another "brave mother of three" from Davao. "He said all he needs is to convince his family. . . . The mayor is smart, he'll run."

"I hope so," Dondon said.

Dondon was the second son of a professor who taught French and German at the premier state university. He had traveled the world as a child, to the United States and to Britain and to Poland and Hungary and Italy and Portugal and Spain. As an adult, he took vacations to Morocco and Tanzania, had

matriculated at the Ateneo de Manila and graduated fr
University of the Philippines' College of Dentistry. He was
litically active, had campaigned for free reproductive heal
care for women and organized dental missions and emergency
aid to typhoon victims. He was not fanatical in his patriotism—
unlike many of his countrymen, did not vote for Miss Universe
candidates on the basis of their Filipino citizenship. He prayed
often. He attempted kindness in most things. He joined the
massive crowd that welcomed Pope Francis at Luneta Park, and
he concluded it was possible to be a good person without being
a devout Catholic.

Dondon liked the mayor from Davao City. He liked that the
mayor was a fresh face in the national political landscape. He
thought that the mayor was different from the usual run of sycophant politicians. He celebrated the announcement of the may-
or's candidacy with Facebook posts—"Duterte for the win!"—and
had no small amount of contempt for the righteous and the politically correct who criticized his choice. He was not, he was
careful to say, strictly DDS. He was not voting for Duterte's running mate, Senator Alan Peter Cayetano. He supported the opposition's vice-presidential candidate, Leni Robredo, whose
closest opponent was not Cayetano but Ferdinand "Bongbong"
Marcos, Jr., the son and heir of the former dictator. Once, arguing in the comment sections against a woman calling for a return
of the Marcoses, Dondon snapped back with a denunciation of
the evils of martial law, including the painful fact his uncle had
been killed in the 1970s under the dictatorship. The woman
apologized. The point was acknowledged. That Dondon cared
nothing for the uncle—"It really didn't matter to me whether he
lived or died, to be honest"—was irrelevant in the exercise of
internet wrangling.

"Run Duterte Run," Dondon wrote.

matriculated at the Ateneo de Manila and graduated from the University of the Philippines' College of Dentistry. He was politically active, had campaigned for free reproductive health care for women and organized dental missions and emergency aid to typhoon victims. He was not fanatical in his patriotism—unlike many of his countrymen, did not vote for Miss Universe candidates on the basis of their Filipino citizenship. He prayed often. He attempted kindness in most things. He joined the massive crowd that welcomed Pope Francis at Luneta Park, and he concluded it was possible to be a good person without being a devout Catholic.

Dondon liked the mayor from Davao City. He liked that the mayor was a fresh face in the national political landscape. He thought that the mayor was different from the usual run of sycophant politicians. He celebrated the announcement of the mayor's candidacy with Facebook posts—"Duterte for the win!"—and had no small amount of contempt for the righteous and the politically correct who criticized his choice. He was not, he was careful to say, strictly DDS. He was not voting for Duterte's running mate, Senator Alan Peter Cayetano. He supported the opposition's vice-presidential candidate, Leni Robredo, whose closest opponent was not Cayetano but Ferdinand "Bongbong" Marcos, Jr., the son and heir of the former dictator. Once, arguing in the comment sections against a woman calling for a return of the Marcoses, Dondon snapped back with a denunciation of the evils of martial law, including the painful fact his uncle had been killed in the 1970s under the dictatorship. The woman apologized. The point was acknowledged. That Dondon cared nothing for the uncle—"It really didn't matter to me whether he lived or died, to be honest"—was irrelevant in the exercise of internet wrangling.

"Run Duterte Run," Dondon wrote.

. . .

It remains unclear who said it first. It went from mouth to mouth, post to post, and by the time the idea took shape and appeared as a slogan on cardboard signs, it was impossible to determine whether the mayor's possible candidacy was the product of a political conclave or a night in a downtown Davao bar.

To hear the mayor tell it, the movement for his presidency had the force of a natural phenomenon, unstoppable and uncontrolled. Billboards sprang up along highways. Posters were taped to front doors. Thousands streamed into rallies. Run, Duterte, run.

"I'm telling the Filipino people, not me," said the mayor. "It's going to be bloody, because I will not sit there as president and just like any other regime, say, 'That's all I can do.' If you put me there, do not fuck with me."

The mayor said he did not want to be president. He had many reasons. He said he was too old. He said he was unqualified. He said he had accomplished enough. He said he had no money, no machinery, no support from his family. Were he running for president, he would end corruption in government, but he was not running for president, because he was uninterested. Declaring interest would be read as naked ambition, he said, and he had no ambition beyond retirement. If he was president, he would abolish Congress. If he was president, he would run the country like a dictator. If he was president, he would reinstitute the death penalty, but he wasn't running for president. If he were, the country would need more funeral parlors, because everyone would be dead, but he wasn't running, not at all. He demanded an end to the posters and the billboards and the phone calls advocating for his candidacy. He said the country had no need for him. He said he did not want to be a hypocrite. He said he was embarking on a listening tour, only a listening tour, and that the many appearances he made, city to city, were just "jamming" with the people, nothing more, unless it was God's will that he run, but even then he was only 40 percent willing, if that. The mayor said no, once, twice, thirteen times, "for the nth time," each refusal reported by the dailies, each bold-lettered headline picked up on the evening news—"Duterte: I Won't Run for National Post in 2016"; "Duterte's Final Answer: I Won't Run for President"; "Duterte Insists: I'm Not Running"—while lists of his presidential promises were published, captioned "Duterte: I'm Not Running but if I Were the President . . ."

The dance lasted almost two years. The deadline for the filing of candidacy passed in October 2015. The mayor's party, Partido Demokratiko Pilipino-Lakas ng Bayan (PDP-Laban), on discovering the mayor was unwilling to commit, instead fielded its own deputy secretary general, Martin Diño.

At the time of his filing, Diño had little to no national profile. His candidacy was so improbable that the Commission on Elections (Comelec) considered classifying him as a nuisance candidate, along with several dozen others, including a seventy-six-year-old taxi driver who had scrawled "Ignacio for President" on his sleeve with a marking pen, a ponytailed gentleman who signed his name as Archangel Lucifer, another man who promised the Philippines U.S. statehood, and Allan Carreon, Intergalactic Ambassador of Planet Earth, whose commitment to national wireless access was trumped only by the confession he had the unflagging support of his extraterrestrial allies.

Diño, after claiming to be insulted by the possibility of his disqualification, withdrew his candidacy. A quirk of Philippine election law allowed for a substitution on the conditions that the replacement candidate belonged to the same political party, and that the original candidate withdrew his certificate of candidacy. The country waited. The mayor continued to say no, whenever he didn't say yes. And when he did say it, finally, it wasn't because of crime, or corruption, or federalism, or war, or God. It was because of that American.

The American in question—or former American—was named Grace. She was the adopted daughter of Fernando Poe, Jr., and Susan Roces, king and queen of the silver screen. Grace had left the Philippines at the age of twenty-two for the United States. She had married a Filipino American, taken on American citizenship, and was happily ensconced in Virginia with her growing family when her father ran for the Philippine presidency against President Gloria Macapagal-Arroyo.

"A lot of people ridiculed him," Grace Poe told me. "They said, 'He's just an actor, he knows nothing.'"

The man who was just an actor swept the polls in 2004, but Arroyo still won in an election rife with accusations of cheating and bribery. Within months of his narrow loss, Da King, as Poe was known, collapsed from a stroke, slipped into a coma, and died before his daughter could come home.

Grace Poe filed for dual citizenship. She sent her children to local schools, renounced the American flag, and accepted a minor government post running the film and television classification board. Nine years after she watched the crowd of mourners at her father's burial, Amazing Grace, as columnists began to call her, landed on top of the senatorial polls on her first outing as a national candidate.

"Who would've thought," she once told a crowd of supporters, "that a foundling would ever become senator? I thank you for giving me that opportunity."

Her run for the presidency was almost inevitable. She was

courted by the ruling party. She was the darling of the news media. She was the candidate of choice among a middle class concerned about corruption and young voters in search of inspiration. At campaign rallies, the loudspeakers boomed the same music they had once played for her father. By the time certificates of candidacy were filed, she was leading a field of three, with a likely 47 percent of the vote over the Aquino-anointed interior secretary Mar Roxas and then–vice president Jejomar Binay.

The single challenge to her candidacy was a petition for disqualification. It had been filed by opponents on the premise she was not a natural-born Filipino.

"They say I am not a Filipino because I am a foundling, and I do not know my real parents," she told overseas Filipino workers in Hong Kong. "But that is not fair. What we're fighting for here is real change for our country."

A tribunal voted 5–4 in her favor. She was permitted to run.

"This is not about politics," Mayor Rodrigo Duterte said. He may have been uninterested in the presidency, but "if this is how the game is played in the country, then the option to run is on the table." He called the tribunal's decision a cheapening of the Constitution. "I cannot," he said, "accept an American president."

One month before the substitution deadline and six months before the election, the mayor announced he would fill the slot vacated on the Comelec roster.

"The die is cast," the mayor said, when asked if he might still change his mind. "I have crossed the Rubicon. Rubicon is a bridge heading to the slaughter."

The press published another headline, one that would finally prove true: "Rodrigo Duterte: I Am Running for President."

Fort Bonifacio, Taguig City, Metro Manila. Late evening,
161 days before the election. Campaign concert.

The mayor is on a roll, on a stage, in a denim shirt. He's talked
about the fucking government, and the fucking airport, and the
fucking drunks, and fucking his two girlfriends at cheap by-the-
hour motels (one fuck at a time, as he's too old to do more, even
with Viagra).

The crowds cheer.

He does not admit to killing men who are hogtied or on their
knees. That way is for cowards. And if you say he's killed, he
really hasn't killed too many. He counts them, one, two, three,
four. He does not lie. He does not need to lie, son of a bitch.

If he becomes president, the druggies should give up and
hang themselves, because he will really kill them. He is not joking. He is serious. He will not allow the nation's children to be
devoured by drugs. Drugs have screwed with this generation,
not like back in the day, when the worst anyone could do was
marijuana. Fair warning. You get into drugs and you keep doing
drugs, you will have to die. Let the human rights activists come.
He doesn't care. You think you have evidence, go file a case in
court. If the people want him to be president, he'll be president.
He'll take it. He'll accept responsibility. He will call on the military. He will call on the police. He will tell them to kill every
drug addict in the country. Those who fail at killing he will have
to kill himself.

Let the activists hunt him down. Let Congress investigate,
threaten impeachment, slap him with restraining orders. He'll
send in the war tanks to wait outside the Session Hall. If they
keep at it, he'll tell the military to go shoot those idiots.

You don't believe him? Try him. Maybe the next government will pardon him, but if those jackasses are out for revenge, he'll be happy to rot in jail. He's fine with that. He's killed two cops this year for getting into drugs, didn't want to do it, but that's his policy. He can't protect people without killing people. Get out of the drug business, he says. Same for the cops who kidnap and kill, who bully commuters and steal their money, who go after the Chinese businessmen and their kin. Stop before he wins, or else he'll tell the armed forces they have three days to hunt down those bastards and put them down. He won't accept surrender, even if they try. He'll have his cops shoot the sons of bitches, drop them to the ground, plant guns on each hand when they're dead—that way it can be said the bastards fought back.

That's why Davao is safe. Go to Davao. You'll see. The streets are safe. He told his cops to send their wives and beautiful daughters alone, out on the streets at night, and they did. They came home smiling, unmolested, without some fucker having made a grab for their tits or their panties or their wallets—that's security. That's the standard. And if one of them recognizes a kidnapper walking about, out on bail, well, that's trouble. Bail means nothing. Stay in jail. It's safer there.

Nothing to fear for everyone else—all you law-abiding, God-fearing citizens have no reason to be afraid.

The crowd applauds.

Dondon, in Manila, was typing away: Duterte for the win!

That Dondon supported the presidential ambitions of the man alternately called the Butcher and the Punisher did not contradict the principles he held dear. He was law-abiding. He paid his taxes. He had never used drugs. He did not worry about the mayor's promise to slaughter criminals and drug addicts, not because he believed the mayor was joking, but because the sort of people who might be killed were not the sort of people Dondon considered necessary to his preservation. Their disappearance from society would eliminate a drain on resources. If they died, it would be for the greater good.

There was concern, in those early days, of the impact the more frenetic Duterte campaigners had on people who were on the fence. Establishment liberals, after all, described the DDS movement's character with the same dismissive contempt as Hillary Clinton would describe her basket of deplorables.

It worried one former governor, Manny Piñol—a Duterte loyalist—so much that he addressed a public letter to all Duterte supporters. Piñol explained that Duterte's opponents had so weaponized the good mayor's language that they had portrayed him "as an unstable, disrespectful, irreverent, bullying and cussing person." Likely aware he could do little to censor his own candidate's violent rhetoric, Piñol appealed instead to the congregation of Rodrigo Duterte. The existing criticism against the mayor, Piñol said, was only "made worse by Duterte's rabid followers, who have been labeled by political opponents as 'Dutertards,' as in Duterte's retarded minions, or who call themselves 'DDS' or Duterte's Die-Hard Supporters." All this could alienate "even those who are still vacillating in their choice for President."

He had, as it later turned out, little cause for concern.

Jason Quizon was born in Pampanga, a province just off the capital region. His father was a potter who brought home four dollars a day. His mother sold crabs, painted nails, cooked for neighbors, and ran a small store from a window cut into their front room. Neither parent had a high school diploma, and both were united in the pursuit of higher education for their children. After a night of rain, Jason's father, a gruff, plainspoken man, would rise at dawn to hunt frogs that they would later sell from the overflowing riverbanks. Jason himself survived on scholarships and part-time administrative work, and on occasion painted Japanese scenery on wooden panels of the sort that graced certain middle-class living rooms.

Through considerable effort, and despite a massive volcanic eruption, all five Quizon children graduated with professional degrees. They were the pride of the village. Jason had graduated an engineer, and so did one sister. Another sister was a nurse. One brother was an accountant who ran a buy-and-sell business. The last was employed as a senior manager for the water service provider supplying the entire western capital region. If their father, the best man Jason knew, still insisted on the daily labor of firing up his enormous wood-burning ovens, that was up to him, but Jason was happy to send money home.

By late 2015, Jason was an overseas Filipino worker, an OFW, of some ten years' standing. "I followed the money where it led," he said. Where it led him was Saudi Arabia, then the United Arab Emirates, then Qatar, then back to the UAE before settling into Qatar again, where he accepted an offer to oversee the laying of pipeline for an oil and gas company as an interface project engineer. He had savings in the bank, was well-liked by most of his employers, and played badminton in his spare time. He bought the house where his parents lived and married the woman he loved, a Catholic who in spite of her tears had accepted the fact that her husband was an unapologetic atheist. They had three children who went to good schools. He read Asimov, watched *Star Trek,* and considered himself a liberal—"not to the extent I'm a libtard though." He believed in the right to same-sex marriage. He considered abortion a woman's right. He was contemptuous of the fact that the Philippines was the last country outside the Vatican without divorce. He believed drug addiction was a disease that required rehabilitation instead of punishment. He was articulate, reasonable, practical, and tolerant.

The reason Jason voted for Duterte can be reduced to a bullet. Or several bullets.

On September 17, 2015, the American missionary Lane Michael White accused personnel at the Ninoy Aquino International Airport (NAIA) of planting a bullet in his luggage. The Comprehensive Firearms and Ammunition Regulation Act, Republic Act 10591, considers the unlawful possession of ammunition a crime. Ammunition is defined as a single unfixed unit. The penalty for those found guilty begins at six years and one day. White claimed that the personnel subsequently attempted to extort ₱30,000 from him. He spent six days in the police aviation facility and was released only after posting ₱40,000 in bail.

The scam was called *laglag-bala,* bullet drop. The way Jason explained it was this. "You go to NAIA. And then suddenly you put your bag on the X-ray machine, and then suddenly the officer will just set you aside and say, 'Oh, you have one piece of ammunition in your bag. So how do you want to go about it? Do you want to go the long way, processing all these, going to the police station and all, miss your flight, or you just give me— how much money do you want?'"

The missionary was not the first, or the last. The parade of suspects included, for example, a woman in a wheelchair on the way from Manila to LAX. She said an airport staffer shoved his closed hand into her bag's pocket, turned his back to her, "and when his hand came out—he was holding bullets!" The staff member took the woman's passport and green card, then returned to suggest the problem could disappear. The cost of disappearance amounted to ₱500.

The stories piled on. A teenager flying to Seoul for a singing competition was released, her flight rebooked. A fifty-six-year-old migrant helper was charged, for a bullet wrapped in a red cloth; her pending case was a barrier to her entry to Hong Kong. A Japanese national, age thirty-three, was charged, then bailed out for ₱80,000. A sixty-eight-year-old woman was arrested for one bullet, .45 caliber.

Finally this: a sixty-five-year-old woman, from Cavite City heading to Singapore, had padlocked her luggage and sewn the outer pocket closed, but she had left one side pocket accessible, enough space for one bullet. She demanded a lawyer.

At best, the bullet drop was an expensive inconvenience; at worst, it cost people jobs and jail time. Terror of a bullet drop swept over travelers, particularly overseas workers. Jason, like many others, took to wrapping his suitcases in plastic. He even traveled with a roll of cling wrap stuffed into his hand-carry, in case a suitcase inspection required rewrapping. He personally knew no one who had been victimized, but he wasn't going to risk it.

It was not strictly the concern of overseas workers. That there were only seven victims named in public was irrelevant, because anyone could be a victim, regardless of class or place of origin. People rode planes and traveled in and out of the capital, but the line between traveling safely and spending weeks in jail had become a narrow one, dependent on the whim of a single airport employee. The fallout landed at the president's feet. Aquino, never articulate when it came to gut issues, ordered a probe into the allegations of extortion, but dismissed the issue as largely sensationalized.

An overseas worker appealed to the mayor from Davao: Mayor, please be our lawyer, we don't have any other ally, be our lawyer.

The mayor said yes. He offered to lawyer for victims for free. He articulated the "more tragic" possibility that innocent Filipinos from the provinces, bullets in their baggage, would land in jails across the world. "This is not just a matter of extortion. This will threaten the lives and freedom of ordinary Filipinos."

He blamed the scam on government agencies and demanded that President Aquino fire all airport ground operations personnel. "You have five days to do that, Mr. President," Duterte said in a press conference. "Mr. President, you have to cross the red light, you should do something drastic. Your lip service is not enough."

Otherwise, he said, "I will lose trust in you."

"This is the problem with Aquino and his public relations team," Jason said. "He doesn't fucking think about what people will think about him. He did not think the *laglag-bala* issue is a big deal for him. For us OFWs, it was a big deal. I know certain people who voted for Duterte solely for that reason."

What Jason liked was that the mayor was a man of action. That he swore like Jason, spoke like Jason, saw solutions instead of problems, as Jason did. Jason saw Filipinos as gullible folk, always willing to leap onto the next bandwagon, always looking for the next racket, quick to outrage, quicker to forgive, susceptible to tall tales and taller accusations, devoid of social conscience until they felt threatened, and so perversely loyal that they made decisions at the cost of their own interests. Idiots all, he said, largely simple-minded.

"And you don't consider yourself a simple-minded voter?"

"No," he said. "I'm not."

It was why, when the mayor talked of murder, of drugs, of tossing the dead into Manila Bay, Jason thought it was all meant to cater to the simple-minded among his fellow citizens, all of whom didn't understand that the tough talk was just fodder for the media. Jason appreciated the political maneuvering. He wasn't one of them. And because he wasn't, he thought the mayor was joking.

It was also why Jason, practical, reasonable, liberal Jason, chose a president who said a mayor should be the first to rape.

Amoranto Sports Complex, Quezon City, Metro Manila, twenty-eight days before the election.

The mayor is wearing a red polo shirt unbuttoned at the neck. It stretches tight at the armpits and pulls snug over his belly. The spotlights flare blue behind him. He holds a microphone in his right hand like a bottle of beer and speaks with the casual ease of a favorite uncle telling the story of the woman who got away.

The mayor is speaking of the woman. He does not say her name. She is the Australian woman sometimes. She is the nun other times. This evening she is the beautiful woman with the face of an American actress.

"Listen," says the mayor, "I'm telling you a story."

The story begins in 1989. More than a dozen convicts are holding a prayer group hostage at the downtown Davao City jail. There are negotiations. The convicts try to break out. They push the women and children ahead of them as shields. There is a shoot-out, a retreat, corpses left behind.

One of them is the woman. The woman is an Australian lay minister. Blond, pretty, dead.

The mayor clucks his tongue as he tells the story. Shakes his head. Pulls at his ear.

"I thought, this was going to be a problem," he says. "The Australian embassy kept calling and calling. The corpse was carried out, then covered. I saw her face. Son of a bitch, she was like one of those beautiful American actresses. Son of a bitch. What a waste. What I thought then was, 'They raped her, they lined up to rape her.'"

He says he was angry. "That she was raped? Yes," he concedes reluctantly. "That too."

The mayor pauses. He cups his right cheek in one palm and tilts his head. Below him, a congregation of thousands lean rapt into steel barricades.

"But she was so beautiful," says the mayor. "The mayor should have been first."

The crowd explodes into laughter.

The mayor offers a rueful smile and rubs his cheek. "What a waste," he says again.

Joy Tan believed in God, and God, she was certain, did not believe in rape and murder. She did not believe the mayor really intended to rape that missionary, but she believed that the mayor could kill. Joy knew what the second D in DDS meant. She did not consider it murder.

When Joy was a teenager, she traveled the two hours to Davao City for a doctor's appointment. Her cousin, also a teenager, decided to come along. He was hoping to apply for a job as a security guard in Davao.

He smoked pot back in their village in Cotabato, a bus ride away, and had also participated in the occasional armed robbery.

They were in the city when it happened. It was ten in the morning of a summer day. Joy was getting ready for the doctor. Her cousin was lying on the floor watching television. The various aunts and uncles and cousins were scattered about. A man, unremarkable in his jeans and T-shirt, the sort given away for free at campaign rallies, walked into the house without stopping to knock.

He was looking for Joy's cousin.

"That's me," the cousin said. "Why?"

"Here's the thing, pal. If you want to make it to tomorrow morning alive, there's a truck delivering corn to Cotabato later at dawn. You should be on it if you still want to live."

The man in the faded T-shirt was calm. So was the family. Nobody said anything until he left. The neighbors would later say the man worked for the mayor's son.

Joy was afraid, but her aunts said it would be okay, because anyway it was her cousin's fault. Because her cousin never listened. Because her cousin was stubborn.

He thought so too. He didn't wait for dawn or the truck heading to Cotabato. He found a ride home that night. It was many years before he dared to travel to Davao again. He was not, as Joy would later learn, terrified enough to practice restraint back home in Cotabato. He still did drugs, still stole when he could, but he never did any of it in Duterte's city.

Joy Tan was born in 1982, in North Cotabato in Mindanao, in a village so close to the rebel fighting that her childhood was punctuated with cannon blasts from Camp Abubakar. War again, her father would say. Sometimes the family would have time to throw pots and pans into gunnysacks before they ran to the local high school, and sometimes the gunfire would be so close that the most they could do was climb into the bunker under the farmhouse.

It was not clear to Joy whom exactly they were running from. No one explained what the war was about. She picked up words from the radio and from her father's snapped orders. It was the MNLF. It was the NPA. It was the MILF. It was the BIFF. It was the bandit groups. All she knew was that Muslims were the enemy. If equipment was burned, if livestock disappeared, if gunfire rang out, she was told that it was the Muslims who did it, and if a Muslim man crossed her path, she'd better run. It went on year after year, cannon fire and then the rush and the wait.

It was the danger that sent them often to Davao City, just across the border, where their extended family had a home in the slums. In Davao, they were told, the mayor kept his city safe.

Joy left home after college for cosmopolitan Cebu province to live with her grandparents. She couldn't find a job she liked, so her grandparents sent her to a six-month culinary certificate course. It was where she met her husband. He was kind. He was sweet. He was also a recovering drug addict, and the cooking class was his family's way of getting him off the street. They said it was better than rehab. Joy and her husband moved to Leyte after they married. He worked as a cook in a restaurant. They had one son. Life was comfortable until the day Super Typhoon Haiyan pounded the province into rubble.

They lost everything, but they lived. For a while it was just that, living. Putting food in her mouth, keeping her son alive, while Aquino's interior secretary traded barbs with the mayor of Tacloban City over government response to the storm. International aid was reported in the news, but none of it came for the small family living in a small town in the province of Leyte.

Joy was angry. She was angry at the Aquino government's neglect. She was angry, two years later, when the government's incompetence sent an entire company of Special Action Force policemen to die in the cornfields of Tukanalipao in Maguindanao. She was angrier still in early 2016, when a riot over the failed delivery of rice supplies in Kidapawan City killed three farmers and injured more than a hundred. She was angry, most of all, because after the typhoon, when she took her family home to seek refuge in Cotabato, her brother and cousins were so deep into their addictions that they were stealing from the family to buy illegal drugs out of Liguasan Marsh. She was so angry that she began writing letters to the director of the Philippine Drug Enforcement Agency, listing names and addresses and details of her own family's drug involvement. She begged the government to arrest the boys, if only to give the rest of them peace.

Joy was angry, all the way to the day when Rodrigo Duterte finally announced he was running for president.

She saw him on television. It was like seeing Jesus.

She ran home whenever her husband messaged her that Duterte was on the air, heading straight for the television to hear Jesus speak. She wept every time, replayed every interview, every speech, every clip she could find. Jesus would save her. Jesus would deliver her. Jesus understood.

Joy also knew what the second D in DDS meant. She wasn't afraid.

To vote for Rodrigo Duterte, you had to believe in certain things. You had to believe, for example, that he was a righteous man. You had to believe he wasn't a rapist, and didn't want to be a rapist. You had to believe he was poor, or was once poor, or had lived with the poor. You had to believe in destiny. You had to believe in God. You had to believe that God had a peculiar preference for deadly autocrats, because the presidency is destiny and Rodrigo Duterte was destined to lead.

To believe in Rodrigo Duterte, you had to believe he was brave. You had to believe he would cut America out of military agreements and that Barack Obama was a son of a bitch. You had to fear China, or you had to love China, or you had to believe, in the face of China's territorial aggression, that Rodrigo Duterte was willing to ride a Jet Ski out into the open sea to plant a flag on the disputed islands China had seized.

To believe in Rodrigo Duterte, you had to believe he was a killer, or that he was joking when he said he was a killer. You had to believe in the specter of a narco state, or you had to believe that he was only playing to the crowd. You had to believe drug addiction is criminal, that drug addicts are not human, and that their massacre can be considered acceptable public policy. You had to believe he could make crime and corruption and illegal drugs disappear in three to six months. You had to believe that a mayor who kept peace by ordering undesirables out of his city could succeed in a country where undesirables were citizens too. You had to believe the intended dead would be drug lords and rapists, only drug lords and rapists, and not your cousins who go off into Liguasan Marsh to pick up their baggies of meth. You had to believe there would be a warning before the gunshots ring out.

To believe in Rodrigo Duterte, you had to believe he was just. You had to believe he was honest. You had to believe he was untainted by the oligarchy and beholden to no one. You had to believe he was your father. You had to believe he was your savior. You had to believe he loved you, because you love him enough to carry his name.

Quirino Grandstand, Luneta Park, Manila. Miting de Avance. Estimated crowd size 600,000. Two days before the election.

The mayor is standing back from the edge of the stage. He says the edge of the stage gives snipers a target. The mayor has been told he's a target, but the mayor is a brave man. He will not hide. He steps forward, closer to his people. Screw the sniper. Go ahead. Shoot him. He is willing to die. He wants to die. He will die gladly for the sake of the Filipino. Best to kill him here, now, tonight, because if he wins, he'll kill you himself. He is not clear about whom he plans to kill, but the thundering crowd knows he doesn't mean them.

He kisses the flag. The crowd cheers. I do not.

I am here to see him speak. I did not take the cab to the Quirino Grandstand to cover the final rally. I am not here as a journalist. I had written my piece, published my three thousand words, called out the misogyny, warned of the bloodshed. I did not write that I wasn't Duterte, would not vote for Duterte, intended to vote for anyone but Duterte. I am a reporter, not the resistance. I am, however, careful to shove my press ID into my back pocket.

The crowd is a writhing, laughing, cheering behemoth. I shoulder myself in, slide past the steel barricades, tuck myself into the wall of bodies between a lanky teenage boy with red hair and a pudgy man taking pictures of his fist against the sky. Someone smiles at me, and glares at the man whose backpack muffles my nose. The man moves forward a step. Drones fly overhead. I try to write on tiptoe, try to suck in the cooler air a few inches above my head, then give up. The air is thick with sweat and excitement and someone's perfume. I smell dread, but it is only my own.

The mayor is on the stage. Red shirt. Short sleeves. "Du30," a shorthand for the mayor's surname, was embroidered over the left breast. His coterie is behind him, around him, blank-faced. Arcs of yellow light flare and beam.

Remember, he says, that he is an ordinary man. Remember that before the campaign, no one knew his face. He has no claim to greatness. He's not bright. He's no valedictorian. He's just a mayor, an ordinary Filipino whose only peculiarity is that he's angry at those sons of bitches. He is a specialist in nothing except death. Now everyone knows who Duterte is, so well that he once nearly got his hand broken after some woman grabbed it and refused to let go. Maybe if she had grabbed something else, he would have given it to her good. Too bad it was just his hand.

The boy beside me laughs. So does the kindly man who makes room for me in the crowd.

The mayor is angry now. Someone should answer for the troubles of the country. Why is it that no single ship offered armed resistance when China began seizing our islands? Why is it that commuters wait daily in lines two kilometers long, only to be shoved into train cars that stall on the tracks? Why are they forced to walk down the highway, the women pissing like frogs by the side of the road? Why are none of the promises kept? Why are Filipinos hungry, sad, on bended knee? What sort of son-of-a-bitch government is this?

Watch him, he says. Look at him.

We look. We watch.

Here is his promise. He will slap a man, kill a man, humiliate a man, for the sake of the Filipino people. If you're looking for a poor man, vote for him. If you're looking to be fed, vote for him. If you have lost faith in government, vote for him. He will protect you from the landowners, the sugar barons, the rich, the elitists, the men who don't understand that if you don't plow your five hectares, you do not eat. Those men are afraid now. Those men are banding together to stop you, those corrupt sons of bitches. This is your time to pay them back for the suffering and the contempt.

Maybe people look down on him, he says. Fine. Who here earned Latin honors in school? Who here graduated cum laude?

Summa cum laude? Why choose the valedictorians to lead the country? Why look up to those who claim to have Wharton degrees? Who among you passed school by the skin of your teeth? Passed by just enough? Passed with a seventy-five?

Vote for people like us, he says. People like you and me. There are many of us. Don't vote for people who defend criminals.

Forget about the laws protecting human rights. Forget about the regulations made by men. Look up to the sky, and there you will see the eternal justice of God. By what right in the universe do those sons of bitches dare to cook up crystal meth? Where in the vastness of the sky do they find the license to feed drugs to the nation's children? What sins did their mothers commit? What faults did their fathers possess? Why destroy the lives and bodies of a one-year-old, a twelve-year-old, an eighteen-month-old? Answer him. He'll follow the law, fine. Due process, presumption of innocence, all that, but he will never allow anyone to destroy the children of his country. He will stake his life on it. So destroy the government and launch your mutinies. He will protect the nation. He is willing to go to hell and pull on Satan's fucking tail. He is not afraid.

I stand there scrawling away in my notebook.

You elitists, I write. Us versus them, I write. Kill you, I write.

The lights burn hot. The woman behind me screams the mayor's name, and in spite of my Latin honors I feel a compulsion to cheer too.

Watch him. He'll do it. He's not asking for years. He's not asking for months. He'll start the day he steps into office. He will go after the corrupt, the criminals, the dirty cops, the drug dealers. Those of you involved in drugs, son of a bitch, he will kill you, you sons of bitches. He will have no patience. He will have no middle ground. Either you idiots kill him, or he'll kill you.

Those human rights defenders protect idiot criminals. He can kill the criminals. He'll do it in front of you. Even if it costs him his life, his honor, and the presidency, he will do it.

Mark his words. Mark it on your ass or on your balls or anywhere else you like, you son of a bitch, because he'll do it.

To prove her love for Rodrigo Duterte, Joy Tan gave up an Asus K424 laptop, the last ₱500 in her wallet, and several dozen Facebook friends. The Asus was a gift from a sibling, but she hocked it for ₱5,000, a quarter of its value, and passed on the money to a group printing free Duterte T-shirts.

Jason Quizon, to demonstrate his commitment to Rodrigo Duterte, booked a flight from Abu Dhabi to Doha, 321 kilometers away, to cast his ballot at the embassy where he had been registered to vote. He told his parents, both of whom he described as "politically benign," that he would hold off on sending them remittances if they didn't vote for the mayor. They did.

Dondon Chan, to show his support for Rodrigo Duterte, took it upon himself to extol the wonders of Davao City. Vote for Duterte, he posted, and the country will be like Davao. He said it in the comment sections, and he said it to friends, and he said it to the random people who made the mistake of questioning his new leader. That Dondon had never been to Davao was a fact he chose not to share.

Ann Valdez, to earn the love of Rodrigo Duterte, embarked on a daily campaign to turn everyone she knew into Duterte supporters. She convinced her husband. She convinced family. She convinced friends. She fought anyone online who had the temerity to choose a candidate other than the man she called Father, hallowed be his name.

Why, she demanded of one friend, would you vote for anyone else?

"Where I come from, most of the people were Duterte," Ann Valdez told me.

On June 30, the day she and her husband moved into their new home, she stuck six five-peso coins onto the wet cement of her front stoop. Thirty pesos, for Du30. Thirty pesos, for June 30, moving day, inauguration day, the day Father became president because Ann had not let him down.

I did not vote for Rodrigo Duterte. The fact that I was a journalist covering trauma did not mean I was inured to death. It was only that I saw death often, reported it often, and hoped, every time, that I would never have to see it again. I wrote about babies in backpacks and missing girls and the massacres of journalists because I believed that the public preferred girls safe and journalists alive and babies whose lives did not end stuffed into a JanSport backpack with flaking purple stitching. When I wrote, I wrote for people like my father, sitting at home with the newspaper open to my column, shaking his head.

That baby, my father would tell me over the phone. *What a terrible thing.*

Journalism, in the end, is an act of faith.

In the three months before the presidential election, I collaborated on an opinion series with the sociologist Nicole Curato. The Imagined President was a series of presidential profiles published in Rappler, mapping the narrative arcs of every presidential candidate. We compared myth with reality in an attempt to understand what resonated with the voting public.

The final installment was published on May 2, seven days before the elections. It ended with a warning: "If Rodrigo Duterte wins," we wrote, "his dictatorship will not be thrust upon us. It will be one we will have chosen for ourselves. Every progressive step society has made has been diminished by his presence. Duterte's contempt for human rights, due process, and equal protection is legitimized by the applause at the end of every speech. We write this as a warning. The streets will run red if Rodrigo Duterte keeps his promise. Take him at his word—and know you could be next."

I regretted those sentences within a day of publication. They were sensational, colorful, with none of the restraint expected of working journalists. I would have expunged them if I could.

On June 30, 2016, we became Duterte. The streets ran red.

II

CARNAGE

6

SALVATION

Rodrigo Roa Duterte won the presidency of the Republic of the Philippines in a five-way race. He won with sixteen million votes, four million more than the Aquino-anointed candidate. It was not a close fight. The vice presidency was a different story, and the results in that race demonstrated the capricious nature of Philippine democracy. Aquino ally Leni Robredo, a human rights lawyer and former congresswoman, emerged victorious in a tight race for the vice presidency against the son of the former dictator, Ferdinand "Bongbong" Marcos, Jr., who appealed for a recount. He lost in court.

The former mayor Duterte wore the *barong tagalog*—the embroidered traditional pineapple silk shirt—with a pair of slacks as he swore his presidential oath at high noon on June 30, 2016. He read a prepared speech from the rostrum of Malacañang Palace. He thanked former presidents and acknowledged the presence of dignitaries. He swore to honor all treaties and international obligations, quoted Abraham Lincoln and Franklin Roosevelt, promised to be uncompromising in his adherence to due process and the rule of law, and conceded that criminality and illegal drug use were "mere symptoms" of ingrained social ills. He used the words *whom* and *indeed* and *democratic*. He was, for the nearly fifteen minutes of his inaugural address, the closest approximation to a statesman possible for a man who had spent the campaign year denouncing enlightenment and civility.

Here were the things he did not do. He did not threaten martial law. He did not order the execution of addicts. He did not call anyone a son of a bitch. He did not use any of the following words: *kill, shoot, die, rape,* or *fuck.* He was not, in sum, the mayor.

The mayor made his appearance later, at forty-five minutes past eight in the evening, shucking the pineapple silk for a striped polo shirt under a navy jacket with the sleeves rolled up.

The event, according to the program released by the government television network, was A SOLIDARITY DINNER WITH THE POOR. The poor appeared as directed. They filled the Delpan Sports Complex in Tondo, a large, orange-walled gymnasium where long plastic tables topped with white tablecloths and foam food containers had been laid out over the basketball court.

Tondo, population 630,363, was the sprawling port area where shanties sat cheek to jowl with Manila's slaughterhouses and churches. Tondo was where photographers had made names for themselves at the turn of the century with stark black-and-white photos of grimy children scrabbling in rubbish, and where foreign missionaries put up their outposts to save the souls of the starving in Jesus's name. Tondo was also where enterprising tour guides once offered the Slum Tour for twenty-five dollars a pop—a "special experience" rated five stars by Tripadvisor.

That evening, his first day on the job, His Excellency President Rodrigo Duterte picked up the microphone and let loose the dogs of war. The sons of bitches would die. They were destroying the nation and its children. Do not go into drugs, he said, because if you do, he will kill you. It might not be tonight, it might not be tomorrow, but it would happen, even if it took all of six years.

"So, those of you who are still into drugs, there's been enough warning during the campaign. Whatever happens to you, listen now, it could be your sibling, your spouse, your friend, your child. You be the one to tell them. There will be no blaming here. I told them to stop. Now, if anything happens to them, it's on them. They asked for it."

His people cheered, even as he threatened to gun down their children. "If someone's child is an addict, kill them yourselves," he suggested, "so it won't be so painful to their parents."

Within hours, the first of the dead men who asked for it was listed on official records as Unidentified Male Person. His body was found at three in the morning abandoned in a Tondo back alley, a five-minute walk from the Delpan Sports Complex where the president had just spoken. The dead man wore jeans, a red shirt, and a pair of blue shoes. Police pegged his age between twenty-five and thirty years old. He was short, a little over five feet. He had been shot just behind the left ear.

A cardboard sign sat on his chest: I AM A CHINESE DRUG LORD.

A concerned citizen sent word to the police. The word was passed from person to person—from the witness to the village watchman, from the watchman to the Port Authority, and from the Port Authority to the homicide investigator, who was told of "a male person alleged victim of summary execution."

There are other terms for this. Extrajudicial killing. Vigilante-style murder. Targeted assassination. In the Philippines, a specific word evolved for this specific sort of death. The word is *salvage*.

.   .   .

Contronyms are Janus words, two-faced and adversarial. An alarm can turn off, or it can go off. A moon might be out as the lights go out. Contronyms mean the opposite of themselves, occupying an abstract category of the English language. He left; she was left. He ran fast; she held fast. He sanctioned the killings; she sanctioned the killers.

Salvage, in my country, is a contronym. It is a hopeful word everywhere else. To salvage is to rescue, regardless of whether the salvaged is a ship or a soul. *Salvage* and *salvation* are rooted in the same word—*salvus,* "to save." So sayeth the book of Luke: "And Jesus said to him, this day is salvation come to this house, as much as he also is a son of Abraham, for the Son of man is come to seek and to save that which was lost."

The entry for the verb *salvage* in the *Oxford English Dictionary* offers three primary definitions. The first is "to make salvage of; to save or salve from shipwreck, fire, etc." The second, limited to American and Australian use, is to take or "make use of unemployed or unattended property." The third definition is the most current: "to save and collect (waste material, esp. paper) for recycling."

There is, however, a fourth meaning. In 2015 the *OED* appended what it called a draft definition to the official entry.

Salvage: *Philippine English.* "To apprehend and execute (a suspected criminal) without trial."

Our use derived first from the Spanish. *Salvaje,* an adjective introduced by the conquistadors, translated into "wild." My people took *salvaje* and adapted it into our verb *salbahe.* "The way it is used in Filipino is different," the historian Ambeth Ocampo told me. "*Sinalbahe* means that the person was savaged, not that the person was good, bad, or a savage. Then we made the Spanish adjective into a verb, *sinalvaje,* and read it with the *j* into a *g.*"

Had martial law never been declared, *salbahe* might eventually have translated into its English counterpart. *Sinalbahe,* "savaged." *Sinasalbahe,* "savaging." *Sasalbahiin,* "will savage." But the Marcoses came in the 1970s, and with them the slaughter. *Salbahe* was anglicized into *salvage.* It was a corruption, not an evolution. The poet and journalist Jose F. Lacaba attributed the translation to the "visual similarity" of the two words. Lacaba calls it an Englishing; Ocampo calls it a Filipinism.

The *Glossary of Human Rights Terms,* published in 1991 by Task Force Detainees (TFD), defines *salvaging* as an "execution committed by government agent(s) in contravention or violation of due process of law" that is "equivalent to the international terms extra-judicial and summary executions." In the seventeen-year period after Marcos's declaration of martial law, the TFD reported at least 1,217 salvagings. Amnesty International put the number at 3,240. The historian Alfred McCoy counted 3,257.

In large part, international publications using the word *salvage* are careful to enclose the word in quotation marks, as *The Washington Post* did in 1994, reporting that in the Philippines, "due process for common criminals sometimes gives way to extrajudicial executions known as 'salvagings.'" The Geneva-based International Commission of Jurists, in a 1984 mission report, noted that "it is indeed general and public knowledge in the Philippines that the police resort to torture and so-called 'salvaging.'" A book by human rights advocate Iain Guest explained that "under President Ferdinand Marcos of the Philippines, security forces did not 'kill,' they 'salvaged.'" The *OED* offers this sentence from 1980, published by Toronto's *Globe and Mail* about martial law in the Philippines: "Another 303 political activists are known to have been 'salvaged' by the military and assassinated."

Salvage-as-murder does not exist in most Filipino dictionaries. Nor does the definition appear in the many English-Filipino compendiums that are available for academic use. But every child in my country knows this meaning. We learn it before we learn how to spell it, we learn it long before we discover that the rest of the world does not hear it with the same dread. To me, even now at thirty-seven, the two words are indivisible in my mind's eye, each informing the other, all salvagings savage and every savage a man with a cocked gun. A salvage yard is not a fenced-in patch of concrete with secondhand cars and vintage lamps for thrifting. A salvage yard is a street corner in Tondo, or the right lane of an overpass at dawn. A salvage yard is a cemetery, unless there is no one to give the dead man a name.

The salvagings would happen at night, so it was at night when I worked. I had never been a police beat reporter. I was used to investigating the slow aftermath of trauma, rarely its beginnings. It was the photographers who taught me. I learned to sit for hours outside the press corps office of the Manila Police District (MPD) Headquarters waiting for the next alert, learned which police mobile belonged to the homicide investigators, learned who to contact for a spot report and which news agency could afford to send a driver with a car big enough to fit just one more reporter. We called ourselves the night shift, when we called ourselves anything at all. The foreign press called us *nightcrawlers*.

"Meet the Nightcrawlers of Manila," wrote *Los Angeles Times* writer Jonathan Kaiman the first summer of the war, promising readers "a night on the front lines of the Philippines' war on drugs." At the center of his story were the photojournalists who "speed through Manila to some rain-slicked slum or dark alley and arrive while the bodies still lay in the streets." It was a dramatic story, all blood and neon, the narrative focused on a freelancer named Linus Escandor.

"In the morning, if you shoot dead people, it's gory, but at night it's almost beautiful," Kaiman quoted Escandor. "You can hide the blood, because of the shadows. It's psychedelic, the colors."

The photographers, said Kaiman, were all looking for what he called "The Shot"—the photograph "powerful enough to shine a light on the crackdown's human cost."

And so the Nightcrawlers were born. "I didn't want the label," photographer Raffy Lerma told me one night, years after the war began. "I didn't want this kind of label. If it stuck, then so be it. I let it be. Then later I found the movie."

The 2014 movie stars Jake Gyllenhaal as Louis Bloom, an amateur cameraman in search of grisly crimes that he films and later sells to a local news station. The synopsis provided by the film's distributor describes local television news as a blood sport: "Lou muscles into the cut-throat, dangerous realm of nightcrawling—where each police siren wail equals a possible windfall and victims are converted into dollars and cents. . . . In the breakneck, ceaseless search for footage, he becomes the star of his own story." That ceaseless search also includes leading his own subjects to their deaths.

"I watched a few minutes of it," Raffy told me. "I found out he was this unethical photographer—"

"He was a psychopath," I interrupt.

"Yeah. Yeah. And it's completely opposite what we're trying to do."

Vincent Go, a freelancer, was less polite.

"That's just nonsense from the white people," Vincent told

me. "I figured they were trying to sensationalize a story about photographers when there really wasn't one. I just laughed it off."

Vincent's first day on the job began at 5:03 in the morning of July 6, 2016.

It was Wednesday, the Eid al-Fitr holiday. The sky was just beginning to brighten. Traffic was scarce on the way to the Quirino Grandstand, where the Muslim faithful were gathering to celebrate the end of Ramadan. Vincent, forty-eight years old, a freelance photojournalist, was driving through Tondo when a uniformed policeman caught his eye. The cop was standing at the center of the Delpan Bridge. A police cruiser, lights blinking, blocked the northbound lane.

The district of Delpan lies at the bottom of Tondo. The ten-lane overpass called the Delpan Bridge arcs over the tenements just before it speeds south over the Pasig River. Vincent slowed at the high curve, made a U-turn, and parked his battered 1997 Mitsubishi Lancer behind the cruiser. Yellow tape and a handful of patrol motorcycles formed a semicircle around a body on the ground.

The dead man lay in the shadow of the parapet wall. He was fair-skinned, barefoot, wore a good coat over a white shirt. His wrists were bound with duct tape. So were his feet. His head had been stuffed into a black trash bag.

Vincent nodded at the police. They nodded back. He lifted his camera, adjusted for the light, and took the first photo.

It was the job, and Vincent was good at the job. Rodrigo Duterte had been president for all of five days. Bureau chiefs had sent word to freelancers that images of salvage victims were welcome. Vincent stayed long enough to document the arrival of crime scene investigators. They found no witnesses.

It was not the first time Vincent had gone looking for a body. The first was when he was eleven years old, and the body had belonged to his father.

Vincent's father, Eddie, was a Chinese immigrant who ran his various businesses from an office in Manila's Chinatown. Precisely what those businesses involved was unclear to Vincent. The Chinese liked money, he said, and his father was no exception. It meant an easy life for the family, even during martial law. Vincent's father went to work. His mother stayed at home. They owned two cars, had a family driver, and sent the four children to private school.

One day armed men with military crew cuts burst into the house where Eddie sat reading the paper. The men tried to drag him away. Eddie struggled, and was hit in the face with the butt of a gun. Vincent, all of eleven years old, jumped one of the men. He was swatted away and was forced to watch as men he would never see again hauled Eddie out of the house to shoot him on the street.

There was no funeral, because there was no body. The family hunted for Eddie. The search lasted months. They went to hospitals. They visited morgues. They interrogated cops. One aunt paid good money to a fortune-teller who told them that Eddie was still alive.

Decades later Eddie's son filed his photos of a dead man lying on a bridge under a dawn sky.

"Manila, July 6, 2016," Vincent typed. "A body bound with duct tape was dumped at dawn on top of Delpan Bridge in Tondo Manila bearing a placard that says, 'Chinese Drug Lord Li Peng Hui.'"

·   ·   ·

In English grammar, *voice* is one of the five properties of verbs. A verb can be either active or passive. *I am writing this sentence* is active. *This sentence is being written* is passive.

The Chicago Manual of Style summarizes voice this way: "Voice shows whether the subject acts (active voice) or is acted on (passive voice)—that is, whether the subject performs or receives the action of the verb."

In the case of the body that Vincent Go discovered, the subject is the body: *A body bound with duct tape was dumped at dawn on top of Delpan Bridge in Tondo Manila bearing a placard.* A body was dumped, subject and verb. Everything else is description. The body does not assist in its abandonment. Neither does it abandon itself. The action occurs upon the body, a passive construction.

Fidelity to the active voice is an early dictum in journalism and in most other writing. "Never use the passive where you can use the active," intoned George Orwell in his 1946 *Politics and the English Language*. The habitual use of the active voice "makes for forcible writing," wrote William Strunk, Jr., and E. B. White. "Use the active voice" remains Rule Fourteen in the fourth edition of *The Elements of Style*.

"Passive voice," wrote the late journalism professor John Bremner, "is preferred by the weak, the cowardly, ashamed to name the fink who told them what they are evasively telling you."

Rule Fourteen, however, does not consider dead men found on Manila bridges at three in the morning. A reporter at a crime scene can point no finger, even if dead men require other men to drive cars, open doors, and pull triggers. You may, if you are so inclined, say that the government salvaged the man in the blue shoes, and you may be correct, but that sentence risks libel charges and government displeasure. We may, thirty-seven years after the fact, speak of the conjugal Marcos dictatorship's guilt in the salvaging of activists, but speaking of the dangerous new government of Rodrigo Duterte requires linguistic care.

A sentence cast in the passive voice is a statement of fact. One in the active voice is an accusation. *The dead man in blue shoes was salvaged,* and the sentence ends there as, according to the homicide report filed on July 1, 2016, "nobody among the crowd could give the exact account anent this case."

In 2016 the verb *salvage* was marshaled again into daily use. Salvaging, by its nature, is a passive construction. The addict was salvaged. The dealer was salvaged. The man in the blue shoes was salvaged, and so was a man whose head had been wrapped with packing tape before the killer drew over it a marking-pen smile.

Here is another grammatical point of interest: only transitive verbs have voice. Intransitive verbs cannot shift from active to passive, or from passive to active. No literary sleight of hand can hold someone else accountable for having sneezed your nose or arrived you late. Nor can anyone else do your dying, because *die* is an intransitive verb. You died. He died. She died. They died. Regardless of whether any of them were salvaged, it was the subject who did the dying, not the man with the gun.

Death, in the end, disappears all voices.

My first night on the job, the night Jerome Roa was salvaged, began at 2:56 on the morning of August 20. It was the eighth week of the war. At least eighteen drug suspects had already been killed in the district of Tondo alone. Four had been shot by unidentified gunmen. Fourteen were killed by police for allegedly resisting arrest.

I stood by the side of the four-lane MICT Access Road in Manila. Jerome Roa, twenty-seven, had been found dead at half an hour past midnight. His body was curled into the seat of a red tricycle, a passenger vehicle with a tin sidecar attached to a standard motorcycle. The tricycle was parked outside Parola Gate 64. One bare foot was propped on a connector railing, the head tucked into the space between the motorcycle and the tarp-covered sidecar. There were no marks on his camouflage-print cargo pants or anywhere on the bright blue shirt hiked over his waistband. Jerome Roa could have been asleep if it weren't for the pair of gunshot wounds at the back of his neck and the blood pooling under the sidecar's back wheels.

Jerome's grandmother stood just outside the ribbon of yellow tape, wiping sweat and tears with a grimy kitchen towel. Her name was Josephine. She was sixty-seven years old. News of a body that had been found sent her running; she ran through the warren of twisting alleys, out through the arch of Gate 18, cutting through the highway past the police cars and the media vans and the windowless facade of a trucking company where Jerome had once worked. Josephine had raised Jerome. He had taken a job with a group of long-haul truckers and learned that getting high on meth could keep him awake longer than caffeine could. Jerome, addicted, lost his job. He lived on the street, sleeping inside any one of the tricycles parked in haphazard lines along the sidewalks. He barely earned enough to eat, let alone enough for a fix. After Duterte was elected, he told his grandmother he quit drugs and promised to stay clean.

The body was gone by the time Josephine found the crime scene. She never saw his face. The police had wrapped her grandson in a blue tarp, then loaded the corpse into the back of a utility truck.

She patted the bloody seat where they found him and spoke quietly.

Jerome, she murmured, *pray for us.*

Josephine was not angry. She understood why Jerome had been salvaged. The killers, she said, might have been unaware her boy was no longer using when they marked him for death.

Salvage is a contronym in the Philippines. It can mean its opposite, sometimes at the same instance. Duterte's war salvages its own dead, repurposing the bodies into a warning for the living, cardboard signs flapping in the wind. I AM A DRUG DEALER, the signs read. FOLLOW NOT IN MY FOOTSTEPS.

After the press convoy drove away, I stayed behind and walked over to a clump of bystanders. They had watched, leaning against tricycles, as the corpse of Jerome Roa was carried away. They had known Jerome too, but they did not weep.

It was dark without the camera lights. "Is it dangerous to live here?" I asked one of them.

No, a voice said, then shrugged. There was no danger for people like them.

"You're safe as long as you behave."

Eloisa Lopez's first night on the job began with five bodies. They were killed at the Malabon Public Cemetery, where the very poor lived in shanties in the shadow of old tombstones. The five had been shot by men riding motorcycles. Three of them were dead on the ground, two died later in the hospital. A scrawled cardboard sign was left behind: DRUG PUSHERS.

Eloisa took pictures. She asked no questions. She was barely twenty years old. Her first published photo had been a picture of a half-dozen people carrying beribboned shovels with the debris of a groundbreaking ceremony in the background that made it onto the front page of her college newspaper, giving her the first thrill of a byline, with *Eloisa Lopez* printed in ten-point sans serif above the fold. She graduated, secured a press ID from a local broadsheet, and supplemented the five-dollar contributing free-lancer rate with weekends shooting birthday parties, christenings, and the occasional restaurant menu. The paint was still wet in the closet-sized apartment she rented when the bodies began dropping.

She trailed the night shift from crime scene to crime scene, a young woman clutching a large camera, dressed in skinny jeans and sneakers. She did not intend to photograph the dead, but the dead were the story. She wanted to know if she was as good as the rest.

The picture that mattered came three months into the war. It was the same cemetery where she had spent her first night. She was too late to see the body. The police had come and gone. All that was left was the father, sitting beside a tombstone, weeping softly, his wife dazed behind him.

"I thought the victim was a drug dealer," Eloisa told me. "It wasn't."

The corpse belonged to a seven-year-old girl. Found by neighbors, naked, bloodied, her panties shoved into her mouth. The suspect was a neighbor who had asked to take the girl for a walk. The press crowded inside the police station. The father stuttered through tears. The suspect cowered in a circle of cops and cameras.

He was drunk, the cops said, and an addict.

The room smelled of sweat and fury. The suspect was lanky, wore an earring on one lobe, where a smudge of red was still visible. He had blood on his ear, on his nose, on his shirt, on the dirty shorts. He jittered in his cuffs. "He denied everything," Eloisa said, "but he looked guilty. He looked exactly like I thought an addict would look."

You fucking son of a bitch, said one man. It was unclear if the speaker was a cop or a reporter. The curses came thick and fast. You fucking goddamned son of a bitch.

Eloisa, crouched on the grimy tile, camera in hand, mouthed the words. Son of a bitch. You fucking son of a bitch. Then she stepped out of the room, walked to the press car, locked the door, and cried.

"That night," she said, "I wanted him to die too."

Inside, the dead girl's father spoke. It doesn't matter if you kill him, he said. It won't bring my girl back.

Eloisa has a picture of that night: the father who wept, the mother who mourned. It was published once, with her name on the byline. She photographed many more bodies after that night, some of them women, most of them men, sometimes just the skulls if all that was left were skulls. She does not know what happened to the man with an earring who killed the little girl.

She hopes he survived.

Extrajudicial killing is not a new term. It has been associated with the executions of hundreds of activists during the Salvadoran Civil War, the purgings of thousands of Chilean Socialists after Augusto Pinochet assumed power in 1973, and the lynchings of emancipated African Americans before the rise of the civil rights movement. In the Philippines, it has been used to describe the "carefully selected and intentionally targeted" executions of suspected Communists during the "all-out war" of the mid-aughts, and during investigations of an alleged death squad operating in Davao City under the infamous mayor Rodrigo Duterte.

The United Nations generally defines extrajudicial killings as "the deliberate killing of individuals outside of any legal framework," as it did when the UN Office of the High Commissioner on Human Rights referred to "the current wave of extrajudicial executions and killings" during the Duterte drug war.

In early September 2016, Glenda Gloria, then my managing editor at Rappler, sent out a company-wide email encouraging all reporters to familiarize themselves with the term. We were to use the phrase "to liberally refer to all killings by state or non-state actors that are made outside court processes, outside the law, outside legitimate police/state operations, and which violate universal standards of the right to life."

In the first six weeks of Rodrigo Duterte's war, according to the police, 899 people were killed, described by Philippine National Police Chief Ronald dela Rosa as "the dead who were just found floating along canals, the dead who were dumped along roads with their hands tied and their faces, eyes, and mouths taped, also those killed by riding-in-tandem, or those who were just shot."

Dela Rosa offered a new name for the dead, one that had never been used before the election of Rodrigo Duterte. They would be called "deaths under investigation." It would later evolve to "homicides under investigation."

"Those aren't EJKs," Dela Rosa said, "because they're not state-sponsored. We term it as plain homicide."

Deaths, Dela Rosa said, not murders. Homicides, he said, not murders. In a single surgical strike, the Philippine National Police stripped the language of intent, and reduced a pattern of executions to common crime.

Members of the House joined in the performance. Deputy Speaker Gwendolyn Garcia questioned the use of the term "extrajudicial killing," citing a Wikipedia definition as her standard.

She proposed the removal of extrajudicial killings from the panel's lexicon. The phrase would no longer be used in all official hearings, investigations, or reports.

The motion was offered, seconded, and approved.

Raffy Lerma's first night on the job was not his first photographing the dead. He had been assigned the night shift in 2007 as a young photographer for the *Philippine Daily Inquirer*. By the time Rodrigo Duterte was elected in 2016, the *Inquirer* night shift had long been discontinued, and Raffy was a thirty-eight-year-old general assignment photographer with a decade of work under his belt. He knew there would be killings and was certain they would happen at night. He volunteered. His editor agreed. One week before his scheduled deployment, he took his camera to the MPD to reorient himself to night work.

"That was it," he said. "I remember, my first ten minutes inside the MPD and there was already a call. We responded to the crime scene."

The location was Pandacan in Manila. There were three victims—police called them suspects—killed in a police operation after allegedly resisting arrest. No reporters were allowed inside the house where the encounter occurred. Raffy climbed up a next-door balcony, shooting down as bodies were carried out of the front door. Neighbors pointed him to a young girl standing by a post, daughter of one of the dead men.

"She was just, you know, standing there. That was the first time it hit me. I was looking at her when they were carrying her father's body out, and she was just there watching. She couldn't cry. She couldn't, I guess, because of the stigma of people getting killed and labeled drug pushers. Like they had been judged. . . .

And she couldn't grieve. I couldn't understand it then. And when the media wanted to interview her, she just left. When the bodies were being lifted into the funeral car, it was like everyone was crowding in, feasting on it, taking pictures of the dead. And I heard it, heard them cursing at the bodies—*you sons of bitches, you animals. . . .* That was the first time that I saw the lust, you know, the wanting for people to be killed. I covered the night shift before, but it wasn't anything like this."

The night shift rode back to the MPD. Five hours later the radio crackled out a flash report. Another body had been found along Taft Avenue. They bolted for their cars. It was a short drive. The body, curled in a fetal position, was inside a white grain sack. The dead man's wrists and knees were bound tight with yellow nylon string. His face was wrapped in packing tape. A cardboard sign was tucked inside the sack, naming the man an addict.

Another message, in smaller letters, had been added to the usual warning: YOU WILL BE NEXT.

Raffy heard a cry, the high keening of a female voice. He looked up to see a woman standing on the elevated concrete planter dividing the lanes, lit by the flashing lights of the police cruisers. She was middle-aged, her hair haphazardly tied back. A towel hung off one shoulder. She wept as she screamed.

Reporters asked if she knew the dead man. She did not.

"Everyone was just doing their jobs," Raffy said, "like it was an everyday thing. And it was the woman who was screaming at us. 'Don't you have hearts? Don't you have a conscience?' I don't know if she really knew the dead guy. Maybe she did, maybe not. But she was being human. Like she was the only one who made sense that night."

7

HOW TO IDENTIFY AN ADDICT

President Rodrigo Duterte did not call for murder, not once. It was a word he avoided with careful precision.

They would "have to perish," said the president. They would be "wiped out from the face of the earth." He would "slaughter those idiots." He would do it himself if he could. Leave them to drown on a boat in the Pacific. Push them out of helicopters. Hang them, "not with rope" but with barbed wire, sharp as blades, so sharp that "when you drop, you leave your head behind when your body falls."

Murder was a word he deployed with great care. When Rodrigo Duterte said *kill,* he did not mean murder. To murder, he said, was to kill a bound man begging for his life.

"I declared war," he said. "That's war. Why do they say it's illegitimate? Why, is it wrong to say *Papatay ako ng tao para sa bayan ko*? Tell me, is there a crime?"

Papatay ako ng tao para sa bayan ko. "I will kill people for my country."

Rodrigo Duterte called himself a killer, "just an ordinary killer," but he was adamant that he was no murderer. Not once, in speech after speech, did he demand the murder of the sons of bitches he promised would die. He blustered. He threatened. He evaded. He was only kidding, he said sometimes. He would pardon himself, he said other times. "Charge me when I step down," he said in a speech at the palace. "'Pardon is extended to Rodrigo Duterte for crimes against humanity,' signed Rodrigo Duterte."

Murder does not require only that the victim die. To call an act murder, according to Article 248 of the Philippine Revised Penal Code, any one of six elements must be present. The victim died with treachery, for example, or the suspect killed "taking advantage of superior strength" or "with evident premeditation." Without any of the elements present, an act of killing is reduced to homicide, a bailable offense.

Duterte's order to kill, according to Rodrigo Duterte, was not a license to murder. Neither did it constitute criminal homicide, as homicide in the Philippines is punished by a term of twelve to twenty years in jail. The president said no cop would spend a single day behind bars for the performance of his duty, and that duty, very often, would be the "duty to kill."

There is no word for "murder" in Filipino. There is *patayin*. There is *paslangin*. Both mean "to kill." While much of our jurisprudence is written and spoken in English, another remnant of American colonization, my own language does not distinguish between the premeditated killing of one human being by another and the accidental death of a person. But Duterte did make the distinction, said it clearly, again and again.

"I never said do it from behind. It's murder," he said. "What

I said was war. I am declaring war against the drug people. I'm declaring war against those who would destroy the youth of the land. I said I will kill you."

Article 11 of the Penal Code offers a number of defenses for killing a person. Article 11.1 protects from a murder charge "anyone who acts in defense of his person or rights." Article 11.5 exempts "any person who acts in the fulfillment of a duty or in the lawful exercise of a right or office." Article 11.6 exempts "any person who acts in obedience to an order issued by a superior for some lawful purpose." Any person proven to have killed under these circumstances is free of criminal liability.

"I am the president now," Duterte said in 2017. "The fight against the drug people will continue to the very last day of my term. That would be six years. Another killing for the night, I don't mind."

It was the necessary fiction of the drug war. Those who threatened the future would die simply because they had lost the right to live. The president would provide bounties. He would enjoin police "to hunt them, and then to kill them." Their own neighbors would put them down if those neighbors had guns— "you have my support," he promised. They would be drowned, stabbed, shot, buried, dropped into Manila Bay, fed to fishes, and sent to purgatory, and none of it would be murder because it was not murder, only justice. It was not a rationalization for the use of force. Nor was it a declaration of war. It was a call for execution.

"Simple justice," he said. "Not murder-murder."

Depending on where you begin the story, it started with a goat.

"I'll give it to you raw," the president said.

Back when he was mayor, there was a Christmas party, a

family reunion, out in rural Mandug in Davao City. "So people got together," he said, "and this addict also came. He saw his sister carrying her baby daughter, and he said, 'So this is my niece.'"

The niece was eighteen months old. The uncle picked up the baby. He said she was pretty, prettier than her mother. Merrymaking continued through the night until the mother discovered her baby was gone.

They found her in the morning on a riverbank. Dead, with her belly torn open. The police caught the uncle. They held him at the police station. The mayor stormed in. He asked the uncle why. "His answer to me? He said, 'Ah, that's really how I am, Mayor, sometimes when I've got no one to fuck, I end up fucking the goats.'"

What the dead girl's uncle said is a part of the story I cannot report with certainty. It is possible it was true. It is also possible that the mayor imagined it. What can be verified is this—that sometime in the early 1990s, a dead baby was found by the river in the village of Mandug, where urban Davao City gives way to dirt roads and small farms. It happened in December, and the journalists who were there never forgot. They still remember the rip in the soft skin, and one of them said the small throat had been cut. They remember how the mayor burst into the police station and sent the media out of the room, and all of them heard the meaty thunk of the mayor's fists through the plywood walls. They remember this too: the mayor's knuckles were red and bruised when he stepped out.

The president told the story many times, and every time the goat was the clincher, the punch line that proved the moral.

"If that's the answer you get," the president asked in Pampanga, "what will you do?"

"You, if you were the mayor," he asked in Manila, "and you're answered with that, what will you do?"

"Guess what I did," he asked the cheering thousands in Tondo.

He never quite explained what he did. "I did do something," the president said. He couldn't say what, "because the media is here." He said it was a lucky thing that someone had given him a snub-nosed Ruger revolver that Christmas. The timing "was just exactly right, son of a bitch, right there at the station."

The lesson the president offered was not that a suspected rapist might have been punished, or beaten, or killed. The moral was inside the man, and what was inside the man was a monster. This was the enemy, the president meant. Addicts. Rapists. Baby-killers. Goat-fuckers. The image sears into the imagination. The small, broken body abandoned in the wild grass, the weeping mother who had been so proud hours before, and the uncle, red-eyed, casually unrepentant, and so high on meth he forgot to be afraid. The addict had raped a baby. The mayor was angry, and the city understood. They were angry too.

Six times the president told the story. Forgive me, he said, "if I am driven also to insanity." It was not enough to end the life of one addict, because there were so many. What happened to the baby in Mandug happened "not one, two, three, four, five, six" times, but "every day, in the whole country."

To identify a drug addict, you must first look at the teeth. Mark the gaps. Note what is missing. You ask a question, and the answer wanders into inanity. A drug addict will stutter and ramble, will grind teeth and grin. Ask the president, and the president will tell you. "You know, you would know a person if he's into drugs. He's smelly, he does not take a bath, he does not sleep, and he keeps on grinding his teeth in front of you. So most of the addicts have lost all their teeth. That's one indication."

The United Nations Office on Drugs and Crime recognizes that the world lacks "a global standard definition of a problem drug user." President Duterte does not recognize this lack. Long before he was elected, he referred to addicts as a class of people, particularly those addicted to crystal methamphetamine, or *shabu*. They were criminals, all of them, maddened by the drugs that were shrinking their brains. The president once heard an American doctor say there was no hope for rehabilitation for a meth addict. It would take a year, he was told, maybe six months, and a little more than a dozen hits of meth, and the human brain would be gone, shriveled, dried up, "destroyed."

Drug addicts "are raping children," the president said, twenty-seven days into his administration. "They are killing fathers. They punch their mothers when their mothers refuse them money. You all know this. They steal. Because they must have the fix every day, they'll take it from other people."

It was a "pandemic," said the president, an epidemic responsible for the deaths of 77,000 in the three to four years before his election. He claimed those 77,000 victims had been killed by drug addicts—"mostly rape, straight murders, rape with homicide, robbery with homicide, robbery with rape and homicide."

"You know, in the wake of the drug contamination in the Philippines, 77,000 deaths, drug-related. Who will answer for that? Who will take the cudgels for those innocent—the young women raped? The ones held up in jeepneys—who will answer for them?"

It was a number he dictated across eleven speeches and repeated in multiple interviews. Seventy-seven thousand dead in three to four years. That toll is not just improbable, it is impossible. Between 2012 and 2015, the four years before his election, the Philippine Statistics Authority reported 37,039 murders and 16,213 homicides. Even if every death was at the hands of a rampaging meth addict, the total is nowhere near 77,000 in four years. Neither does the president's claim square with this fact: There is no definitive way to singularly attribute a rape or murder to drug use.

But meth addicts, explained the president, were "really crazy." They were "out of their senses." They had "no cognitive value." Rehabilitation was "no longer a viable option." They were "beyond redemption," more suitable for suicide than for sympathy. They raped for the sake of raping, an egregious departure from the days when men raped only the attractive. "Back in my day," the president said, "rape victims were all actresses, all beautiful, and you can't blame the rapists that they went mad because the women were really so beautiful." His war was necessary because any woman can be raped. Leave your house, and your wife will be raped. Your nanny. Your children, "even the babies eleven months, eighteen months old—like it happened in Davao."

Watch their mouths. Smell their hair. Listen to them mumble and see if they sleep. They have no fear. They have no shame. They assault the sons and daughters of hardworking parents who slave away as overseas workers in the Middle East. They are pedophiles and madmen, bestial and bizarre, and when the monkey rides their backs, they will kill for the fix with no questions asked.

"A lot of them," said the president, "are no longer viable as human beings in this planet."

In my country, medicines are good, and drugs are bad. Medicine, or *gamot,* refers to all substances for clinical treatment. Drugs, or *droga,* even without appending the word *illegal,* is understood to mean crystal methamphetamine, cocaine, heroin, marijuana, or any of a slew of other narcotics the law formally calls dangerous drugs. A drugstore is a pharmacy legitimately selling ibuprofen, and President Duterte certainly was not referring to the regulation of premenstrual syndrome when he intoned "My God, I hate drugs, and I have to kill people because I hate drugs."

Numbers were important to the president, because numbers demonstrated the enormity of the problem: the army of mindless monsters whose extermination would require the entire might of the national government. The country had three to four million drug addicts, he said, possibly more, all probably violent, even though official government studies accounted for the prevalence of drug use, not of addiction. The surveys conducted by the Dangerous Drugs Board (DDB) made no distinction between a problematic user—the sort of violent addict that the president raged against—and the teenager who smoked a joint at a birthday party. Both can be classified a "current drug user"—anyone who used any illegal drug once within a thirteen-month period, according to the DDB in 2015.

The estimated number of illegal drug users in the Philippines has remained fairly consistent for almost a decade. In 2008 the DDB's National Household Survey estimated there were 1.7 million current drug users in the country. In 2012 there were 1.3 million. In 2015 the DDB estimated 1.8 million.

The 2015 study was completed during the term of former president Benigno Aquino III. It fell to the new DDB chairman, the career bureaucrat Benjamin Reyes, to present the numbers three months into the new administration. It meant that in the year Rodrigo Duterte took power, the same year he raised the specter of the country as a narco state run by drug barons and rampaging addicts, the Philippines' current illegal drug users, estimated by the government itself, clocked in at roughly half the global average. Less than half were meth users. The drug of choice for most of those surveyed was marijuana.

Chairman Reyes was asked more than once about the discrepancy between the president's numbers and the DDB's official survey results. He said both figures were credible. One was scientific, he said, the other was from the intelligence community. "Personally, I don't know how they conduct intelligence gathering," he said.

In a television interview with reporter Christian Esguerra, Reyes, caught between principles and his principal, attempted to placate both and failed.

"Why the disparity?" Esguerra asked. "You have intelligence sources that say there are around four million drug users. But the official figure, as far as the DDB is concerned—it's only one point eight million."

"Well, in the campaign you need to look at several data sources, and all those data sources are valid," Reyes answered. "We have a source coming from a survey. We have a source coming from intel figures. As long as they are gathered using a methodology, valid methodology, that means those figures can be used."

"Sometimes the president even uses six million," Esguerra responded. "Now, the figures are important because this is the basis for policy, right? This is among the questions raised to you at the forum in—"

"It's how you use the figures. If you are using figures to target populations, I would rather use the figure which is higher. I would rather overtarget than undertarget."

Chairman Reyes was fired the next day.

"Get out of the service," the president told him on national television. "You do not contradict your own government."

The contradiction was not with the government. It was with the president.

The DDB was wrong, the president said. His count of drug addicts—never merely drug users—fluctuated from three million to 3.7 million to four to five to six million. He attributed his initial count of three million to Dionisio Santiago, who once headed the DDB's enforcement unit, the Philippine Drug Enforcement Agency (PDEA).

Dionisio Santiago had run for a Senate seat in 2016. He lost, even with the support of the president. When Duterte, then still a candidate, offered up his three million figure at campaign rallies, he would point to Santiago for confirmation. Santiago, when asked, called the number "a guesstimate" based on the "realistic situation on the ground."

After Reyes was fired, Santiago was appointed to head the DDB.

The PDEA, in answer to questions posted by *The Philippine Star,* said its estimate was derived from a statistic publicly available from the UN Office of Drugs and Crime.

Here is the statistic the government relied on: globally, 5.2 percent of people between the ages of fifteen and sixty-four were illegal drug users.

The Philippine population between the ages of fifteen and sixty-four numbers 65.1 million.

"Using the UN percentage on drug users," wrote the PDEA, "65.1 million multiplied by 0.052 is equal to 3.4 million. Therefore, the country's estimated number of drug users is 3.4 million."

Here is what those numbers mean. The Philippine government, absent any actual field surveys, extrapolated 3.4 million Filipino drug users from the average number of drug users worldwide, a number that had very little to do with drug prevalence in the Philippines. That number became fact to the president. It was quoted, expanded, then misrepresented into a three-to-eight-million-strong zombie army of goat-fucking meth heads responsible for the rape and murder of 77,000 supposed victims.

"By their reasoning, you might say, the world's estimate of drug prevalence is so and so, our population is a hundred million, so our estimate of drug prevalence is so and so multiplied by a hundred million," said Jose Ramon Albert, formerly the country's chief statistician and senior research fellow of the Philippine Institute for Development Studies. "That's a biased estimate either upward or downward, depending on whether the world's estimate of a prevalence is higher or lower than the country prevalence."

The numbers ballooned, shrank, and ballooned again, as government lackeys struggled to catch up. The president would add numbers on the fly then call them conservative estimates. It was reasonable, said the president, to assume that in the years since the number was released, more had turned into addicts.

"So three million plus one million is four million," he said once.

"Give it a liberal addition," he said another time. "Maybe, make it 700,000. So, 3,700,000. The number is quite staggering and scary."

A Reuters investigation concluded that "data on the total number of drug users, the number of users needing treatment, the types of drugs being consumed and the prevalence of drug-related crime is exaggerated, flawed or non-existent." It cited antinarcotics officials who called the numbers "overestimates" but conceded they were valuable in bringing the community together to fight what was once "a lonely battle."

"I don't see it as a problem," Wilkins Villanueva, PDEA's Metro Manila regional director, told Reuters. The president "just exaggerates it so we will know that the problem is very big."

Later the police would compile statistics about how 11,321 of the country's 42,065 villages were considered "drug-affected." It was, said the Philippine National Police, "indicative of the worsening drug problem that has victimized mostly the underprivileged and impoverished sector of the society."

Drug-affected, like *drug user*, is a loose term. A *drug-affected* area was one with "a proven existence of drug user, pusher, manufacturer, marijuana cultivator or other drug personalities regardless of number." One user, one addict, one dealer, one man with pot in his pocket, and the village was marked.

The word *proven* was also undefined.

In July 2016 the Philippine National Police formally launched the drug war by issuing Command Memorandum Circular No. 16-2016. The circular was released by the office of Chief of Police Ronald "Bato" dela Rosa, President Duterte's former Davao City police chief who once told me he considered himself Duterte's "loyal soldier." Even the PNP was unwilling to stand by the president's figure of millions of addicts, instead quoting the same 1.8 million the DDB offered.

Absent any written orders from the executive, the PNP announced that the program was based on the "pronouncement of President Rodrigo R. Duterte to get rid of illegal drugs during the first six months of his term." That deadline, repeated in campaign speeches, was the single commitment that came close to an actionable policy plan from the president.

The operation would be called Project Double Barrel.

"One touch of the barrel, two triggers will be set off," Police Chief dela Rosa was happy to inform the media. "There's a barrel that will target from above, the high-value targets. And there's a barrel that will target from below, the street level."

The first of the metaphorical two barrels was directed toward what the government called high-value targets: the drug syndicates and financiers known colloquially as drug lords. The second barrel would target street dealing and daily drug use. The operation had its own name: Tokhang.

Tokhang did not exist in any of the local languages. It was a portmanteau designed especially for the drug war, derived from the Visayan words *toktok* and *hangyo*—"knock" and "plead." Tokhang meant "house-to-house visitations, led by the police, to persuade suspected illegal drug personalities to stop their illegal drug activities." Those on the drug lists were invited to surrender at village halls and police stations and to admit their crimes. Tens of thousands swore oaths, turned in their own pot-smoking friends, and were sent home with the admonition to sin no more.

Tokhang was Dela Rosa's own brainchild, the velvet glove over the iron fist. It was, the police said, an invitation, not a demand. If it so happened that a suspect was killed, it was because he had pulled out a gun.

Kill them all, said the president. The drug problem would be eradicated in three to six months. He would resign or die if he failed.

But if it wasn't to be murder, the police had to have a reason to kill them.

That reason was the caveat built into the president's every speech, the sort that could be typed out in police reports and presented to the "bleeding-heart human rights people" who complained that the president was a butcher. Kill them if they resist violently. Shoot if they fight back.

Get them before they get you.

．　　　　．　　　　．

In 1978 the Marcos government held the first parliamentary elections after the declaration of martial law. By then, Ninoy Aquino had spent most of the previous five and a half years in solitary confinement. He established a new party and assembled a slate of twenty-one candidates. Aquino's party was the only viable opposition to challenge the dictatorship's massive machinery, whose chief candidate was the appointed governor of Greater Manila, First Lady Imelda Marcos herself.

"The electoral deck is stacked against the opposition," Aquino wrote from his cell in Fort Bonifacio. "But fight we will!"

The word for "fight," in Filipino, is *laban*.

Lumaban siya. He fought.

Lumalaban siya. He is fighting.

Nanlaban siya. He fought back.

Aquino's new party was named People's Power—Lakas ng Bayan. Its shorthand was Laban. The Laban Party lost nearly every seat in 1978. Eight years later the yellow-clad protesters who crowded the length and breadth of Edsa during the People Power Revolution thrust out thumb and forefinger into the letter L. The word on their lips was *laban*. It was the word that interrupted prayers and songs, that was shouted at approaching tanks, that was scrawled on handmade cardboard signs clutched by elderly nuns.

It was, in 1986, what the people did in the name of my generation. I was born free because of a word.

Nanlaban sila. "They fought back."

Thirty-seven years later the word *nanlaban* belonged to the police. The yellow ribbons of the revolution were replaced with crime scene tape.

"*Nanlaban siya*," the cops told us, night after night, bodies at their feet. "He fought back."

Nanlaban, under Rodrigo Duterte, did not mean only that a man had fought back. It meant he had fought and died. Nanlaban is judgment and justification, verb and noun, a shorthand for the dead bastards who deserved what they got.

Here then was the assumption of resistance in the drug war: you fought, and then you died.

8

HOW TO KILL AN ADDICT

I lived in an old apartment building for eight years, just two blocks from the broadcast network where I once worked as a producer. When I began working the night shift in the drug war, I learned to acquire cigarettes by the double ream and canned tuna by the box. I ran out of fresh laundry often, so I found myself a field uniform instead and bought a half-dozen white button-down shirts with sleeves I would fold four times to just above my elbow and far too many pairs of the same navy slacks. By the fourth month of President Duterte's war, my dog had chewed through my microwave cable and a rough square foot of my kitchen floor. I gave him up the second time he got sick. I like to think he understood why I had to give him away. He was a very good boy, and I missed him very much.

My building was five stories high and stood squarely between a bar and a missionary convent. I never saw the nuns, but occasionally, just after dawn, when the bar's speakers cut from Nicki Minaj, I could hear the sisters of St. Charles Borromeo singing hymns from my bedroom windows.

I was sitting at home on one of those mornings when a photojournalist I knew sent me photos of a crime scene I had missed. The deaths had been reported as a police encounter. My witnesses had said it was murder. I was investigating the official statements and needed to verify the placement of the guns.

The photojournalist told me to be careful. These were cops, he said. The men were armed. "I know," I answered. "I'll be fine."

Within minutes he had sent me another picture, unsolicited, of an activist's corpse. He had taken it years ago. She lay on the wild grass, broken and bloody, her face beaten into unrecognizability. This, he said, was the risk I was taking.

"Thanks," I said.

He sent a smiley face. "Coffee later?"

I could, if required, enumerate the many reasons why it was necessary for me to move out of my apartment. The roof leaked. The commute took too long. Far too many people knew my address. But mostly I moved because I couldn't unsee that picture of the woman. The grass had gone dark under her head. I had, after seeing her, taken to imagining footsteps shuffling up the metal fire escape. The hallelujahs morphed into furtive mumbling.

The new apartment was in a university town, in a building just off the main avenue. It was apartment suburbia. Trees spread overhead. Cyclists and joggers streamed past the pink dormitories. It was a town of college professors and golden retrievers and girls in white sneakers walking to yoga studios. The president might have banned all public smoking during his first year in office, but my new neighborhood made room even for that. The coffee shop across the street had a roofed deck fenced in by trees. Ashtrays lay on the outdoor tables, birds sang in the early morning, and a small creek gurgled just past the café. The waitresses smiled. The other diners wore headphones. It would have been possible, were I so inclined, to leave my laptop on the table and find it untouched ten minutes later. That was where I wrote, working through packs of cigarettes and paying for the privilege with a cappuccino every two hours. Had I not been a journalist, the practical impact of Rodrigo Duterte's election on me would have been limited to my tobacco consumption and little else.

As it happened, I *was* a journalist, and I spent the nights in the mechanical absorption of organized killing. I needed to find a logic to every crime scene, a chronology to the questioning. Was it a salvaging, a drive-by, a buy-bust, or a body dump? Was the killer a cop or a vigilante? How many, what time, who called it in? Was there a sign by the body, were the hands bound, was there a gun on the ground, was the body stuffed into a bag, was the head packed in plastic?

The steps were clear, as I ticked through one, then two, then three. Confirm the street corner. Find the investigating officer. Sidle up to the bystanders, ask if they knew the corpse's name.

We don't know, someone might say.

The family is coming, someone else might interrupt.

Stand still. Listen for the wailing. Find them in the crowd, run both recorders. Apologize. Condole. Keep the voice low and keep the questions simple. Who was he, what happened, where are you from, when did you see him last, how did you know he was gone?

Take me to that moment, I would say. Tell me your story.

I moved through the checklist: each point an anchor to keep the chaos in place. Count the bullet casings as the cops put down the bright numbered tags. Watch the techs empty the pockets for IDs, for plastic packets of meth, for cash, for cell phones. Check for the name of the morgue. And write down everything, every detail in sight.

Blood thick, tomato ketchup on asphalt.
Tape over mouth, excess folded over chin.
Cop uses own shirt, wipes blood from hands.
Bond paper inside wallet, Times New Roman, all caps. Typed,
*   I am a dealer.*
Shorts, Hawaiian print shirt, slippers tossed between legs.
Killer walked away. Did not run.

Here was the bridge where a person was shot every week— "Every Monday," said the street sweeper. "We don't go out when it happens." Here was the morgue man, loading the corpse on the stained stretcher into the van.

The nights in the field ran long. I did the job. I ran the interviews. I hounded the cops. I appeared, for all intents and purposes, to be a functioning member of the news media, by which I mean I filed stories occasionally and invented believable excuses when I didn't. Sometimes a mother would ask if I could help fund the burial. Sometimes a grandmother would tell me there was no money for school. One woman would plead every so often for a loan—for food, for power bills, for rent, for funds to visit a son in jail. I paid for none of it, because there were rules to reporting, and one of those rules was that I could never fund a source, because paying a source meant buying a story. *But no one will know,* said the woman whose son had been killed with a bullet in the gut. *I'll know,* I said.

I tell this story not to demonstrate my virtue but to explain how conscience has very little to do with surviving the field. I found it was possible, for example, to note that a father might weep over the fact that he could buy no candles for his dead son, then find myself paying my Amazon Kindle bill that amounted to the cost of a small coffin. I followed the rules because the rules were all I had left.

In the early years of the war, I fell in love, I learned to ride a bike, and I discovered firsthand just how much blood could fit on the inside of a grown man. The world kept turning, and people kept dying, and for the next few years I sat under the leafy green and wrote about the dead.

A buy-bust operation, much like a romance, is an intimate affair. The alleged drug dealer is identified and surveilled. His comings and goings are noted, his accomplices investigated, his preferences are observed, and the nuances of his everyday interactions are filed away for future use. The pursuit is a careful operation. It is a courtship of sorts. An undercover cop, called the poseur-buyer, poses as an illegal drug user at the suspect's doorstep. He declares his intent. He promises good faith. The goods are handed over, the question asked and answered. Cops use the same word for fulfillment as is used for newlyweds: *consummation*.

"After the consummated transaction," read one police report, "poseur-buyer and companion arrested the suspect."

Only when the suspect is killed during the operation does another phrase appear, and it appears with surprising regularity. In the black-and-white of a Philippine spot report, "suspect sensed presence of lawmen" comes just before "suspect drew his firearm." It is the final intimacy between killer and killed. On one side the recognition of an enemy, on another the appreciation of a threat. One leads to another: the choice to defy, the weapon drawn, the finger to the trigger, the dead man on the ground. On paper, it is a single line. On the field, it is a death sentence.

Consider, for example, one day in the drug war, a year into the administration of President Rodrigo Duterte.

It began at twenty minutes past midnight on August 15, 2017, when cops conducted a buy-bust operation that resulted in the confiscation of fifty grams of crystal meth and the death of two men.

It took the cops less than twenty-four hours to bag thirty more corpses.

At 12:20 a.m., suspects Bernard Lizardo and Justine Buca-cao, "after sensing that they were dealing with an under-cover police poseur, fired successive shots at the operating team, and tried to elude arrest that led to a brief firefight which resulted to the death of the suspects."

At 12:40 a.m., suspects Jimmy Gongon and Bartolome Marin "sensed the presence of operatives" and drew arms, resulting in "the instantaneous death of the two suspects."

At 1:40 a.m., a suspect, "a certain Alvin," had just con-cluded a sale when he "sensed he was transacting with a policeman" and "shot towards the approaching operatives which prompted the policemen in the area to return fire that resulted in the death of the suspect."

At 1:45 a.m., suspect Christopher Tecson "sensed that the poseur buyer was a Police Officer" and "shot the Police and a brief firefight ensued that resulted in the death of the suspect."

At 2:25 a.m., suspect Wilfredo Alapide "sensed that the police undercover was a police officer and tried to escape." Police pursued, and "a gunfight ensued between them that resulted to the instantaneous death of the aforesaid suspect."

At 3:00 a.m., suspect Jessie Andales "noticed the approaching operating team and fired his gun to the direction of the police officers, which prompted the latter to retaliate and gun fight ensued." He "sustained gunshot wounds in different parts of his body," was rushed to the hospital, and was declared dead on arrival.

At 3:30 a.m., suspect Jefry Miranda "found out" he was facing a police undercover officer and proceeded to "shoot the police officer. Gunfire ensued between the suspect and operatives that resulted to his death."

At 4:30 a.m., a suspect known only as "Alias Macoy," after a "consummated transaction," resisted arrest, "drew his firearm and fired at the poseur buyer but missed." The police backup personnel "retaliated killing the suspect on the spot."

The thirty-two who died in that twenty-four-hour period did not constitute the national toll. All thirty-two were killed in a single province. On that day, the police stations of the province of Bulacan conducted sixty-seven operations and engaged thirty-two men in armed encounters. All thirty-two died of gunshot wounds.

The next day the government news service offered up the headline of "drug dealers killed," even as the police were unable to name several of the dead. (The last was referred to only as "an identified one.") The Bulacan police chief, Police Colonel Romeo Caramat, Jr., told the public that "it is quite obvious that many of those killed are no longer in their right minds because instead of surrendering like most of those arrested, they are inclined to fight it out with our policemen."

More than a hundred suspects "who yielded" were arrested. All thirty-two suspects who offered armed resistance were shot and killed. There were no injured cops. There were no wounded suspects. To believe this narrative is to believe that local cops clocked a 100 percent kill rate, higher than the already improbable 97 percent reported by a Reuters investigative team in 2016, higher than the 83 percent of the notorious police shootings in Rio de Janeiro.

"Luckily," wrote one Bulacan lieutenant colonel, "there were no casualties on the PNP side."

Were they murders? The cops did not call these deaths murders. If they were not murders, was every Bulacan policeman, including the rawest of recruits, a marksman of such astonishing talent that every random armed encounter was met with such fatal accuracy? If they were not murders, how was it possible that police reported no casualties after twenty-five separate gunfights inside a single twenty-four-hour period? And if they were not murders, did every suspect who shot at the police miss the target?

Luck, said the police.

Good, said the president.

On August 16, 2017, a day after the violent deaths of at least thirty-two of his citizens by agents of the state, the president expressed his hope that more would die.

The carpet was red at the Heroes' Hall inside Malacañang Palace. The crowd that had risen from carved wooden chairs to applaud the arrival of the president was pressed, coiffed, and conscious of the cameras streaming their faces over public television. They had gathered to celebrate the nineteenth founding anniversary of the Volunteers Against Crime and Corruption (VACC), a group that had thrown its support behind the president during the campaign.

President Rodrigo Roa Duterte wore the traditional, formal pineapple silk shirt, the *barong tagalog*. Even with the two top buttons undone, it was a rare bow to ceremony by a man who preferred to work in short sleeves and plaid. He strode to the lectern. A uniformed aide handed the president a thick binder. It held the second iteration of what the press had come to call the narco list—the names of all public servants who were, according to the president, involved in the business of illegal drugs.

The president greeted the audience. He congratulated the VACC. He waved a copy of his address and said the victims of crime and corruption deserved better than a two-page speech. In forty-six minutes of extemporaneous remarks, he addressed the deaths of the previous twenty-four hours.

"Thirty-two died early in Bulacan in a massive raid," said President Duterte. "*Maganda 'yun.*"

In Filipino, *maganda* means "beautiful." It can also mean "good." It was unclear what the president meant that afternoon in August, but there was a reason every English-language local news organization chose to use the word *good* instead of *beautiful*. *Good*, as egregious a judgment as it was, was far less outrageous than *beautiful*. *Beautiful* would have offered an element of pleasure, a romanticizing of brutality, the impression that the commander in chief of a democratic republic was not just pleased but delighted by the ruthless killing of his citizens.

Those of us who wrote of the president and his frequent incitements to violence did so in good faith, offering the benefit of the doubt to a man whose rambling threats had come to target members of the free press. We translated his *putang ina* into "son of a bitch" instead of "son of a whore." We repeated his spokespersons' smiling excuses, their explanations that the president should be taken "seriously, not literally," that his words required "creative imagination" in their interpretation, and that it was only "heightened bravado" that had him encouraging his soldiers to rape on the battlefield.

I quoted the president's statement on my own social media page: "'Thirty-two died early in Bulacan in a massive raid,' said President Duterte. 'That's good.'"

A reader left a comment. "For the record, he did not say 32 dead was a good thing," he wrote. "Duterte said it was beautiful. Let not the perversity be lost in translation."

Here then is what the president said in the late afternoon of August 16, 2017.

"Thirty-two died early in Bulacan in a massive raid. That's beautiful. If we can kill another thirty-two every day, then maybe we can reduce what ails the country."

The president has called many things beautiful.

Pajamas were beautiful. Roads were beautiful. Federalism, the Scout Rangers' houses, trains, the King of Cambodia's mother in her youth, all beautiful. An actress who was raped was beautiful. A white missionary who was murdered after being raped by convicts was beautiful—although the president said he should have had her first. The president's girlfriend—the older one—was "more beautiful than the other one." The island of Mindanao was beautiful. So were the daughters of Davao City, and his own daughters, and the city itself, "even if everyone is dead." In no particular order: a song written about him, the language used in the introduction of the International Narcotics Control Board brochure, his German ex-wife, being called mayor instead of president, his rapport with the military and police. Filipino women were beautiful "and they smell good." It was, he said, "a mayor's happiness to look at beautiful women." His sidearm was beautiful. The Church of Duterte was beautiful—"Nothing sinful here, you can drink all you want and have all the women you want until your wife kills you." The country would be beautiful after he eliminated corruption, criminality, and drugs. It was beautiful to humiliate U.S. president Barack Obama, the U.S. secretary of state, the United Nations, the UN Human Rights Commission, and the European Union. The female mayor of Taguig City was beautiful. Melania Trump was beautiful. So were motorcycles, especially the 750 Harley Davidson Sportster. And the economy. Corpses that had "only had one bullet hole in each head"—that was beautiful. Beaches in the Visayas, auditoriums in Iloilo. The candidates of the 65th Miss Universe Competition. His circumcised penis. Filipino women who marry Russians. The "white and lithe women of Cagayan de Oro." Certain hospitals. The sky at dusk. The defense secretary's hair. His nurse. His relationship with China. The Nighthawk .45 pistol. Linens at the Peninsula Hotel. The vice president, whose knees he noted particularly—"I wanted to tell her, 'Ma'am, maybe next time you just wear shorts.'" The red shoes worn by a reporter. Disciplined citizens. The Miranda Bridge. The City of Marawi. Middle Easterners. The "beautiful race of Muslims." Chinese-made sniper rifles. Jericho handguns. American-made Barretts. The Glock. A woman named Lia he had met whose "distribution of flesh is almost perfect."

And on August 16, the killing of thirty-two men by the police officers he had promised to protect—that was beautiful too.

The subversion of the word *beautiful* was not unique to Rodrigo Duterte. In the 1970s, another autocrat had redefined beauty for Filipinos: Imelda Marcos, the Iron Butterfly, half of the conjugal dictatorship, whose pursuit of beauty had emptied the national coffers.

"It is not expensive to be beautiful," she said. "It takes only a little effort to be presentable and beautiful. But it takes some effort. A for effort. And unfortunately, people think of beauty as luxury, beauty as frivolity, no, or extravagance. Beauty is a discipline, beauty is art, is harmony, in the ideological sense and in the theological sense, beauty is God and love made real. And the ultimate reach in this world is beauty."

By the day the thirty-two were killed in Bulacan, President Duterte's pursuit of beauty had already failed. He had won the presidency promising to end the evils of drugs, crime, and corruption within three to six months of his administration. "No excuses," he had said, before extending his own deadline another six months.

A year into his presidency, on the stage at the Heroes' Hall, the man who had promised no excuses made many that day: That the country was too much unlike the city of Davao, where he had succeeded in enforcing his own discipline. That his agencies were corrupt. That the country had no unity. That municipal mayors had been bought by drug lords. That the media was "beating up on me." That the human rights community "make so much noise." That even the United States of America, as powerful as it was, had failed to solve the problem of drugs. That he had been working and killing and fighting, and still people complained.

"When you kill them, look what happens," he said. "I think there will be an outcry again. They will grieve again for justice over the thirty-two that were killed in mass joint operations."

On that day, he stood before an applauding crowd of the political elite and presented a thick binder of names.

It was a long list. "But with God's help, this will be a death certificate someday."

To kill a drug addict, says the president, you have to be on duty. You have to have a warrant in your pocket or watch crystal meth exchange hands. You have to announce your authority—it's a rule that you can't break. Say you're a cop. Announce you're there for an arrest. Demand that the addict give up, surrender, and follow you to the station for an inquest and investigation. Your duty is to take the addict into custody, and if he resists, your duty is to overcome. When he shoves a hand into his pocket, you have to reach for your gun. If the addict's weapon is lethal—and of course it is, because the criminal is an addict, and all addicts are armed—it is your duty to shoot him.

Is it murder?

Is it homicide?

Are you responsible for the killings?

To kill a drug addict, it is necessary to be afraid. Fear is a condition. You can have no intent beyond survival. You do not operate in anger, or bias, or in the dregs of an afternoon's drunk. You are afraid to widow your wife. You are afraid to orphan your children. You pull on your trigger, and if the trigger is attached to a machine gun instead of a revolver, you can't help where the bullets go. You hit the addict. You hit the five people behind him. The addict dies. The five others die. Ten people, a hundred die. The bullets ricochet.

"If you kill the five people behind him," said the president, "you are in the performance of duty. That is excusable."

The question is not who you are at the time of the killing. It is what you are. "As long as it is in the performance of duty," said the president, "if you squeeze [the trigger of your] M-16, and you hit a criminal, you hit the whole world, that's okay. That's the way it is. Where are you at the time? What are you?"

What you are is a cop, and when the choice is between a dead cop and a dead addict, the duty is clear—"It's your duty to kill." An ordinary man who slams a bullet into another human being can argue self-defense. A man with a badge who empties the barrel of his gun into another human being does not only have the right to claim self-defense. He also enjoys the presumption of regularity in the performance of his duty.

This was legal, said the president. This was correct. The same line is echoed down the ranks. "The presumption of regularity remains with the law enforcers and unless proven otherwise in the court of law," said PNP spokesperson Police Brigadier General John Bulalacao in a statement to the Supreme Court. "It's what really happened on the field," former Quezon City police chief Guillermo Eleazar told me in an interview. "That's where you have your presumption of regularity."

Like most Philippine jurisprudence, the presumption of regularity is borrowed from the Americans. Its roots lie in the Latin phrase *omnia praesumuntur rite et solemniter esse acta donec probetur in contrarium*. "All things are presumed to have been rightly and duly performed until it is proved to the contrary."

In the modern Philippines, regularity in the performance of duty is discussed in both the Rules of Court and the Revised Penal Code.

In the Rules of Court, Section 3, Rule 131, the presumption of regularity is considered "satisfactory if uncontradicted, but may be contradicted and overcome by other evidence." Cops are presumed to be performing their official duty regularly. Any evidence offered otherwise removes the presumption. Article 11.5, of the Revised Penal Code says "any person who acts in the fulfillment of a duty or in the lawful exercise of a right or office does not incur any criminal liability." It is a defense after the fact, meant to be raised in court.

Under Duterte, the claim of presumption of regularity became the justification for why very few of the thousands of incidents of drug suspects killed in "legitimate police operations" have been prosecuted. Those cases are often marked solved. The killer is known, and the killer is no murderer.

The presumption of regularity is an argument of good faith. The cop killed the addict because the addict fought back— *nanlaban*. Actions, unless proven otherwise, are considered normal and appropriate and correct. The cop is trusted because he is a cop. The addict is a criminal, "and if he resists arrest violently, you are free to kill them." Overcoming resistance was a duty that every cop owed to God, the Constitution, and the law of the land.

Listen to the president. "I told the police, 'Don't abuse.' You can kill them legally. And why do you have to kill them illegally?"

To kill a drug addict, every element must be present. The cop in the performance of duty. The criminal rejecting authority. The violent threat, the risk to life, the show of deadly force. Those elements aligned at least 6,252 times during the drug war, though it is unclear if it took 6,252 cops to kill 6,252 suspects, or if some cops performed their sacred duty more than once.

The elements aligned when a cop killed a young man in front of his twenty-year-old cousin, who said the cop raised a hand in a thumbs-up after reporting the suspect was dead.

The elements aligned when thirty-one police officers "had no other option but to retaliate" and took out three armed scavengers "in open defiance," including a man identified only by the name *Buhay*—life.

The elements aligned with Allan Formilleza, police staff sergeant, a seventeen-year veteran of Quezon City Police Station 6.

Formilleza was not alone on the day he pulled the trigger. Official documents filed after the incident list three others who walked down Road 10 with Formilleza: his team leader, Captain Emil Garcia, and two rookies, James Aggarao and Melchor Navisaga, both ranked patrolman.

It was a standard operation. The four were conducting a visit under Operation Plan Tokhang. Their destination that day, August 21, 2016, was the home of suspect Marcelo Daa, Jr., located in Payatas, Quezon City.

Tokhang required that the cops seek out drug personalities, knock on their doors, and invite them to surrender to authorities. But in this case the cops had no time to knock. The suspects "sensed" the presence of the police officers. All five drew guns. They fired.

The cops took cover. They announced they were police officers. One of the suspects, Efren Morillo, shouted back, *"Hindi kami papahuli ng buhay!"*

We will not be caught alive.

The cops had no choice.

"Our team retaliated," the officers wrote in their joint affidavit. That retaliation resulted in the "instantaneous deaths" of the suspects. They reported a death toll of four. Marcelo Daa, thirty-one years old. Rhaffy Gabo, twenty-three. Anthony Comendo, thirty-six. "A certain Jess," age and name uncertain. All *nanlaban*.

Was this legal?

Was it committed in self-defense?

Was it committed in the performance of duty?

Was it committed on the order of the president?

Police Captain Emil Garcia, interviewed by a television news crew just outside the crime scene, said that the suspects were armed with a revolver and a .45 caliber. "As we approached the room they came out of, suddenly, they fired at us."

The police enumerated the evidence recovered by crime scene operatives. They included five pistols, two small heat-sealed plastic sachets of suspected crystal methamphetamine, and various drug paraphernalia.

An after-operation report, filed by the team's station commander a week after the fatal incident, offered a concluding assessment of the operating team: "For awards and commendation."

The theory of regularity, as posited by David Hume, presupposes that effects follow causes with invariable consistency. Hume requires three conditions to determine regularity. First, a cause should come temporally before an effect. Second, the cause must be contiguous to the effect. Third, the instances must have resemblance: All like causes must lead into the same effect.

Thus, a shoot-out.

An addict resists; a cop fires back. Cause before an effect.

An addict grabs for a gun; a cop pulls the trigger. Cause proximate to effect.

Thousands of dangerous suspects offer violent defiance. Thousands are neutralized in the hands of the police. Cause and effect, one story bleeding into the next in near-perfect repetition.

"Now, if you pull out your gun," said the president, "if you fight back, and this cop, in his head, goes, 'Oh no, he might get me first, I could really die,' he can shoot. What are the factors involved? First of all, self-defense. The criminal really will kill you. Second, performance of duty. Because the law says you have to overcome his resistance by whatever means."

Regularity, Hume claimed, requires a regular connection, built on a routine succession of cause and effect. The mind will infer the effect from the cause.

Suppose resistance is an effect, not a cause. Follow the chain of causation a single step backward. Why would a suspect, in the face of likely lethal force, still choose to resist? Why did five men, four of them local residents, in the presence of their girlfriends and sisters and children, without the benefit of prior discussion, all make the split-second decision to simultaneously raise the guns they so conveniently carried on a Sunday afternoon, all committing, at that moment, to either likely death or a lifetime on the run? "We will not be caught alive," one of them was supposed to have told the cops. The cops who, according to their own story, were simply "ambling to the location" to peaceably converse with the men in the house.

We will not be caught alive. We have chosen to risk death.

His Excellency the President has an answer. They were addicts. They all resisted violently because all addicts did. They were "sick with paranoia and are always armed." This was "standard behavior," the president said.

"They really fight back, because they are paranoid, hallucinate all the time, and almost always carry lethal weapons to fight it out."

If a killing wasn't to be murder, it had to have a reason. The individuals were to be killed if they resisted violently, and they resisted violently because they were addicts, and because all of them tended to violence, all of them should be killed.

It would be reasonable then to assume that, given the millions of alleged paranoid psychopathic addicts, millions too, not thousands, should have been killed—killed legally—in police encounters across the country. Yet the police, in their attempts to defend their actions, emphasize the opposite statistic. Millions who could have died did not die, said police spokesperson Bulalacao. The peaceful surrender of 1.3 million suspected addicts and dealers was proof the mass killing was not state sponsored. "If the claims on [extrajudicial killing] are true," Bulalacao told the press, "then these surrenderers and arrested suspects should not be alive as well. The ratio of those who died and those arrested and surrendered is 0.3 percent only, which would logically rule out EJK."

So said too the chief of police of Quezon City, under whose watch the Tokhang operation of August 21 took place. He claimed fatal encounters made up only 6 percent of antidrug police operations, "a small percentage," as General Eleazar called it.

Which is it then? That they are addicts who by their nature will resist and therefore must die, or that they are addicts, who by the fact of their surviving demonstrate the professionalism of the police?

In the end, the presumption of regularity depends on what the mind infers. To kill legally, as the president has ordered; to fulfill a duty, as the president has defined; to continue to work, to do the job, to destroy the enemy—to do all this, the country must make the irrevocable connection between an addict and a gun. It is a connection that the president has made in speech after speech. That is what is normal, acceptable, *regular*.

Here, for example, is Police Staff Sergeant Allan Formilleza, explaining to me precisely why he believed that a young man named Efren Morillo had waved a gun and howled that he would not be taken alive.

"That's how addicts are," Formilleza said. "Always out of it. That's how they are."

Here is another story about what happened in Payatas, Quezon City, on August 21, 2016.

There were five of them that day. Marcelo Daa stood playing pool at a table set up under a shed out in the front yard. With Marcelo were his neighbors Jessie Cule, Anthony Comendo, and Rhaffy Gabo; and Marcelo's childhood friend Efren Morillo, who had long since moved away but dropped by that day.

Marcelo worked as a truck driver's assistant. He lived, with his partner and three children, in a house just a few feet from the shanty where his mother had given birth to him thirty-one years earlier. Unlike many of the Payatas settlements, the Daa home sat in a remote clearing, requiring a long walk downhill from the main highway, through a patch of woods where the thick canopy of trees did little to mask the stench of the nearby dump site. The Daas lived in a lonely huddle of squat houses pieced together from tarps and plywood, their tin roofs weighed down by large rocks and washbasins and a chipped *Blue's Clues* doorstop lying on its side. A sixty-foot ravine curved around the edges.

It was a hot afternoon. The minutes ticked by slowly. Marcelo and Jessie and Efren played pool. Anthony and Rhaffy drowsed in hammocks, then walked into the house to eat. The women—Marcelo's mother, aunt, sister, and live-in partner—watched television. The children chased spiders in the wild grass.

The rattle at the front gate came at a little past three in the afternoon. The young men looked up from the pool table. Seven people stood outside: five men, two women. None of them wore their uniform tunics.

One of the men pulled out a gun. "Nobody runs," he said.

The five young men raised their arms. They were bound, cuffed, and beaten. The police didn't carry enough handcuffs, so one cop ripped out a length of electric wire from the shed roof. The cops ransacked the house. They pocketed a cell phone, a tablet, a lighter, a bong, pieces of aluminum foil, a weighing scale, and a new bottle of rubbing alcohol.

"They took my hearing aid," one of the women told me later. "It's why I can't hear you so well, because they took my new hearing aid."

One of the men stepped outside the house. "We didn't find anything."

Marcelo's father, sixty-nine, was down in the valley, working on his patch of banana trees when he heard the commotion. He hauled himself up the hillside and found all five young men, including his son, sitting cuffed and bound by the side of the house. The yard was crowded. One of the policemen, who called himself the commander, shoved Marcelo's father. The commander called Marcelo's father a criminal mastermind and tried to grab him by the arm.

"They told me they had a mission," Marcelo's father said. "They told me they were cops."

Marcelo, still cuffed, called out to his father, "I'll take care of this. This is my fault. Go."

Marcelo's father went. He wished he hadn't.

The cuffs came off when Marcelo's father left. Marcelo's weeping sister was sent away. The five young men were led into the backyard. A cop in a red sweatshirt, the man witnesses named Allan Formilleza, took charge of Efren and Marcelo. He pushed both of them into the makeshift tarpaulin shanty just off the backyard.

The two were told to sit. They sat: Marcelo on the wooden chair, Efren sideways on its arm. Police Staff Sergeant Allan Formilleza raised his gun and aimed the barrel.

Efren spoke fast, the words tumbling over each other. He said he knew nothing. He said he was clean. He said he was a vendor, sold fruits and little else. He said he had nothing to do with anything.

"Really?" asked Formilleza. "Really?"

The bullet slammed into Efren's chest, just under his heart.

He lay limp on the packed-earth floor, his head tilted away from his killer, as Formilleza shot Efren's friend Marcelo once, twice, thrice, in quick succession.

There was more shooting from the backyard. Formilleza walked away.

"You know what to do," he told his men outside the shed. "Call the crime scene operatives. Leave the evidence behind. Say they all fought back."

The other women were kept inside the house. Another Daa aunt, living less than a mile away, heard the commotion and made for the trees bordering the Daa property. She stopped just short of the backyard. In an affidavit, she said she saw Rhaffy and Anthony sprawled on the ground, bleeding from gunshot wounds. She said she saw Jessie Cule, on his knees, injured, still alive.

A man who might have been a cop stepped into her path. She began shouting, screaming, until the man shoved her out the gate. It was a low gate, less than four feet high, made of recycled wire mesh.

She heard one of the cops call out, "Sir, one of them is still breathing."

There were two more gunshots.

A teenager who had climbed up into a tree saw the shooting from above. He told Jessie's girlfriend that Jessie was the last to die. He said Jessie had thrown his arms around the legs of the cop who held the gun.

"That's what I can't accept," Jessie's girlfriend told me. "He knelt. He hugged the police. If he sinned, he sinned against the law. He didn't sin against the police, for them to kill him like that. He was crying. It meant he didn't want to die. Because he wanted to live. He was begging."

Marcelo's partner ran out of the house. She saw three bodies in the backyard. None of them belonged to Marcelo. The cops held her back. She watched them as they stole food and cigarettes from her own small store. They sat at the pool table. They ate off her family's plates.

Marcelo's mother had found her husband on the road. She understood that her son was in trouble and went running up the hill, past the gate, past the pool table, past the main house where her mattress had been torn apart, past a kneeling Jessie Cule, dead with his head resting on his clasped hands and his chest slumped on the drenched grass, past the rain-wet bodies of Rhaffy Gabo and Anthony Comendo, all the way to where Marcelo Daa sat propped against the tamarind tree his mother had planted in the year he was born.

His right leg crossed over his left. The bullet hole was a black star over his left eyebrow. Blood streamed out of his mouth.

His parents slept at home that night.

"Why would we leave? They got what they wanted, didn't they?"

.   .   .

The rules of engagement governing operating procedure during most of the drug war can be found in the *Revised Philippine National Police Handbook,* issued in 2013.

Rule 7 begins with a single sentence: "The excessive use of force during police operation is prohibited."

There are no exceptions. Police might, in the performance of duty, use necessary and reasonable force. Police are enjoined to consider a number of factors that contribute to the determination of "the reasonableness of the force." The number of aggressors, for example. The nature and characteristics of the weapon. The assailant's physical condition. The place and occasion of assault.

The responsibility of maintaining reasonable force falls on the officer in charge of the operation. The officer must exercise control over all police officers and "exhaust all possible means to apply the necessary and reasonable force to protect lives and properties during armed confrontation."

The word *reasonable* is used so often and so casually across the police handbook that a reader might conclude the handbook's original crafters nurtured a deep and abiding faith in the rational faculties of their police officers. An officer must exercise "sound discretion." A police officer's goal is merely to "subdue" clear and imminent danger. Force must only be "sufficient to overcome the resistance." The use of a firearm requires that the danger must be "actual, imminent and real." A later revision to the *PNP Handbook* allows the use of weapons only to prevent, repel, and immobilize.

"As much as possible," reads the manual, "avoid hitting the head or other vital parts of the body. Wounded persons/suspects must be given first aid and/or brought to the nearest hospital at the first possible opportunity."

The performance of duty, as defined by law and operating

procedure, must be proportional, rational, reasonable, *regular*. It presumes police officers are operating in accordance with the standards of their own code.

Yet in speech after speech, His Excellency Rodrigo Duterte, commander in chief, ordered his own men to violate not just the spirit but the letter of the law.

"Shoot him," he said at the Naval Forces Eastern Mindanao Headquarters during a wake for soldiers killed in action. "Grabbing for something is a hostile move. Don't wait for them to take out a gun. Like that. So now if they're just scratching themselves—well, that's too bad."

"If there is a weapon," he said at the Ninth National Biennial Summit on Women in Community Policing, "if it's lethal, it can kill you, and [if] he refuses to surrender and offers a violent resistance—you just have to kill him."

"If you are confronted with the violent resistance," he said at the twenty-ninth annual convention of the Prosecutors' League of the Philippines at the Royce Hotel and Casino, "thereby placing your life on the line, shoot them dead. We all know that. That is my order."

"You have no obligation to anyone you killed," he said in a visit to the Battleground Command Post in Marawi City. "Because, and I repeat, you are working in the performance of your duty. This [suspect's] duty is to surrender, not to fight back. If they fight back—well they shouldn't fight back because they will die."

"Now if he fights back," he said at the eleventh founding anniversary celebration of the Armed Forces of the Philippines' Eastern Mindanao Command, "and you feel he's holding a .45 gun, and that you will really die, look, kill the son of a bitch. He's asking for it, as they say."

The president offered every cop a promise. He would believe them if they claimed to have killed in the performance of duty.

Every cop charged and convicted who followed his orders would be pardoned. "Don't be afraid. Don't be afraid to kill for as long as it's those idiots, if they start to fuck with your city."

This, he claimed, was why he had won every election since 1988.

"My secret is simple," he said, as he congratulated newly elected mayors at Malacañang Palace.

"It's all about sincerity. When you say, 'Son of a bitch, don't do it, or I'll kill you,' you're not the one doing the killing."

He cocked his head, smirked: "Psst, police." He pointed to the side, downward, as if ordering an imagined cop to deal with the problem.

He laughed.

"Thank you," he said. "Congratulations."

The man who sat across from me had good teeth. He did not grind his molars. He did not stutter. He did not hallucinate. He had yet to rape a child, a goat, or his own mother. He smelled of nerves and Safeguard soap, and while I did not ask if he considered himself paranoid, I would have understood if he was. He had also, by his own reckoning, never touched illegal drugs, even if the cops listed him as a "drug personality." He stripped off his shirt to point out two dark scars on his narrow chest—one under the right breast, and one on his left.

On the morning of August 21, Efren Morillo, fruit vendor, father of two, put on his brother's shorts and his father's shirt and told his mother he was going to Payatas in Quezon City, back where his old pal Marcelo still lived. Marcelo owed him money, and Efren wanted to get it back.

When the bullet slammed into his chest, Efren Morillo decided not to die.

He made the decision in the split-second between the gun firing and the sudden flood of blood soaking his underwear. He lay limp and still on the ground, forcing his breathing to slow as Police Staff Sergeant Allan Formilleza shot Marcelo Daa a bare five steps away. Efren prayed through the gunshots. He prayed through the screaming. He prayed for the strength to live as he thought of his two small children. He prayed, hard, as the cop walked away.

Efren waited. He listened until he was certain he was alone, then staggered to his feet. He took a minute to talk to the dead. *Help me,* he told them, then threw himself down a ravine.

It did not occur to him he could die. All he wanted was to get away. An hour and a half later he emerged from the hills onto the highway, a bloody figure clutching guava leaves to his chest.

Kill them if they make a move, said the president. Kill if they refuse to surrender. Shoot them in the head, shoot them in the heart, shoot them dead.

Here was the presumption of regularity. Shoot, and shoot to kill.

Here then was the irregularity, the failure in the operation that Rodrigo Duterte had warned his cops against.

Five men were shot. Four men were killed. The fifth man lived.

Efren Morillo found the highway past four in the afternoon, more than an hour after the bullet punched through his chest. He didn't dare go to any Quezon City hospital. He was afraid the cops would find him and finish him off. He found an old friend near a gas station. He begged for a ride to a clinic in Rizal, near his home. The friend was terrified but helped Efren into the back of a jeep. There was no doctor present when Efren arrived. The nurse attempted to bind his wounds, but the blood was pumping out in a fountain, soaking through gauze and tape. Efren stayed conscious. He asked a gasoline boy to run to his house and get his mother. Hours passed before she arrived at half past ten in the evening. She had gone to Payatas and was told he was dead.

The clinic stood beside another police station. Soon the Rizal cops were inside. They asked Efren what had happened. They called the Quezon City cops and promised Efren they would help. Efren told them everything.

The ambulance left for Quezon City Police Station 6 after eleven in the evening. Cops stepped up to the window to look inside. Efren, stretched out with his mother sitting beside him, screamed and screamed. He was in pain, but it wasn't why he wailed.

"I kicked up the drama," he said. "I heard one cop say, 'This kid's strong. Shot at three p.m.—he's still alive.'"

The ambulance sat parked at the station for close to half an hour. It was midnight when Efren was carried into the emergency room. The Rizal police left, and the Quezon City police cuffed him to his bed. They told him he was being charged with assault, a full hour before doctors discovered that the bullet had entered Efren's chest and exited between his ribs, just under his lungs. He spent ten days in the hospital with his left wrist locked to the hospital bed.

The Morillos sold their house. Efren's bail was paid, and so were hospital expenses. The cops, in spite of their claim that Efren was a drug dealer, did not charge him with the possession and sale of illegal drugs.

Efren went to court. He fought back.

He filed administrative charges. He filed criminal charges. The list was long: frustrated murder, murder, robbery, and planting of drugs and firearms. A human rights law firm, the Center for International Law (CenterLaw), took on his case pro bono, and invited the nonprofit organization Physicians for Human Rights (PHR) to perform an independent forensic analysis on evidence regarding the shooting deaths of Marcelo Daa, Jessie Cule, Anthony Comendo, and Rhaffy Gabo.

PHR, which won the Nobel Peace Prize in 1997, helped develop standards to document human rights abuses and was a partner in investigations into torture and extrajudicial executions. Dr. Homer Venters, who had overseen more than a hundred assessments of survivors of torture and injury during interactions with security forces, conducted a preliminary analysis of the forensic documents. He concluded that Efren Morillo's account "was consistent with the available evidence."

A second, independent analysis was written by Dr. Nizam Peerwani, an expert forensic consultant for PHR and a fellow of the American Academy of Forensic Sciences. Dr. Peerwani concluded that the QCPD "failed to provide empirical evidence to substantiate their allegations that the four victims were shot when they drew their weapons on the police." The extensive PHR report pointed out mistakes in the protocols of scene of the crime operatives (SOCO). It included the "highly unusual" failure to perform "comprehensive postmortem toxicology" on the bodies, "especially since the encounter between the operatives of Batasan Police and the Daa family was an alleged 'drug raid.'"

Dr. Peerwani's findings list the paths of a number of bullets as downward—consistent with witness testimony that the men had been kneeling when they were killed. Rhaffy Gabo, according to his report, was shot twice in the back.

Dr. Peerwani concurred with Dr. Venters: "It is my opinion that the autopsy findings support the eyewitness narrative provided."

.   .   .

There was, first, denial. Morillo was lying, said the police. The witnesses were lying. The allegations were a "cinematic, thespian, histrionic, dramaturgical interlocking script of narration of events." They were "baloney." They were "a complete lie." They failed to consider the presumption of regularity in the performance of duty.

It was a standard operation, said the cops. They filed new affidavits, and the story began to change.

There were in fact three policemen on the scene, they said, not four. Police Captain Emil Garcia, whose name had taken top billing in multiple police reports, who had been present in uniform in the aftermath, who had stood before cameras to say that "suddenly, they fired at us," who had described the suspects down to the make and model of their guns, retracted all claims that he had been present at all. He was not there, he said; Allan Formilleza was the team leader. Garcia said he had misreported his presence at the near-fatal armed encounter, explaining it away as merely "a small mistake."

There were many more small mistakes.

There had, in fact, been seven suspects, not five.

Three, not one, had escaped, possibly with a large cache of drugs.

There had been no stealing. They did not take the Daa family's food or eat off the Daa family's plates. It was only that Formilleza hadn't had time for lunch and was so hungry, he had asked one of his men to buy him food. He ate and drank, and while he admitted to having used a glass owned by the Daa family to drink water, he certainly never touched their spoons or forks or plates.

Then the final, astounding new revelation: There had been only a single shooter, not a team of cops.

Garcia had not been present. The rookies had not drawn their weapons. Only Allan Formilleza, with his one police-issue gun, had believed his life was in danger. He had fired in the name of God and the law and the Constitution. He had fired fourteen bullets into five moving targets. Twelve bullets had hit the suspects in the head and torso. Formilleza then walked away without sustaining a single gunshot wound.

Was it murder?

Was it homicide?

Was he responsible for the killings?

"And, as you were saying," the prosecutor asked Formilleza, "you drew your gun in exchange of the fire of their guns that were also discharged by these two men and then subsequently by these three men, correct?"

"Yes, sir," Formilleza answered.

"So, after the incident, Mr. Witness, what happened next?"

"The three malefactors fell on the ground."

"And then?"

"And then Efren Morillo was able to escape, utilizing the river towards Montalban."

"Efren Morillo was not one of those three?"

"No, sir."

"He happens to be one of those who had an encounter with you?"

"Yes, sir."

"So, Efren Morillo was able to run away?"

"Yes, sir."

"And what happened to the four?"

Morillo's lawyer, CenterLaw defense counsel Gil Aquino, interrupted. "Your knowledge is misleading, sir. The witness said three men."

"Sustained," said the judge. "Re-form your question, Prosecutor."

"So," rephrased the prosecutor, "you made mention that the three malefactors apparently were neutralized. Correct?"

"Yes, sir."

Here is another word for death. The word is *neutralized*.

Project Double Barrel, laid out in Command Memorandum Circular No. 16-2016, seeks, among other goals, the "neutralization of illegal drug personalities nationwide." Human rights lawyers argue it is an order to kill. On the basis of that word, they have challenged the entire drug war apparatus at the high court.

Nowhere in the memorandum, or elsewhere in Philippine law, is the word *neutralization* defined. "Neutralize means to kill," wrote the lawyers of the Free Legal Assistance Group.

The government insisted that *to neutralize* meant only "to overcome resistance." Whether that meant to disable or to kill depended on the exigencies of the moment. Those moments are many. Twenty-six-year-old Raymond Yumul of Concepcion in Tarlac was neutralized. Jeffrey Cruz of Carcel Street in Quiapo was neutralized. Samar native Wilfredo Chavenia was "neutralized while the other suspect managed to escape." John Ryan Baluyot of Olongapo City was "completely neutralized." Two unnamed male suspects, distinguished only by the color of their shirts—one white, one gray—were both neutralized. Fernando Gunio of Quezon City, who "sensed the presence of police operatives," allegedly pulled out a handgun and fired, forcing the police to "neutralize the said suspect." Forty-two-year-old Arnel Cruz and fifty-one-year-old Oliver Reganit "were neutralized before they could hide in the middle of the cornfield." Renato dela Rosa, alias Jay-jay Toyo, after allegedly opening fire, was cornered and "subsequently neutralized by the responding police officers."

Each of these men is dead, but in the official reports of all these cases, none of them were referred to in the narrative of events as killed. They were neutralized, verb and noun, as was narrated by the Bulacan officers who shot Justine Bucacao and Bernard Lizardo: "Neutralized suspects sustained gunshot wounds on different parts of their bodies."

The debate remained at the Supreme Court, but President Rodrigo Duterte, during an evening interview at Malacañang Palace, had already offered his own definition of neutralization. He said the government had "no hand in extrajudicial killings." He said he was requiring state media to publish the lists of drug-linked incidents to which he was privy in his briefings. "You can see who is dead, and who isn't," he explained.

"But it is not really that many," he said. "As you can see the symbol, there is A-A-A-A-A-A, that's arrested, and N, it's neutralized—those are dead."

In court, Police Staff Sergeant Allan Formilleza sat in the witness box. Morillo had a companion, he told the prosecutor, but Morillo ran away.

"What happened to his companion?"

"He entered into, into—he ran into the shanty."

"And then?"

"We learned eventually [he] was in trouble already."

Morillo's companion was Marcelo Daa, and the trouble was that Marcelo Daa was dead, dead of a bullet in the ear, in a story that could not be made to make sense, no matter how many times it was told: men falling magically to the ground, police commanders disappearing into thin air, rookie cops frozen still, a lone hero taking down four armed suspects on the run, none of whom, in the barrage of bullets, managed to injure Police Staff Sergeant Allan Formilleza.

All four were neutralized, dead on the scene. All of it was justified in the performance of duty.

It was the truth, said the police. It was reasonable. It was appropriate.

It was regular.

On March 17, 2023, more than five years after the fifth man staggered past his friend's corpse, the Quezon City Metropolitan Trial Court Branch 133 acquitted Efren Morillo of assaulting officers of the Philippine National Police. Three of the cops allegedly present at the shooting admitted that none of them saw Morillo fire a gun—the rationale used to justify the deaths of Morillo's four companions.

In the case of the killings in Payatas, according to the court, the presumption of innocence trumped the presumption of regularity. By all intents and purposes, four cops of the Philippine National Police lied officially and on the record. Police Captain Emil Garcia lied. Police Staff Sergeant Allan Formilleza lied. Patrolmen James Aggarao and Melchor Navizaga lied. The discovery of those lies, and the subsequent case that was lost, were due only to a single irregularity in the daily circumstances of fatal police encounters under the administration of Rodrigo Duterte. That irregularity is named Efren Morillo.

"But I've always told you that if you have to shoot, shoot them dead," Duterte told police at Camp Crame. "And this is what the human rights idiots are trying to complain about. You know, when I say, 'I'll shoot them dead,' I'd prefer they'd shoot them in the heart or in the head. That's the end of the problem.

Because if we'll just arrest them with the money, billions of it, they can always go out, have the best lawyers. And that is why all these years, the country has always been on the edge when confronted with cousins of senators and the mayors."

Efren Morillo is not the cousin of a senator or a mayor. He cannot read. He cannot write. His lawyers work for free. His family continues to live in fear. He is an irregularity, not because he is poor or illiterate or brave, but because he is alive.

Five men were shot. Four men were killed. The fifth man lived.

9

MY FRIED DOMINGO

Lieutenant Colonel Robert Domingo's office in Plaza Hugo was casual and workmanlike, much like Domingo himself. He was short and square and solid, his white T-shirt tucked into his uniform trousers. His blue uniform tunic hung on a rack nearby—"You don't need me to wear this, no?" he asked. On the wall behind him was a framed print of the Philippine National Police Academy Class of '99.

The city of Manila is divided into fourteen police districts. Each police station—referred to as PS-1 to PS-14—has its own commander, who supervises not only the main station but the precincts scattered across their designated area of operation. Domingo's district of Santa Ana, population roughly 195,000, was established by Franciscan priests in the sixteenth century in the name of Saint Anne. The police station, PS-6, hunkers under the stone shadow of the Church of Our Lady of the Abandoned, whose bells rang to signal the Philippines' liberation from the Japanese occupation.

Colonel Domingo, the commander of PS-6, was happy. He was happy, he said, that the Duterte government had thrown its weight behind the police force. He was happy with the promised increase in pay. He was happy that cops had been provided with legal assistance. He was happy that they all had the support of the president—"we now have backup, you know." Certainly he was happy that his eighteen-year-old son, whom he had once insisted come home early every day, could go out at all hours and come home without a scratch. Domingo's streets were safe. Late in the night, out in Tondo, in Punta Santa Ana, in Zobel Roxas, in all the places in Manila where crowds gathered and every drunk once sat jawing with a bottle of beer, there were no more people, only quiet.

"So, our patrols would go around ten, eleven at night, blinkers on, and send everyone inside for their own good," Domingo told me. "And people would thank us. 'Sir, thank you, sir, it's good you caught him.' That's what they'd say. 'Sir, thank you, sir.'"

The man they had caught, the one whose takedown had elicited such appreciation from the citizens of Santa Ana, was a man Domingo called Buwaya, "the thorn in our side."

Buwaya, so the story went, was the toughest, meanest son of a bitch ever to set foot in Santa Ana. *Buwaya* was an alias that means "Crocodile." Everyone had something to say about Buwaya: cops, village captains, the tricycle driver who stopped by the curb where I sat at midnight. They said Buwaya was big and bad, a monster of a man, six feet tall and maybe an inch over. They said he emptied his revolver into the air on New Year's Eve. They said he stole from neighbors. They said he broke into a mayor's house. They said he beat up his sister. They said he broke down doors and shot bullets through plywood walls. They said he was mostly drunk, or high, or both.

Long after the war on drugs was declared, so said the cops of Santa Ana, Buwaya was still pushing drugs and raising a middle finger at law and order. His takedown was a success story, the sort of community cooperation that was proffered up to journalists as proof of concept.

"He didn't believe in Tokhang," Domingo told me. "So, we encountered him."

The word *encounter* is both a noun and a transitive verb. You encounter turbulence. You encounter opposition. You encounter a roadblock, a thief, a typo, a budget overrun, a dear friend, a dog on the road home, an ambush in the mountains.

Chance characterizes an encounter, regardless of whether it leads to an exchange of phone numbers or a joust on horseback. You might encounter traffic. You might encounter rain. You might, were you so inclined, slick on red lipstick on the off chance you encounter an ex-boyfriend wandering down the same grocery aisle. Encounters are casual, undesigned. You can plan for an encounter, but you do not plan for the timing of its occurrence, or else it would be marked on a Google calendar.

"We encountered him," Domingo told me.

We killed him, he meant. He did not say it out loud, but I was expected to understand that Buwaya was dead, and that his death was at the hands of the cops.

It is usage that is not unique to the Philippines. In September 2017, the *Oxford English Dictionary* inserted a draft addition to its official entry for the word *encounter*.

Encounter, n. South Asian. A violent incident resulting in the killing of a suspected criminal by the police. Often with modifying word, as false encounter, police encounter, etc.

Below the addition, the dictionary offered a caveat in fine print:

Sometimes euphemistic, with the implication of a deliberate act depicted as a chance incident.

Buwaya's death began with a ballot box.

One day in July, so the cops said, the roughly eight hundred residents of Santa Ana District Village 767 gathered at a basketball court. The village officials spoke. They were all going to vote, they explained, to make sure there would be no talk of finger-pointing or witch-hunting. There would be due process. There would be rules. There would be names on the ballots, and every man and woman would have a say.

Tell us who the drug dealers are, they said. Make a list. Put the worst men at the top. Anonymity is acceptable, no need for you to sign your names.

Everyone lined up. There was a table. On the table was a box, and in the box went the lists. The officials tallied up the votes, signed the results, and handed the results to the police.

Buwaya came up first. He was, by popular acclaim, in a manner good and fair and democratic, judged to be a danger to the public by a jury of his peers.

On the morning of August 28, 2016, twenty cops reported for duty at the corner of Estrada Street. An undercover cop was sent up the stairs to knock on Buwaya's door. Drugs were offered. Money exchanged hands. Buwaya recognized the gun's bulge and drew out a revolver.

The cop was faster on the trigger.

"They voted for him," Domingo said.

.   .   .

I knew none of this when I dropped by PS-6 for my first inter-view with Domingo. I did not ask about Buwaya—I had never heard of Buwaya. It was Domingo who told the story. Buwaya had fought back, he said. Buwaya was dead.

Buwaya's family had their own story to tell. I found the nar-rative in a Supreme Court petition filed by CenterLaw on behalf of the survivors and witnesses of the killings in Santa Ana. The suit, filed more than a year after Buwaya's death, charged PS-6 with "systematic violence" and detailed harassment, physical threats, illegal arrests, and failure to investigate killings. It named police officers including, among others, one Robert C. Do-mingo. Thirty-nine witnesses filed affidavits.

One of them was Valerie, the common-law partner of Ryan Eder, alias Buwaya.

Valerie told the story in the stilted language of court deposi-tions. Men had burst into their bedroom with guns drawn. "One of the men aimed his gun at Ryan," Valerie said, in an attach-ment marked Annex-T. "The other man knelt and aimed his gun at me. We jerked up in bed."

Ryan, terrified, pleaded with the armed men. He swore he would surrender. He promised he wouldn't fight back. He began stripping off his white T-shirt and gray-and-orange basketball shorts to prove he was unarmed.

The man holding the gun to Ryan's head gestured at Valerie. "Take her downstairs," he said.

"Please don't hurt Valerie," she heard Ryan say.

A gunman grabbed Valerie by the arm and dragged her out the door, down two narrow flights of stairs, all the way to the first floor, where she was when she heard two gunshots ring out.

Valerie said there had been no drug bust, no drug dealing, no resistance. She said the cops had arrested her on charges of illegal drug use, along with Ryan's mother and cousin. She said she was taken to a room and told to stand by a table where guns and sachets of white powder had been arranged. Pictures were taken. "This is all for the cameras," the cops assured her.

She said the cops extorted ₱30,000 from her family on the promise she would be released. She said the cops had lied.

"They shot and killed Ryan," she wrote from jail. "He never fought back."

Domingo, badge number 0-08627, was smoking a cigarette. It was late afternoon.

He blew out the smoke.

"If it's your time to die, it's your time to die," he told me.

The chief of PS-6 was not a coward. The reason he was not a coward was that his commanders were not cowards. His president was no coward. His chief of police was no coward. Domingo told his men, all 280 of them, that they couldn't dare be cowards themselves. The bureaucracy of the drug war covered Domingo's desk: faxes with information from concerned citizens, a folder from headquarters with instructions on how to testify at court proceedings, letters from village captains attesting that their jurisdictions were free of drug infestation—70 percent of Santa Ana was clear of drug dealing, Domingo said.

These, he said, were the golden days of the Philippine police.

Domingo was a Tondo boy, born and bred. His father was a librarian; his mother had died when Domingo was thirteen. The family lived off the income from a small rental inherited from a grandfather. Domingo earned a degree in radio broadcasting from the Polytechnic University of the Philippines and paid for it by driving pedicabs and working at a fast-food joint. He entered the police academy straight out of college. "I joined the PNP because I wanted to," he said. "The PNP never told me to join. I wanted to be a cop."

He was assigned the traffic beat and worked his way up. He was promoted to spokesperson of the National Capital Region Police Office, from whose podium he announced recruitment opportunities and bans on the wearing of baseball caps inside shopping malls. He was, he said, a member in good standing of the National Geographic Society. He liked to read. He enjoyed the cinema. He also, unprompted and on record, informed a German correspondent that the policewomen of Santa Ana were all beautiful women with a shared appreciation for white men. "They are all single," Domingo told the correspondent, who sported a decidedly western nose. "They all like Caucasian."

I had come to interview Domingo about three people his men had killed in another encounter. The story had gone viral. One of the young men, a twenty-year-old named Jefferson Bunuan, was a straight arrow who wanted to be a cop so badly he was studying criminology on a scholarship. I had spoken to residents and tracked down village officials, but was unable to secure an interview with Domingo himself. I was, at the time, still in the process of introducing myself to the Manila homicide investigators while leaving business cards and boxes of Dunkin' Donuts. It was possible I went through the wrong channels, appeared at the wrong time, or messaged the wrong numbers, but it was also possible that Domingo was reluctant to speak to another reporter after having been crucified online for the death of a minor. In the absence of a response, I did what many local journalists have done before me. I called in a favor from a white man.

His name was Carsten Stormer. It was his name that got me

through the door. Stormer was an old friend, a German correspondent based in Manila whom I had met in the aftermath of the Maguindanao massacre. Domingo liked Stormer. Whether it was because of Stormer's charm or Stormer's last story—he freelanced for *National Geographic*—Stormer had gotten away with shadowing Domingo while rolling a video camera. He had ridden in Domingo's squad car. He had interviewed Domingo in his office. He had followed Domingo going door to door during a Tokhang operation.

I had viewed raw footage of the ride-along. Domingo sat in the back seat, Stormer and his camera in front.

"We will go to the lairs of the drug users, the drug pushers!" Domingo announced.

He spoke in English, enunciating each word. Note the word choice. He did not speak of visiting the *residences* of illegal drug suspects. He was leading the Western world to the *lairs* of drug pushers and drug users. They would knock on their doors, Domingo explained, and offer the option of surrender and cooperation.

Domingo stepped out of the patrol car and strode down the Santa Ana streets trailed by uniformed cops and a local village official. The official was acting as Domingo's guide. Domingo had asked for a subject to visit.

Was anyone, asked Domingo of the official in Filipino, ready for a visit?

"Nothing's going to happen to him," Domingo assured the official. "I'm just knocking on his door. Just knocking, and it's just for the purpose of this."

"Yes, sir," said the village official. "I explained it to him."

"Well, it doesn't matter. Let's go to him. It's all we're doing." Domingo paused. "Does he have a gun?"

"No, sir!"

"That's it, we're just going to knock on his door, tell him he needs to change. This is just for video."

"Yes, sir—"

"Just for a documentary."

Stormer was accompanied by a translator. The translation, for the sake of the rolling camera, did not happen in real time. They walked to the lair of the drug user: a modest clapboard house with potted plants and a wooden gate.

"Nog?" Domingo called out. "Nog? Nog, it's Colonel Domingo, Nog. Nog, it's Colonel Domingo. You know me, Nog, don't you? Don't you know me, Nog? You know me, Nog."

Domingo spoke to the camera. "This is where we go in the Philippines," he said.

The gate was open. Domingo swung it shut, then knocked. "Hey, Mister Nognog!" he called out.

Domingo turned back to the camera and spoke in English. "Like that. Can we start?"

The man named Nog was a confessed former drug user. A Tokhang operation at that point was unnecessary, because Nog had surrendered long before Domingo's visit. He knew, as Domingo knew, as the village official knew, as the cops knew, as Stormer at that moment did not know, that the entire performance had been arranged strictly for the benefit of German television programming. None of it made Nog appear any less afraid.

A voice filtered out from inside the house. "Just a second, sir, I'm just getting dressed."

"That's okay, put on any shirt, Nog."

"Just a second, sir. Wait a bit."

"Come on, Nog, it's just for a documentary," Domingo said in Filipino.

"I'm here, sir."

The man who appeared on the sidewalk was tall and gangly, ribs visible under his skin as he struggled into a green polo shirt. He had barely thrust his hands into the sleeves when Domingo called out the first question in English.

"Are you a pusher, or are you a user?"

"I tried it a few times, sir," Nog answered in Filipino, "like I told you before."

Prodded, Nog admitted, low-voiced, that he was a drug user.

"Did you ever sell drugs?"

"No, sir." Nog stood with his arms clasped behind his back. The nerves showed as he attempted a smile.

"But didn't you operate before?"

"No, sir."

"Well, that's all," said a smiling Domingo. "All I'm telling you is that you need to change."

Nog bobbed his head. "Yes, sir."

"That's all from me. You need to change, to refrain from illegal activities, live your life, you know? To get away from illegal drugs."

A small boy wandered up to the brown gate.

"Don't you have kids?" Domingo asked. He signaled for the boy to come closer, then gestured to the man behind the camera. "His kid," he told Stormer, then went on with the lecture as Nog nodded along. "You have to change. Look at your son. What if something happens to you and you're gone? Your boy will be an orphan."

Nog ran a hand through his son's hair.

"Can you swear an oath?" Domingo asked.

"Yes, sir, I already did before."

"Well, you'll swear now," Domingo said. "Swear with your body."

Both men raised their right arms. Domingo recited a phrase at a time. Nog repeated each line.

"I—say your name—promise to cooperate with the Philippine National Police in avoiding any illegal activities that involve me in the use and sale of illegal drugs. May God have mercy on me."

Later that day, a translator explained to Stormer that the visit had been a performance, and little else.

"I wasn't going to air that," Stormer told me.

The footage went unreleased.

Colonel Domingo possessed the single quality most prized by long-form feature writers, myself included: he made for good copy. He might have been cautious when I first walked into his office, but he soon began expanding on the glories of the drug war. Every question I threw his way was an opportunity for a story, a punch line, or a soliloquy on the national situation. "We are very dead serious against illegal drugs," he said. "This is not for us, this is for my son, and the future generation of this beloved Republic of the Philippines. We don't want this Republic of the Philippines to become a narco state."

He walked the company line, and he did it with panache. The sound bites came thick and fast. His policy on erring cops was "zero tolerance," his men were the nation's "first line of defense," the drug pushers killed were always "in flagrante delicto." He was, in large part, a chubby-cheeked Dirty Harry who delighted in his own script. "If they get the jump on me, then they get the jump on me. Maybe I'll get the jump on them. You've only got one life."

The golden age, as viewed from the desk of the commander

of Police Station 6, was a marvel of discipline and community spirit. Every cop in the country had "the total backing" of the commander in chief himself. Combat pay had been increased. Lawyers had been provided to defend the police. Crime was at an all-time low. It was already possible for teenagers to wander about the streets playing Pokémon GO without having their phones plucked out of their hands. Most of the police caseload was petty theft—a stolen saucepan, a purloined gas tank, a robbery in a jeep. The only recent murder had resulted from a drunken argument over the relative saltiness of a roasted pig.

Policemen were no longer afraid of criminals, and the people, Domingo said, were no longer afraid of the police. Note the distinction: criminals, not people.

"Now it's the other way around," Domingo said. "They're the ones we're hunting. They're the ones who are hiding. They're the ones who are leaving."

It was all because of Rodrigo Duterte.

"What sort of president is he?" I asked.

"Legendary," he said. "Legendary."

I worked my way carefully toward the reason I had come for an interview. Domingo's cops had killed three young men during what the police recorded as a shoot-out. The case had been marked solved.

It had been, said Domingo, another case of *nanlaban*.

I had seen a picture of the dead. It had been taken just after cops secured the crime scene.

The picture was of a room, seven feet wide, roughly ten feet deep. A metal bunk bed stood flat against the back wall. A foam mattress took up most of the floor, covered with a grimy sheet that might have once been white. There were three people in the picture. All of them could have been asleep if it weren't for the blood. Mark Bunuan, half-blind with cataracts at seventeen, was on the lower bunk. His feet were flat on the floor, bony knees bent, as if he had been sitting at the edge of the bed before he fell back. A gun rested on his chest, cupped under skinny fingers. Twenty-seven-year-old Tutong Manaois, alleged dealer, lay curled on the floor, tucked against the right wall. The blood spilling from his head pooled under the gun that was positioned next to his hand. Twenty-year-old Jefferson, the scholar whose death had caused such an uproar, lay sprawled on his stomach like a boy asleep after a long day of play. One foot was spattered with blood. A purple polka-dotted Hello Kitty pillow lay beneath him. Red soaked through the back of his orange shirt.

The picture was complete. Three young men in a square room. Three guns, perfectly placed. Encountered, neutralized, the case solved. All were involved in illegal drugs, said Domingo. Impossible they were otherwise. The room was too small, so tiny that Domingo refused to believe they were there to sleep. What else would they have been doing, he asked, other than getting high?

"They were really among the drug personalities," Domingo told me. "They were really in our drug watchlist."

"All three?" I ask.

"Yes," he said. "They were really in the watchlist."

There were many lists.

The president had his own. He warned all public servants on his list to repent, resign, or die. Then he went on television and read their names. The list included judges, police officials, congressmen, generals, mayors. The president accused them all of involvement in the narcotics trade. The president said he had "intel" implicating the people on his list, and while his own staff said they had no knowledge of this intelligence, they said he was likely right, because he was the president.

Several of them did die. In the town of Datu Saudi Ampatuan in Maguindanao, in the south, the mayor and nine of his men were killed in what was reported to be a police shoot-out. The mayor of Ozamiz City in Misamis Occidental was shot dead in an encounter that also killed his wife, his brother, his sister, and eleven others. The mayor of Ronda was murdered as he slept inside his office in the town hall, just seven months after his vice-mayor was ambushed by unidentified gunmen. The mayor of Albuera was placed in police custody after allegedly being found with high-powered firearms and eleven kilos of crystal meth. He was killed inside his jail cell by cops who said they shot him in self-defense. In Tanauan City, an unknown sniper's bullet killed the seventy-two-year-old mayor as he stood singing the national anthem just outside the city hall. He too had been called a narco politician and had been stripped of supervisory powers over the police.

The president's list had several iterations, compiled into thick folders that the presidential staff hauled to the podium. He would read a few of the names out loud, occasionally offering personal commentary—"You've been ambushed twice, and you're still alive, you animal?" One of the lists came out just before the midterm elections.

"If your name is there," said President Duterte, "son of a bitch, you have a problem, I will really kill you."

Local watchlists, sheafs of which were printed on A4 sheets and handed out to cops, were not called narco lists. That name was reserved for the high-value targets that the president collected. The targets that local police commanders pursued were the lower end of the government's double barrel—street dealers, meth addicts, small-time pushers. They were given a catch-all term: drug personalities. Cops called them drug lists, sometimes watchlists. They were compiled by what were known as BADACs—Barangay (village) Anti-Drug Abuse Councils. Each member was a volunteer, selected from the pool of residents and approved by the elected village captain.

It was easy, one village captain told me, to identify a drug addict. It was "the aura" that gave it away. "I can tell from the eyes."

There were many informants, said Domingo. They supported the government because they were "tired of what's happening." Some went directly to the police. The names were culled from village captains, councilors, residents, and a range of sources, sent via text messages and anonymous dropboxes, compiled into lists that landed on desks like Domingo's.

Every new surrender was an opportunity to collect more names.

My photographer and I were sitting in his office when Domingo explained the intelligence-gathering process. Domingo was on his feet. "For example, Domingo surrenders." He pointed to himself. "He's asked, 'Where do you get your drugs?' 'From him, from Pedro.' After that, someone talks to Pedro. 'Pedro, where do you get your drugs?' 'Sir, from Patricia.'"

He pointed to me.

"Two points to Patricia. 'You, where do you get your drugs?' 'From Patricia.' Three points. You can form a link there, right? You can form it. This person gets from Pedro, and Pedro gets from Patricia, but this other person goes directly to Patricia, and this other person goes through Pedro to go to Patricia. And whoever's name gets mentioned the most, we eliminate that one. It means, this person, this one is moving [drugs]. Right? So, we go to the village hall. We ask them who this person is, and then we knock. 'Patricia, maybe you can stop, because our interview validation shows you're the one people keep talking about. You're the one they keep pointing to.' 'Sir, yes, sir.' And then we say, 'If you have time, if it's okay with you, you can surrender.' 'I'll see, sir.' If she doesn't show up, that's fine, but we monitor."

Those who choose to surrender sign a waiver—they vary across cities and stations—promising a new understanding of how "my involvement in drugs has no good effect." Surrenderers were moved to another watchlist—Reformed—and monitored for good behavior.

"After this we conduct again a second visitation," Domingo had explained to Stormer, "validation coming from the village hall. He's from the village hall," he said, pointing to the official who had accompanied Domingo up to Nog's door. "He will validate it, and if this guy will again be doing that, we will report it. And we will go to apprehend him. We conduct an operation against him."

By August 2016, the month I met Domingo, a little more than a month after President Duterte's declaration of war, at least 144,202 names were listed in the national drug watchlist. Each station operated with a quota—a percentage derived from the national government's unfounded estimate of drug users in the population. It mattered little whether the quota was filled by the surrendered, the arrested, or the dead. Domingo's share of Manila's quota was two thousand. A little less than half had surrendered. Several dozen more were dead. Across the country, the toll of bodies rose with increasing velocity.

This, said Domingo, did not mean the deaths were state sponsored. Percentages mattered, and the number of dead were far fewer than the numbers of those who had, like Nog, raised their hands to swear never to sin again.

"The numbers of those who have surrendered are up to seven

hundred thousand [across Metro Manila], but those killed are only at three thousand," Domingo told me. "That's probably not even ten percent. It's just that so many of them fight back."

The story I meant to write about Domingo was an investigative report on the killing of Jefferson Bunuan. That version was never published. Many of my sources withdrew their statements. Witnesses and survivors were afraid. "Have you seen *The Purge*?" one of them asked me. I hadn't. It was a film, he said. He had seen it with his friends. It was about America after an economic collapse, when the ruling party passed a law endorsing an annual purge when all crime, including murder, was legal. "It's like that here at night," he told me. "There's a purge."

I wrote a softer feature instead, on the district of Santa Ana, the man named Buwaya, and the crusading cop who idolized the president and carried out his war. I enumerated allegations against PS-6. I laid out the case made by human rights activists that Jefferson Bunuan's death was an execution. I put Domingo's more inflammatory comments side by side with the president's own.

I called the story "Legendary." I ended it with a parallel, between the president and Domingo. The president, during his campaign, had said that none of his children were involved in drugs, but he would order them killed if they were.

Domingo's own son also wanted to be a cop. I had asked Domingo about the president's promise. Would Domingo kill his own son, if his son was an addict? "Reality bites, but it's true," Domingo had answered, shrugging. "He'll be worthless, right? That would be it, from my point of view. He'll be useless."

It was, I had thought, a damning portrayal of the president's illegal drug war. I did not hear from Domingo. I did not hear

from the families. I was certain I had made some mistake somewhere that would make me or my sources a target—a general
unease that I could explain only by the fact that I had just written
about men who had killed a seventeen-year-old on a bunk bed.
Witnesses had withdrawn their statements. I could not withdraw
my byline.

One night, late in 2016, I dropped by Police Station 1 on Raxabago Street in Tondo. It was early in the evening. There were no
bodies yet, but there had been a tip that a pair of marijuana farmers had been apprehended at PS-1. The marijuana in question was
a scraggly potted shrub barely a foot high that stood on the front
desk beside the daily logbook. I introduced myself to the on-duty
cop. I asked to see the station commander for an interview. The
officer disappeared into the commander's office. We waited.

Colonel Domingo came striding out. "Trish!"

I was vaguely aware that Domingo had been transferred out
of PS-6. It was a regular exercise, commanders moving in and
out of stations every few years. He seemed pleased, almost delighted to see me.

He pointed out the marijuana plant. It was six months old, he
said. The street value was a little more than a dollar. The plant
had been confiscated behind a shanty. It was likely there had
been more.

"Look at this," he said, pulling at one of the leaves. "It's cute,
right?" And then he laughed.

A pair of skinny men I had not noticed had folded themselves
into a corner of PS-1's small reception area. They were cuffed together. At Domingo's pointing finger, they hid their faces behind
their shirts. The marijuana had been found in their possession.

"These two, they're okay, they weren't hostile," Domingo

explained. He addressed them directly. "You didn't have guns, right? You should be thankful. You didn't fight back."

Domingo looked at me. "I didn't kill them," he said, grinning. "That stuff we found would have been enough to get them killed. That's killing stuff."

"What do you mean by 'killing stuff'?" I asked.

He told me to look at the men. I looked. "See, you can't kill their sort, when you know they won't fight back. Come here, come here, show them, here, we found these too. They're seeds."

He shook out a handful into his palm.

"Those are seeds?" I ask.

"Seeds," he said. "Part of what we confiscated." He ordered one of the cops to empty a drawer. "Spread them out. They're seeds."

There was one last thing he wanted to show me.

Here, he said, leading me to his office. Look, he pointed.

I started laughing.

On the wall, dead center, was a framed and printed screenshot of the feature story I had published for Rappler a month before. The photo was pixelated, ripped from a Facebook post and badly cropped. The header showed Domingo himself, photographed in all his uniformed glory, smoking a cigarette, and sitting on a sagging plastic table beside graffiti that read "fuck the system, fuck the police."

The commander smiled. "You write like John Grisham," he said.

"Thank you, sir."

We smoked a couple of cigarettes. He introduced me to the men who strolled in and out of his office.

"This is my friend Trish," he told them.

.   .   .

I hadn't been called Trish since my freshman year in college, when a well-meaning friend told me the name didn't suit. Trish, I was made to understand, was a name meant for cheerleaders and A-plus students, smiling girls with nice manicures and breezy hair whose drivers picked them up after class. Trish didn't trip over her own feet and didn't cuss when she did. Trish was classy. Trish was friendly. I was Pat, not Trish.

I'm Pat, I would say, when I introduced myself to sources. Call me Pat.

Domingo was the exception. He had decided on Trish, and Trish I would remain. It pleased Domingo to use it, and I didn't correct him.

Trish, Domingo would begin, when he called late at night. Sometimes he would call to tell me he had read one of my stories. Sometimes he would talk about his day. Sometimes I called, for background on one case or another. He was the single police source I did not hesitate to contact.

My editor advised me to maintain a relationship with Domingo. Best to have someone on the inside. Safer during a war. "That's the kind of source you keep," Glenda told me. And then she grinned. "Okay, Trish?"

In early January 2017, almost seven months into the drug war, a young transgender woman was killed on the border of Manila and the city of Navotas. Her name was Heart de Chavez. She had chosen the name Heart, grown her hair long, taken hormone pills, and found work washing towels at a beauty parlor while moonlighting as a housemaid.

She began dealing drugs just as President Duterte was elected. It was an enterprise that terrified her mother, Elena, who had heard the president's threats.

Heart brushed off the warnings. She said no cop would take notice of a ten-dollar deal. She was wrong. She was put on a watchlist of more than a hundred suspects. A letter was sent. Police officers visited. Heart surrendered and was one of thousands of alleged drug personalities who personally swore oaths to the Navotas City authorities. She was invited to attend a three-day, all-expenses-paid seminar for drug users and dealers.

On January 10, 2017, seven masked men barged into the home she shared with her mother and her sister, Arriane. It was Heart they were after. One man held her by the hair and pounded her head into the table. Another man caught Heart by the front of her thin black sweater and dragged her out of the house.

Ma, Heart screamed. Help me.

One of the men stayed behind. He aimed a gun at the women. When he left, mother and sister scrambled to their feet and ran out the front door.

They met one of the masked men. "Sir, please, where is my daughter?"

"At the corner," he said. "We put her in the mobile."

Mother and daughter ran, stumbling, and caught up with two more men wearing masks.

"Sir, please, where is my daughter?"

"She ran."

Witnesses said they saw the men walking down the street, Heart in tow. The man in the lead held his gun with both hands. He ordered everyone back into their homes. Doors were locked. Windows were shuttered. Heart's screams could be heard up and down the street. One teenager listened as Heart was kicked into a shanty while begging for help. Neighbors heard three gunshots in quick succession and a fourth ten seconds later. Arriane and Elena rounded the bend, Arriane barefoot, clutching a baby, Elena limping along in the dark.

They found Heart inside an empty house with a bullet in her cheek.

The spot report filed hours after the killing did not detail exactly how Heart de Chavez had died, only how her body was found. There was no reference to armed men or Heart's screaming, only that a "dead male body was found inside a house" in San Jose, Navotas City.

The family accused the Navotas City Police of murder. Navotas denied responsibility. The chief of police said the death was likely drug-related, and that it was possible that Heart was killed by fellow users or dealers. No evidence linked the police to the killing. "We don't go into homes and kill people," Chief of Police Dante Novicio told me. It was a difficult case to solve because the killers had been masked. "So," he said, "this will remain unsolved."

Heart's family told me another story, of what happened just before Heart had been killed.

The city of Navotas shares a boundary with the seamier side of Tondo in Manila, so close that the De Chavez family did their shopping at the Pritil Public Market just inside the area of responsibility of Manila Police Station 1. Heart had been arrested by Tondo cops who belonged to the Pritil Police Community Precinct (Pritil PCP), one of four precincts under PS-1's supervision. According to Heart's mother, Elena, cops from the Pritil PCP demanded ₱50,000 for Heart's release.

"I went weak," she told me. "I told them, 'Sir, I don't have that money.' My daughter was crying, she was saying, 'Ma, don't leave me, they might take me out and kill me.'"

Elena left the precinct. She pawned her husband's pension for ₱7,000. She returned with the money, and said the police were unsatisfied. They opened her wallet to check for more and found nothing. Heart was released. She was dead three days later.

I found the Pritil Precinct on Herbosa Street in Manila. It was a small white box set in a bigger compound, with a parking lot to the left and a creek at its back. Between the creek and the building was a narrow veranda with a plastic table and a couple of motorcycles, separated from the parking lot by a blue-painted grill gate. A gaggle of cops sat at the table.

The commander met me at the back gate. His name was Edwin Fuggan. I introduced myself. I told him why I was there. I described Heart and the circumstances of her arrest.

He was reluctant and turned his face away as I spoke.

No, he said, no De Chavez had been picked up, arrested, or questioned on January 7.

I pulled out my recorder. He stopped answering questions. If I wanted to know more, he said, go to their headquarters at Police Station 1.

The officer on duty at the PS-1 desk was a friendly sort. All the PS-1 men were. The desk officer's name was Adonis Sugie. He did not blink at my recorder, and he remembered Heart.

"She didn't make it here," Sugie said. "She was picked up by the Pritil PCP. So we were asked to verify previous cases, but that was negative, so she was released."

"Did you verify here or at Pritil?"

"Pritil handled it because that's where she was picked up. They had an operation there. She wasn't alone, there were many others. They verified them, called in the names to see if they had warrants, pending cases. That came up negative. So she was released immediately."

"How come Pritil told me there was no such person? That they verified no one?"

"No, they did catch them . . . but maybe, ma'am, with so many people, maybe they forgot. But I remember her. She was the one who surrendered to Navotas."

"Is she the one who looked like a woman?"

"Yes, she was gay, this one was gay. The wake lasted two weeks. Almost two weeks."

I asked to speak to the station commander, Fuggan's boss. Sugie led me straight into the office of my friend Domingo. I told him about Heart's death. I told him about the accusations. I summarized the allegations of extortion committed by cops under his watch and said I needed official comment.

Domingo asked if the family was willing to speak to him. I made the phone call. They were. Domingo made his own call. He asked for Fuggan to appear.

Domingo sent out for coffee. For half an hour we smoked cigarettes and discussed pulp literature and the future of Philippine cinema. When a uniformed Pritil PCP commander, Police Captain Edwin Fuggan, walked in, every seam straight, Domingo stood up to introduce me.

"Ma'am," Fuggan said, shaking my hand. This time, he did not turn away.

He sat down as we waited for Elena and Arriane de Chavez.

The door opened.

"That's him—" said Elena.

Fuggan rose quickly. He crossed the room and slung an arm around the older woman.

"Good afternoon, Mother," he said.

We all sat around Domingo's desk just under the framed picture of my old feature story on Domingo. My recorder was rolling, a massive Zoom H4 with a microphone head. I set it on the table between Fuggan and Elena.

It was a small room. Domingo was not shy about demonstrating his displeasure.

"Tell me. You remember who you paid?" he demanded of Elena.

"Yes, sir," she said in a low voice.

"Point it out on video too! I will sue!"

Fuggan was quick to join in. "How much money was taken from you? I'll return it."

"Seven thousand—" Elena answered.

"Here's what we'll do," Fuggan said. "If anything was taken, I'll pay it back, son of a bitch."

He turned to Elena. His voice was amiable, almost ingratiating. "Mother, I'm the PCP commander."

"Yes, sir."

"You should have—"

"Here's the thing, buddy," Domingo interrupted. "You sons of bitches, you sons of bitches, those son-of-a-bitch cops of yours, you didn't keep them in line with the stealing. You sons of bitches, you should be the ones killed—"

"That's really what happened, sir," Elena said. "I even showed it to them. I pawned my husband's pension."

"Yes, I heard," Fuggan said.

"Get the pictures! I'm not going to allow—"

"We'll handle it, the cash that was taken, I'll give it back," Fuggan said.

"Yes, sir," said Elena.

"Give it back, you sons of bitches," Domingo growled, "because all of you, all of you sons of bitches, you can't keep your cops in line, you sons of bitches. Point them out! Son of a bitch, if I see them, Sugie, I'm going to kill those cops."

Sugie was standing patiently by the door.

"Sugie, they may think I can't—"

Fuggan, interrupting, turned to Elena. "So when did it happen?"

"—and I haven't popped my Valium yet!"

"Just the other day—" Elena said.

"And wasn't it just verification," interrupted Fuggan, "because she wasn't from around here?"

"Yes, sir."

Domingo was at the tail end of a diatribe when I heard my name. "Tricia knows I take Valium, right, Tricia?"

I didn't, but decided the appropriate answer was agreement: "Yes, sir."

Fuggan was trying to lead Elena to safer ground. "And didn't I tell Heart she should clean up her act, because it's now the time of Duterte?"

Elena was not following. "That's what I told her, sir. I said she should stop with the drugs."

"Do you agree?"

"She stopped with the drugs," Arriane, the sister, interrupted.

"If I'm not mistaken," Fuggan tried again, "I called you 'ma'am.' Didn't I say that?"

Fuggan had suddenly discovered that he knew Heart and her mother. He turned to me.

"Ma'am Patricia, I remember!"

"Yes, sir," I said.

"I remember you now," he told Elena. "You were sick, and I told both of you to go home. I told your kid, 'You should stop, sis.' I called her sis, because she told me she was gay."

"Yes, sir," Elena said.

"But I didn't—"

"She hadn't left the house for three days," Elena interrupted. "A neighbor went to our house and asked Heart to pick up drugs. She really wasn't going out then."

"So it was really your neighbor's fault she got in trouble!" Fuggan concluded. He turned to Domingo. "Now I remember, sir. I was eating then, and I said, 'Okay, you should take her home, she isn't from here.'"

Fuggan, memory refreshed, said he had been at the Pritil Precinct on the night Heart was arrested. He had seen Elena de Chavez. She was elderly, he said, ill and confused. He had approached Elena. He was sympathetic. He called her Mother. He had been told by his cops that Heart was being held for verification.

Fuggan called Heart a "suspicious" character. The reason she was suspicious was because his cops hadn't recognized her face on the street.

"That's our first move," he told me. "We doubt you if you're not from here, because all our cops know if you're from here or not. It was really just for verification."

He had trouble defining what he meant by *verification*.

No evidence of criminal activity had been found on Heart's person. Heart, Fuggan said, had not been arrested. She had not been detained. The word, instead, was *held*. Heart had been held, and it all went easily enough. Fuggan said he had comforted Elena. He said he had lectured Heart. He said he had told them to go home. Whatever extortion might have occurred had happened outside of his knowledge, but he was willing to pay its costs regardless.

Inside the office of the chief of PS-1, Domingo was still performing righteous indignation.

"You sons of bitches, if you don't all stop this, I'm the one who'll take you apart personally. After all, since regular people can't kill you, I'll kill you myself. All of us are cops here, son of a bitch, let's just shoot it out. That sort of shamelessness isn't allowed, son of a bitch. You sons of bitches, look at what is happening to this country. If you have to steal, steal from Gokongwei.

Steal from the rich. But her"—he pointed at Elena—"she's dirt poor! For fuck's sake, she doesn't even have the money for a ride home. Not even for a ride home! That's the sort of person the government should be protecting, the poorest of the urban poor. And the cops are dipping into their pockets?"

It was an impressive lecture. Fuggan, his voice low, ventured to defend himself: "I only told her to live a better life."

Sugie returned with a pile of index cards. Each card had a police officer's name and ID picture. All were cops from the Pritil PCP. Sugie had been ordered to collect them so Elena could identify the cops who had extorted money from her family.

Domingo stood over Elena. He instructed her to view each card carefully.

For a while, the office was quiet, the only sound the shuffling paper and the television playing outside.

"Don't be afraid," Domingo said. His voice boomed in the small room. "You're speaking to the commander here. I am the commander! I am the chief! Do not be afraid."

"We'll help them, sir," Fuggan added.

"I am the commander," Domingo repeated.

Elena murmured as she paged through the names. "This one," she said, pointing to a picture. "I think this is one of them."

"We'll call them," Fuggan said.

She said there were five cops who extorted funds for the release of her daughter. She came up with four index cards. Domingo fired off a referral for the investigation of four Pritil police officers. The case was alleged extortion.

Here, he told me, you can take a picture of the document.

We left. I shook hands with Domingo. I thanked Fuggan, who called me ma'am.

We were well away from the police station when Elena told me she knew who the fifth cop was. She had been afraid to say the name.

"It was Fuggan," she told me later. "Fuggan put the money in his own pocket."

I met with Arriane and Elena again a few days later. A cop had met with her family, Arriane said, and offered a wad of bills. Seven thousand pesos, the exact amount Elena claimed had been extorted by the Pritil police.

The cop was only a messenger. He said he had been sent by Fuggan.

I called Domingo. I told him I had come across new information that required a statement from his precinct commander. There were more phone calls, back and forth. I spoke to Fuggan again. I explained he could refuse comment, but if he agreed, it should be on video. We agreed on a time and a date, the location Domingo's office.

Domingo called me the night before the interview. It was late, near midnight. There was none of the usual joking banter from the other side of the line.

It was a short call. He said he had a question.

"Do you consider me a friend, Pat?"

He asked the question more than once.

Be honest, he said.

Do you consider me a friend, Pat?

Do you consider me a friend?

Pat, do you consider me a friend?

I remember being reluctant to say yes. If I agreed, he might ask me to withdraw the story, and I did not want any claims of a conflict of interest. If I disagreed, I did not want to risk an angry cop with two hundred armed men at his disposal. I skated around the answer, then agreed. Yes, sir, I consider you a friend.

He did not say why he asked. I didn't know what it meant, or if I should be afraid. I sent a message to my editor, Glenda, the next morning. I was concerned, I said. Domingo was in a mood. I was keeping my GPS open so Rappler could track me. *"Heading into Raxabago PS1 Manila,"* I wrote. *"Will be charming and harmless and reassuring."*

I met Fuggan at PS-1. Domingo was not present. It was a straightforward interview.

Fuggan said he "didn't know anything about anyone asking for money." He said he could not imagine "any reason why any cop would be involved in extortion." He denied the incident, called it exaggerated, and said he was certain it never happened.

"Cops don't do that," he said, "because we know it's wrong."

He admitted sending money to Elena. The funds had come from his own savings. It did not mean he was guilty. He was "only helping." It was "out of the goodness of my heart."

I published the story. Heart's murder, as promised, went unresolved.

I heard little from Domingo after that. I didn't notice, because for those three months I was deep into an investigation of cops from Manila Police Station 2, near Moriones Street. Witness testimony described a series of executions of young men shot dead by a cop who had acquired himself a nickname whispered among the residents of the neighborhood of Delpan. They called him the Demon of Delpan. In the aftermath of publication, I got an approving call from Domingo, who clucked over the rights violations I had described in detail. He reminded me, somewhat smugly, that unlike the men I had profiled, he and his men understood what human rights were.

Just days after that call, on April 27, 2017, a team from the Commission on Human Rights, acting on a tip from an informer, made a surprise inspection of Domingo's PS-1. The CHR is an independent government body, created in the aftermath of the martial law atrocities. Its chairman at the time, Chito Gascon, a former student activist, was one of the last voices inside the Duterte administration willing to speak against the slew of killings. Gascon was an Aquino appointee, and by law, except for cause, could not be replaced until his own term ended.

The CHR had been told that a secret detention facility was hidden inside PS-1, a cell tucked behind the office of Domingo's Drug Enforcement Unit (DEU). The tipster said it was where alleged drug suspects were locked up, even if their names weren't on the books. If true, it was an extortion operation: suspects were released only after police successfully extracted funds from their terrified families.

Domingo, still in plainclothes, demonstrated the sort of coolness required of a former spokesperson of the Philippine National Police. He gave a smiling tour of the station to Gilbert Boiser, who led the CHR team while trailing a pack of journalists. Eventually Boiser walked into the DEU office, where he found three civilians already inside. They were, explained the police, suspects waiting to be processed.

Domingo told Boiser he knew of no secret facilities.

Photojournalist Raffy Lerma saw one of the male suspects flick his eyes toward a bookshelf. The bookshelf stood flush against a corner of the room.

"Is anyone in there?" Boiser called out.

Every journalist in the room heard a muffled voice shout from behind the wall, "We're here!"

Boiser, whose informant had already shown him a hand-drawn map of the room, tried to pull the bookshelf forward. Nothing happened. It was Raffy who knelt to find the lock hidden behind the lip of a lower shelf. He released the bolt. The bookshelf swung open like a door. A woman stepped out, thin, blinking in the light. "Please," she said, "don't leave us here."

They staggered out, one by one, nine in all. Behind them was a narrow corridor, roughly three feet wide and sixteen feet deep, so narrow that it was impossible for the twelve people who had once been crammed inside to stand with their arms stretched sideways. There was a broken urinal where detainees had piled bags of their own excrement. There was no light that night. There were no windows. The back of the cell was lined with steel bars, covered from the outside with a sheet of galvanized iron.

A few of the detainees managed to speak to reporters. They claimed cops had held them hostage, some for as long as eight days, for amounts as high as ₱100,000. One of them, who showed bruises from a beating, said the police promised he would be hurt worse if his family failed to produce money. "They said we would be killed."

None of their names were recorded in the police logbook. None of them had been charged.

Domingo insisted the jail was newly constructed. Before the rolling cameras of three national news networks, Domingo informed the public that the detainees were lying. "It's their word against ours. So we will fight that [to] the end."

At least a dozen journalists were crammed into the station that night, all of whom had been kicked out of the DEU office by cops who had just realized they were in trouble. I was not there that night. Another reporter had sent me word. "*Your Domingo was caught,*" she messaged.

None of the detainees were released to the Commission on Human Rights.

"Those are our arrests," insisted Domingo's officers. "You can't take them."

The story hit the headlines of every major broadsheet, many of whose beat reporters had been present for the raid.

The next morning the bookshelf was gone. A single sheet of legal paper had been stuck to the wall just above the entrance.

TEMPORARY STAGING AREA, it read.

Domingo was briefly relieved of duty. The Commission on Human Rights filed complaints at the Office of the Ombudsman against Lieutenant Colonel Robert Domingo, Police Corporal Dylan Verdan, Patrolman Berly Apolonio, and other John Does for arbitrary detention, grave threats, delay in the delivery of persons to the proper judicial authorities, grave coercion, grave misconduct, and conduct prejudicial to the best interest of the service.

The complaints were dismissed in 2020.

Domingo called me, some time after the CHR raid.

"Trish," he began, "you believe me, don't you?"

10

SOME PEOPLE NEED KILLING

In early January 2017, the wife of a South Korean businessman appealed for government assistance in the pages of the *Philippine Daily Inquirer*. Her husband, Jee Ick Joo, had disappeared on October 18 of the previous year. Neighbors claimed that at two in the afternoon, armed men had shoved the fifty-three-year-old, struggling, into his own vehicle before driving away. The family's household helper had also been abducted. The helper, later released, said the men involved were cops claiming it was a drug bust.

The story unraveled. The police officers who dragged Jee Ick Joo out of his Angeles City home on a pretend drug bust had been waving a fake arrest warrant. They took him to the national police headquarters, where a drug unit cop, armed with a roll of packing tape and surgical gloves, strangled the detained businessman. They demanded ₱8 million in ransom from his wife, got ₱5 million, then refused to provide proof of life.

The story made the international news. The South Korean embassy called for an investigation. The Senate held hearings. Two police officers were charged with, one later convicted of, the crime kidnapping with homicide. There were reports the victim's head had been wrapped in packing tape and his corpse cremated—before a panicked funeral parlor employee flushed the ashes down a toilet.

It was seven months after the declaration of the drug war. More than seven thousand were dead, and only then was Rodrigo Duterte finally willing to concede his cops had done wrong. "I apologize for the death of your compatriot," he told the South Korean government in a public address. "We are very sorry that it had to happen."

The chief of the Philippine National Police, Ronald "Bato" dela Rosa, stood before the media and said the police would "focus on internal cleansing." He said he would have preferred to kill the cops involved, if only it were legal. He called the crime offensive. He would "melt in shame if I could."

President Rodrigo Duterte called the incident an embarrassment but refused Dela Rosa's offer to resign. On January 30, 2017, the president suspended the same police institution he had empowered from participation in the war against drugs. Police antidrug units were dissolved. He called the police "the most corrupt, corrupt to the core." He called them criminals. The war would continue, but there would be no more police operations against illegal drugs.

On that night, every drug war journalist I knew gathered at the press office of the Manila Police District. We waited. There were no crime scenes that night. No drug addict died; no dealer was shot. Not in Manila, not in Caloocan, not in Cebu or Navotas or the slums of Quezon City. The president had spoken, and for the first time in seven months—with the exception of Christmas Day—no new names were added to the death count. It came as no surprise that the cops kept their guns holstered, but the vigilantes did too. There were no salvagings, no drive-by shootings, no masked gunmen kicking down doors of suspected meth dealers. The uniformed militia stood down, and so did, if the reports were to be believed, the killers they employed. The death toll stopped at 7,080.

The war, or what had been called the war, ended with the flush of a toilet.

The suspension of the drug war was not an act of hypocrisy, or of hypocrisy alone. Here were senior antidrug cops who had believed they could kill a wealthy foreign national inside the national police headquarters after demanding millions from his wife, and here was the president, who, like everyone, had been witness to impunity on the streets, announcing his shock. To tell cops they were trusted while telling cops they were corrupt; to guarantee their protection while pledging to kill them; to rage daily against the inconvenience of human rights while railing in outrage when human rights were disregarded; to hold the high ground while glorying in mass graves; to profess vulgarity while promising morality; to denounce laws while pledging to uphold them; to believe in the likelihood of one murder while denying the possibility of all others; to claim to be a killer while repudiating killers—this was the magical reality of Rodrigo Duterte, one that had been applauded, broadcast, and imitated across the nation with willing alacrity.

George Orwell's contribution to understanding autocrats everywhere is necessary here. The word is *doublethink,* the ability to hold two contradictory ideas in mind simultaneously while accepting both. It was, Orwell wrote in *Nineteen Eighty-Four,* the power "to tell deliberate lies while genuinely believing in them." It was to use facts only when convenient, to disavow their existence when contradictory, and "to deny the existence of objective reality and all the while to take account of the reality which one denies." How dare the cops murder? How dare they not kill? Thus, the Orwellian lie, stripped of its subtleties.

The lie, however, requires proper delivery to be accepted as fact. In 1961 the American historian Daniel J. Boorstin published *The Image,* a book that introduced the term *pseudo-event.* The pseudo-event is not spontaneous. It exists primarily for the purpose of being reported. It has an ambiguous relationship to reality. It is, when successful, a self-fulfilling prophecy. The pseudo-event is not propaganda, because it happened. The facts, artificial as they are, provide a bulwark against criticism. "While propaganda substitutes opinion for facts," wrote Boorstin, "pseudo-events are synthetic facts which move people indirectly, by providing the 'factual' basis on which they are supposed to make up their minds."

In the case of the drug war's suspension, the pseudo-event was the image of General dela Rosa, at Malacañang Palace in his white dress uniform, head bowed, eyes to the ground, explaining his sorrow and his shame. It was the presence of Rodrigo Duterte, on a podium in Sarangani province, threatening corrupt cops that "they will suffer" for their sins.

Within days of the war's temporary suspension, Amnesty International released a scathing report claiming that police had been fabricating evidence and assassinating drug suspects for pay.

The drug war was in trouble. The world was paying attention. The government had been caught committing what could only be called murder—there was no way, after all, to claim that the killing of a bound and defenseless man was covered by a presumption of regularity.

Enter the vigilantes.

.   .   .

It was the afternoon of February 9, 2017. CNN Philippines carried the press conference live. The national media were in attendance. The gold stars of the PNP's top brass were on full display. All of them were surrounded by assorted investigators and enforcers, some of whom forced back the bent heads of the three suspects arranged behind General Ronald "Bato" dela Rosa.

"They did kill him," the general said. "They abducted him, then killed him, then put him in a sack." This "him" was sixteen-year-old Charlie Saladaga. Between his abduction on January 1 and the discovery of his body a day later, Charlie had been shot in the face, stuffed into a sack, and tossed into the breakwater of Isla Puting Bato in Tondo, Manila. His fourteen-year-old sister identified his kidnappers as members of a local gang called the Confederate Sentinels Group (CSG).

After Charlie's death, the police said the CSG had threatened the Saladaga family—at least once at gunpoint—so badly that Charlie's mother, Cristina, finally walked over to the Manila Police District to file a complaint. Soon after, police raided the CSG's outpost on Road 10 in Village 105. Law enforcement operatives confiscated several items, including cell phones, a .38-caliber revolver, two homemade shotguns, and a variety of scattered ammunition. CSG members were arrested.

"This is their uniform," Dela Rosa told reporters, holding up a black shirt with the words CSG, TONDO 2, BARANGAY 105 printed on the back. "Confederate Sentinel Group. A civilian volunteer organization that apparently became a vigilante group killing robbery suspects. That's why they targeted the kid. They killed him. They said he was a thief."

A police official held up an enlarged photo of a gangly young man splayed on the ground. Part of his body was still inside what appeared to be a torn sack. "This is the picture of the kid who was salvaged, then stuffed into a sack," Dela Rosa said.

He claimed the suspects had confessed. "They are here now," said the general. "We've confiscated their guns, all their guns, and they have admitted to what they've done."

He called one of the suspects to the microphone and ordered him to repeat "what you told me earlier."

"It was our Commander Maning who—" the suspect began.

"Properly, speak properly," interrupted Dela Rosa.

"It was Commander Maning," said the suspect.

"What?"

"Commander Maning, sir."

"Who is he?"

"He's the one who gave us orders."

Manila Police District chief Joel Coronel took over the podium for Dela Rosa and admitted that the PNP had accredited the CSG as peacekeepers. He said they had never been authorized to carry arms. He said they had been operating in Tondo at least five months. He said the police had "monitored through several complaints that this group has been engaged in summary killings" and that there were "about ten persons engaged in these extrajudicial or vigilante killings," although Dela Rosa also said the group may have had up to two hundred members.

Coronel said the CSG killed to protect the drug trade and other criminal activities. It targeted suspects from enemy gangs and murdered "to instill fear and panic in people." He said victims wrongly believed the killers were policemen.

Dela Rosa said the PNP had discovered, from cell phone messages and tactical interrogation, that the CSG had been responsible for at least three more homicides before Charlie Saladaga was killed. Those cases, he announced, were now "considered solved." Charges would be filed. Three of the suspects were already in custody. The PNP would conduct a manhunt for three others, including the alleged mastermind, Ricardo Villamonte, alias Commander Maning.

The press conference was an unexpected event. Charlie was not the first sixteen-year-old to die; nor was he the first to be shot in the face or thrown into the water—an option for corpse disposal so happily endorsed by the president himself.

But Charlie was special, because Charlie was the answer to a public relations crisis. As General dela Rosa said, the arrests were "a solution of some of the DUI [Deaths Under Investigation] cases, or what the media refers to as EJK—extrajudicial killings—which were presumably being attributed to the police."

"It dispels some accusations," Dela Rosa said, "that these DUIs were sanctioned by the police, or were the work of the police."

The accusations were not all dispelled, because the cops didn't arrest all the killers. Because they didn't, some of them talked. Some of them talked to me.

I had been planning the moment for months, was afraid every day that it wouldn't happen, that the vigilante would withdraw, disappear, never be in contact again. We met at a gas station. He rode a motorcycle. He nearly ran away when he saw my photographer, because he was told he would be meeting a woman and was afraid he had been set up. He came back when I stepped out of the tinted van and lit a cigarette.

"I'm Pat," I said. He nodded.

I gestured to the open van door. He hesitated, then stepped in.

He said nothing during the ride. I don't remember if I said anything, only that I was certain, at that moment, that this man had killed and could kill again. His knee jerked. I was relieved.

I know his name, photographed his identification, but the name I will use is Angel. Angel's shirt matched the motel couch. So did mine. We talked about his family at first. About his education, about the elections, about the state of the nation.

"What did you think of that press conference?" I asked.

Angel had likely never read Boorstin, but he saw the press conference for what it was.

"It was like the cops were putting on a show. 'Let's pick these guys up, put them in front of people, say they're guns for hire.' So that's what happened. Like they were showing off. But they knew that the guys they caught, they were like us: we were their men on the ground."

The police's alleged man on the ground took his orders from Commander Maning. The cops were correct, he said. Maning had told Angel they were forming a group. "He told us our job was to clean out the thieves and drug dealers. He said we'd try to clean up Tondo."

Angel had wandered into the CSG mostly by chance. His friends had been recruited. They had told him to bring his guns. There was a meet, they said. It was for surveillance. Come along, we have a job.

"I found out later that every time they said we had a job, they meant we were going to kill," said Angel. That first night the men sent in Angel first. He went down the side of a road and found himself a corner. The target came strolling by.

"I wasn't ready when they shot him," Angel said. "I went, 'Oh.'"

Oh, he said, and then everyone ran. Angel did not remember how many gunshots were fired, only that there were two gunmen on the run the moment the corpse hit the ground.

Angel became one of the CSG's veteran vigilantes. At its height, sometime between July 2016 and early 2017, my sources said, CSG Chapter 2 in Tondo had an estimated twenty to forty members. They were garbage truck operators, jeepney drivers, scavengers, security guards, construction workers—a small army of true believers who, at least at the beginning, considered themselves soldiers in Rodrigo Duterte's war against drugs.

Angel could not remember the name of every man he killed. He remembered instead where each of them was shot. Sometimes a target was waylaid outside Tondo, because if you kill where you live, "the area gets hot." There were the two men in Payatas. There was the one in Caloocan. The last one was in Blumentritt, and Angel isn't sure if he was ever given a name.

He said Commander Maning set the bounty for each dead target. It ranged from ₱30,000 to ₱40,000, although it once went as high as ₱100,000. "We only got paid if we killed," Angel said. The money was split among the members of the kill team: driver, shooter, lookouts, backup, finisher. Angel said the lowest he had been paid was ₱8,000.

"The police knew," said Angel. "They couldn't not know. We couldn't have operated in that area if they didn't know."

Commander Maning's CSG—CSG Tondo Chapter 2—was part of a larger organization. The Confederate Sentinels Group Incorporated was registered at the Securities and Exchange Commission in 2009. Its stated intent was to work "within the purview of social welfare and development." Its founder, Alvin Constantino, told me that the group lived by Matthew 25:35–46, "that part where Matthew says, 'Feed the hungry, give drink to the thirsty, clothe the naked and welcome the strangers.'" The group was meant to be "protectors of the weak and needy." Members belonged to medical, rescue, and marshal units. It was the marshal unit that partnered with police as force multipliers.

While the group ran an annual fundraising effort and received occasional donations from its chapters, the most the national CSG had ever raised in a year was ₱120,000, less than half the organization's actual spending. Constantino said his family provided the bulk of the CSG's budget. They treated the organization as a family operation.

"That's our offering to God," he said, "ourselves, our treasure, our time, our effort, to glorify his name."

The CSG's roughly thirty chapters were spread across the country. In 2016, the year the CSG publicly supported the candidacy of Rodrigo Duterte, it had two chapters in Tondo, Manila. Constantino claimed that Chapter 2 had never progressed beyond "a probationary chapter."

He was categorical in his insistence that the CSG had nothing to do with the recruitment of Chapter 2's members. It was the police, he said, who called to inform him that a new chapter from Tondo was "ready for orientation." It was the police who introduced him to Commander Maning, the police whom Constantino trusted, and the police who allowed Commander Maning to join patrols, ride in mobile units, and direct traffic. It was the police who had direct command and training supervision over every one of the CSG's marshal units—a characterization the PNP chief denied in an interview with me. "So the police give the instructions," Constantino said. "My people just do what they're told, because those are uniformed personnel."

The national organization's advocacy, he said, "does not include vigilante killings."

But the CSG's vigilante activities were no secret to the residents. "They were the killing arm of the police," a community volunteer told me.

Rumors of an armed group of vigilantes spread across the tenements and shanties of Tondo's Village 105. The men would patrol late at night, sometimes at dawn. One resident who saw them pass by on his way home asked who they were. "They're the CSG," he was told. "They're the ones who kill the drug users and dealers."

With every death, the CSG reached new levels of notoriety. "Even the village watchmen were afraid of them," said one resident. One woman I spoke to said she was afraid one of the children would get shot in the crossfire. Most of the walls in the area were made of plywood. "They shoot like cowboys," she said.

"At first I didn't believe the story," said a visitor to the tenements. "But I was friends with some of the members, and they were pretty vocal about what they called their job. They were real, and they were killing."

The target lists were spoken of in whispers. Brothers and fathers and sons were sent out of Tondo to hide. "I couldn't sleep knowing the names of people who were about to die," said one Tondo resident who had heard the list read out. "I went to each of their mothers. I told them to run."

The deaths were sometimes reported in the news, part of the count of alleged drug suspects gunned down daily across the country. One of the reported Tondo deaths, a man named Ernesto Sabado, had been released from jail in a robbery case only days before he was killed. Residents said Sabado had been dragged out of his home. "They shot him outside the hall," one source told me. "In the hallways of the building, in front of everybody."

A news report noted that Sabado had been killed "in front of his pleading mother." Another tabloid reported that Sabado had been "shot dead by his neighbor and two cohorts who forcibly entered his house in Tondo, Manila." The reports quoted an investigator, who said authorities were hunting down three suspects.

One of them would later be paraded at a Camp Crame press

conference, head down, towel over his head, surrounded by police dignitaries, arrested for the murder of Charlie Saladaga.

I sat across from another killer in another hotel room. "I was scared of killing at first, but not anymore," he told me. "It's like drugs. You get addicted. Then you're not afraid."

I called him Simon. It wasn't his real name. He told me to call him any name I wanted. Where he came from, Simon said, weasels were shot with no questions asked, and he did not want to die.

Neither did I. The day before I opened a hotel room door to Simon, I had sat in a conference room with my photographer and Rappler's management, assessing the danger of a second interview with a vigilante. "Make sure he's unarmed," Glenda told me. "Pat him down before you record."

No problem, we said.

We waited in the hotel room. The doorbell rang. My contact delivered Simon to the door.

"I'm Pat," I said. I shook his hand.

"I need to use the bathroom, ma'am," the killer said.

I gestured. He went. I reminded my photographer of the rules. "You have to check him for a gun," I said.

He cocked his head. "What happens if I find a gun?"

It was a question that had not occurred to us the day before. The bathroom doorknob was turning. We didn't search Simon.

He stepped out of the bathroom and sat gingerly on the edge of the bed. I showed him the mic. Hooked the clip to his collar. Laid out the backup recorders on the bed. Did he want a cigarette? Yes, he did. He lit up. I lit up.

I pressed the record button.

"Tell us your name," I said.

Simon called himself an ordinary man. He owned a gun. He was religious. He had a wife and children. He believed that drugs "make people go crazy," and he voted for President Duterte because he believed Duterte was right that drug addicts should die. He lived in Aroma, a sprawling slum in Tondo, where sagging two-story tenement buildings opened onto dirt roads layered with garbage and last week's rotten Happy Meal.

"Every kind of dangerous person lives in Aroma," Simon told me. "Killers. Addicts. The men on the Most Wanted lists. They come to Aroma to hide."

In the story Simon told, police officers promised CSG Tondo Chapter 2—"we're what you call vigilantes"—payment for every corpse they delivered. He had been recruited by Commander Maning. Maning gave the orders, and the men would follow. This man, that man, get it done, do the job—you, you, and you. The names of targets were announced at the CSG Chapter 2 outpost. The photos were stuck to the walls. The targets included meth users, drug runners, thieves, and the occasional philandering husband. Simon estimated the gang's death count at roughly twenty over a seven-month period.

"After Duterte was elected, the killing was automatic, one after another," said Simon.

In the first two years of the drug war, Simon killed two more men. By *kill,* he meant he pulled the trigger. He had other roles in other operations. He conducted surveillance. He acted as a lookout. He drove the getaway van. There was very little he was unwilling to do, because success at what he calls "the job" meant one less criminal threatening the future of his children. Simon claims he was never paid, but he stayed on anyway. He believed in the cause.

"I'm really not a bad guy," said Simon. "I'm not all bad. Some people need killing."

. . .

The list of dead targets grew longer, said Simon. He knew most of them by their aliases: Toyo, Joseph, JC, Antonio, Pinuno, Sitoy. "We were confident," said Simon, "because if we showed the police our ID, or even if we didn't have ID to show, we'd just give them our names and say we were Commander Maning's men. They'll hold us at the PCP. . . . They'll take us for a ride and hold us. If they prove we're positive [as the CSG], they'd let us go."

Not every target was killed on police orders, said Simon. One woman on the target list, a dealer the locals called "Mommy," knew there was a hit out for her and refused to leave her house. "So they took it out on her son instead."

"It depends on the orders," said Angel. "Doesn't matter if you're a kid or an adult. That's how it works. If Maning says to kill someone, because the police paid him, he'll say, 'Go, drop the guy, he's pissed off a lot of people inside. Do it.'"

Once Commander Maning announced a target, the surveillance team would fan out, four to seven men. They would watch the target, sometimes for days, from across an alley or the stoop of a corner store. They would listen when plans were made, befriend neighbors, and note when children came home. Sometimes the surveillance men would look through windows or knock on the door to purchase a sachet of meth—no problem, no worries, here you go, the folded hundred-peso bill just a quiet deal between friends.

Once the target was "positive," a team would be selected. "Someone would go, 'You, you, and you, go with him so it's safe,'" said Angel, pointing at imagined cronies. "Four in front, the rest to the side. In every area you have a backup. That corner, two backups there. Those in front are on motorcycles. On the other side, two more. The target safely down, and no screw-ups."

Sometimes they would use a van one of the members owned, sometimes a motorcycle with unregistered plates. If the target survived the first shot, another man would be waiting. He could be sitting at an outdoor canteen with a bowl of noodles. He could be on his phone, standing by the side of the road. He moved only after the target fell and the shooter ran. If the target twitched, he would fire the killing shot. They called him the finisher.

"I finish the job," Angel said.

It took time for the vigilantes to develop more efficient methods for murder. They made mistakes along the way. They said they accidentally shot a twelve-year-old. That they killed a man wearing the same color shirt as their target, while the target ran away. They said they occasionally panicked and found themselves bunched into a cramped knot at the mouth of a narrow alley, just as their armed target walked by.

"I told them that's how we would get screwed," said Simon. "If anyone sprayed us with bullets, then we'd all be dead. I said, 'We go corner by corner. One man at every corner. Let the enemy run, and we rip into him wherever he goes.' That's how we got Sitoy."

By then, it was seven months into the drug war. The target, Sitoy, was a short, cocky meth addict who liked to hang a pair of grenades on a string around his neck. Simon told me Sitoy was so dangerous, he sometimes forgot one of his grenades in the canteen where he ate. They said he dealt meth when he had the money and scored drugs with the barrel of his loaded shotgun when he was broke.

Simon said Sitoy's execution was "on the orders of the police."

A team was selected, surveillance initiated, the time and place set. The six, possibly seven killers took up their posts along the row of tenements. They waited in the dark. The mosquitoes were biting. Nobody moved until an hour past midnight, when Sitoy walked out into the open.

The vigilantes began firing.

"We shot him in the ass," said Simon, "so he couldn't run. And then he went for his grenade. The pin was taped down, and he was ripping it off. So we shot him again."

Sitoy dropped to the ground, bleeding from a chest wound. "When he cried, I felt bad for him," Simon said. "He was begging, 'Don't, don't!'"

Simon said they shot Sitoy at least six times: once from the back, once on the arm, once in the chest, and three times through the skull.

The vigilantes called the police. The cops came in with a bomb squad. The killers went home.

According to the police report, Sitoy, "who is determined to kill," was holding a hand grenade. Police said imminent danger to the public had prompted their officers to shoot.

The bomb squad extracted the fragmentation grenade from Sitoy's hand. Investigators confiscated two sachets of suspected meth and a fan knife. They reported that "a cursory examination of the cadaver showed gunshot wounds."

"We were the ones killing the addicts—the ones with bounties on their heads, the ones who were real criminals," said Simon. "But who ended up looking good in the news when people like Sitoy with his grenade were killed? The police. But they didn't kill him. We just called them whenever there was a body."

Four of my sources said that a certain police commander had ordered the extrajudicial killings of criminals and drug suspects from the last quarter of 2016 to early 2017.

I first heard the commander's name from a broadcast journalist. He was working at a television network and had been probing the CSG long before I picked up the story. His station had withdrawn its approval for the investigation. It was too dangerous, they said.

The reporter had managed one phone interview with a vigilante before the story was canceled. In the interview, the vigilante had named the police commander who gave Maning marching orders.

I was home the day I found out. The reporter was on the other end of the line, and I was pacing, hoping to find out who had ordered the killings.

"You know him, Pat," the reporter told me.

"I do?"

"The Station 1 chief," he said. "My source said it was Domingo who ordered them to kill."

If the CSG Chapter 2 killers were to be believed, my friend Domingo had outsourced murder to the vigilantes of Tondo. Simon said Domingo gave Commander Maning the target list. He said cops under PS-1 along Raxabago were also involved. Police would give vigilantes the all-clear whenever there was a job inside Tondo, "so we wouldn't accidentally shoot at each other."

"It was Domingo," said Angel. He later pointed to Domingo's face in photographs. "That's him."

The protocol was efficient. Whenever a target fell, Commander Maning would order one of the CSG members to pick up payment from Domingo. The instruction was to "get it from the chief."

"That meant money," said Angel. The funds would be divided among the kill team, after Commander Maning took his cut.

"Domingo was well known," said Angel. "People knew that if you got caught with drugs, you could pay to get out. Or if you were a snatcher, you could pay too. When it's Domingo, you could always get out."

There was a television news report after Sitoy was killed. Sitoy, the shotgun-carrying, grenade-tossing suspected meth addict whom Simon's team had shot in the ass. The report was broadcast in the morning and included an interview with the operating team's station commander.

"This one who died, the one with the grenade, he got himself trapped," said Lieutenant Colonel Robert Domingo, station commander of MPD PS-1. He looked into the camera. "He moved to pull the pin, so no choice. Our cops had no choice, right?"

I called Domingo when I was investigating the story. He picked up immediately. He had assumed I was calling about the secret jail. I told him I wasn't. He was pleasant, as always, friendly, as always, but refused to comment. "Maybe not, Trish," he said over the phone. I told him the accusations were specific and criminal. I said he shouldn't refuse to comment without knowing what the allegations were. He would get back to me, he said.

He messaged within the day. He had been advised not to comment. I asked for his email address, and sent him a long list of questions anyway.

He acknowledged receipt, but my friend Domingo never told me if he ordered the killings.

I had been attempting to interview Commander Maning for months. I sent intermediaries. I hired fixers. I extracted promises from local watchmen and clerks and the village captain, all of whom said Commander Maning could not be reached, was unavailable, maybe another time, yes, he might come by. Under no circumstances was Rappler willing to allow me to go personally into the tenements where we believed Commander Maning lived. I waited at the chairwoman's office and went home only after the sun began to set. Commander Maning did not appear.

Get out, my editor, Chay, would message. *It's getting dark. Don't risk it.*

I tried one last time. My flight out of the country was booked for the next day, the same day we published. We wanted to make sure I was out of reach.

I sent a message to a village hall clerk. It was a Hail Mary, nothing more.

You know, she texted back, *he might stop by today.*

I called Chay. Give me one more day, I said.

Just one more, she said.

I found him outside the village hall, just inside the grill gates. The Rappler car was still moving when I caught sight of him. I had seen him only in pictures, but in every picture, he stood the same way.

I leaped out of the car. The man in the yellow shirt was just pushing open the gate.

I was certain then. I am not a beat reporter. I have no expertise in the conduct of ambush interviews, have failed as often as I succeeded the few times that they were necessary. I was also uncomfortable at the thought of thrusting my recorder at an unsuspecting civilian who may or may not have been carrying a gun. None of it mattered, because this, finally, was Commander Maning.

"Sir," I said, and stepped into his path. He looked up. "Are you Ricardo Villamonte? Are you Commander Maning?"

Yes, he said.

He told me he had just taken his child to school. He was reluctant to speak. He tried to step around me, but I followed in an awkward tripping dance. He tried to get on his motorcycle. I smiled, and stood in front of the handlebars.

I told him I was a reporter. I asked if he could answer my questions. I pressed record. "We're on the record, sir. Were the police wrong in their accusations against you?"

"They were really wrong," he said. "We weren't doing anything. We were even helping them out. How come we're the bad guys now?"

"How about the cops? Didn't they push through with the charges against you?"

"It's gone. Our case was dismissed."

"Was that the case that Cristina Saladaga withdrew?"

He nodded.

"Okay. There are people who told us that the CSG are vigilantes. Is this true?"

"How can we be vigilantes? We're not going anywhere. We're not doing anything. We're just helping the village."

Yes, he said, he was part of CSG Tondo Chapter 2. Yes, it was a cop who had selected him to lead the chapter, for no other reason than that he was already the president of the Aroma tenement coordinators. Yes, he and his men helped patrol the village, but it was "for peace and order, so that there would be no snatchers and no riots, and we told off the ones who are trouble."

He had, in fact, been awarded for his work. Applauded. Recommended. Robert Domingo had signed Maning's certificate himself. It was a precinct commander under Domingo who had chosen Maning as leader. No, he had never been paid to kill. He had never been ordered to kill. He had never ordered anyone to kill. He said he had been dragged into the allegations, had nothing to do with any of it.

"Did they see anything?" Commander Maning asked me. "What right do we have to kill? We're not cops."

I gave him name after name of dead men.

Did you kill him?

This man?

That man?

I know nothing, he said. We know nothing. Ask the cops. No more questions. No comment.

"No comment on what, sir?"

"On everything that happened. No comment."

Ask the cops, he said again.

Then he swung a leg over his motorcycle and sped away.

Simon said the murder of Charlie Saladaga had been a mistake. "They should have surrendered him first," he said, "because even if you say he's a troublemaker, he didn't have a fighting chance. It's the drug lords we should have been killing. Those feel good to kill. The addicts, it feels good to kill them too. But the ones just taking drugs, they're just victims. Unless of course we catch you in the act taking drugs—that makes you a target."

In Village 105, talk of murder centered mostly on whether the dead deserved it. Sitoy had died because he was an addict and a hitman. Toyo had died because he was a drug dealer. Sixteen-year-old Charlie Saladaga had died "because he was a trouble-maker." His murder, which would later so outrage the generals in Camp Crame, caused little consternation among the members of CSG Tondo Chapter 2. The vigilantes called him a house-breaker, a thief, a young punk who did what he liked and felt up women when he could. "We caught him again and again, even before I was CSG," said Simon.

"It was nothing to them," said Angel. "The CSG were brag-ging. They were saying, 'Look what happened. Which punk is next? Who else is left?'"

Charlie had been warned, said the vigilantes. He was trouble, said the village captain. They were happy he was killed, said one clerk at the village hall. "Neighbors complained," said Angel. "He was stealing, snatching from people along the highway."

Charlie, they said, was personal business. Personal meant Charlie had never been part of the police kill list. It was a side job for CSG members. "Some neighbor was probably pissed because they lost a lot when Charlie stole from them," Angel said. "So they paid two, maybe three thousand pesos"—at most sixty dollars.

None of the killers had hidden their faces. "I told them that was their mistake," said Simon. "They should have known they would be recognized. 'Why'd you grab him without wearing masks?'"

In Tondo's Village 105, shanties built from plywood crowded each other inside the hollow shells of old tenements. Teenagers crouched sniffing solvent inside burnt-out buildings. Outside, on the sodden passages that passed for streets, piles of leftovers scavenged from the back alleys of fast-food joints were packaged for resale for about fifty pesos, or a dollar a bag. Village 105 was where a twenty-two-year-old could knife five people without once getting caught, and where a man could witness a murder one evening and get shot in his living room the next.

The elected village captain, Leny Reyes, said 105 was no more violent than other places in the country. "As our president said, 'If you want to change, go home to your provinces,'" said Reyes.

For Reyes, 105 had become a more peaceful place in the years since a strongman from the south took his seat in Malacañang Palace. She said she could count on one hand the number of people murdered in the last two years. "It's why we thank the president," she said. "We see how things got better here. He did a lot for us. Not that I think he can hear me, but big thanks to him. First to God, second to him."

Allegations that an active vigilante team had been operating unchecked under Reyes's watch aroused little concern.

"What they're saying, about the killers, yes, there were killers," Reyes told me. "But there are snakes everywhere, aren't there? Even in Makati City or other places, they're there. That's why I said, when night comes, people should be inside their homes. If you have nothing to do, don't wander around. That's what I say. God made the night for sleep, the day to work, right? So things like that wouldn't happen if people just stayed quiet in their own homes."

While Reyes was vague about her relationship with Commander Maning and the rest of CSG Tondo Chapter 2, she was clear where she thought blame for the death of Charlie Saladaga lay.

His death, said Reyes, was his mother's own fault. "Let me tell you about that boy," Reyes began.

In December 2016, by Reyes's reckoning, Charlie and at least two of his friends had broken into the home of a local village official. According to Reyes, the young men stole computers and "everything they could get their hands on." The teenagers were caught, but Charlie managed to escape.

Reyes has four sons, all of them professionals, all college graduates, all employed, one of them working at Stanford Hospital in the United States, another a nurse in Norway. It all depends on the parents, she said. Living in Tondo doesn't mean being immersed in drugs and violence.

"Sometimes it's the mother, she's negligent," she said. "You need to look after your kids."

Had Cristina Saladaga been a dutiful mother, said Reyes, Charlie would be alive.

Rappler published the story as a seven-part series titled "Murder in Manila" in late 2018. I did not interview Charlie's mother or the rest of his family. They had gone into hiding.

"Isn't it strange," Simon asked me, "that it's the families of the dead who have to run?"

I never saw Simon again. He left the hotel room at a little before seven in the evening. He had a job, he said. The cops were coming. He didn't want to be late.

I met Cristina Saladaga more than a year after her son's death, in a damp shanty in another city in the national capital region. The roof leaked, but her photocopied court testimony was safe in a plastic envelope.

The last time Cristina saw her son, it was New Year's Day, 2017. Charlie had hauled the family off to Luneta Park, where crowds gathered to watch the city's fireworks display. The whole family went, even Charlie's father, whom they thought was too drunk to go. They watched the singing, saw the bright lights. Charlie fell asleep on the parade grounds. They went home at dawn, laughing, after shaking Charlie awake. He went back to sleep at home.

When he awoke in the morning, he stripped off his shirt and slipped out the door, telling his mother he would be back after a computer game. He left his slippers at the door. At noon Cristina sent Charlie's little sister Exmila out to look for him. I'm still playing, he said when she found him. Don't wait for me. They didn't look for him again until dusk, when Exmila stepped out and found her brother at the market surrounded by men. She saw them drag him away. She knew them, most of them. CSG Chapter 2 members, armed men, one of them Commander Maning.

"How did you recognize them?" I asked. "Did you know them from before?"

"Yes," she told me. "They're the ones who kill us."

Charlie, she said, looked scared.

The men told Exmila to go home, and she did. She told her mother nothing. She told me she was scared.

Cristina looked for her son. Filed a missing persons report. Hunted for him at the government welfare desks. Went to Maning, once, twice, because she had heard from Charlie's friend that Maning and the CSG had been seen with her son. Maning said they had let Charlie go and hadn't seen him again. She sent her eldest son, Cristopher, off to the funeral parlors, and he came back with no news. After Charlie disappeared, there was word about a body. A child in a sack, out in the breakwater, dead.

Cristina went to the cops then, to the homicide desk. They showed her a picture—the inside of a sack, and a barefoot boy wearing the shorts her Charlie had worn. Her husband went to the morgue and found their boy, a hole in his face, just under the left eye. She went back to the cops. She got lucky, she said, because the man she talked to was a good cop. His name was Major Rosalino Ibay, then head of the District Intelligence and Operations Unit. He listened; he asked how she knew it was the CSG responsible. She said she had heard it from someone who had heard about it too. It was in his office that Exmila finally told her mother what she saw.

"Ma, they took him."

"Who took your brother?" Cristina asked.

"It was them—it was them."

"Who?"

"It was the CSG, Mama."

It came out, all at once. How her brother had been taken. How she had seen who took him. How the CSG had sent her home, telling her not to speak. And then word had spread, that the Saladagas knew, that the Saladagas had gone to the authorities, that they were going to talk.

"They came to our home, ma'am, so many of them," Cristina told me. "They came to the house."

"To the house in the tenements?"

"Yes. They brought guns."

They were having dinner. Cristina remembered the corned beef and rice. It was past eight in the evening. They came all at once, men and women both, all armed, more than a dozen of them lining the sides of the narrow apartment. Cristina knew some of them by name. She knew Maning. She knew the man in the baseball cap and the other with a .45 pistol. She saw the guns aimed at her family and felt the food go sideways in her throat. They were looking for her other son, her Cristopher.

They said they had heard the family was blaming the CSG for Charlie's death. They said they had killed Charlie, and they would kill Cristopher too.

She told them her boy was with his girlfriend, in another building. Go to him, she said, and when they left, she rushed out the door trailing one daughter, out the building, down the alleys, out to the highway, where they waited for Cristopher. And then they ran.

In the aftermath of the press conference at Camp Crame, those who escaped the police raid lay low. They were afraid of arrest. The vigilantes hauled their guns everywhere, even to the shower, where they bathed with their pistols wrapped in towels. Police released statements that "a hot pursuit was immediately conducted" against Commander Maning.

"That's when I lost heart," Simon said. "We don't have a salary, we're volunteers, and if we die, we get nothing. It's our parents who'll have to pay for our funerals. I know [General dela Rosa] knew about us. But he was on TV. Of course, he wanted to be a star."

Dela Rosa told me that while he was unaware of any allegations that CSG Chapter 2 vigilantes were under police orders, it did not make sense for police to arrest vigilantes they actively colluded with.

Were it true, he said, it would have been "foolish" for the PNP to arrest its own hitmen. "That would have gotten them implicated," Dela Rosa said.

On the day Cristina Saladaga was meant to appear before the prosecutor, she retracted her sworn statement, including the complaint of murder and kidnapping that she had filed against men who had already confessed to the assassination of her son. In her affidavit of withdrawal, she explained that she had been "thinking repeatedly about the events" leading up to Charlie's death. She asked to "dismiss all charges of kidnapping with homicide and murder" against all the men implicated. She said she had come to realize that the entire complaint was the result of "a misunderstanding."

More than a year after the charges were dismissed, I spoke to Rosalino Ibay, Cristina's good cop, who had investigated the CSG before he led the raid of the CSG outpost. There was justice in solving the case, he said, but justice had "not prevailed." He did not believe police officers had been working with the CSG. His tactical interview with the suspects resulted in only Commander Maning's name—"It just so happened," he said, "that the Station 1 Commander at the time of the raid was Sir Robert Domingo."

Late one night in 2019, a year after I released the story, a few months after I found Cristina, I got a call from a source. Get to the police station, I was told. The cops had taken Cristopher. Cristina was at the station with her daughter.

Go, the caller said. Make noise. Throw your weight around. Tell the cops you're doing a story. Tell them you're watching.

I pulled on my boots, grabbed my recorder, and called for my photographer.

Cristina was outside the station. She believed Cristopher had been tortured. She said he was being prepared for release. She was sure he would be salvaged before dawn.

Please, she said.

I spoke to the sergeant. I took down his name. I chattered away at men on duty, flashed my ID, told them the sad story of a terrified mother and the boy she had lost. Cristopher was fine, they said. Cristopher was safe. I asked them to let Cristina see her son. "Just to reassure the mother," I said, smiling. They let her see him through the grills.

A pseudo-event is not spontaneous. It exists primarily for the purpose of being reported. It has an ambiguous relationship to reality. It is, when successful, a self-fulfilling prophecy.

Cristina was still inside the station when I left. She refused to go home. The sergeant offered her water and a bench to sit on. I waved goodbye. The sergeant waved back.

11

DJASTIN WITH A D

WITNESS: NESTOR LOPEZ, UNCLE

Tondo, Manila

PAT: Is it true the cops were kicking him?

NESTOR: Yes.

PAT: Can you tell me what happened?

NESTOR: They would shoot him, then slap him, then kick him. Then they would shoot him again, then slap him again. Three cops were taking turns.

The head count would start at one and end at nine. JR first, then Djastin, Otil, Jesy, Jopet, Eray, BL, and Luinor, all the way to little Igiboy, one through nine, every night, for years. Less than nine, and Lito Lopez was out in the alley, calling out names, sending one teenager in pursuit of another until he was satisfied where each of his nine were.

The count changed the older they got. Sons and daughters moved in and out and back again, trailing girlfriends and boyfriends and a steady stream of toddlers tumbling in their wake. Nine became eleven, became twelve, thirteen. Nobody got married, although it was understood that when someone moved in, that someone was considered husband or wife.

One night, sometime in late 2017, Lito began counting again. The count was loud, because Lito was drunk. Even as he slurred and stumbled, he remembered which daughter had moved out, and which son had brought in his woman. He knew his youngest had decided to move in with a godfather. He accounted for the four grandchildren who had decided to sleep with their grandma.

Lito remembered all of it, except for one fact. He turned around and around in the tiny house, peering into bunk beds, pulling up blankets.

Djastin, he called out. Has anyone seen Djastin?

He roused one of the older boys. Go to the railroad tracks, he said. Tell Djastin to come home.

His wife, Normy, asked Lito if he had gone mad.

Djastin, she told him, was dead.

The Lopezes lived in the slums of Tondo, on a chunk of land bisected by railroad tracks and lively with extended families. The houses slouched behind a row of warehouses with narrow alleys just wide enough to drive a motorcycle. A single two-way road opened at the mouth of the slums, feeding straight to the main thoroughfare of Jose Abad Santos Avenue, the snarl of traffic lined with a McDonald's, a Shakey's, and the showrooms of Honda, Nissan, and Mitsubishi.

Sometime in the 1980s, the seventy-five-square-meter lot that the Lopezes occupied had been a two-floor rooming house.

In those days, the family patriarch, Lito's father Cornelio, was running a business that involved room rentals, passenger jeepneys, a small grocery, a glassware shop, and the export of shaped and polished tin. Cornelio was past master of the art of turning out tin pots, cake pans, and ice buckets. He included among his triumphs the shining torch carried by no less than Miss Universe herself during the Marcos-sponsored beauty pageants that were a constant in the 1970s.

It is unclear whether the turn in the family fortunes was the result of a fire back in the 1980s, or whether Cornelio—his opinion muttered to anyone within earshot—was right in that it was due to having to feed several dozen human beings.

In the years since, four ramshackle homes had risen on the scorched property. Each was an irregularly shaped single-story room. Three of them opened into one alley. Cornelio and his wife, Gloria, lived in one home with two of their grown sons. Another son lived behind them, and Gloria's nephew just next door. The smallest home belonged to Lito and Normy, where they lived with their children and their children's children, a household of sixteen people in all, babies included.

The Lopezes shared the single toilet inside Cornelio's home, flushing with a dipper of water collected in the early morning. They shared a single prepaid power account, whose reference number—a twelve-digit code that Normy recited every day—was necessary in the topping up of the dollar's worth of electricity each household required. They shared work, most of the men scraping tin whenever Cornelio had clients. They shared food, served out of big open pots.

In all, twenty-eight members of the Lopez family, ranging from two years old to eighty-two, lived shoulder to sweaty shoulder in four boxes each roughly the size of a standard parking space. They lived beside call center agents and electricians, bookies and bodega owners. Avon ladies moonlighted as fish ball vendors. Grandchildren wandered door to door, clambering into laps, pulling coins out of pockets, curling into whatever corner had an electric fan running.

Djastin Lopez, pronounced *Jastin*—"I wanted his name to be special," said his mother, "so he got a silent D"—was born on New Year's Eve 1991 to Normy and Lito Lopez.

Djastin had his first seizure at four years old. Normy carried him through a Manila flood straight to a hospital emergency room. Doctors ran a gamut of tests and diagnosed him with epilepsy.

Every epileptic attack was the same. Djastin's arms jerked. His teeth chattered. His eyes rolled to the back of his head—*tumirik* in Filipino. It gave Djastin his nickname. "Tirek!" his younger sister would shout.

They took him to the public hospital every time he convulsed, until a doctor taught Normy what to do when he began seizing. Keep him cool. Give him space. Put a wrapped spoon between his teeth. Wipe him down with a damp towelette. Fan him while he rides out the spasms.

Djastin grew up under the bright sun of his mother's affection and prescription phenobarbital when she could afford it. He dropped out of school in the third grade, after one teacher, terrified he would die on the classroom floor, had suggested homeschooling instead. Djastin agreed. He said staring at the blackboard gave him headaches. He learned at home instead and could be counted on to read passages from the family's pocket-sized Bible.

He was a good son, they said, even with the drugs. He fell in with the local boys, who taught him what marijuana could do. His family was uncertain where or when he learned to use meth, only that he did.

His mother lectured Djastin. His father warned him. His

grandfather found all manner of other work to keep him busy, so Djastin made his money running errands for the tin business. He was arrested once, just after he turned twenty, caught in the net of an antidrug operation targeting one of his friends. He was released on bail one year later. The case was dismissed.

Djastin went home, to his mother and father and the girl-friend he called his wife. He was a father of two by the age of twenty-one. He was good with children. His smiles were rare, but he often broke into a laugh dandling one or the other of his nieces on his lap.

He was twenty-four years old the year Rodrigo Duterte was elected. The Lopezes did not vote for the mayor from the south, but they weren't particularly afraid, even when the newly inaugurated president appeared at a basketball court nearby to threaten his people with summary execution.

The stories began trickling into Tondo. This man killed in a police operation. That man salvaged by vigilantes. That boy who was shot as his mother ran for help. Djastin's family worried. Djastin said it was all right. He might have been using crystal meth, but he was no dealer.

Djastin was at home in the early afternoon of May 18, 2017. He was slow that day, tired. Seizures had sent him to bed, and it had only been a day since the last convulsion.

His mother, Normy, heard his phone beep.

"Later," Djastin typed. "I'm resting, and we're eating."

He climbed up to the upper bunk bed and slept tangled with his girlfriend. Normy arranged herself on the lower bunk, half-asleep herself.

Djastin's phone rang from the top bunk.

"Who is this?"

A pause.

"Why? What do you need?"

He clicked off. He told his mother it was someone asking him to come by the railroad tracks.

Sleep, she said. Stay home.

He promised he would.

The text alerts kept coming, beep after beep.

"It's nobody," Djastin told his girlfriend. "All these numbers sending texts and calling. I don't know any of them."

Finally, at four p.m., Djastin climbed down and said he was going out for a snack. He put on a yellow Nike T-shirt. He had several, all knockoffs in a rainbow of colors.

Djastin's girlfriend left the house. Normy had a telenovela she wanted to watch and walked to her father-in-law, Cornelio's, home, where he had the working television that day. Cornelio stopped Djastin on his way out. He handed his grandson money, down payment from a client to purchase aluminum. Djastin was to commute to the supplier in another city.

Do it quickly, Cornelio said.

Djastin left. Normy sat down to watch her show. She was still watching television when Djastin's grandmother Gloria sent her son Nestor after Djastin.

The railroad tracks ran across a grassy field, two turns and a five-minute walk from the Lopez home. Shanties lined both sides.

It was near dark. Men "who looked like cops" appeared along the tracks. One woman, a vendor who was looking for her children, swore she saw one of them aim a gun at Djastin.

Djastin, she said, had raised his arms.

Please, he had said, don't shoot. Please don't shoot.

·   ·   ·

Djastin's uncle Nestor stood a few meters away. He had followed Djastin on his mother's orders but he froze in place when the cops burst past him.

He saw a young man running.

He saw the raised gun. He heard the pistol bark.

Nestor Lopez did not realize it was his nephew who had fallen, only that someone was shot, and that someone did not scream when the cop shot him in the chest.

Djastin's eyes rolled back. His body jerked. His mother would have known what to do, would have fanned his face and put a wrapped spoon between his teeth and wiped him down with a damp towelette until he rode out the spasms.

But there was no Normy. There was only the cop, who reared back and slapped Djastin Lopez in the face.

"They shot him after they slapped him," Nestor said.

The cop shot Djastin again, slapped him, kicked him, and shot him again, heavy palm smacking into juddering cheek, the bullets ripping holes the size of a toddler's thumbnail quadrant by skinny quadrant, bang into the right pectoral, into the left abdomen, into the epigastric, the heavy slugs ripping open lung and muscle and liver and kidney and heart. His chest filled with blood. His organs congested. The fish balls he had eaten only hours before sat heavy in his gut.

He was twenty-five years old.

At forty minutes past six in the evening, a blotter entry was filed on the logbook of Manila Police District Station 7 Jose Abad Santos (PS-7). It noted a phone call from the field about a "police operation along railroad track," and the subsequent dispatch of the station duty investigator.

Normy was sitting outside Cornelio's house. Another of Djastin's uncles came running.

Quick, he said, call Djastin.

She couldn't. Her phone was broken.

That uncle ran back to the tracks. He returned in minutes. "Tirek is gone," he said. "They killed him. They shot him."

Normy ran. Her children leaped up to join her. JR, the hairdresser. BL, the gambler. Lui, her little girl, raced to the tracks on her own. No, Normy said, it wasn't Djastin, couldn't have been Djastin. She caught the sleeves of neighbors scuttling into their houses.

What was the dead man wearing? she demanded. Tell me what he was wearing.

Gray, they said.

Not Djastin, she panted, relieved. Yellow, she repeated to herself. He was wearing a yellow Nike T-shirt.

They raced to the railroad tracks. A crowd had formed. Cops lined both sides of the tracks. A handful of civilians sat on the grass, under guard.

Normy tried to push past the cops.

"You can't go there," one of them said.

She asked them why. She told them she wanted to know if it was her son lying on the grass.

No, said the cop. Stay out of it.

She wept and pleaded. She asked what the man was wearing. She asked about his shorts. Camo, someone said. Yellow and green.

She sagged. Those were his shorts. Maybe it was someone else. Same shorts, wrong shirt, it couldn't be, it might have been.

She ran again, burst past the cops. She got close enough to see a body, but it was dark, and her eyes were bad.

A flashlight winked on.

It was one of Normy's sons who said it.

"Mama, it's him."

Around them was whispered murmuring, the story passed on, lips to ear, the words louder at each iteration until it exploded out of fifteen-year-old BL Lopez.

"You sons of bitches, you killed my brother! You slapped him and shot him, you heartless bastards! He would have been dead with one shot! One shot, he was so skinny! Why did you have to keep shooting my brother?"

Normy hushed him.

He wouldn't hush. "You think you're the shit with your guns. What if you didn't have guns? I wish my brother had a gun too. He would have taken you down with him."

The cops heard him.

One of them turned. "Fucking idiot," he said. "You want me to send you after your brother?"

The funeral parlor's van waited behind Normy, called in by the cops. She didn't want to give up the body. If it really was Djastin, she told the police, she wanted to choose who handled his body. She was a practical woman, despite the grief and confusion. She knew the cost of burial in the hands of the cops' favorite morticians.

I want my own funeral parlor, she said. Please, give me that much.

They told her she needed signed paperwork from the village captain.

JR, her eldest boy, held Normy steady. Go, he told her. I'll take care of this.

She left. Don't let them take him, she said.

The body was zipped into a bag and loaded onto a stretcher.

Cornelio heard about the shooting too, and when he did, he ran. Cornelio, a former boxer, all wiry sinew and beetling eyebrows, whose eighty-year-old grip bent sheets of aluminum daily, pushed through the crowd and snatched the edge of the stretcher. Had Cornelio been younger by twenty years, by thirty, he would have left the cops where they were. Cornelio Lopez wasn't an idiot. No, he would have gone home to borrow a gun. Then he would have walked back into the circle of yellow tape. He would have been quiet. He wouldn't have said a word. And he would have executed the son of a bitch who killed his boy.

Instead, Cornelio held on to the stretcher where his grandson lay.

You can't have my boy, he said.

A cop turned. Big man, with big hands.

He seized Cornelio's arm. Shoved a hard elbow into Cornelio's chest.

Cornelio nearly fell.

The cop pulled out a .45 pistol.

The crowd began shouting, "Why'd you have to hurt the old man?"

Cornelio staggered upright.

"Had Djastin gotten sick and died, it wouldn't have hurt so much," he told me later. "But son of a bitch—one, two, three, four, five, six, seven, eight. Eight gunshots until ten, maybe more than ten. They just went at him, son of a bitch. Even a buffalo wouldn't have survived that."

Normy found the village captain. He signed the papers. He promised the body would be released to the family. She raced back, stopping only at her own front door, where Lito sat weeping with all the other children.

By the time she made it back to the tracks, the cops were gone. Cornelio, raving, had been led off by neighbors.

Nobody knew where the body had been taken. Normy and her sons hailed tricycles, trudged up and down Severino Street, knocked at funeral parlor doors.

No, sorry, not here, sorry.

She tottered down the stretch of road, convinced, in spite of evidence to the contrary, that her son was still alive. She wept. She screamed. A stranger took pity on her, told her there was another funeral parlor she could visit, just off Lardizabal Street.

She walked into the office of Archangel Funeral Homes and asked if a body had come in from the railroad tracks.

There was, the clerk confirmed. But no, Normy wasn't allowed to see him.

She took JR's phone. Please, she asked one of the morticians. Take a picture.

The mortician returned.

It was then, holding the phone with the picture of her dead son's face, that Normy believed.

The earliest police report, filed the same day and prepared by PS-7 chief station commander Alex Daniel, described the incident that killed Djastin Lopez as an "armed encounter."

The report was brief. A police team had been conducting anti-illegal drugs operations at the railroad tracks on or about 6:35 p.m. in Tondo, Manila, when a police officer "spotted a male person acting suspiciously."

There was no description of the suspicious activity, but it had been reason enough for Police Staff Sergeant Gerry Geñalope of the Station Drug Enforcement Unit "to accost the suspect."

At his approach, "the latter pulled his firearms and shot the police officers twice but missed."

The death on the tracks was summarized in a single sentence: The officer "returned fire using service firearm [to] defend himself and his team that resulted to the death of the suspect."

Geñalope was described as both complainant and victim.

"Upon verification," wrote the PS-7 chief, "the above-named suspect is listed on our Drugs Watchlist Personalities and suspect for killing of Michael Turla y Panganiban, transpired on May 14, 2017, at about 1:30 p.m." Turla was a thirty-nine-year-old who had been found murdered on the railroad tracks four days before Djastin was killed. Turla's live-in girlfriend had woken up to gunshots and went out to see her partner dead on his back. Cartridges from two different pistols were found at the scene. There were no initial witnesses. Perpetrators were only described as "two unidentified malefactors both armed with unknown type of firearms." Investigators pointed to Turla's alleged involvement in illegal drug activities as a possible motive. He had previously been jailed.

Police, in explaining Djastin Lopez's killing, named him a suspect in Michael Turla's murder.

Homicide had assigned a case investigator, who generated his own report dated the same day of the killing. The "fatality," Djastin, was "lying on his back on the railroad track covered with his own blood."

The homicide investigator's report expanded on the Michael Turla connection. The investigator said the police team had stumbled upon a suspicious character they later discovered was a murder suspect. Moreover, he claimed, the operation that had killed Djastin Lopez was a targeted maneuver, "an Anti-Criminality Operation and Follow-up Operation" seeking the apprehension of one Justin Cacay Lopez, aka Tirek, "who was then a suspect in the killing of Michael Turla."

Investigators said the murder suspect had been seen sitting on the railroad tracks. Police Staff Sergeant Gerry Geñalope had "notic[ed] the presence" of the suspect while simultaneously introducing himself as a police officer.

The suspect had "pushed away" Geñalope.

The suspect had been "able to evade arrest."

The suspect "immediately" drew out a firearm and fired, missing Geñalope, who, "sensing his life [was] in total jeopardy," had no other choice "but to fire back against his armed aggressor, who sustained gunshot wounds and fell on the ground." Geñalope then "promptly approached" the suspect, intending to bring him to the hospital.

The suspect "aimed his firearm and fired another shot."

Thus, wrote the homicide department of the Manila Police District, "Geñalope had no other recourse but to protect his life and retaliate."

The suspect "died on the spot."

The report enumerated all the evidence found at the scene. It described the gun that was allegedly found in the suspect's possession—a .45-caliber pistol, serial number 297076, with live ammunition loaded in one chamber—as well as five cartridge cases, three bullets from a 9-millimeter pistol, and a heat-sealed plastic sachet containing a white crystalline substance suspected to be crystal meth.

On June 9, less than a month after the incident at the railroad tracks, the Crimes Against Persons Investigation Section of the Manila Police District released a progress report on the death of Djastin Lopez. "This pertains to the buy-bust operation turned shooting incident resulting in the neutralization of an alleged drug suspect."

On paper, the antidrug operation that turned fatal because of a suspect's sudden "suspicious activities" evolved into a drug buy-bust operation. Djastin the suspicious actor was discovered to be Djastin the murder suspect before becoming Djastin the drug suspect. Nowhere in the reports was there mention of a poseur-buyer, a consummated operation, or money that exchanged hands. There was also, in the end, no mention of a dead man named Michael Turla.

I first met the Lopez family at Djastin's wake, a little more than a week after he was killed. I knew nothing of the police narrative when I stood in front of his casket. Most of us on the night shift were already struggling to access police reports. The two-page documents that had previously been so ubiquitous had become almost as rare as CCTV video footage. What used to be a straightforward request, journalist to cop, had become a convoluted bureaucratic process that was likely to be refused—especially, it seemed, if the request appeared under the Rappler letterhead.

We began relying on the families for documents. The Lopezes attempted to access a copy, but were told they needed to provide death certificates and autopsy reports first. On the day Djastin was buried, the Lopezes knew nothing of the police narrative, had read no official report, were uncertain, in fact, as to whether Djastin had been shot by police at all. They had suspected Djastin's death would be justified by charges of resisting arrest, as had happened with hundreds of drug suspects killed by police. They did not know their dead son had been accused of murder, post-mortem.

It also meant that none of them knew the killer's name.

Cornelio wanted to challenge the killer to a duel. "Call in your second," he muttered as he puttered around his home. "I'll look for a gun and you bring yours."

Djastin's coffin lay on a street close to the family's home. Laundry hung in lines just beside the body. A tarp hung on a makeshift oilcloth wall, printed with a pixelized picture of an unsmiling Djastin, his face floating beside the Virgin Mary's on a bank of clouds. The dates of his birth and death were italicized in blue. Over it all was the logo of the funeral parlor, along with the name, address, and multiple phone numbers of SRB Sanctuary Chapel.

The funeral parlor staff loaded Djastin's coffin into the back of a black SUV. The village hall sent an official vehicle. Djastin's sisters combed their hair, slicked on lipstick, and held on to their small children. The vehicles moved slowly as the mourners walked beside the short convoy. Rap music played on a mobile speaker.

Djastin's father, Lito, shuffled behind the funeral car. He kept his hands pressed flat against the bumper, wrists rigid, forehead knitted in concentrated effort. That the vehicle was powered by an engine was irrelevant. Lito was going to push his son's coffin all the way to the North Cemetery, and no one could stop him.

The Lopezes secured a letter from the Commission on Human Rights supporting their request for a copy of Djastin's police report. The report was released.

It named the suspect as Justin Cacay Lopez, twenty-three years old, single, and jobless. That "Justin" had been twenty-five at the time of his death was only one of the errors.

"We told them, that's not my son's name," Normy said. "You caught him, killed him, and you misspelled his name. Maybe you were looking for the wrong man. That's what Lito told them. Maybe you were looking for a different Justin, not him."

The Lopezes filed a request to correct Djastin's name. The request was later noted on a police progress report. "Moreover, Mr. Luisito Lopez signifies his intent to rectify the name of the deceased read as JUSTIN LOPEZ y CACAY to read as DJAS-TIN LOPEZ y BACCAY."

Normy laughed. It was not a happy laugh.

"I said, gee, didn't they do a good job? They killed my son and didn't know what his name was. The name they knew was Justin. And Cacay, not Baccay. Who is this Cacay?"

Normy Lopez filed a murder complaint at the Office of the Ombudsman in September 2017, with counsel from the National Union of Peoples' Lawyers. She began to volunteer with the group Rise Up for Human Rights. She spoke at protests. She wrote a poem, published by the papers, called "My Most Beloved Son"—a title that caused more than a little consternation among her eight surviving children.

"He was the sick one," she explained. "He needed me the most."

Threats, or what Normy considered threats, came in the immediate aftermath.

It started with Luinor, called Lui, the eighth child and youngest daughter, who had been thirteen and in eighth grade when Djastin was killed. Word of Normy suing the police had spread throughout the village.

Lui was on the street, running errands for Normy, when a

man walked up to her and asked her for directions. Beside him were some other men, in police uniform.

Do you know a Normita Lopez? the man asked.

No, Louie said.

She was sure the man didn't know who she was. It was just chance that he had asked Normy's daughter about Normy. Lui walked away, carefully casual. When she was sure she was out of their sight, she ran, skidding down the alley, looking over her shoulder, afraid men would be racing behind her.

Normy was asleep beside one of her grandchildren when Lui burst in and slammed the front door shut.

"Mama, Mama, they're coming to kill you!"

She threw herself over her mother and sobbed.

"Who said?" Normy asked. "Who's going to kill me?"

The cops, said Lui.

Normy was at home that night, putting one of her grandchildren to sleep. It was past nine. The television was still on, but everyone else was in bed.

The front door was ajar. Normy looked up. Two faces were pressed against the opening, watching her.

She had never seen them before.

Yes? she called out.

Nothing, one of them said. We're garbage collectors.

No garbage collectors had ever appeared outside her front door. Trash was collected at the mouth of the alley, and certainly not at nine in the evening.

The faces disappeared.

She locked the door and prayed.

In the aftermath, Lui, who had long been going to school alone, insisted that her mother walk with her, and be there, outside, every afternoon. She began to suspect every unknown man and every uniformed security guard. Might be a cop, she would tell her mother. "Ma, I'm scared," she would say. "They might be looking at me." Eventually she refused to attend school. She trailed her mother everywhere. She was afraid to leave her mother alone. She didn't know what she could do if the cops came, only that she wanted to be there. "I thought maybe I could save Mama," she said.

The Lopezes didn't buy newspapers, but one day Normy picked up a tabloid that someone had left outside their house. She read the back page—"I always start with the puzzles"—and made her way through the paper.

"Before I made it to the first page, I saw it," she said. "There was news about an epileptic who had died in an extrajudicial killing. So I read it. It was him. I asked, where did this come from? I wondered how it had happened, where did that come from? I didn't know how that newspaper got here. . . . I still wonder."

The tabloids weren't alone in picking up Djastin Lopez's story.

"New Win vs. Tokhang," wrote Rappler. "Ombudsman Orders Murder Charges vs. Manila Cop."

"Grieving Poet-Mother Gets Sliver of Victory as Ombudsman Orders Dismissal of 'Tokhang Cop,'" wrote ABS-CBN.

"Cop Axed for Killing Epileptic in 'Drug Raid,'" headlined the *Philippine Daily Inquirer*.

The *Inquirer*'s story included a quotation from President Duterte's spokesperson. "We welcome it," Salvador Panelo said, "as President Duterte says, his administration will not tolerate abuse on the part of police officers."

The official document arrived in March 2019, almost two

years after Djastin Lopez was killed, via registered mail from the Office of the Ombudsman.

It was addressed to Ms. Normita Lopez.

The ten-page joint resolution decided on OMB-P-C-17-0388 (for Murder and Planting of Evidence of Illegal Drugs and Firearms) and OMB-P-A-17-0461 (for Grave Abuse of Authority, Grave Misconduct, Oppression and Conduct Unbecoming of a Public Officer), both cases filed by Normita B. Lopez, Complainant, against Police Captain Jojo Salanguit, Police Staff Sergeant Gerry G. Geñalope, and 14 John Does, all of the Station Enforcement Unit of Police Station 7, Jose Abad Santos Avenue, Manila Police District.

Charges were dismissed against all but one of the respondents.

"Wherefore, let an information for Murder be FILED against respondent Police Staff Sergeant GERRY G GEÑALOPE before the proper court."

It was the first reported resolution from the Philippine Office of the Ombudsman against a member of the police force operating during the war on drugs.

The resolution also found Geñalope guilty of grave misconduct. The penalties were dismissal from the police service, cancellation of public service eligibility, forfeiture of retirement benefits, and perpetual disqualification to hold public office.

On the day Normy Lopez received her certified copy, she and Lito made the trip to the North Cemetery, where Normy proceeded, page by page, to read the decision out loud to the son buried under a bright blue marker. She wept as she read.

She told Djastin that Geñalope was no longer a cop. It wasn't enough, but the murder case still lay ahead. She wanted Geñalope in jail, and while she wished all the other officers had been charged too, she still looked forward to meeting them face-to-face. She wanted to ask them why they did it, why they shot her son who had his hands up.

If Geñalope went to jail, she would visit him every day, if only to make sure he was still behind bars.

The first attempt to offer a settlement was directed at Lito.

There was a meeting, arranged by the village captains. One spoke on Geñalope's behalf and made an offer of money. Lito said he would consider it. He said the decision was his wife's, not his. He went home and told Normy.

No, she said. Absolutely not. "Tell them we'll settle if you can give back my son's life," she told him. "That's fine with me. Give me back my son's life. They can keep the money if they can give me back my son's life."

The second settlement offer was delivered by another cop, a friend of Geñalope's.

The cop called Lito and told him to go to a billiard hall. Normy followed him and brought her youngest with her. Keep watch, Normy told Igiboy. Igiboy was twelve and armed. He carried a wooden stick, to spank anyone who threatened his father.

They trailed Lito to a street corner. They saw the cop approach. Lito stood listening as the cop talked. They were ten or a dozen steps away. Normy strained, but tricycles were rattling, and cars were honking, and she couldn't hear a word.

The conversation ended. Lito walked away. He didn't see Normy.

"Love!" she called out, as loud as she dared.

He stopped. So did passersby. She blushed, embarrassed.

They walked home together. He told her that the cop had repeated the settlement offer.

It's there, the cop told him. Take it. There's nothing else you can do.

Lito answered the same way he had answered the village captain. He would think about it, but the decision was his wife's.

She was outraged. "I got angry at Lito when he told me," Normy said to me. "Why didn't you tell them? You should have told them, 'See you in court.' That's what I always tell him. If someone comes up again, just tell them, 'See you in court.'"

The third and final offer came from a retired police officer. He was an older man, a family friend who used to go to the horse races with Lito.

Come, said the message, but don't go inside yet.

They found out why soon enough. Geñalope, they were told, was inside the cop's house. The cop came out and explained that a settlement would be better, that the money for the legal battle could go to the Lopezes instead.

Lito went in. Geñalope was gone, but there was an offer, a large amount.

Normy apologized to the retired cop for his trouble. "Tell them I won't withdraw the case," she told him. "We're talking about a life here. My son's life. Can any amount of money bring him back? Of course not. So I'll fight it out in court, whatever the outcome." She told him the amount didn't matter. She told him she couldn't accept money at all. She told him Geñalope and the rest should suffer for what they had done.

"Maybe it would have been okay if my son hadn't surrendered," she told me. "His arms were raised, and they still shot him. And they weren't happy with just that, they shot him again and again after. I said, 'One gunshot to that son of mine, that skinny boy, he would have died with one, but they battered him with bullets.' "

She told the cop there would never be a settlement.

The old cop said he understood.

I heard the story days later, sitting on the cramped floor of the Lopez home across from Normy, recorder blinking red, notebook in hand. Lito sat beside her.

That final offer wasn't the end of the story, she said. "I need to tell you about Lito."

Lito blinked.

"He got angry with me," Normy said. " 'Why did you answer that way?' That's what he told me."

"Who told you?" I asked.

"This one."

This one was Lito, sitting quietly beside Normy.

"He got angry at me. He said, 'Why did you—why did you say that? You should have said you'd think about it.' I told him, 'Why would I think about it?' I was crying then. 'Why would I think about it?' I asked him. 'This is your son's life we're talking about, you son of a bitch.' People were staring at us already. 'You money-grubbing son of a bitch, you animal,' I told him. We were in Divisoria Market, and I was yelling at him. Louie was telling me people were staring. 'Well fuck him!' I said. 'He's only after the money. His son is dead and he'll trade him for money. It's easy to earn money.' I was so angry."

It's a lot of money, I said.

"I don't need money!" Normy began to cry. "Whatever happens we'll have food every day. But not my son."

Lito sat staring at the floor, big hands on his lap.

I asked him the next question. "What did you tell her?"

"Nothing," he said.

"He was angry," Normy interrupted. "He was cursing at me too. He was angry."

"Do you still want the money?" I asked Lito.

"So I messaged the lawyers," Normy continued. "And I complained about what he did—"

"No," Lito answered me. "It's up to her."

"—and I told them what he said, and that's why the lawyer talked to him after. Fine, you take the money," Normy ended, with a glare at Lito.

"No," he said. He shrugged, still not looking up. "What she wants goes for me."

"I'm not changing my mind," Normy said.

Their children, said Lito, had advised him to accept the settlement. One of their sons said it was for their future.

"What if Normy says no?" I asked Lito.

"Then there's nothing we can do," he answered.

Another voice broke in, sharp and angry. "Can I just say something?"

I had forgotten Eray, who had been listening to the interview. Eray was twenty, the Lopezes' sixth child. She had been sitting outside the circle of Normy and Lito and myself.

Yes, I told her. Go ahead.

"What if one of us is killed?"

"Nothing will happen to you," Normy said. "I filed the case already."

I turn to Eray. "Are you afraid?"

"Yes," she said.

I asked if she supported the court case.

"I'm afraid now. Of course I am, we might get hurt. After she lost Djastin, it's like he's the only one she cares about."

Normy was crying again. "We just need to pray, and the Lord will not forsake us. I cling to Him."

"Of course, you don't know what [Geñalope] is thinking," Lito told her. "Of course, he's stressed. He committed a crime and might do something stupid—"

"Especially," interrupted Eray, "since he knows he's been fired anyway."

"Do you know—" began Normy.

"We're up against cops," Eray said. "You think he won't touch us if he becomes a cop again, do you think he'll stay away?"

BL appeared at the door, looking for keys.

Get them from Jopet, Eray said.

There was a moment of quiet, then Normy spoke. "See, that fucking money is tearing us apart."

Nobody spoke.

"Do you think," I asked, "that you can wait another three years if your children are afraid?"

"I think of them," Normy answered quickly. "That's why I keep thinking of where I can get money. For them. I'm not thinking of myself. My head spins thinking about it. None of you know what I have to go through. What I'm thinking of having to do. I just don't tell you—can you believe, your brother's killer is still alive, and he's doing this? And he's a cop! We fight seventy-five percent and twenty-five percent, I think of—" She broke off. "It's all just money."

"Think of what other people are thinking," Eray said.

"He won't touch you."

"What if one of us is taken? You don't know what he's thinking."

"Are all of you siblings afraid?" I asked.

"I don't know about them. Me, I'm really scared."

"Can you keep this up three years, Normy?" I asked.

"Yes," she answered. "I can do this. Not just three years. I know it's a long process."

"And if it hits a decade?"

"I don't know. I just want to fight." She broke down into sobs. Stood up, walked the three steps into the bedroom, and slammed the door.

I shut down the recorder.

She'll be okay, Lito said.

He said he knew of another case, another dead neighbor whose family refused to settle. The offer was six thousand dollars. The killer was jailed, the house needed repairs, until finally the family decided they needed the money. By then, the offer was withdrawn.

"I just don't want it to come to that," he said.

Normy spoke at protests, signed affidavits, knocked on doors, and volunteered to interview mothers of other dead boys. She held them and wept with them and convinced them to fight, even the one mother who had burned her son's documents.

The case of Djastin Lopez moved slowly through the courts. And as it did, a virus causing "unexplained pneumonia" began spreading across the city of Wuhan in China.

I met Normita at a street protest, two years after the pandemic lockdowns began. We had spoken many times across the months of the pandemic, on video when we could, over the phone when the internet signal failed in Tondo.

She waved, smiling. We hugged. It was loud on the road. We walked to a spot beyond the barricades. She slipped off her mask. I bent my head and tried not to jog the recorder.

"How's Djastin's case?"

"It's fine," she said. "Geñalope was jailed."

I stopped walking. "What?"

"He surrendered. Because there was a warrant."

"So, no more settlement?"

She giggled, nervously. "There might have been."

"Will you accept it?"

"You know—can we go off the record?"

I have no recording of the ten minutes we spoke quietly by the side of the road, in the shadow of the People Power Monument. I remember there were tears. When she had calmed, I crouched in front of her and asked what I always asked.

"Can we go on the record now?"

Maybe she shouldn't have told me, but she did. It was only months later, at another protest, when she looked around at the other mothers and lifted a finger to her lips that I understood that the story she told me was one she had yet to tell her friends. I was there to find an ending and thought I did, in the quiet weeping of the small woman whispering into my recorder, saying she regretted it all.

What happened was this. One day, she saw her husband, Lito, stick his hand into his pocket and pull out a thousand-peso note. One of her children had been asking for money. He handed over the thousand, and over the course of the week handed out more thousands. It took that long, a week, for him to tell her. He had taken money, an entire fifty grand as initial payment, with the promise that the family would drop the charges. When he told her, she cried, then screamed, then she stopped speaking altogether, climbed out of the bottom bunk that they shared and laid out a mat in front of the door to sleep alone and weep. It was too late, she thought, because most of the money was gone.

"So there was a meeting after that," she said. "I went along. He didn't take me along, but I followed him going to the village chairman he knew who had brokered the settlement. I followed because I thought maybe Geñalope was there and he might kill— or that something bad would happen. I went. We went, Luinor and me, my daughter. I saw them there. And I didn't want to agree to the settlement. But it's not like I could do anything because Lito was there and who knew what would happen because he had already taken the money. And still it took a while, a long while, until I finally said yes. And that was only when Geñalope's daughter tried to hug me—what could I do?"

What she did was take the money, with the promise of withdrawing from the case involving the death of Djastin Lopez. They sat in a restaurant, Normy and Lito; Geñalope's wife, Edna; and their lawyers. There were no official terms of settlement set on paper, only an understanding that the family would stop pursuing the criminal case, and Geñalope would leave them be. The Lopezes sealed the deal against the advice of their lawyer.

The money helped. Helped pay for the power bill for the entire extended family. Helped purchase the materials for the aluminum business. Helped to buy mobile data and clothes for Djastin's children, who lived with their mother and the new husband. The money went fast, with everyone coming to Normy because they knew Normy had money.

In court, People of the Philippines vs Staff Sergeant Gerry Geñalope for Murder was provisionally dismissed. Private complainants Nestor and Normita Lopez failed to appear. Geñalope's lawyer argued that the accused had "already exhausted the trial dates without any witness being presented." The prosecutor did not object.

I shouldn't have done it, she told me that day on the street.

I shouldn't have said yes, she said.

It is a refrain: I regret it. Until now I regret it. I regret it every time I see Djastin's picture. I'd stop it if I could. If we never signed, I'd take it back. If we never got the money, if it hadn't been spent, I'd give it all back.

I have never spoken to Gerry Geñalope, former police staff sergeant. I had sent messages and a letter to his lawyer asking for comment. Both went without response. It was his wife, Edna, who spoke to me, over the phone, in a recorded conversation that took place long after her husband was released from his short stint in jail.

It's over, she told me. There has been forgiveness on both sides.

She does not know if Gerry shot Djastin, she said. She has never asked her husband. They have not spoken of the events on the railroad tracks. All she knows is what she saw on television, and what she read in the summons that arrived. He was charged and arrested, and while she might have been present at the meeting with the lawyers, she refused to confirm any payments were made. Neither does she deny it. "Maybe there was no money paid," she said. For her, the case is over, forgiven, done.

"Does your husband know you're speaking to me?" I asked.

"No," she said.

I told her he should know I was looking for him. The book would tell a story, Djastin's story, and while I would write down what she said, her husband had a right to speak too.

She would tell him, she said. She would let me know.

I have yet to hear from Gerry Geñalope.

Her husband is a good man, Edna told me, was a good cop. She had been so proud. This was the first time there had been trouble. It wasn't his fault at all. All he wants is to be a cop again.

"I don't know what really happened, ma'am," she told me. "He was just a cop doing his job."

12

MY FATHER IS A POLICEMAN

Rodrigo Duterte was not the first politician in the world to declare war on a domestic issue. Wars on poverty, pornography, hunger, obesity, cancer, and drugs have been launched and fought by presidents and potentates long before Duterte moved into Malacañang Palace. None of these wars have so far been won. None of that matters, because for the politician, the declaration is a victory all its own. The headlines are printed. The campaigns get their slogans. The solution is left to whoever comes next, or to God. But metaphorical wars were of no interest to Rodrigo Duterte, as he is a man who has no love for metaphor. He declared a war on drugs, and when he said kill, he meant dead.

There was dissent in the aftermath. There was an opposition. There were lawyers and priests and activists, but for those of us documenting Duterte's war, the protests were no more than a whisper in a hurricane. Life went on as normal for most everyone else. It was possible that little was said in the hope that the death toll would remain low and the war would be short. Maybe those who had voted for death thought they had voted for a metaphor. There are places in my country, after all, where death is a polite abstraction: a coffin, a bouquet, a sprinkling of holy water. In those places, a person can expect to live and die without ever having seen a bullet, or what a bullet does to a body when fired at close range.

One day in December 2020, all of that would change.

His name was Anton, and he was about to die.

Had he known this, he might have said something else that Sunday afternoon in late December, when he stood lanky and shirtless as the big man stalked across the lawn. But Anton was drunk, and Anton was angry.

What he shouted instead was this: "You wouldn't be so brave if you didn't have that gun."

"You son of a bitch," the big man said. "I'm arresting you."

One brawny arm snatched at Anton, but then there was Sonya to contend with.

Short, gray-haired Sonya, Anton's mother, had flung herself between the big man and her twenty-five-year-old son. All three stood on the dirt edge of the grassy lawn at the base of a two-foot-high front porch. It was an awkward embrace. The big man was dragging Anton from the safety of the porch wall by the hem of his black cotton shorts; small Sonya skidded on the dirt with her arms wrapped around her son's waist; and Anton was caught in the push and pull, flailing like a marionette.

Someone said stop, please stop. Someone shrieked for the authorities. Someone, a child, raised her voice in a long wailing scream. Sonya was thrown off her feet. She clamped one hand on the porch ledge and kept the other arm wrapped around Anton. When Anton's older sister thrust herself into the fray to shield her brother, the big man shoved her away, the side of his closed fist jammed into the side of her neck. She held her ground even as the big man caught her head in the crook of his elbow.

Only when a small hand yanked at her hair did she let go. The hand belonged to the big man's twelve-year-old daughter. The girl had been lurking quietly on the edges of the fray when she reached up to snatch a fistful of hair. Anton's sister doubled over, almost to her knees. She snatched at the girl's hair on the way down.

Suddenly five people were locked in the moving muddle of arms and legs. The big man's daughter wailed. The big man shouted. He held on to Anton with his right hand. With his left, he pulled out a gun.

The video clicked off.

When I began writing this book, I had never seen a murder committed. Every scene I wrote was a reconstruction. The investigations I published for Rappler were a patchwork of police reports and expert opinions and recorded testimony that I delicately extracted from terrified bystanders. Paragraphs were punctuated with "according to" and "in the story she told." Sometimes I arrived at the crime scene half an hour after the gun went off. In most cases I arrived days later, copied down the graffiti, and counted the fading splotches of blood.

I interviewed everyone I could, filling in the picture, conceding the contradictions, determining what had been witnessed and what was secondhand rumor. I spent much of my time sorting through the convoluted grammar of official police reports.

The occasional video clip offered corroboration, not confirmation. Killers were masked. Recordings were rare. Witnesses were too frightened to remember to pull out their phones, and CCTV footage, when available, was often too grainy for identification.

I lived, for as long as it was necessary, inside the crime scenes I pieced together in my head. Everything mattered. A direct quote published by a broadcast network. An official statement on a wire story. A picture posted by a cop's wife. Much of what I knew had gone through the filter of memory, trauma, self-interest, and my own constantly shifting judgment. I laid all of them out in blocky handwriting on brown sheets of butcher paper taped up to my office wall. Not even dates of death had the automatic legitimacy of simple fact. The official police report for one death, for instance, had been conflated with a two-week-old murder whose only connection was the fact that both victims had been salvaged in the city of Manila. The picture was never complete, but it was as close to the truth as I could get.

This story, however, was complete. And it came with video.

NIGHT SHIFT MESSAGING GROUP

12:20 a.m. Ezra Acayan [Photojournalist]: [Facebook Video Link]

12:20 a.m. Ezra Acayan [Photojournalist]: "A Paranaque City police officer shot dead two unarmed victims at point-blank range in Purok 2, Brgy. Cabayaoasan in Paniqui, Tarlac at around 5:10 p.m. on Sunday. (Video: PNP source) Oplan Kandado level 1 activated re Shooting incident transpired aao 5:10 PM today Dec 20, 2020 at Brgy Cabayaoasan, Paniqui, Tarlac wherein victims are identified as mother and son Sona Anthony y Rufino, 52 yo, and Frank Anthony Gregorio y Rufino, 25yo perpetrated by the Suspect identified as PCPL JUNEL NUESCA, member of crime lab soco, Paranaque City, on board nmax color red, wearing black jacket, black helmet, black tshirt and blck long pantd, fled away goint to Tarlac city."

12:22 a.m. Ezra Acayan [Photojournalist]: Word is he's from the Parañaque SOCO.

12:38 a.m. Vincent Go: Damn it. We were in Tarlac yesterday.

5:20 a.m. Alyx Arumpac [Filmmaker]: Just watched the video again. Jesus, it's really horrible. He shot them because the mother shouted at his daughter.

5:22 a.m. Alyx Arumpac [Filmmaker]: It's really that easy to kill.

9:29 a.m. Pat Evangelista: Woke up late. Can't find the video. Did they take it down?

9:29 a.m. Alyx Arumpac [Filmmaker]: I think it's down, but I saw it in another post somewhere.

9:35 a.m. Vincent Go: Knew it would be removed.

9:35 a.m. Vincent Go: [video attached]

The eleven-second clip that went viral was first published at 9:52 on the evening of December 20, 2020, almost a year into the pandemic and nearly five hours after the murders. It appeared on the Facebook account of the Metro Manila newspaper *The Daily Tribune*. The broadsheet claimed the video had come from a PNP source. Faces had been blurred, including that of the twelve-year-old girl. An extended version of the video was shared more than two hours later on the personal account of Ronjie Daquigan, a municipal councilor from a neighboring town. Daquigan, who described himself in his profile as a publisher and editor in chief, provided a caption for the clip.

> *Mother and son from Paniqui tarlac . . . shot and killed by para-ñaque policeman pcpl Junel nuesca of soco Crime lab. . . . a brutal crime where the helpless mother and son were slaughtered like chickens last Sunday around 5.10 in the afternoon.*

Daquigan described the victims, Sonya Gregorio, fifty-two, and her son Frank Anthony, twenty-five, as residents of Paniqui Town in the province of Tarlac. Tarlac, in Region 3, was a three-hour drive from Manila. The clip was filmed sometime after the hair-pulling incident.

The recording begins with a burst of sound—a chorus of screaming voices, many of them young. The person who is recording the video, later identified as Anton's sixteen-year-old cousin, is standing on the porch a few feet away, at an angle just slightly overhead.

In the video, Anton faces the lawn, angled away from the camera. Sonya is behind him, her back to the porch wall and her arms clamped around Anton's chest. A heavyset man wearing rubber slippers, a pair of shorts, and a dark blue T-shirt prowls around the pair. His name is Jonel Nuezca, an off-duty cop living two houses away from the Gregorios. Nuezca's grip shifts from the hem of Anton's shorts to the center of his waistband.

A man in a gray shirt, later described as a male relative, attempts to calm the situation. He pleads with Nuezca. "We can talk this out," the relative says. He covers Anton's mouth, as Anton begins to curse. Anton goes silent. Nuezca stops pulling at Anton's shorts, even as he keeps his grip. For a moment, it seems the peace will hold.

The cop turns to look down at Anton. "You be the cop so you can get a gun."

"Let my son go!" Sonya snaps back.

"Let him go? I'm arresting him!"

"He's not leaving!"

Anton says he wants to change his clothes. "You tore my— Stop yanking at me!"

"Yes," adds Sonya. "Stop dragging us, you keep dragging us. We're not leaving."

The cop's twelve-year-old daughter, who has been circling her father and the Gregorios, sticks out a skinny arm to shove Sonya. "Let go of him!" she demands.

Sonya jerks.

Anton laughs. "Your Papa brought you up, and you turned out like that?"

The child's answer is a snarling howl: "Just let go!"

"You let go," Sonya retorts. "We won't! We're in our house!"

The young girl, her small face framed by a curtain of hair, bellows back the single sentence that would ricochet across Philippine cyberspace:

"My father is a police"—she pauses for breath—"man!"

Sonya answers in a taunting singsong. "I don't care-eh-eh-eh-eh-eh!"

The words, and the tune, are ripped directly from a sprightly Korean pop song by the band 2NE1. It is the sort of response designed to infuriate a twelve-year-old girl.

It infuriates the cop instead. "Son of a bitch, you want me to end you now?"

The gun barks.

Bang, and Sonya falls. Every screaming voice goes silent.

Bang, bang, and Anton falls.

A twitch from Sonya.

Bang.

The screaming begins again.

The cop's daughter watches. She does not scream.

I saw the video four days before Christmas. My brain clicked through the images. It was like watching a movie based on a book I had already read. The sequence was correct, but there were elements missing. I played the final minute again, then again, and understood what I was looking for only when I attempted to write down what I had seen. I was listening for the thunder. It seemed to me that something as final as a fatal gunshot would demand more pomp and fanfare. There should have been an explosion, a mushroom cloud, something, somewhere, signaling the sudden turn from life to death.

Instead, it was quick. There were four gunshots in the space of less than five seconds—tap and *bang,* brief and innocuous. The tinny smack of a hammer pounding into a nailhead had little practical difference from the crack of a bullet smashing into a human brain at close range.

I discovered that I had spent a decade seeing death in slow motion. I had built moments movement by movement: the head turning, the arm rising, the finger jerking on the trigger. I packed in detail with every death. I traced the flight of the bullet from autopsy reports and witness testimony. I listed the witnesses, noted the reactions, integrated what someone had thought and seen and heard into walls of text attempting to reconstruct the last minutes of a man's life.

The truth was simpler: It takes longer to type a sentence than it does to kill a man.

The video had flooded cyberspace by the time I saw it. The views were in the millions. It was deleted, reposted, shared, then uploaded again.

The comments surged onto my timeline: "I hope you resist arrest, you sonofabitch." "Why," bemoaned one celebrity, "did it have to come to this?"

The hashtags trended. #StoptheKillingsPH. #CopsareTerrorists. #MyFatherisaPoliceman. It was "heartbreaking." It was "a moment of outrage." It was a "culture of death."

"Say their names," implored the posts. "Justice for Sonya and Frank Anthony Gregorio."

All of us who had ever covered the drug war knew this story. We couldn't say all the names if we tried. It had happened so often that many of us kept folders on our hard drives organized not by date but by hour of death. The little yellow stars that my friend Vincent would use to mark the location of corpses on a map were so densely crowded that it was impossible to distinguish one body from the next.

According to the sixteen-year-old who shot the video, the cop and his daughter walked away. They did not kneel or scream for help. They did not run. The cop pulled the trigger with the same easy assurance as a man flicking down the spark wheel of a cigarette lighter.

"It happens every day," Ezra Acayan of Getty Images posted on Facebook. "And you all have been playing blind and refusing to LISTEN because there wasn't VIDEO. Wake up."

"Your Father said he would protect the cops," wrote broadcast journalist Barnaby Lo. "So why wouldn't they kill with impunity? You clapped for him every time. All so you can feel safe? You feel safe now?"

"Yes, an outrage," said veteran publisher Inday Espina-Varona. "But Philippines, that's been happening for the last year.

I see some drug war cheerleaders screaming today. You did this. With your Father."

I won't pretend I wasn't angry, but like most of my colleagues, there had been no particularity in my outrage. That was a constant thing, like cigarette smoke, so present I barely noticed. I was furious instead at everyone who announced their indignation after ignoring a four-year parade of coffins. It couldn't have been the blood that shocked, because blood had pooled on the streets for years. It was the casual pull of the trigger. There was no space for an alternative narrative, no time between the gunshot and the thump of a dead body to claim the dead man pulled a gun, no room to say he deserved it, she deserved it, that all of this was just propaganda. These were the only facts available. The child, confident her father was a cop, the cop asking the mother and son if they wanted to die, the gun, the trigger, once, twice, again, both dead in an instant.

"This is not who we are," read a last Twitter post.

This was exactly who we were.

A little more than an hour after the murders, Police Staff Sergeant Jonel Nuezca, a twenty-three-year police veteran, surrendered to officers of the Philippine National Police.

Nuezca worked out of the Parañaque City Crime Laboratory in Metro Manila. He kept a home in a red-gated field a short walk from the Gregorios' home. His wife's family still lived in Tarlac—Nuezca himself was not a native of Paniqui Town. He was home and off duty on December 20, just as the rest of the country attempted some semblance of holiday celebration after nine months of the world's longest pandemic lockdown. Nuezca's service firearm was unmuzzled, contrary to holiday tradition during previous administrations. Two weeks earlier PNP Chief

Debold Sinas had told the press that muzzling guns made cops hesitant under fire. Sinas was confident that the "majority of our police officers now have self-restraint and are disciplined."

In the late afternoon of that Sunday, several of the young Gregorios were scattered across the property. Sonya Gregorio's youngest daughter, inside the house, was recuperating from a recent appendix operation. Anton was in the yard with several other young people. He had succeeded in firing off a *boga*. The *boga,* an improvised noisemaker made of PVC pipes or bamboo tubes, was on the prohibited list of firecrackers, which also included the more interestingly named Grandpa Thunder, Good-bye Philippines, and Judas Belt. It was the explosion that had sent Nuezca, his wife, and his daughter rocketing into the Gregorio property uninvited.

A heated argument broke out. Nuezca, according to the story the family told, threatened to arrest the drunken Anton. Nuezca was already dragging Anton across the lawn, but Sonya flung her arms around her son, using her body as a shield. Someone ran for the village hall for help. Someone screamed for everyone to stop, because Anton's younger sister was terrified, and her stitches might come loose. One of Anton's older sisters thrust her body between Anton and the cop, only to be shoved away. There was hair-pulling and pleading and weeping. A series of neighbors and relations attempted to referee.

According to a police report, Anton and Sonya were shot at ten minutes past five in the afternoon. Within twenty-four hours of the shooting going public, the Tarlac police chief, the secretary of the interior, and the Central Luzon police chief had made public statements promising justice and no special treatment for Nuezca. The provincial prosecutor filed two counts of murder. The Senate called for a probe. PNP Chief Sinas condemned "the criminal act committed by one of our police personnel" and assured the public that "the PNP does not and will never condone any criminal act of our police officers."

Video released by former Duterte aide Senator Bong Go showed the president watching the shooting on a cell phone held by Go. "The president is angry," Go told reporters.

In a rare moment of transparency, police released Nuezca's record to the public. Nuezca had applied as a rookie to the National Capital Region Police Office. He had served for eleven years in Taguig City, one of the country's central business districts, then three more with the Parañaque City Police. He was later assigned to Parañaque's police crime laboratory. In the span of ten years, he racked up at least six administrative cases. The milder cases involved a refusal to undergo drug testing in 2014—he was suspended for a month—and another, later dropped, had resulted from failing to attend a court hearing as a prosecution witness.

Two other cases pertained to deaths. In 2016, the year President Duterte declared his war on drugs, the PNP Internal Affairs Service (IAS) investigated charges of homicide against Jonel Nuezca for the shooting deaths of two drug suspects during a buy-bust operation. The case against Nuezca was dismissed. According to the IAS, Nuezca, part of the backup team, had been nowhere near the site.

Similar charges were filed in 2018, this time for the death of a single drug suspect. The police claimed the dead man had engaged cops in a shoot-out. Nuezca was one of the three policemen involved. The IAS spokesperson told the press they had been unable to determine "who among the three policemen was responsible for the suspect's death." The case was dismissed.

In the late evening of December 21, the president addressed the murders of Sonya and Frank Anthony Gregorio on national television.

"This cop is an isolated case," President Duterte said of Nuezca. "He's sick in the head. Crazy."

The government performance of accountability continued over the next few days. A spliced and much-edited video clip, posted by Police Regional Office 3, the office supervising the province of Tarlac, was captioned: "We never tolerate: Police Regional Office 3 Regional Director Police Brigadier General Valeriano T. De Leon [giving] Nuezca a beating for his wayward act unacceptable to all."

The "beating" was a lecture delivered to Nuezca about Nuezca's inability to control his temper. "Weren't you taught to practice deep breathing?" The police director was in uniform fatigues, sitting ramrod straight, across from a cuffed and properly penitent Nuezca.

"Sir, I admit, sir, my mistake," Nuezca said. "I was carried away by too much emotion. I regret what I did, sir. I regret it a lot. First for my family, sir."

Brigadier General De Leon informed Nuezca that he was to be removed from the service. He had "dragged the whole organization." He had killed "like a dog." He would be prosecuted.

"With the exception of drug organizations, everyone is angry at you," De Leon pontificated. "That's what you should regret. No one is on your side after what you did. For that, you have to pray hard. People are really angry at you."

By and large, the united front of the national government and its armed militias succeeded in redrawing the long blue line. As in several other instances when facts and public opinion were wavering in favor of the victims, the government quickly recast the erring police officer as the exception to the ranks of men and women whose duty it was to serve and protect. Certainly, there were lapses in the narrative. A female patroller wrote a Facebook post defending the murders—"You can brutalize me, but don't you dare yell at my kid." A police chief from Catanduanes, promptly reassigned, announced that even old women owed respect to police officers. The PNP spokesman, in a briefing to the press, said that while the police respected all accusations made against Nuezca, hopefully the public will be "fair and just and give attention to the heroic acts [of the police], over this particular case of Nuezca."

Sergeant Jonel Nuezca, police veteran, who throughout his career had been investigated and cleared of a variety of charges, was stripped of his badge and rank. In the story the government told, he was not a cop, but a madman.

"You son of a bitch cops, I love you all because you're doing the job, you've seen how much I love you . . . but you sick men, you crazed lunatics—and I'm sure that by now, he should not be allowed to go out because that was double murder," President Duterte said during his weekly public address. "I don't think you can escape the rigors of justice because it was caught on TV, even I was in disbelief. You are useless. That was unfair, and too brutal. Jail him. Don't let that devil go."

It might be better, he added, if Nuezca were fried alive.

Out in Paniqui, Tarlac, Florentino Gregorio, husband to Sonya, father to Frank Anthony, stood in front of an ABS-CBN camera.

"It's a big thing," Florentino answered. "Especially because it was our president. I thank President Duterte for his care for our family. It means a lot to us."

Two days before Christmas, we drove out to Tarlac. It was a three-hour drive on the North Luzon Expressway, past tollbooths and miles of sugar plantations. The pandemic hadn't

slowed down the holiday traffic. The rest stop parking lot was
crowded with packed vans and masked families strolling to Star-
bucks to the tune of "O Come, All Ye Faithful."

The late president Corazon Aquino had been born in the
first-class municipality of Paniqui in Tarlac, which had also been
one of the only holdouts against Duterte during the 2016 elections. Paniqui was largely prosperous. Sonya Gregorio, formerly
Rufino, had been born to a tenant farmer who was awarded land
through the agrarian reform law. Sonya, one of only two siblings
who graduated from college, met Florentino Gregorio early in
the 1990s in Metro Manila. She was a schoolteacher at the Philippine Normal University. He had a job as a water deliveryman.

She was pretty, he said, so pretty he decided not to charge her
for deliveries. "You owe me so much, maybe you want to pay
me back with a date," he would say, laughing.

They were married in 1991. She called him Pa when she was
pleased and Florentino when she wasn't. He liked that she was
smart, that she was tough, and that she never complained when
things didn't go her way. When he left to work overseas, she
raised their children. He wanted a quieter life out of the city when
he came home. The family moved to Paniqui, where there was
room in the Rufino property. Florentino drove dump trucks.
Sonya taught school. They raised seven children and bought a
tract of land after several of the children moved out and married.
The pandemic, and the havoc it wreaked on daily work, provided
the opportunity for the family to begin building a new home.

When we arrived, the house, with its peaked tin roof, stood
tall and unfinished on a large lawn. On one of the posts, someone had stuck the round blue logo of the Tarlac Truck Drivers
Association. Journalists stood by with cameras. Mourners, many
of them family members and townspeople, milled about under
tarpaulin tents that had been loaned out by the local govern-

ment. Funeral wreaths on tall stands fenced in the elevated porch, hung with shiny white ribbon printed with the names of the senders in black and gold felt-tip pens. Many came from the PNP high command. Condolences from Police General Debold Sinas. Condolences from Regional Director Police Region 3 & Staff. Condolences from Police Colonel Renante C. Cabico, Provincial Director, Tarlac Police Provincial Office. Condolences from the Officers, Men & Women of Paniqui Municipal Police Station. There were flowers from senators, from congressmen, from the secretary of the interior, from the governor of Tarlac, from provincial board members, and from a handful of councilors from Paniqui Town.

I was standing on the porch with a group of photographers when Raffy Lerma tapped me on the shoulder. Two feet below us, where the lawn gave way to dirt, a young man in his twenties was crouching over a pair of candles that had guttered in the breeze.

"Can I borrow your lighter?" he asked me. He gestured to the bright blue Bic poking out of my pocket. I handed it down. "Ma will kill me if I let the candle die out," he said with a small smile. A splotch of dark blood still stained the base of the cement wall.

"What's your name?" I asked.

"Luis," he said. "Youngest son." A half-dozen shutters clicked.

The line of giant funeral wreaths snaked their way up the front steps, all the way into the front room, where Anton's wife sat quiet and still. The coffins lined the unpainted walls. The white starburst on Anton's forehead was still visible in spite of layers of makeup. An extravagant flower arrangement from President

Rodrigo Duterte stood in the place of honor between the two coffins. Each coffin was decorated with a large colored sticker in full view of all the mourners and the half-dozen cameras marching in and out of the tiny room: CONDOLENCE FROM MAYOR MAX ROXAS; VICE MAYOR BIEN ROXAS.

Political signage is not rare in the Philippines. Graduation congratulations and Christmas greetings on tarpaulin banners are holiday standbys. Plastic tents—the sort borrowed for wakes, feeding programs, and mass weddings—are routinely printed with the faces of current officials. There are sidewalks in my city tiled with the mayor's initials. This, however, was the first time any of us had seen government compassion advertised on a coffin lid.

It was Florentino Gregorio, Sonya's husband, who received visitors paying their respects. He was the sort of man, present in every Filipino family, who was content to sit quietly at family dinners and offer encouraging smiles as his wife held court. I was not his first interview. He was exhausted by the time we sat down across from each other, three feet apart, his son's coffin at my back, his wife's behind him.

Trauma interviews are difficult in and of themselves, but during the pandemic, they slipped into the macabre, with none of the intimacy that could sometimes spring between a reporter and a subject. *Trust me,* I wanted to tell him, but it would have been odd assurance coming from a masked stranger holding a recorder clamped to the end of a borrowed three-foot-long selfie stick. I asked him about his wife. How they met. How they fell in love. How she would wake him before dawn every day after she loaded the washing machine for which the family had so carefully saved. How she would prepare coffee—"always two cups, and we would go to the terrace, around three a.m., just the two of us"—

and how they would talk, about the house, about the children, about the plants she was propagating in plastic pots.

"When she knew I had a trip out, she would say, 'Pa, bring me home plants,'" he told me, red-eyed. "So I bring her the plants. Pebbles for the garden. Anything she wanted."

Sometimes it was garden soil she wanted, and he brought sacks of it back to Paniqui, all the way from Pangasinan.

"Very good," she would tell him. It was what she said when she was pleased, a relic of her days as a schoolteacher. "You were very good."

"Do I get a prize?" he would ask.

"Yes." His prize, often, was a kiss.

His eyes crinkled over the blue mask. I laughed. He laughed. Then there was shouting. A cop, assigned to the family, strode into the living room carrying the body of a young girl.

Florentino leaped up. "That's my granddaughter." His voice broke in panic. "What happened?"

"She fainted outside," said the cop.

The bad blood between the Gregorios and the Nuezcas had begun as a property dispute. Sonya's sister Mary Rose, an elderly woman living in another city, had prevailed upon her younger sibling to sell a small tract of land on her behalf. Sonya sold it to the Nuezcas.

Money was exchanged, but then the deal went sour. There was a dispute over right of way. The feud escalated. There was trouble with the title, accusations of bad faith, a claim, later disproved, that the property was in hock, a fraud case filed in court, and a judge's decision, according to Mary Rose, in favor of the Gregorios. The relationship between the two families had reached a point that police had to be called in at least once—due, said the Gregorios, to intimidation from Jonel Nuezca.

When Florentino's phone rang on December 20, he was still on the road, up in Binalonan, driving back to Paniqui after making a delivery. There was very little information. All he was told was that Anton had been shot.

They never told him Sonya had been shot too.

The story flashed across global headlines. *The Washington Post* reported that the murders "cast a harsh new light on the rampant abuse of authority by police under President Rodrigo Duterte." *The New York Times* described the "wave of outrage directed at the government and a police force that many say acts with impunity." Senator Leila de Lima, jailed on spurious allegations of drug dealing, denounced the "execution-style" slaying: "Because of Duterte's murderous statements and encouragements to kill, the police are killing with the smallest provocation!" The human rights organizations that the president so gleefully denounced sent out their statements: "As with many incidents of recent police violence, the killing by Nuezca of Sonya Gregorio and her son Frank was brazen and underscores the impunity that prevails in the Philippines," Human Rights Watch deputy Asia director Phil Robertson said. "It took place in the context of an enabling environment for police violence that President Duterte himself has encouraged."

Out on the lawn of the Gregorio home, I spoke to Mark, Sonya's eldest. The family, faced with an advancing army of journalists, had designated the twenty-nine-year-old grocery cashier as their spokesperson. By then, the government had sent troops to secure the Gregorio property. The Department of Social Welfare offered therapy for the terrified young witnesses. Mark, who on filing charges did not feel safe surrounded by cops wearing the same uniform as the man who murdered his mother and brother, was reassured. One of the uniformed men had leaned in to speak to him: "Don't worry," said the cop, "we won't let you down."

"There are people who say this is the president's fault," I said. "They say there are many dead, and that's because of a culture of impunity."

"No, no," Mark said emphatically. "No, we can't blame it on everyone. However great your leadership is, if your members are bad, or your subordinates, then it doesn't matter. It's not up to the people on top, the highest ranks. Everywhere, all organizations are like that. You can't blame the head, or the president, or whoever is leading the company, because it's all up to the subordinates."

After Mark left to speak to his father, a young photographer sitting beside me rolled his eyes. "I can't believe he said that."

"Quiet," I snapped. "Not here."

A week after the murders, I rode back to Tarlac for the funeral. Many of us from the national media were milling on the lawn. The Gregorio children and grandchildren sat at long plastic tables. A protective detail dressed in camouflage gear camped outside a neighbor's porch. Distant relatives, previously unknown to the family, stood watching on the fringes. I met three: a retired cop, a government clerk, and a tricycle driver, all of whom had discovered the family connection over a group chat.

"What happened to us was terrible," said one, shaking his head. "We had our pictures taken too," another said.

Dozens of men and women packed the lawn. Many of them held up cell phones to shoot video and take selfies. All of them were dressed in approximations of the official police patrol uniform: portable radios hooked on belts, black trousers, and short-sleeved, bright blue collared shirts emblazoned with blocky yellow letters. They were, in fact, not cops, but force multipliers, volunteers accredited by the PNP. Most of them had driven the half hour from neighboring Nueva Ecija. The group called them-selves the Philippine Hotline Movement Incorporated (PHMI). *Hotline* might have been a misnomer—"We don't really have a hotline." One member, a woman, led the group in loud prayer and implored the Lord God to grant his people wisdom.

It was unclear why the PHMI had appeared suddenly on the damp lawn of the Gregorio home. Some said they were there to mourn with the family. Some claimed that the Gregorio father and son were members. Others said that a cousin or an aunt or a grandmother was part of the organization.

"We partner with the police," their regional secretary, Risa Ramos, told me. "Our main motto is 'Together we can stop crime.' And we join the police in monitoring and reporting. That's our number-one thing at the Police Hotline."

The two-kilometer convoy to the cemetery began at a little before nine in the morning. The PHMI lined the muddy path leading to the funeral cars.

"They look like idiots," Vincent Go said, when I caught a ride with him to the cemetery. "That's the thing with Filipinos. They put on a uniform, and suddenly they think they're kings. Even during the pandemic, even in the villages, even if they're just security guards. They're so proud of their outfits, their vests, something changes inside of them. Clueless morons thinking they're enforcing the law, but really they have no goddamn clue what they're doing."

"They're not cops," I said.

"Yeah, they're just morons."

We parked across from the Paniqui Garden of Angels. It was a massive compound. The tarp at the front entrance announced a 20 percent burial plot discount for anyone who paid cash on the spot.

I told Vincent about my interview. The family, I told him, did not believe the president was in any way responsible.

"They're the perfect example of folks who can't see the bigger picture," Vincent said. "They have no idea how it came to this. They're ordinary people who haven't seen what we've been seeing these past four years, all those dead, all the stories, all the anguish from all the families left behind. This family will probably get justice, and they'll be satisfied. What about the more than thirty thousand still looking for the truth? When will they find peace?"

At the cemetery gates, a handful of cops in fatigues guarded the entrance.

"They really need bulletproof vests and bandoliers?" a photographer beside me muttered. "Is there a war?"

The coffins were laid out under a large temporary pavilion. A green carpet of artificial grass surrounded the two open graves. The tent was packed. The family surrounded the coffins, the journalists surrounded the family, the cops surrounded the journalists, while a loose crowd of observers, holding cell phones aloft, surrounded the heaving scrum. An old woman wailed, beating her fist in the air above Sonya Gregorio's open casket. Sonya's children broke down sobbing, one after another, while a red-eyed Florentino Gregorio, still firmly masked, took one child, then another into his big arms. Shutters clicked, cameras rolled, the mass of humanity tightening around the Gregorio family.

"Please," begged Mark in tears. "Please move back."

As it happened, I was standing on the sidelines, attempting to maintain a six-foot distance from the rest of the gaggle, unable to keep myself from stepping forward every few minutes to hold up a phone recorder in the gaps between the cameramen's shoulders. I stepped back when Mark asked, but I can't pretend to have stood on any moral high ground. I understood that we were there uninvited, and that the family had the right to mourn quietly, but my guilt at covering the wild mourning of December 27 was equally the result of the terror of a Covid infection. Under different circumstances, with no pandemic and a documentary to produce, I might have been in the scrum myself, rolling a Panasonic AF100 as the family pleaded for the media to back away.

"You have your footage," the police field commander told the media. "Please step back."

I didn't venture in again. There were enough cameras taking footage that I was certain would go online in hours. I could afford to walk away and note down the fact that the wreaths, so carefully arranged outside the Gregorio home, had been tossed down onto the memorial park's lawn with little to no regard for the importance of their senders.

I heard a man's voice shout: "Justice for Sonya and Frank Anthony!"

"Justice!" answered a chorus.

On the cemetery lawn, just behind the coffins, the men and women of the PHMI had gathered in a semicircle. Two cameras broke away from the scrum and joined me as I crossed the damp grass to watch.

The man who led the cheer wore the PHMI's bright blue shirt. He was a small man. He held a cell phone, panning this way and that for a video that I later discovered was streaming live over Facebook. He turned to us, with our lenses and cameras, grinned, and held up one finger in question—*One more time?*

It seemed he got his answer. He turned back to the waiting enforcers, raised an arm like a conductor, and shouted again.

"Justice for Sonya and Frank Anthony!"

"Justice!" roared the volunteers.

He did this two or three more times, as some of the Gregorio family limped out of the tent to walk away from the fresh graves.

He introduced himself as Gerona town councilor Ronjie Daquigan, president of the Tarlac Media Association, president of the Prime Alliance Publisher, editor in chief of Ronda News, and "Reporter of the Philippines." He was the same Ronjie Daquigan who had released cell phone video of the Gregorios' murder over his Facebook page.

Daquigan was a proud member of the PHMI. Their duties, among many others, included peace and order, security, traffic assistance, monitoring, and rescue operations. They had big plans, including the pursuit of justice for Frank Anthony and Sonya Gregorio.

"We will call the group 'Justice for Nanay Sonya, Justice for Frank Anthony, and Justice for All,'" he told me. "It's not just for Nanay Sonya and Frank, but for the many other victims of brutal crimes that are happening but are not exposed like this one that was exposed because of a viral video."

I asked what the PHMI had to say about the fact that a cop had killed the Gregorios. "In this incident, as far as I know, it was only because of a quick impulse by this cop who was at fault," said a woman who introduced herself as the PHMI regional director.

"Only this cop?"

"Yes, just this cop."

"The government has no fault here?"

"No, none, none at all."

·   ·   ·

Frank Anthony Gregorio committed a petty offense. The orders banning firecracker use had authorized police to make arrests, even as Anton's violation was the sort often negotiated with warnings and an occasional fine. It was, after all, a homemade firecracker released in the middle of an open field inside private property days before the New Year, but Jonel Nuezca decided it was a crime, and Jonel Nuezca had the law on his side. Anton was defiant. So was his mother.

On December 3, 2020, three weeks before their murders, President Rodrigo Duterte had delivered a speech applauding the work of the police. No cop should be afraid to kill in self-defense, he said. "But if you're uncertain or you suspect they'll draw first, kill them so it's done. One less idiot in this world." It was another enumeration of the president's greatest hits: drugs destroy the youth, every drug dealer is armed, human rights are for the weak, cops are the last bulwark against criminality.

"I'm telling the law enforcement, the uniformed personnel: Do your duty," President Duterte ordered. "Do it in accordance with law, but be alert and be wise. They make one mistake, shoot them."

Staff Sergeant Jonel Nuezca, in shooting them both dead, had been following the orders of his commander in chief.

Here is what I think would have happened had there been no recording. I think that Jonel Nuezca would have called down his brothers in blue. I think he would have claimed that young Anton, likely drunk, possibly high, had fought back during an attempted arrest. I think Nuezca would have said that Sonya Gregorio had gotten in the way. I think the Gregorio lawn would have been empty of the white anthuriums sent by the high command of the Philippine National Police. I think that whatever investigation was conducted, if any had been conducted, would have cleared Jonel Nuezca, as he had been cleared twice before.

I do not think that His Excellency President Rodrigo Duterte would have made the same promise of justice for the family. I think the murders on the lawn of an unfinished house in Paniqui Town would have been one more story reported by local media, and, while I would likely have doubted the official narrative, if I had heard about it at all, it would not have occurred to me to leave the relative safety of my study in tree-lined Quezon City to pull on a KN-95 mask and drive three hours to Tarlac two days before Christmas to ask a weeping man how his dead wife liked her coffee.

"They hate you, you know," a freelancer told me later that day.

"Hate us?"

"The other media. They hate you night shift people. They think you're all self-righteous jerks."

I shrugged. We stood smoking outside a mall halfway between Manila and Tarlac. One journalist blew out smoke and railed against the family's perceived support for the Duterte government. A rumor, unverified, had been circulating that the Gregorios had raised their fists in the Duterte salute.

Those of us who followed the dead could afford to bemoan, as Vincent did, the family's inability to "see the big picture." It was easy to follow the parade of coffins and imagine these last two deaths as inevitabilities, the natural consequence of violent rhetoric from above and wholesale impunity below. But cut out the microphones and the Twitter feeds and the line of blue-shirted volunteers, and all that would have been left was a single family who, one Sunday afternoon, watched mother and brother snatched away. Widen the frame just a little, and there would have been me, sitting on a plastic chair on the Gregorio lawn, asking Mark Gregorio, twenty feet away from his mother's coffin, who he'd voted for in the election of 2016. The story would have become this: a family in mourning with a crusading media looking to make a parable out of a private tragedy. I was the person watching from the outside, looking to lay the weight of democracy on the shoulders of a grieving family. They had their dead. I had my guilt.

In the first week of January 2021, Jonel Nuezca stood before a judge to face charges of murder.

He pleaded not guilty.

He returned to jail to await trial, and was convicted eight months later. On November 30, 2021, almost a year after the incident in Paniqui, Jonel Nuezca, former policeman, was pronounced dead at the New Bilibid Prison Hospital at 6:44 p.m. He was, reported the Bureau of Corrections, walking with a cellmate when he collapsed unconscious.

While Nuezca was not the first high-profile inmate during the Duterte administration to die under allegedly questionable circumstances, a preliminary report from the National Bureau of Investigation "indicates that Nuezca died of cardiac arrest." The spokesman of the Bureau of Corrections said there were no signs of torture or violence. Nuezca, he said, had no enemies, and no suspicious incidents were recorded previous to his death.

"But for those asking if there was foul play, based on our initial investigation and questioning of his fellow inmates, his death points to natural causes," the spokesman said.

I cannot, with any certainty, report the true toll of Rodrigo Duterte's war against drugs. Numbers cannot describe the human cost of this war, or adequately measure what happens when individual liberty gives way to state brutality. Even the highest estimate—over 30,000 dead—is likely insufficient to the task.

When the intention is to lie, numbers can make extraordinary liars. Even government agencies fail to agree on how many the police killed in alleged antidrug operations. The PNP's Directorate for Operations put those deaths at 7,884 in August 2020. The government's communications office, two years later, lowered the total to 6,252 in May 2022. The last of the DUI numbers was released in 2019, but the number is meaningless in determining drug-related deaths, conflated as it is with every possible variation of homicide.

The truth is almost certainly much higher. A study by Columbia University's Stabile Center for Investigative Journalism estimated that government figures were "a gross underestimation of the extent of drug-related killings in the Philippines." The Supreme Court demanded all documents on the "total of 20,322 deaths during the Duterte administration's anti-drug war." The Commission on Human Rights chairperson Chito Gascon said the number of drug-related deaths could go "as high as 27,000." International Criminal Court prosecutor Fatou Bensouda said that "between 12,000 and at least 20,000 killings" were committed in relation to the drug war.

"Baseless and bloated," said the interior secretary. "Propaganda attempts," said a PNP spokesperson. When the government launched its "Real Numbers" campaign, the intent was to "clarify the confusing and divisive numbers." An assistant secretary complained of the "patently false" information spread across the international community. "We're here because a narrative is being pushed down our throats, right?"

"Our only appeal [to the media] is to be fair," PNP Chief dela Rosa said. "Just don't bloat the data too much. Don't paint our drug war as truly evil."

Upon Dela Rosa's retirement, I asked him if he believed that the drug war he had overseen had been successful. He said that it was the gratitude of the people that assured him that it had been. They would thank him, he said, and hug him, and sometimes weep, they were so grateful. "The Filipino masses have learned to love their policemen. . . . They love, trust, and respect their police force."

There is a phrase that has been used whenever police officers sit down to brag about their prowess in the field. It is also a phrase that appears in a certain species of police report. In each report, the suspect is killed by the police in supposed shoot-outs or after the suspect allegedly presented a threat. The suspect is discovered dead, or almost dead, but that discovery occurs only after "the smoke of gunfire subsides." In Binondo, for example, "after the smoke of gun battle subsided" two suspects were "seen sprawled lifeless inside the rooms of the small house." In Santa Cruz, "when the smoke of gunfire subsided," police reported the subject "lay in the cemented pavement mortally wounded." The same is true for a man in Tondo, found dead just after "the smoke of gunfire subsided," and in Jose Abad Santos, where another subject was found lying on another cemented pavement dead of gunshot wounds—"after the smoke of gunfire subsided."

It is a florid phrase, more than a little baroque, blurring the line between actual fact and dramatic hyperbole. There is, after all, no cloud of smoke bursting out of a modern Colt .45-caliber police issue after a firing, certainly not enough to obscure the dead body of a full-grown man. And still the words are written and filed, registered as entries for the official record, as was the case for ten police reports signed by various homicide investigators at the Criminal Investigation Branch of the Manila Police District.

Slaughter dressed up in bureaucratese dulls the senses, and

over time can anesthetize an entire population to the horror happening right where they live. Objective reality is winnowed away by each succeeding government report. The dead perish again, into nonexistence.

"Only" is a qualifier, and the manner in which it is used by the Duterte government is meant as a diminution. Take, for example, the answer offered by PNP spokesperson Benigno Durana, Jr., at the 2018 Real Numbers forum, back when the police were admitting to having killed 4,410 drug suspects, an average of six suspects killed by police per day. The trouble, he said, was that "drug suspects can be armed, drug-crazed heavily armed," and police could not be expected to "lay down their lives for these criminals."

"But again," Durana said, "we are very sensitive and we are actively listening to the suggestions, comments, even criticism of some quarters in our campaign against illegal drugs." It was why, Durana said, killings by police went down that year: an average of 105 killed a week went down to 69, all the way to a recent average of 23 deaths weekly—"only twenty-three deaths on the average."

Applaud their sensitivity. Salute their restraint. Only six thousand or seven thousand are dead. Only two thousand of thirty thousand are drug-related. Only 23 have been killed by the police of a possible 105. They are numbers on a board, accomplishments on a checklist, only criminals, not quite human. It is when a government can append "only" to any number of deaths that it is possible to grasp what was lost.

To Normita Lopez, mother of nine, "only" is not a diminution. Her Djastin is not her only son, but the son she lost was her only Djastin, the boy she carried through a flood, the boy the cops killed, the boy whom she will describe as her most beloved son.

On September 15, 2021, the International Criminal Court

authorized the commencement of an investigation into the campaign against illegal drugs, concluding that there was reasonable basis to proceed, "in the sense that the crime against humanity of murder appears to have been committed."

The decision, signed by Presiding Judge Péter Kovács, Judge Reine Adélaïde Sophie Alapini-Gansou, and Judge María del Socorro Flores Liera, noted that "President Rodrigo Duterte has publicly encouraged extrajudicial killings in a way that is incompatible with a genuine law enforcement operation."

"I would like to reiterate my statement," Duterte said in March 2023. "You sons of bitches in the ICC, I don't care. You know why? Early on in my presidency, if you were listening, [I said] I would stake my name, my honor and the presidency itself."

I do not know how many more lives have gone unlived, as Djastin's has, but Normita lives, and she will remember him. The truth of the numbers might disappear into official lies, can be wrongly confirmed, badly certified, and misprinted in historical accounts, but that truth is not unknowable, only unknown, now, today. It is truth nonetheless. And truth will outlive the killers. It will be remembered and retold. The smoke of gunfire will subside, and someday, one generation, two generations from now, there will be a phalanx of men and women who will stand up to be counted, who will raise their hands, who will say, on the record, *They killed my family too.*

III

REQUIEM

13

ACTS OF CONTRITION

Jason Quizon had booked a flight from Abu Dhabi to Doha to vote for Rodrigo Duterte at the embassy there. He was a liberal and an atheist, an engineer with progressive values and a champion of rational thought who had worked his whole life for the ease his family now enjoys. Duterte's language did not bother Jason. Duterte spoke like a drunk, much like Jason's father after a night chugging Red Horse beer. Let Duterte threaten. Let him babble away. All of it was fodder for the gullible masses. What Jason liked was that Rodrigo Duterte was a man of action.

Jason did not regret his vote when the bodies began dropping. It was okay, he said. This was a drug war.

One day, early in the drug war, Jason saw a photo. He couldn't help seeing the photo, because most everyone did. It was a picture of a barefoot woman, a tattoo on her right shoulder, sitting at a highway intersection while cradling a man's corpse between her legs. A torn sheet of cardboard with a single handwritten word—PUSHER—lay forgotten on the asphalt.

The photo credit belonged to Raffy Lerma. "A weeping Jennelyn Olaires hugs partner Michael Siaron, 30, a pedicab driver and alleged drug pusher, who was shot and killed by motorcycle-riding gunmen near Pasay Rotonda on Edsa. He was one of six killed in drug-related incidents in Pasay and Manila yesterday."

In the days, weeks, months that followed, the picture became iconic in the Duterte drug war. It acquired its own title, *La Pietà*, reminiscent of Michelangelo's marble sculpture of the Blessed Virgin Mary cradling the limp body of the dead Christ. The photo made its way to Jason's social media timeline: the dead man, the crying family, and the woman, screaming that her partner wasn't guilty, not at all. Jason calls it a striking photo, but he didn't believe the story. "These kinds of people" were what he called them. The poorer sort, the squatters, the unreasonable and unthinking, "the kinds of people who in your mind do drugs."

One day, Jason saw another story. He couldn't help seeing the video either, because most everyone did. The dead boy was a seventeen-year-old eleventh grader named Kian delos Santos. Police claimed Kian was killed in a spontaneous shoot-out, *nanlaban*. CCTV footage contradicted the story and showed officers dragging the teenager past a basketball court.

The witnesses spoke. They said officers handed Kian a gun before telling him to run. They said Kian tried to run, only to be shot, at least twice in the head. Those witnesses testified to Kian's last words.

Don't, Kian said.

Please stop, Kian said.

I have an exam tomorrow, Kian said.

"You know, he's a young kid," Jason says. An innocent boy

who didn't look like an addict, didn't look like a squatter, was a student who could have been Jason's brother or sister or son. "And that's when I had to look back," he said. "I had to question how many of those who died before, like the *Pietà,* were similar to Kian—even if they didn't look like Kian."

On that day, Jason Quizon stopped believing in Rodrigo Duterte.

He will say it to anyone who asks. He will admit his mistake; he will tell his story; he does not care because he doesn't give a fuck if he's judged for his honesty. Filipinos are classists, he says, sometimes racists, only no one wants to talk about it. But he will, he tells me. "You know how if you're in a mall, in a sloppy shirt, how the guard will look at you, how the saleslady will treat you? It's there; it's happening. I'm not immune to those kinds of things."

Here is Jason Quizon's confession, his act of contrition. He was conned and allowed himself to be conned. He is disappointed, not in Duterte, but in himself. Jason regrets his vote. He regrets the fact that maybe ten more people voted for Duterte because he told them to vote for Duterte.

For Jason, Rodrigo Duterte is a liar and "the most cowardly person to ever hold that position."

When Jason Quizon voted again, he did not vote for the Duterte daughter, or the Marcos son. He is still disappointed, not only in himself, but in his people too. When it comes to elections, he says, Filipinos are still fucking morons.

Dondon Chan voted for Rodrigo Duterte. He made the turn against Duterte early, just after the president permitted the long-contested burial of Ferdinand Marcos at the Cemetery of Heroes. Dondon had been a Duterte supporter, had sometimes lied in the president's defense, but he would never support the glorification of a dictator. So Dondon went to one protest, and then to the next. He followed the news. He watched Duterte's continued isolation of the opposition. Then he saw Congress shut down the ABS-CBN Broadcasting Network.

He is regretful, but he is a practical man, a Jesuit-educated dentist who admits to a life of comfortable privilege. His opposition to Duterte did not demand any emotional breast-beating, only a concession that he was wrong. In the summer of 2020, Dondon Chan and a pair of friends created a social media group. They called it Kwentong Ex-DDS—Ex-DDS Stories—a place where confessions could be made by people who had voted for Duterte and regretted that vote. The entire project is something of Dondon's own confessional. "You wouldn't think of doing this if you didn't go through it."

There are more than seventy thousand members in a group that started with a few hundred. Dondon is careful with them, protects them when he can, because it's not only the DDS who attack but also the people who have despised Duterte from the beginning and blame those who once voted for him. Serves you right, they would say. That's karma for you.

The people who regret voting for Duterte have many reasons for stepping away. They are angry at the country's deepening relationship with China. They are unhappy with the loss of ABS-CBN, the media network that had been padlocked under the Marcos dictatorship and now struggles to survive without a franchise. They are distressed by the government's failure to manage the Covid-19 pandemic. Some, the Catholic faithful, have been thrown by the fact that the president called God stupid. Others speak of having supported a drug war they did not understand.

There is a word they use often, Dondon says. The word is *pagsisisi*. It can mean many things. Regret, for some. Guilt, for others. In Filipino, the fullest translation of *pagsisisi* is *contrition*. To be contrite, from the Latin *contrītus*—"bruised, crushed; worn or broken by rubbing"—means, in its modern and figurative sense, according to the *OED,* to be "crushed or broken in spirit by a sense of sin, and so brought to complete penitence."

Here is Dondon Chan's confession, his act of contrition. He was wrong, and because he was wrong, it is necessary to act.

Ann Valdez voted for Rodrigo Duterte because she had found in Duterte a father. She had never had a father, and Father Digong was the man she chose. On the day he was inaugurated, she moved into a new home, where she had built Duterte into the foundation, sticking six five-peso coins into the wet cement of her front stoop. Thirty pesos for Du30, for June 30, moving day, inauguration day, the day Father became president because Ann had not let him down.

She was happy when he won. She was happy with her home. She was happy too when she found out she was pregnant with her second child, before she lost the baby in a public hospital where the doctors ignored her and the nurses laughed when she couldn't push the baby out. She left then, left the new house, left the country, went off to work as a domestic helper so that some-day she could afford the cost of a private hospital.

She was in Macau when the pandemic hit. She had time on her hands, and spent that time on social media, on the public page of her town of Baler. When Duterte was attacked, she de-fended. She began trolling critics of the man she called Father. She stole their photos, posted them on her own timeline, named them and shamed them until their wives and children were dragged into the mix. "I bashed them," she says. It got worse and worse. She made up an account under a different name, her first time. She hounded actors, public figures, everyone who criticized Duterte. *You sons of bitches,* she would say. *You idiots. You dumbasses.* She said things she never would have said as Ann Valdez.

It began to occur to her that she might be wrong. She started reading the criticism, discovered that it was possible the critics might have had a point. Once, in a fit of curiosity, she sent a message to one of them, a Filipino living in the United States. She asked him if he was paid to be antagonistic. He responded. He said no, certainly not. He was comfortable, living well, and could afford to pay off his own trolls if he wanted. He made sense, she thought. She felt guilty then. She tried to apologize to people she had harassed, only to find that she had been blocked by some of them.

As the pandemic lockdowns tightened in the Philippines, she worried for her son and her husband. She saw how her local government made exceptions for the powerful, had allowed officials to travel to Baler without so much as a rapid test, while most of the province endured long quarantines outside the borders. She became angrier and angrier and finally, one day, she opened her social media and called the governor an idiot. Then she thought, why just the governor, if the health secretary had failed too? Why just the health secretary, if the president was in command?

And so she wrote, and kept writing.

The attacks came quickly, so quickly that she didn't have time to hide her own private photos. Fake conversations were circulated. They said she was paid $5,000 to criticize the government. They said she was cheating on her husband. They said terrible things, so terrible that for a while even her own husband believed them.

"They can make up anything about me," she tells me, "but

they won't get anywhere because I'm a real person, a real person speaking. That's what I'm fighting for. I'm the one who was lied to. I loved Duterte, but I was lied to. I believed everything, but it was all lies. It hurt so much because I loved him. That's where I get my strength now, all my posts, everyone can feel my anger. I am really angry. Because I kept the faith, but my faith was destroyed. I was used."

She kept writing. She kept posting. She appeared at the Philippine embassy in Macau, registered to vote, and posted her own picture with her middle finger raised against the president. She discovered that her husband had also turned against Duterte and had, for a full month, been defending her to all and sundry in private messages to her detractors.

Here is Ann Valdez's confession, her act of contrition. She had loved a father, and he did not love her back. She was angry, so angry, that the moment she had saved enough, she sent money to her husband to demolish the house she built, with her tribute to Duterte on the front stoop. "I said, 'Have it destroyed. Demolish it. Raze it to the ground. We'll build again.'"

Joy Tan voted for Rodrigo Duterte because she believed in his war. She was born and raised in Mindanao. She had visited Davao. She had family involved in illegal drugs. When Duterte announced his candidacy, it was like Jesus had spoken. She knew who he was and what he stood for, and even if she was Catholic, she swallowed the cursing and the threats and the slew of rape jokes because Rodrigo Duterte was what the country needed for the sake of ordinary people like herself.

The first few months, when he was giving speech after speech, Joy's husband would text her to come home. Duterte is speaking, he would say. So she would rush back, plunk herself in front of the TV, and watch. She would quote what he said on her Face-book page. She would talk about what he said online. She had voted for him, and she was proud.

It was her husband who first turned, on the day the dictator was buried a hero on Duterte's orders. *Son of a bitch,* her husband said. *I knew it.* Her husband's grandfather had been murdered under martial law, killed, the family believed, because he was a political rival of Imelda Marcos's family. *Why,* asked her husband, *are they burying the traitor?*

Joy still believed in Duterte, but the hits kept coming, one after another. She felt attacked when Duterte called God stupid. She wept when Kian was killed, because Kian was a boy who had an exam, much like her boy whom she tutored. She was terrified when Duterte didn't take the Covid-19 virus seriously enough— "That fucking idiot corona," Duterte had said, "I'm looking for it so I can slap the moron." Then the president reversed, institut-ing lockdowns across the country so stringent that Joy could barely acquire asthma medication for her gasping son. It was, for her, the last straw.

She began to speak. Wrote online. Spoke of the dead, the lost, the mothers.

The impact was immediate. Her relatives unfriended her. Her grandmother cut her off; so did her siblings. She could not go home to Mindanao, because her friends sent a warning: you might not leave the airport alive. One brother called her a Com-munist in public, an accusation that made her a target. One aunt called Joy's father over the holidays and told him if he didn't si-lence his daughter, she would. There were no more birthday greetings, no more Christmas calls, no hellos from family across the world. And then the threats surged online, fast and hard, some anonymous, some from people she knew.

We will skin you alive, they told her.

When you leave your home, we'll put a bullet in your skull.

We hope Digong rapes you.

We hope Digong shoves his finger up your vagina.

The words hurt Joy, those first few months, "because I'm just a typical housewife." Then she saw the protests on the streets, and how protesters were picked up and jailed. She was afraid.

Tomorrow, she thought, I might be the next victim. They could call me a terrorist, a drug addict, anything.

She saw one mother killed, an activist who was on the way to the store, looking to buy food for her children.

And then she thought this: I will be braver.

She volunteered for the opposition. She joined feeding programs. She stayed up at night arguing on online forums. "I said, 'If they put up a lizard to run against Duterte, I'll vote for the lizard.' That's the way I think now. And if someone says, 'You'll be dead tomorrow,' I say, 'Well, everyone dies, but at least I won't die DDS.'"

One day, as she worked at home during the pandemic, her son asked her if she voted for Rodrigo Duterte. I did, she told him.

"This is your fault, Mama," he said.

She agreed. She told him Mama could sometimes be wrong.

She is mother to a young boy, wife to a loving man, but because of her, she says, mothers are childless, and wives are widows. She will do what she can, she will confess her sins, she will feed the hungry and volunteer for the victims, she will walk far and speak as often as she can, she will endure the threats and accept the risks, and maybe one day, her son, her boy, will tell the story of his mother who had sinned and did penance for her wrongs.

"I have one son," she tells me. "I won't let even a mosquito land on his skin. Even if he's a big boy now, I smear mosquito repellent all over him, again and again. And then I think, he can become an EJK victim, just like that. That's what I'm afraid of now, because I keep reading about the victims, and I can't understand why I let all of it pass. Why did there have to be a Kian who only wanted to take his exam?"

Here is Joy Tan's confession, her act of contrition. She believed in Rodrigo Duterte, and she voted for him because she did. "He is a demon," she says, "and I enabled him." And because she did, young boys like hers are dead.

Duterte's loyalists could kill her, but even that wouldn't be enough. Nothing, she says, "will ever atone for what I did."

Epilogue

WE ARE DUTERTE

It is four minutes past eight in the morning, and thirty-six years to the day since the Edsa Revolution. A pair of confetti cannons explode overhead. I pick up a handful. The confetti is red and blue and white. There is no yellow.

I am standing on Epifanio de los Santos Avenue, on Edsa, holding a notebook and a leaking pen, recording what the government calls a commemoration and what the papers call a celebration. It is neither. I am covering a wake, and the mourners are yet to arrive. The press is the audience. Our public is at home.

There are no presidents here, past or present. The last to have attended an Edsa anniversary was Corazon Aquino's son, the year before Rodrigo Duterte unbuttoned his shirt collar and became commander in chief. Today the interior secretary is the guest of honor. The city mayor is present, as well as the chairman of the National Historical Commission. The former commander of the 15th Strike Wing of the Philippine Air Force is present as well.

His name is Antonio Sotelo, and in 1986 he had ignored orders to attack the protesting rebels—a defection from Ferdinand Marcos that brought air-to-ground rockets, a handful of choppers, and several dozen soldiers to the civilian cause. Today, his aging presence is noted as proof "that the spirit of Edsa remained strong and alive."

The national anthem is sung. The flag is raised. The pledge of allegiance is read. Wreaths are laid, the necessary prayers broadcast over the loudspeaker. There is no mention of Benigno Aquino, Jr., the man they call Ninoy, who stepped off a plane in white and landed in red, whose wife put on a yellow dress and led millions in revolt.

The commemoration—or celebration—is over in under seven minutes. A white wreath, the smallest of the four lining the monument's yellow-tiled base, stands mounted at the center of the temporary red carpet. There is no message on the ribbon, only a name. RODRIGO ROA DUTERTE, it reads, the gold seal glinting in the morning sun, hanging limp over the circle of mums, with a few mustard bromeliads wedged under a plastic rosette. Rodrigo Roa Duterte, nicknamed Rody, sometimes called Digong, sometimes Du30, whose government had allowed the burial of the dictator Ferdinand Marcos in the Cemetery of Heroes with a twenty-one-gun salute.

The phalanx of uninterested cops, clubs clipped to their belts, slouch over their riot shields.

The first of the Ferdinands to walk on the sandy beaches of my country was Ferdinand Magellan. Ferdinand the explorer, Ferdinand the adventurer, Ferdinand, who took the Spanish king's ships and the Spanish king's men to the islands where the Spanish crown would plant cross and flag and name as tribute to Philip the Second. Las Islas Filipinas passed from white king to white president to brown, Ferdinand to Ferdinand, Magellan to Marcos, conqueror to dictator, Ferdinand Edralin Marcos of the north, whose reign bled a nation and killed the best of its children. Here is Ferdinand the Second, palm to the Bible, the other raised in oath, I, Ferdinand Romualdez Marcos, Junior, do solemnly swear. Here are the Ferdinands, President Ferdinand the First, buried a hero, followed by President Ferdinand the Second, dearly beloved son, followed by Congressman Ferdinand the Third, young and smiling, waiting in the wings.

The votes are in. The jubilant crowds have poured into the driveway of the Marcos-Duterte campaign headquarters, spilling out into Epifanio de los Santos Avenue itself, where the citizens of the revolution once marched to overthrow Ferdinand Marcos, Sr.

I am a product of him, said the son of his father.

I am his son, he said. I am the same name.

On the day the name wins, in 2022, there is chanting and laughing and dancing and arms raised in victory. The cars rattle past. Tiny flags wave. A campaign volunteer weeps, a young criminology student who will someday be a lawyer. She says it will be her life's mission to clear the Marcos name. A single shout soars over the honking horns: "Edsa is ours."

Think of the same highway, five lanes on each side, in the early light of a Sunday morning in 1986. Think of it crowded, kilometer after kilometer, with a moving mass of men and women, sweating through white T-shirts tucked into jeans, carrying crucifixes and boom boxes and umbrellas, in baseball caps and Christian Dior boaters and sweaty ponytails and grimy straw hats. Think of the tanks charging down the asphalt, think of the helicopters circling overhead, think of the fortifications conjured out of sandbags and tree trunks and lampposts and telephone poles, think of the masses snapping like a cordon around the rebel camps: the grim-faced nuns, the grandfathers bent over radios, the matrons passing out sandwiches, and the fresh-faced girls clutching their handfuls of flowers. Think, finally, of the priest in jeans and boots on the front lines, the hem of his white cassock in one fist as he roars in defiance at the dictator's soldiers, *Are you going to shoot fellow Filipinos?*

Yes. The answer is yes.

Yes, said Rodrigo Duterte. Shoot to kill. He can't be blamed because he had issued a warning. He told the addicts what would happen. Tell the police precincts, he said, let everyone know. If Duterte sees you, he'll snatch you up and deal with you himself. He has a barge down the Pasig River—he'll load you on and toss you out. Good for you if you're already dead.

"You know, they have to realize that they do not have the monopoly of evil in this. It's not as if because we're in government, we can't do anything other than play the good boy. The enemy is evil—which is the lesser evil now? The ones who cooked the drugs and fed it to our children or us who had them killed?"

There is no blood on the scene. The body had been abandoned at the high point of the bridge in the shadow of the cement parapet. He is a big man, with big, bare feet. He wears red basketball shorts and a sleeveless blue-and-white jersey. Truck headlights play over the thick plastic tape wrapped around his head like a helmet. Someone had scrawled on the brown cardboard sign left beside him: DRUG PUSHER. DO NOT IMITATE.

Camera lights flash. A radio reporter barks a dispatch. Ten-wheeler delivery trucks rumble past the crowd of onlookers. The dead man lies perfectly symmetrical, flush against the wall, the still center of the roaring circus that is a Manila crime scene.

I am kneeling just outside the yellow tape when I hear her scream. It is a wordless, keening cry. I see her face first, pale in the distance, blue-and-red police lights shooting off her hair. She comes running from the bottom of the bridge before flinging herself to the pavement beside me.

"Please, let me touch him," she begs the cops. "Why won't you let me touch him?"

Her name is Ivy. She says the dead man is her husband. His name is Rene. She knows him by his feet.

The investigator tries to cut through the packing tape mask. The scissors break. He takes out a cutter. The blade slices from the edge of an ear and traces the line of jaw and chin and cheek to curve under the other ear.

The face underneath is slack and damp. A thin dark line runs over his neck. Rene Desierto had been stabbed nineteen times. Cause of death was recorded as asphyxiation by ligature. He had been garroted. His death is an execution.

Welcome to Manila, the flight attendant says. *Mabuhay*.

Mabuhay. "To live." A greeting, according to our dictionaries. The Filipino aloha, say the travel guides. It is the salutation extended by the tourism services, the cheerful greeting of every pageant queen, the cursive sign over airport lounges, the Monday special in Fil-Am restaurants. No Filipino born in the Philippines opens a door and sings out *mabuhay*. We pick up the phone and say hello, good morning, how are you, how may I help you—yes? *Mabuhay* is a performance, offered up to the outside world as its public face. Ninoy Aquino had long been dead by the time a restaurateur launched a campaign in 1993 to replace the word *welcome* with the word *mabuhay* to demonstrate "our people's warmth of character," and to "enhance our nationalism."

He might have laughed had he known, but he was dead, his last words spoken inside an airplane to the correspondents who would write of the man who had warned them all to have their cameras ready.

Died *of,* died *on,* died *at;* the prepositions matter, even in the intransitive. Ninoy Aquino died of a gunshot wound, a single bullet to the back of the head. Died on the tarmac, the red bleeding into white linen. Died fourteen minutes past one in the afternoon, Philippine Standard Time. Died, in the airport that would bear his name, in the country he had hoped to lead. The prepositions are correct, but they are not sufficient, because Aquino, former journalist, understood that a story requires intent. Died *for,* he said. It is a preposition that became a religion, with Aquino the sacrificed Christ nailed on the cross of the revolution.

Mabuhay, says the flight attendant, as the plane taxis down the runway. Mabuhay, welcome to Manila, feel at home. Listen to it spoken with a bob and a smile, shoulders back, head tilted, a practice as personal as an automatic door, in a country where the only proper articulation for mabuhay is a scream. Here, in Manila, it is wisdom and warning. *I hope you live.*

In Davao, Rodrigo Duterte, nicknamed Rody, sometimes called Digong, sometimes Du30, speaks one last time as President of the Republic, onstage at the inauguration of his youngest son, who had just been elected mayor as his father had once been, as his sister had just been, before that sister was elected vice president beside the Marcos son.

What a queer coincidence, said the president, that for a single moment, the president and vice president–elect of the Philippines are both Dutertes.

Forget that their name is Marcos. Forget that their name is

Duterte. Forget that their name is Aquino. Duterte the First begat Duterte the Second. Aquino the Second begat Aquino the Third. Marcos the First begat Marcos the Second begat Marcos the Third, presidents begetting presidents, begetting vice presidents, rotating and revolving and rotating again. Their names live in airports and amphitheaters, on paper bills and street signs, along the highways where the corpses are still being found. Forget the names of their sons and daughters and remember their dead instead.

Remember Djastin, Djastin with a D, not Justin or Justine, Djastin, with a D, the D chosen to make him special, Djastin with a D, whose mother used to carry him to the hospital through the knee-high floods whenever he trembled and seized, Djastin with a D, whose name police misspelled on the report that lied about his death, Djastin with a D, the D silent, as Djastin would always be, always twenty-five, always there on the railroad tracks, shot then slapped, then shot again, gasping out Mama, help me Mama please.

Remember all the children we cannot name. Remember the father whose last word was Love.

We are Duterte, said the man with the gun.

Remember these names: Constantino de Juan, father of Christine, dead on a blue couch with the bullet buried in the cushion. Buwaya of Santa Ana, born Ryan Eder. Remember Heart, Kian, Toyo, Joseph, JC, Antonio, Pinuno, Sitoy with his hanging grenades. Remember Charlie Saladaga, sitting in a park with his face to the sky, watching the fireworks on New Year's Eve, the day before he disappeared.

Remember this name: Mark Andy Ocdin, the last of Duterte's dead, killed on the last Sunday of Rodrigo Duterte's presidency, on the same railroad tracks where Djastin dies and lives and dies again whenever Normy Lopez closes her eyes. Mark Andy Ocdin is the third of his brothers to die in the war, jailed on drug charges and set free before men wearing masks shot him in the gut. Andy ran down a narrow alley, where he fell into the arms of a woman who opened a door and dragged him in. By the time Andy was killed, shot six times just down the street from his grandmother's house, the Ocdins knew which hospital was equipped for gunshot wounds, even if none of the Ocdin boys ever came out of the emergency room alive. They knew not to push when the police refused to release an official report and knew to double down for the death certificate because the church sent burial assistance only when the back page was filled out with a cause of death. (It was multiple gunshot wounds for Andy, the same as for JR, just two years after Anthony was found salvaged with his fingernails ripped out.)

The Ocdins knew which village councilor had a tent to lend for the wake, and they also knew where to buy the balloons—five dollars for ten, stamped with WE LOVE YOU MARK ANDY in faded blue ink. They knew the funeral parlor would have a suit for sale, one-size-fits-all, eighteen dollars, with undershirt and socks provided, no shoes required. They knew which neighbors would volunteer to carry the coffin—"All my sons were carried by their friends," Cristina tells me. Here he lies, Mark Andy, the last of the dead sons, the rattle of the passing train juddering through painted plywood and the wilting white mums, as the voice of the dictator's son crackles over the radio, "*that I will faithfully and conscientiously fulfill my duties as the president of the Philippines . . .*"

The Ocdins knew to wear white to the funeral, not black, because white was holy and clean and respectable, and they wanted everyone to know their dead boys were too. They knew how many people could fit into a hired jeep for the ride to the cemetery, where a hundred dollars would cover the fee to re-open Anthony's niche to make room for Andy. They knew everything, the Ocdins did; even if Cristina sometimes forgot how many of her children were left—five, not four, as one neighbor corrected—she will remember how many the government has killed.

Vincent and I are sitting at my kitchen table. He lights a cigarette. I pour another shot of gin.

"Nine hundred and ninety?" I ask.

"At least," he says.

Vincent had stayed to document the dead long after the papers stopped publishing photos of the daily slaughter. Sometimes he went to crime scenes alone, the only journalist left following the morgue truck. He printed out the names of the lost and taped them to his dining room wall, a sight so morbid even Raffy complained when he came over for a meal. Once, when the call came on a Sunday night, he brought his toddler along, leaving her in the car with his wife just long enough to do his job. He marked every crime scene on a map, a yellow star for every corpse he saw. By the time Ferdinand Marcos, Jr., was elected, Vincent had collected at least 990 stars. The phrase "at least" is important, as Vincent only started pinning locations seven months after the first surge of bodies.

Vincent did not vote for Rodrigo Duterte in 2016, because he didn't vote at all. Had he voted then, he might have voted for Duterte, because Duterte had promised to kill the corrupt.

"If he had really concentrated on the corrupt, yeah, I would have supported him," Vincent tells me. He leans back in his chair. "That's what Filipinos really need, somebody like him who was determined to do that sort of thing, the unconventional thing—but for the good. Not just for popularity."

"He already claims he killed addicts and dealers for the good," I say. "For the future of children. For your children."

"He killed drug users. Users. They're also victims . . . drug addiction is a disease. But he never killed the source of the drugs, and up to this day the market is flooded. Was it stopped? No."

"But if he killed the corrupt," I venture, "you would have no problem?"

"None." He pauses. "Even now. And I wouldn't have focused on the killings that deeply. I would just tell him, 'Good job.'"

"There's my epilogue," I tell him.

He laughs.

Some people need killing, a vigilante told me once.

Consider this sentence. It is an active sentence, not passive. Some people need killing.

The subject is the people. The object is the killing. *Killing* is not the verb here, *need* is. They needed to die. They chose their own deaths. They earned their dying, had it coming, traded the right to live. Some people were killed because they needed to be killed. It is a presumption of regularity, cause to effect. The language does not allow for accountability. The standard is arbitrary and is generally accepted. Some people are addicts, dealers, criminals. The execution of their deaths is a performance of duty. All that is required is the determination of who deserves to live.

But *kill* is a transitive verb. The subject can be named. The cops killed Djastin Lopez. The war killed Djastin Lopez. Rodrigo Duterte killed Djastin Lopez. Ask Normy Lopez. The direct line from order to trigger to bullet to death can be drawn and drawn straight. The subject killed; the object died.

Are you going to shoot fellow Filipinos?

"I have asked myself many times," Ninoy Aquino once said, "is the Filipino worth suffering, or even dying, for? Is he not a coward who would readily yield to any colonizer, be he foreign or homegrown? Is a Filipino more comfortable under an authoritarian leader because he does not want to be burdened with the freedom of choice? Is he unprepared or, worse, ill-suited for presidential or parliamentary democracy?"

Five months after I was born, thirty-seven years ago, my people said that no man should die because a dictator said he must. My people said it in front of tanks. They said it in front of guns. They knelt and they sang and they prayed and they were brave, and because they were, I was born free.

"I have carefully weighed the virtues and the faults of the Filipino, and I have come to the conclusion that he is worth dying for," Ninoy Aquino said in a speech delivered in 1980.

The Filipino is brave, he explained. The Filipino values life. The Filipino is patient, is dignified, is good. The Filipino is a good follower, and with a good leader, a Filipino can attain great heights. The Filipino is deserving of the sacrifice, "because he is the nation's greatest untapped resource."

I see him in the dim light. He has weighed my people in his mind, imagined their virtues, found them deserving. The Filipino is worth dying for, says the man dressed in crisp linen and blood.

I tell him about the dead. Suspected criminals, addicts, dealers, thieves, men who carry grenades slung around their necks, men who have sold meth to children, men who, by most standards, do not qualify as anyone's untapped resource. Are they worth dying for? I tell him about the living, who voted for a killer, applauded the dictator's son, and called his own son a coward. Are they worth dying for?

He weighs their faults. He calculates their worth. He does not have an answer.

Across from him is another man, slouching back into his chair, plaid shirt unbuttoned, legs spread, a gun on his belt. Son of a bitch, the mayor says. You stupid son of a bitch. The Filipino is worth killing for. The dead do not count. They do not deserve to live.

My grandfather ruffles my hair. Survive, he says. He lights a Dunhill with a match, lets the ash spill onto the tile, offers me the pack.

The dying is not the point, he says. I am the surviving majority.

Duck for cover, and live.

Are you going to shoot fellow Filipinos?

We are Duterte, my people reply.

Ask not for whom the sirens wail.

Ivy found her husband, Rene, on top of a bridge, his head wrapped in tape. She knew him by his feet. They were big and bare, as they had been most of his life.

Many things have happened in the years since he died. Ivy lost her job. She tried to cut open her wrists twice. Occasionally she wrapped her head in packing tape, in imitation of her dead husband. She said she wanted to know how it felt. There were days she believed his death was her fault. She has many reasons. If she had run up the bridge faster, she might have pumped his chest in time. If she had never filed a missing person's report, his killers might have let him live.

The last of the reasons comes from their young son. Once, during an argument, Ivy had told Rene she wished he were dead. Their boy remembered. "It's your fault," her son told her. "You wanted Daddy to die."

I'm writing a book, I tell Ivy.

Tell them our story, she says.

I see Ivy every few months. I carry a box of chicken for her son, sometimes doughnuts. She sets an ashtray on the plastic placemat. I push my pack of cigarettes across the table, along with my recorder.

We light up, before I press the button.

"We're on the record," I say.

Acknowledgments

This book is a record of the drug war fought in the six years between 2016 and 2022 under the administration of President Rodrigo Duterte. My writing, however, is informed by more than a decade of field journalism in the Philippines. I am grateful to the hundreds of men and women who have generously shared their stories. Thank you, particularly, to Ivy Desierto, Christine de Juan, Normy Lopez, Efren Morillo, Cristina Saladaga, Lady Love, and the Daa and De Chavez families. All of them have chosen to bear witness in the aftermath of unimaginable horror. I remain in their debt and am in awe of their courage.

My drug war reporting first appeared as a series of stories called "Impunity" for the online news organization Rappler, where I worked as an investigative journalist. Portions of those stories appear throughout this book. Rappler's unstinting support, despite threats and limited resources, was crucial across the early years of the drug war. I am especially grateful to multimedia head Beth Frondoso, for the careful insight that protected me in the field; to investigative head Chay Hofileña, for her dedication to documenting this story; to chief executive officer Maria Ressa, for encouraging independent journalism at great personal cost; and to my indefatigable newsroom manager Glenda Gloria, Rappler's wartime consigliere, who was the compass that has always led me to my true north, both literal and imagined.

No amount of words can sufficiently describe the dedication of the many men and women who have contributed to documenting what I have come to call Duterte's war. Some have been credited in this book; many others, for reasons valid and varied, cannot yet be named.

I am fortunate to have worked in the company of some of the bravest and best of Philippine journalism. I am especially grateful to photojournalists Ezra Acayan, Raffy Lerma, and Vincent Go, as well as filmmakers Alyx Arumpac and Carsten Stormer, whose commitment to the stories they covered held long after the bodies were carried out.

I have also benefited from reporting by ABS-CBN News, CNN Philippines, GMA Integrated News, MindaNews, the Philippine Center for Investigative Journalism, *The Philippine Daily Inquirer*, *The Philippine Star*, Reuters, TV5, and *VERA Files*. Their work has been invaluable in the writing of this book, as were investigations by Amnesty International, Human Rights Watch, and the Commission on Human Rights, whose late chairman, Chito Gascon, honored his charge with the same quiet fortitude he displayed during a lifetime spent as a freedom fighter. Many thanks as well to Society of the Divine Word missionary Flaviano Villanueva, Vincentian priest Danny Pilario, and Brother Jun Santiago of the Redemptorist Congregation, for the tenacity that sustained so many of the families who continue to deal with the aftermath of the drug war.

Many cases included in this book are here in part because of exceptional work by human rights lawyers. I am grateful for the trust given to me by the Center for International Law, the Free Legal Assistance Group, and the National Union of Peoples' Lawyers, with particular thanks to Tin Antonio, Gil Anthony Aquino, Joel Butuyan, Kristina Conti, and Chel Diokno. I am grateful, especially, for the rationality and vigilance of my own legal counsel, Theodore Te, who, no matter the circumstance, always saw four lights.

Throughout the writing of this book, I was the recipient of many kindnesses from many people. I am grateful for the generous guidance of Karina Bolasco, Gina Chua, Caloy Conde, Sheila Coronel, Kiri Dalena, John Molo, Vergel Santos, Miguel Syjuco, Alfred Yuson, and the late Luis Teodoro and Melvyn Calderon; for the astute observations of advance readers Rupert Compston, Jon Morales, Raffy Tima, Mariz Umali, and Hidde van der Wall; for the encouragement of Erwin Romulo, my former editor at *Esquire Philippines;* for the creative contributions of Ricci Chan, Geloy Concepcion, Mark Nicdao, and Ellen Ramos; and for the companionship and advice of fellow writers from across the world: Susan Berfield, Andrew Sean Greer, Suzy Hansen, Sydney Jin Choi, Pardiss Kebriaei, Meg Kissinger, Amanda Oliver, Safiya Sinclair, Stobo Sniderman, Andrew Solomon, and Tara Westover. Sincerest thanks to Dondon Chan, Joy Tan, Jason Quizon, and Ann Valdez for trusting me with their stories, to relatives Boo Chanco, Louie Chanco, Ying Chanco, Maria Teresa Chanco-Goodrich, and Maria Chanco-Turner for their grace and honesty, and to Maria Pilar Davidson and Mark Evangelista, for the hospitality that offered much needed respite. Kimberly dela Cruz, Alex Evangelista, Aiah Fernandez, Bianca Franco, Jodesz Gavilan, JC Gotinga, Monica Orillo, and Nicole Revita were critical to research. Cecille Santos and Roque Angub provided logistical support far beyond the call of duty. Historians Paulo Alcazaren, Macky Blanco, Brian Giron, Aaron Mallari, and Roy Mendoza offered sound judgment. Fact-checkers Michelle Abad, Lian Buan, Krixia Subingsubing, and Rambo Talabong conducted a meticulous review to correct inaccuracies and my own failures of memory. Particular thanks to the thoroughness of journalist Mike Navallo, whose hard work and judicious counsel set this book on firmer foundations.

I am immensely grateful to my agent, David Granger of Aevitas Creative Management. It was Granger who believed I could write a book, did not believe me when I said I couldn't, and remained an encouraging voice across years of bad drafts and frantic phone calls. It was also Granger whose infallible judgment brought me to Random House.

I am grateful to my publisher Andy Ward, deputy publisher Tom Perry, assistant editor Chayenne Skeete, design director Greg Mollica, publicity director London King, marketing manager Michael Hoak, and legal counsel Carolyn Foley. I am particularly thankful to production editor Craig Adams and copy editor Janet Biehl, whose careful reading and endless patience made this book the best version of itself.

I am most deeply grateful to the vision of my editor Mark Warren, who understood what this book was meant to be long before I ever did. He refused every easy evasion, demanded the seemingly impossible, demonstrated the infinite range of the English language, and in the end made certain I did not, in his words, fuck it up. Working with him was an education. It was also an honor.

I am grateful to the Logan Nonfiction Fellowship and the Headlands Center for the Arts, where parts of this book were written; to the Civitella Ranieri Residency Program and the Corporation of Yaddo, for the safe refuge in community of artists; to the De La Salle Democracy Discourse Series, the New America Fellows Program, and the Whiting Creative Nonfiction Grant, for the essential, incalculable support; to the Dart Center for Trauma and Journalism, for the resources that contributed to the ethical coverage of the war; and to the Council on Southeast Asia Studies at the Whitney and Betty MacMillan Center for International and Area Studies at Yale University, for the privilege of their welcome.

I would also like to acknowledge the writing that has heavily influenced the structure and storytelling of this book: *The Womanly Face of War* by Svetlana Alexievich; *We Tell Ourselves Stories in Order to Live* by Joan Didion; *1919* by John Dos Passos; *Billy Lynn's Long Halftime Walk* by Ben Fountain; *The Face of War* by Martha Gellhorn; *We Wish to Inform You That Tomorrow We Will Be Killed with Our Families: Stories from Rwanda* by Philip Gourevitch; *The Things They Carried* by Tim O'Brien; *Nineteen Eighty-Four* by George Orwell; "Fatal Distraction" by Gene Weingarten for *The Washington Post;* and *The Right Stuff* by Tom Wolfe.

I am grateful to my mother, Felicia, who told me stories, and to my father, Bobby, who listened to all of mine.

I am fortunate too in the friends who are family up and down the stairs of the Loyola commune: poet Mikael de Lara Co, who understood the dynamic equivalence of truth; photojournalist Eloisa Lopez, who walked with me in the dark of the streets and her own memory; writer Pocholo Goitia, who answered every phone call in every time zone to untangle sentences; bassist Joko Maymay, who told me exactly where to find my cojones; activist Voltaire Tupaz, who offered joy and sunsets despite my better judgment; and reporter Sofia Tomacruz, who ferreted out every error, reread every word twice, and added far more than twenty-three. I am especially fortunate in my friendships with Nicole Curato, the sociologist who drew me a map of the world and shoved me out of the classroom into seventeen years of journalism, and Paolo Villaluna, the filmmaker who has been my quiet writing partner of more than a decade, whose extraordinary perception continues to be a source of both exasperation and inspiration.

Most of all, I am grateful for the sanity and compassion of Dominic Gabriel Go, who held my hand through the war and long after. My Dominic, who thinks I am braver than I am and better than I can be, without whose faith this book would never have been possible.

Notes

A Note on Translation

Translations in this book are literal when possible. The author recognizes that nuances do not always render naturally into English, particularly as utilized in everyday conversation. The author, and translator Mikael de Lara Co, have determined that fidelity to the original meaning is the primary imperative to render the truest accounting. They have on occasion deviated beyond literal translation into dynamic equivalence.

This is most evident in the translation of curse words. *Putang ina,* for example, translates literally into "whore of a mother." The phrase can mean "son of a bitch," "son of a whore," "motherfucker," "fuck," "shit," or "damn," depending on context. In these cases, the author prefers to utilize the expression that most accurately captures the intent of the moment.

Direct quotes from official documents such as police reports and court filings are reproduced in the original English.

A Note on Quoting Rodrigo Duterte

The former president generally speaks extemporaneously. He has voiced more than once his unwillingness to read from prepared remarks. His speeches are sometimes rambling and often circuitous. They can last hours and range over many subjects while interspersed with personal anecdotes, denunciations of his critics, and patently offensive statements that are sometimes described as humor or hyperbole by his spokespersons. While the author has attempted to remain true to the nuances of the president's shifts in tone and topic, there may be differing interpretations as to the intent of the president himself. It is, however, important to note that every statement Rodrigo Duterte makes in public is received as the official language of a head of state.

The author relies on video recordings as the primary source for statements attributed to Rodrigo Duterte. Each of the statements published in this book, whether rephrased for narrative purposes or directly quoted, have been independently confirmed by fact-checkers Michelle Abad, Lian Buan, Mike Navallo, Krixia Subingsubing, and Sofia Tomacruz against recordings released by official government channels or the news media.

The author has used a chronological database as a guide for crafting this book. Researcher Jodesz Gavilan extracted transcripts from press releases sent to palace reporters or downloaded documents directly from the website of the Presidential Communications Operations Office. The author's database is by no means a complete accounting of all Rodrigo Duterte's official utterances. It begins in 2014, when then-mayor Duterte addressed the budding grassroots movement calling on him to run for the presidency—"I would like to tell you now that I have no presidential ambitions"—and ends on June 27, 2022, at an oath-taking of newly elected government officials in Davao City. When limited to the six years of the Duterte administration, the database covers 1,184 speaking events, comprising over four million words in a 19,204-page document.

Direct quotations, translated or otherwise, are prefaced in the notes with "quoted from." Rephrased statements are prefaced with "drawn from." Speeches, interviews, and press conferences without official transcripts were individually transcribed from available recordings. When video or transcript was unavailable, the author cites news coverage, academic articles, watchdog reports, and government releases.

A Note on Due Diligence

Unless previously interviewed or cited from published reports, the author has reached out to all individuals accused of varying activities in this book. On May 12, 2023, letters of invitation were sent out to the official addresses of six individuals. Each recipient, or their representative, was informed of the existence of this book and its general scope. The author invited each recipient to an interview or to the opportunity to answer questions by email correspondence. All were offered fourteen days to respond as well as the right to view questions on request. The list included former President Rodrigo Roa Duterte, former National Police Director General Ronald "Bato" dela Rosa, Police Lt. Col. Robert Domingo, Police Maj. Emil Garcia, Police Maj. Edwin Fuggan, and former CHR Region XI Director Albert Sipaco, Jr.

Because former President Duterte holds no public office, and has not established any foundations since the end of his term, a letter of request was sent via fast courier to the office of his former special assistant, Senator Christopher Lawrence "Bong" T. Go at the Philippine Senate Building. The author holds a notarized affidavit of service certifying the letter's delivery. A copy was also sent over email to Go's media relations office and through an email address given to the author by the former president's current assistant, who was endorsed by the office of Senator Go.

The letter invited the former president or his representative to answer questions pertaining to the Davao Death Squad and the enforcement of the Philippine drug war. On May 16, 2023, the president's assistant responded through email requesting questions from the author. They were sent the next day, on May 17.

The questions totaled to thirteen. Many were an attempt to reconcile competing narratives, or to verify claims made by the former president himself. "You have often referred to having killed criminals, but the number varies. Can you categorically say how many individuals you have personally killed?" How did the president see himself as child of poverty with a governor for a father? Was the shooting of Octavio Goco the result of an accident, a duel, or an intentional shooting? Who were the assassins he was referring to when he said criminals were legitimate targets for assassination? What did he do to the suspected addict who allegedly raped a baby in Mandug? What was the basis for the 77,000 people the former president claimed had been killed by drug addicts? Did he believe, given the presumption of regularity, that an officer of the law could kill legally? If the slew of deaths during the drug war were not to be called extrajudicial killings, what was the president's preferred term?

Other questions sought responses to public allegations. What was the president's response to claims he subsidized vigilante group Alsa Masa, or to accusations he ordered targeted executions through the Davao Death Squad, or the story that his mother secured him his post as a Davao City prosecutor?

The list ended with the question of whether the former president considered his drug war a success.

His representative sent the former president's regrets on May 23, citing prior commitments and conflicts in scheduling. The author responded reiterating that emailed answers were sufficient.

There has been no further communication as of publication.

Epigraph

vii **"is instill fear"**: Rodrigo Duterte quoted in Jeffrey M. Tupaz, "Where Crime Suspects Live Dangerously," *Philippine Daily Inquirer,* February 15, 2009.

Prologue

xi–xiii **the Kill List . . . "casualties in the Duterte administration's war"**: Beginning July 7, 2016, the *Philippine Daily Inquirer* published what it called "The Kill List." The list was updated twice a week. Its final update was published on February 16, 2017, just after the Philippine National Police (PNP) was suspended for the first time from participation in the conduct of the drug war. The list totals 2,127 names, with 104 killed by the police and 1,022 by unknown hitmen.

xii **"threaten to destroy my country"**: Rodrigo Duterte, quote from speech at the Opening Ceremonies of Agrilink/Foodlink/Aqualink 2017, World Trade Center, Pasay City, October 5, 2017.

xiii **silence possible informants**: Bea Cupin, "Dela Rosa: Drug Syndicates 'Killing Each Other,' " Rappler, July 14, 2016.

xiii **"those who perished"**: ABS-CBN Investigative and Research Group, "Map, Charts: The Death Toll of the War on Drugs," ABS-CBN News Digital, July 13, 2016.

xiii **"summary killings"**: Office of Senator Leila de Lima, "De Lima Blames Duterte for Rash of Killings in PH" (press release), Senate of the Philippines, March 12, 2021.

xiii **"alleged vigilante-style killings"**: Department of the Interior and Local Government, "Sueno to Bato: Do Quick Probe on Vigilante-Style Drug Killings" (press release), August 8, 2016.

xiii **"summary executions of criminals"**: Resolution No. 9, Senate of the Philippines, 17th Congress, 2016.

Chapter 1: Positive

3–7 **My name is Lady Love . . . It was a blow that started it . . . "We are Duterte"**: Love-Love's narrative is drawn from interviews by the author. The first interview in 2016 was conducted in the presence of Love-Love's guardian. A second interview was conducted in 2023 after Love-Love came of age. She has consented to the use of her first name and nickname in this account of her story.

5 **villages**: A *barangay* is "the smallest political unit in the country." It is, according to the Philippine Statistics Authority (https://psa.gov.ph), smaller than a town or municipality. While the literal translation may vary depending on usage, *village* is used throughout the book in place of *barangay*. The village captain (*barangay kapitan*) is an elected position with a fixed term of three years.

5–9 **babies were zipped into backpacks . . . layer cake of cars and corpses . . . cornfields in rebel country . . . out of the mouth in rivulets**: This account of the aftermath of Super Typhoon Haiyan, the fatal clash between rebels and police officers in Mamasapano, and the siege of Zamboanga City is drawn from Patricia Evangelista, "The Baby in the Backpack," Rappler, February 2, 2014; Patricia Evangelista, "The Mourners of Mamasapano," Rappler, February 18, 2015; and Patricia Evangelista, "Blood from the Sky," Rappler, October 17, 2013.

6 **1,254 times:** This figure is a tally of every instance President Rodrigo Duterte spoke the word *kill,* based on the author's database of transcripts between July 1, 2016, and June 30, 2017. The true number is likely higher.

6 **promising to kill people:** Rodrigo Duterte, drawn from speech at Baden Powell Day (Founder's Day) of the World Scout Organization of the Scout Movement and Investiture Ceremony of the Boy Scouts of the Philippines, Malacañang, April 3, 2017.

6 **jobs to be had killing:** Rodrigo Duterte made this statement to overseas Filipino workers repatriated from Saudi Arabia, in an exchange that was overheard by media present on site. See Christina Mendez, "Rody's Job Offer to OFWs: Kill Drug Addicts," *Philippine Star,* April 17, 2017.

6 **repent, resign, or die:** Rodrigo Duterte, drawn from speech at the mass oath-taking of newly appointed government officials, Malacañang, January 9, 2017. Duterte also made this statement in a series of meetings with mayors held in Malacañang on January 11, 2017. The *Philippine Daily Inquirer* reported Duterte's remarks by interviewing mayors present at these meetings. See Leila Salaverria, "Duterte Tells Mayors: Repent, Resign or Die," *Philippine Daily Inquirer,* January 12, 2017.

6 **threatened to kill human rights activists:** Rodrigo Duterte, drawn from speech at the Inauguration and Ceremonial Switch-on of the 135-Megawatt Circulating Fluidized Bed Combustion of the Palm Concepcion Power Plant, Malacañang, November 28, 2016.

6 **medals for killing:** Rodrigo Duterte, drawn from speech at Thanksgiving Party After Elections, Davao City, June 4, 2016.

6 **journalists they could be legitimate targets of assassination:** Rodrigo Duterte, drawn from media interview at press conference, Davao City, May 31, 2016.

6 **"find these people and kill them, period":** Rodrigo Duterte, quoted from speech at Proclamation Rally, Tondo, Manila, February 10, 2016.

8 **the reporter Wilfred Burchett . . . "a warning to the world":** George Burchett and Nick Shimmin, eds., *Rebel Journalism: The Writings of Wilfred Burchett* (Cambridge, U.K.: Cambridge University Press, 2007).

9 **Seven, twelve, twenty-six:** These numbers refer to the toll of recorded killings on three separate nights during the drug war. For details, see Non Alquitran, "7 More Drug Suspects Killed," *Philippine Star,* June 22, 2016; Patricia Evangelista, "The Drug War: Monday," Rappler, Octo-

ber 21, 2016; Reuters, "Another 26 Killed Overnight as Philippine Drug War Gets Bloodier," *South China Morning Post,* August 17, 2017.

9 **kill the addicts:** Rodrigo Duterte, drawn from speech at the Solidarity Dinner with the Poor, Delpan Sports Complex, Tondo, Manila, June 30, 2016.

9 **kill the mayors:** the 25th Annual Convention of the Vice Mayors' League of the Philippines, Malacañang, June 28, 2018.

9 **kill the lawyers:** Marlon Ramos, "Duterte Warns Drug Lords' Lawyers," *Philippine Daily Inquirer,* December 9, 2016.

10 **children, but they were killed:** Rebecca Ratcliffe, "War on Drugs Blamed for Deaths of at Least 122 Children in Philippines," *Guardian,* June 30, 2020.

10 **they were collateral damage:** Rodrigo Duterte, drawn from speech at the Department of Agriculture Launch of the National Color-coded Agriculture Guide Map, Malacañang, March 7, 2017.

10 **His name was Maximo:** Maximo Garcia, interview by the author, August 30, 2016. For a full investigation of the death of Danica Mae Garcia, see Patricia Evangelista, "Danica, My Danica," Rappler, September 6, 2016.

11 **oldest democracy in Southeast Asia:** Julio C. Teehankee and Cleo Anne A. Calimbahin, "Mapping the Philippines' Defective Democracy," *Asian Affairs: An American Review,* 47:2, 97–125 (2020).

11 **the murders of thirty-two journalists . . . bombardment of Zamboanga City . . . arrogance sent forty-four unsuspecting policemen:** This enumeration refers to the 2009 massacre in Maguindanao that killed fifty-eight people, including thirty-two journalists; the 2013 siege of Zamboanga City by rebel forces; and the 2015 Mamasapano clash that killed forty-four Special Action Force policemen.

12 **In the world as imagined . . . Duterte had your back . . . might give you a warning . . . an end to drugs:** Nicole Curato and Patricia Evangelista, "The Punisher," Rappler, February 19, 2016; previously published for the Imagined President series.

12 **"Hitler massacred three million Jews":** While historians cite a death toll of 6 million during the Holocaust, Rodrigo Duterte, on his return from Vietnam, understated the number in a speech delivered in Davao City, Philippines, September 30, 2016.

12 **Her name was Christine:** Christine, interviews by the author. The first interview was conducted in the presence of Christine's guardian in 2016. A second interview was conducted in 2023 after Christine came of age. She has consented to the use of her name. For a full investigation of the death of Constantino de Juan, see Patricia Evangelista, with additional reporting by Lian Buan, Kimberly dela Cruz, Alex Evangelista,

and photographer Carlo Gabuco, "This Is Where They Do Not Die," Rappler, November 25, 2017.

14 *rap,* for **"discuss"**: "Rappler's Mission Statement," Rappler, February 22, 2021.

14 **the late summer of 2011:** This account was previously published in Patricia Evangelista, "Rappler at 10: Employee No. 6," Rappler, December 12, 2021.

16 **fake news:** Pia Ranada, "Duterte Calls Rappler 'Fake News Outlet,'" Rappler, January 16, 2018.

16 **paid hacks:** Rodrigo Duterte, drawn from Second State of the Nation Address, Batasang Pambansa, Quezon City, July 24, 2017.

16 **tax evasion and cyberlibel:** For an account of charges against Rappler, see Lian Buan, "List: Cases vs. Maria Ressa, Rappler Directors, Staff Since 2018," Rappler, February 25, 2019.

16 **license to operate was revoked:** "Statement on Affirmation of Revocation of Rappler's Corporate Registration," Securities and Exchange Commission, June 29, 2022.

16 **reporters were banned:** "Duterte Himself Banned Rappler Reporter from Malacañang Coverage," Rappler, February 22, 2018.

16 **her new pink raincoat . . . Jhaylord was his mother's favorite . . . carrying a Barbie doll:** See Patricia Evangelista, "In the Name of the Father," Rappler, December 15, 2016; Patricia Evangelista, "Execution at Cessna," Rappler, September 21, 2016; and Patricia Evangelista, "Jerico's Angel," Rappler, November 7, 2016.

16 **"I'd like to be frank":** Rodrigo Duterte, quoted from speech at the tenth anniversary of the Eastern Mindanao Command, Panacan, Davao City, August 26, 2016.

Chapter 2: The Surviving Majority

17 **the first of the white men . . . It was 1521:** The fictional account of Ferdinand Magellan's expedition into the Philippines was drawn from "The Fredding of Ferdinand Magellan," in Mario P. Chanco, ed., *How to Become a Father: A Collection of Humorous Essays, Legends, and Sketches* (Manila: Philippine Book Co., 1951), and Chanco, "Filipinos Laugh Easy," *Sunday Times Magazine,* November 13, 1949. The original account of the expedition, which lasted from 1519 to 1522, was written by Antonio Pigafetta, an Italian scholar and explorer who joined Magellan's voyage. For a translation of Pigafetta's *Il primo viaggio intorno al globo,* see Antonio Pigafetta, *The First Voyage Around the World, 1519–1522,* ed. Theodore J. Cachey, Jr. (Toronto: University of Toronto Press, 2007).

18–24 **"indulged far too often" . . . "deceptively light" . . . "always**

cheerful and earnest": Carmen Guerrero Nakpil, foreword to Chanco, *How to Become a Father.*

19 **Lapulapu of Mactan . . . Ruy López de Villalobos, failed:** Jose S. Arcilla, S. J., *The Spanish Conquest,* vol. 3 of *Kasaysayan: The Story of the Filipino People,* ed. Theresa Ma and Jose Y. Dalisay, Jr. (Mandaluyong City: Asia Publishing Co., 1998). See also Jose Amiel Angeles, "The Battle of Mactan and the Indigenous Discourse on War," *Philippine Studies* 55, no. 1 (2007): 3–52.

19 **Only in 1565:** The Legazpi expedition's process of colonization carefully balanced pacification and aggressive campaigns, soliciting the involvement of indigenous elites. It also introduced, with greater force and in more organized ways, the Christian religion to convert the native population. The joint venture of the sword and cross continued until 1571, when Manila fell to Spanish control and became the capital of the new colony. For a discussion of early pacification campaigns, see Abisai Perez Zamarripa, "The *Principales* of Philip II: Vassalage, Justice, and the Making of Indigenous Jurisdiction in the Early Colonial Philippines," in *Norms Beyond Empire: Law Making and Local Normativities in Iberian Asia, 1500–1800,* ed. Manuel Bastias Saavedra (Leiden: Brill, 2022). For a discussion of the participation of indigenous militias (particularly Visayans) in the conquest of Manila, see Stephanie Mawson, "Philippine *Indios* in the Service of Empire: Indigenous Soldiers and Contingent Loyalty, 1600–1700," *Ethnohistory* 63, no. 2 (2016).

19 **My people were taught to kneel:** For a discussion of the politics and discourses in the process of conversion, see Carolyn Brewer, *Holy Confrontation: Religion, Gender, and Sexuality in the Philippines, 1521–1685* (Manila: Institute of Women's Studies, St. Scholastica's College, 2001).

19 **Philippines rebelling against Mother Spain:** John Offner, "Why Did the United States Fight Spain in 1898?" *Organization of American Historians Magazine of History* 12, no. 3 (1998).

19 **In 1898 the United States declared war:** The United States was forced to grapple with a world whose colonies were beginning to break from the yoke of empire. The U.S., in positioning itself as a colonial power late in the nineteenth century, deployed the discourse of exceptionalism, presenting itself the true agent of the civilizing mission. Unlike previous empires, the United States would engage in colonialism as a tutelary endeavor, supposedly geared to aiding its colonies toward self-rule. See Julian Go, "Introduction," in *The American Colonial State in the Philippines: Global Perspectives,* ed. Julian Go and Anne L. Foster (Durham, N.C.: Duke University Press, 2003); various authors, *The American-Spanish War: A History by the War Leaders* (London: Chas. C. Haskell & Son, 1899).

19 **America's manifest destiny:** "The World of 1898: The Spanish-American War," Hispanic Division of the Library of Congress Online Resource, June 22, 2011.

19 **125,000-strong volunteer army:** Various authors, *American-Spanish War.*

20 **Battle of Manila . . . Aguinaldo, returning from exile . . . "for the sake of humanity":** As a consequence of the Philippines—then a Spanish colony—being embroiled in the Spanish-American War, the United States intervened in the ongoing Philippine revolution that sought to end Spanish colonial rule. The United States negotiated with the Spanish forces in Manila and agreed to stage a "mock battle" to secure the "peaceful" surrender of Spanish forces. This happened within the context of the negotiations for the eventual surrender of Spain to the United States that would signal the end of the war. The "Mock Battle of Manila" happened on August 13, 1898, and concluded in the signing of the Articles of Capitulation that also paved the way for the Americans to establish a military government in the Philippines. Teodoro Agoncillo, *History of the Filipino People,* 8th ed. (Quezon City: Garotech, 1990). See also Jely Galang, "Ang Pamahalaang Militar ng Mga Amerikano sa Pilipinas Bago ang Digmaang Pilipino-Amerikano," *Philippine Social Sciences Review* 62, no. 1 (2010): 197–229; and Moorfield Storey and Marcial P. Lichauco, *The Conquest of the Philippines by the United States, 1898–1925* (New York: Knickerbocker Press, 1926).

20–21 **Filipino troops ringed Manila . . . "little brown brothers":** Daniel Immerwahr, *How to Hide an Empire: A History of the Greater United States* (New York: Farrar, Straus & Giroux, 2019).

20 **The treaty, signed in Paris:** After the Treaty of Paris was signed, the United States released the Benevolent Assimilation Declaration. It became the blueprint of the American exceptionalist rhetoric that justified the empire's takeover. For a copy of the declaration, see James Blount, *The American Occupation of the Philippines, 1898–1912* (New York: G.P. Putnam & Sons, 1913).

21 **"Go, bind your sons":** Rudyard Kipling, "The White Man's Burden," *McClure's,* February 1899. For discussion, see Mark van Ells, "Assuming the White Man's Burden: The Seizure of the Philippines, 1898–1902," *Philippine Studies* 43, no. 4 (1995).

21 **America answered with an iron fist:** The Philippine-American War remains among the bloodiest wars in Philippine history. For more discussion, see Milagros Guerrero and John Schumacher, *Reform and Revolution,* vol. 5 of *Kasaysayan: The Story of the Filipino People,* ed. Theresa Ma and Jose Y. Dalisay, Jr. (Hong Kong: Asia Publishing Co., 1998).

21 **African American soldiers:** Scott Brown, "White Backlash and the

Aftermath of Fagen's Rebellion: The Fates of Three African-American Soldiers in the Philippines, 1901–1902," *Contributions in Black Studies* 13, no. 5 (1995). See also Immerwahr, *How to Hide an Empire.*

21–35 **My grandfather was born . . . great-great-grandson of a Chinese tradesman . . . surname had evolved into Chanco . . . sixth of seven children . . . lived on San Antonio Street . . . learned Spanish at home . . . hunkered down in the capital . . . acquired the nickname Mao . . . community paper from the first floor . . . smoked Rothmans . . . largely comfortable . . . the Beautiful Wife . . . friends with Ninoy . . . old Mercedes-Benz . . . grandfather was one of many journalists . . . more prosaic . . . "*Gone with the Wind*" . . . "support of Marcos was cynical" . . . "a crusading journalist":** These accounts of Mario Chanco's life are drawn from the author's interviews with members of the Chanco family: Felicia Evangelista, the author's mother, on May 9, 2022; Louie Chanco, the author's uncles, who provided genealogical records, on July 12 and September 25, 2020; Jose "Ying" Chanco and Pedro "Boo" Chanco III, both on July 4, 2020; Maria Gugay Chanco-Turner, the author's great-aunt, on September 25, 2020; and Maria Teresa Chanco-Goodrich, on October 3, 2020.

22 **the 73rd U.S. Congress signed:** Milagros Guerrero, *Under Stars and Stripes,* vol. 6 of *Kasaysayan: The Story of the Filipino People,* ed. Theresa Ma and Jose Y. Dalisay, Jr. (Hong Kong: Asia Publishing Co., 1998).

22 **colony to commonwealth:** Patricio Abinales and Donna Amoroso, *State and Society in the Philippines* (Lanham, Md.: Rowman & Littlefield, 2005).

22–23 **a West Point–educated army colonel . . . blowing up bridges . . . brother survived:** This account by Maria Gugay Chanco-Turner refers to Antonio "Tony" Pabalan Chanco, who graduated from the U.S. Military Academy at West Point, Class of 1937. According to an account in the March–April 1998 issue of *The Assembly,* the former alumni magazine for West Point graduates, Chanco entered West Point at seventeen in 1934. Under the Japanese occupation during World War II, he served as the commanding officer of an engineer battalion of the 91st Division of the Philippine Army. He led a battalion of "virtual recruits . . . whose goal was to scorch the earth. Every bridge, every locomotive engine, and every communication facility was to be destroyed." Louis Morton, *The Fall of the Philippines* (Washington, D.C.: Center of Military History, 1993), narrates the division's exploits, including the detonation of Bataan's Layac Bridge to buy time for retreating U.S. forces. Tony Chanco was among those captured by the Japanese when Bataan fell in April 1942. He escaped the Bataan Death March, was recaptured by a Japanese noncommissioned officer, and was later sent home to Manila, to be nursed into health by his family. He joined Ramsey's Guerrillas, led by Lt. Col. Edwin Ramsey, and served with them until the end of the Japanese occupation in 1945.

22 **over a hundred thousand:** Edward Drea et al., *Researching Japanese War Crime Records* (Washington, D.C.: National Archives and Records Administration, Nazi War Crimes and Japanese Imperial Government Records Interagency Working Group, 2006).

22 **"atrocity report":** The report documenting a Manila massacre witnessed by Mario Chanco is *Report on the Destruction of Manila and Japanese Atrocities* (Washington, D.C.: Office of the Resident Commissioner of the Philippines to the United States, 1945). The destruction of Manila during the last months of the occupation, however, was a result of bombardments from both the Japanese and the American armies. It was, as historian Ricardo Jose puts it, "an orgy of rape and murder." See Ricardo T. Jose, *The Japanese Occupation*, vol. 7 of *Kasaysayan: The Story of the Filipino People,* ed. Theresa Ma and Jose Y. Dalisay, Jr. (Hong Kong: Asia Publishing Co., 1998).

23 **ended its "high mission":** Maria Serena I. Diokno, *Up from the Ashes*, vol. 8 of Ma and Dalisay, *Kasaysayan.*

23 **"faithful copy of the U.S. Constitution":** Raul Pangalangan, *Law and Newly Restored Democracies: The Philippines Experience in Restoring Political Participation and Accountability,* no. 13 in IDE Asian Law Series (Japan: Institute of Developing Economies, 2002).

23 **"brand-new automobiles":** Mario P. Chanco, "U.S. Shipping 'Gets Thur Fustest,'" *American Chamber of Commerce Journal* 12, no. 12 (1945).

24 **founding member of the National Press Club:** "Veteran Newsman Passes Away," *Manila Bulletin,* July 19, 2001.

24 **"tongue-in-cheek side comments":** "Chanco, Veteran Scribe; 79," *Philippine Daily Inquirer,* July 19, 2001.

24 **Most Outstanding Young Man:** Felix Bautista, "11. The Most Outstanding Young Man in Journalism," *Sunday Times Magazine,* December 4, 1955.

24 **Fulbright fellowship:** U.S. Foreign Service to Mario Chanco, November 26, 1962.

24 **digest called *The Orient*:** The digest was published by Chanco's Manor Press on Evangelista Street. The name *Manor* is a portmanteau of Mario and Leonor Chanco's names.

25 **"the most decorated war hero":** The falsehood of Marcos's claim of heroism during the Japanese occupation has been documented in National Historical Commission of the Philippines, *Why Ferdinand E. Marcos Should Not Be Buried at the Libingan ng mga Bayani* (Manila: National Historical Commission of the Philippines, 2016).

25 **declaring martial law:** *Proclaiming a State of Martial Law in the Philippines,* Proclamation no. 1081, s. 1971, signed on September 21, 1972.

26 **The conjugal dictatorship:** The term *conjugal dictatorship* went into general use after former Marcos press secretary and right-hand aide Primitivo Mijares used it as the title of a memoir, first published in 1976. Mijares's book, and his testimony at the U.S. Congress led to his death, as well as that of his youngest son, Boyet Mijares. Primitivo Mijares, *The Conjugal Dictatorship of Ferdinand and Imelda Marcos* (1976; reprint Quezon City: Bughaw, 2017).

26–29 **Imelda danced with President Ronald Reagan . . . war correspondent . . . first wave of martial law arrests . . . on both sides:** Raymond Bonner, *Waltzing with a Dictator* (New York: Random House, 1988).

26 **thousand pairs of size eight-and-a-half:** John Lyons and Karl Wilson, *Marcos and Beyond* (New South Wales: Kangaroo Press, 1987).

26 **entirety of a Sotheby's auction:** On March 22, 1986, a former Sotheby's employee disclosed to the *Los Angeles Times* that then–first lady Imelda Marcos bought out the entire contents of philanthropist Leslie R. Samuel's apartment just before it was to be auctioned. It included a $5 million collection of rare seventeenth- and eighteenth-century English paintings, furniture, and pottery. Bob Drogin, "Imelda Marcos' Shopping Gave 'Spree' New Meaning," *Los Angeles Times,* March 22, 1986.

26 **was rife with corruption . . . estimated five to ten billion dollars:** Jovito Salonga, *Presidential Plunder* (Quezon City: University of the Philippines, 2000); Belinda Aquino, *The Politics of Plunder: The Philippines Under Marcos* (Quezon City: University of the Philippines, National College Public Administration and Governance, 1999).

26 **imprisonment of 70,000 . . . torture of 34,000 . . . murders of 3,240 activists:** Alfred W. McCoy, "Dark Legacy: Human Rights Under the Marcos Regime," in *Memory, Truth-telling and the Pursuit of Justice: A Conference on the Legacy of the Marcos Dictatorship* (Quezon City: Ateneo de Manila University, 1999). Also see *Report of an Amnesty International Mission to the Republic of the Philippines 22 November–5 December 1975* (Amnesty International, September 1976); and *Report of an Amnesty International Mission to the Republic of the Philippines 11–28 November 1981* (Amnesty International, September 1982).

26 **Martial law ended, on paper:** *Proclaiming the Termination of the State of Martial Law Throughout the Philippines,* Proclamation No. 2045, s. 1981, signed January 26, 1981.

26 **"We love your adherence":** Raul S. Manglapus, "Buttery Toast in Manila," *New York Times,* July 10, 1981.

26 **That adherence failed again:** For a discussion of the political career of Benigno Aquino, Jr., his dealings with the Marcos dictatorship, and his time in exile, see Walden Bello, "Benigno Aquino: Between Dictatorship and Revolution in the Philippines," *Third World Quarterly* 6, no. 2 (1984): 283–309.

26–27 **In 1980 he was allowed . . . three years lecturing at Harvard . . . worth dying for:** This account of Benigno Aquino, Jr.'s, activities in the United States draws from Ninoy and Cory Aquino Foundation, "Exile Begins," Ninoy Aquino, n.d., https://www.ninoyaquino.ph/exile -begins.html; Mary Humes, "The Scholarly Life of a Leader," *Crimson,* September 21, 1983; and Benigno Aquino, Jr., speech at the Asia Society, New York, August 4, 1980. For a full copy of Aquino's speech, see "The Filipino Is Worth Dying For," *Manila Times,* August 22, 2010.

27 **same white suit . . . "You have to be very ready" . . . military boarding party . . . jetway leading to the terminal . . . Gunshots rang out:** One of the most enduring accounts of Aquino's final flight was written by his brother-in-law, an ABC correspondent traveling on the same flight as the late senator. See Ken Kashiwahara, "Aquino's Final Journey," *New York Times,* October 16, 1983. Also see "Puso at Diwa ni Ninoy" (video), January 31, 2013, RTVMalacanang, YouTube.

27 *A hundred yellow ribbons:* Tony Orlando and Dawn, "Tie a Yellow Ribbon Round the Ole Oak Tree," Arista Records, 1973.

27 **"a soldier who shot Ninoy":** Jeannette L. Andrade, "'Crying Lady': It's Destiny That I Saw Ninoy Killing 33 Years Ago," *Philippine Daily Inquirer,* August 21, 2016.

27 **"I return from exile":** "Undelivered Speech of Sen. Benigno Aquino, Jr., upon His Return from the U.S.," *Official Gazette,* August 21, 1983.

28–31 **The campaign for the presidency . . . The revolution ended:** Alexander Magno, *A Nation Reborn,* vol. 9 of *Kasaysayan: The Story of the Filipino People,* ed. Theresa Ma and Jose Y. Dalisay, Jr. (Mandaluyong City: Asia Publishing Co., 1998).

28 **At least eighty people:** Ruben Alabastro, "The Other Philippine Election Tally: The Dead and Wounded," Associated Press, February 13, 1986.

28–32 **Volunteers were beaten . . . Armed men burst . . . campaign director Evelio Javier . . . baseball caps . . . makeshift fortifications . . . *Are you going to shoot* . . . six tanks, eight jeeps . . . They did not run . . . stood with arms outstretched . . . Some of them were crying . . . They held the line . . . MARCOS FLEES . . . "worthy of ancient Greece" . . . Joan of Arc . . . storming of the Bastille . . . "next to follow their example" . . . showing them the way:** Monina Allarey Mercado, ed., *An Eyewitness History: People Power, the Philip-*

pine Revolution of 1986 (Manila: James B. Reuters S.J. Foundation, 1986).

28 MARCOS CONCEDE: Mark Fineman, "Killed by Sniper After Rally: 'Foot Soldier' Archie Dies as He Lived—for Aquino," *Los Angeles Times,* February 12, 1986.

28 **Cory Aquino led an independent count:** Reynaldo Santos, Jr., "1986 Comelec Walkout Not About Cory or Marcos," Rappler, February 25, 2013.

28 **thirty young computer programmers:** The number was cited in Seth Mydans, "Observers of Vote Cite Wide Fraud by Marcos Party," *New York Times,* February 10, 1986. However, most contemporary sources say that thirty-five computer programmers walked out of the Philippine International Convention Center in Pasay City. They were thereafter called the "Comelec 35" and the "Marvelous 35." See Nancy Carvajal, "1986 Comelec Tabulators Fear Marcos Return," *Philippine Daily Inquirer,* February 24, 2016.

28 **condemning the elections as fraudulent:** Catholic Bishops' Conference of the Philippines, Annex X, International Observer Mission, *Report to the President of the United States of America on the February 7, 1986, Presidential Election in the Philippines* (National Democratic Institute for International Affairs and the National Republican Institute for International Affairs, 1986).

29 **"widespread fraud and violence":** Ronald Reagan, "Statement on the Presidential Election in the Philippines," February 15, 1986.

29 **Ramos defected:** Jack Reed, "Enrile and Ramos: Former Loyalists Turn on Marcos," United Press International, February 22, 1986.

29 **"The full moon":** Phil Bronstein, "Lessons of Philippines' 'People Power' Revolution, 30 Years Later," *San Francisco Chronicle,* February 29, 2016.

29 **one of six planned . . . Highway 54 . . . In the late 1950s:** John Paul Olivares, "Epifanio de los Santos Avenue, Quezon City: The History of Landmarks along Edsa," *Lakbay ng Lakan,* September 14, 2019; Paulo Alcazaren, "The Road from Highway 54 Toward a More Inclusive and Safe EDSA," *Philippine Star Life,* February 24, 2022; Ambeth Ocampo, "Who Was Epifanio de los Santos," *Philippine Daily Inquirer,* June 29, 2018.

31 **aftermath of the Edsa Revolution:** Mark Thompson, "Philippine 'People Power' Thirty Years On," *Diplomat,* February 9, 2016.

32 **motorcades were out in full force:** Human Rights Violations Victims Memorial Commission, "The Events Surrounding the 1986 Snap Elections," Human Rights Violations Victims Memorial Commission, February 12, 2021.

32–33 **a full-page advertisement . . . eleven-point agenda . . . COW-ARD Manifesto:** Photograph in the manifesto expressing support for the Marcos-Tolentino tandem, *Bulletin Today* (now *Manila Bulletin*), January 28, 1986. Reuel Aguila (former president of GAT) documented the events surrounding the manifesto's publication and subsequent reception in "Kabilaan: Pagtatala ng Kasaysayan Hinggil sa Pag-endorso ng Ilang Kasapi ng Galian sa Arte at Tula sa Kandidaturang Marcos Tolentino," *Talababa* 1, no. 3 (2006).

33 **traitors, cowards, and collaborators:** E. San Juan, "What Shall We Do with All of Marcos' Hacks?" *Philippine News,* October 22–28, 1986.

33 **The signatures, I was told, were strictly voluntary:** Ernesto Hilario (journalist), interview by the author, September 25, 2020, and Luis Teodoro (journalist), interview by the author, July 8, 2020.

36 **"gone off with the hordes":** The column describing Mario Chanco's reaction to the People Power Revolution, "Some of Our Panaderos Are Missing," is a framed family copy assumed to have been published by the *Evening Post.*

Chapter 3: Mascot for Hope

40–45 **The economy struggled . . . She captured the presidency:** Patricio Abinales and Donna Amoroso, *State and Society in the Philippines* (Lanham: Rowman & Littlefield, 2005).

40–42 **had its sequel in 2001 . . . a scandal involving illegal gambling payoffs . . . political elite of church . . . tried for plunder . . . State prosecutors resigned . . . "lost the moral authority to govern" . . . "strong and serious" . . . evacuated Malacañang Palace by boat . . . calling the event mob rule:** Carl H. Landé, "The Return of 'People Power' in the Philippines," *Journal of Democracy* 12, no. 2 (2001): 88–102; Yvonne Chua, Sheila Coronel, and Vinia Datinguinoo, "Can Estrada Explain His Wealth?" Philippine Center for Investigative Journalism, July 24, 2000; Jody C. Baumgartner and Naoko Kada, *Checking Executive Power: Presidential Impeachment in Comparative Perspective* (Westport, Conn.: Praeger, 2003); Paul A. Rodell, "The Philippines: Gloria 'in Excelsis,'" *Southeast Asian Affairs* (2002); "Philippine Leader Resigns, Beset by Scandal," Associated Press, January 20, 2001; *Estrada v. Desierto,* G.R. No. 146710-15, March 2, 2001; "Erap's Last Stand: Revisiting President Joseph Estrada's Final Days in the Malacañan Palace," *Tatler Philippines,* July 28, 2020; and Seth Mydans, "People Power 2 Doesn't Give Filipinos the Same Glow," *New York Times,* February 5, 2001.

42 **main campus in Diliman:** Patricio Abinales, "Fragments of History, Silhouettes of Resurgence: Student Radicalism in the Early Years of the Marcos Dictatorship," *Southeast Asian Studies* 46, no. 2 (2008): 175–99;

and Arnel de Guzman, "U.P. After the 'Storm,'" in *Tibak Rising: Activism in the Days of Martial Law,* ed. Ferdinand C. Llanes (Mandaluyong: Anvil, 2012).

44 **"received a salver":** Alfred Yuson, "Pinay Wins It Big in London," *Philippine Star,* May 16, 2004.

45 **"build a strong republic":** Gloria Macapagal Arroyo, "Second State of the Nation Address," *Official Gazette,* July 22, 2002.

45 **Cold War–era antisubversion:** *An Act Repealing RA No. 1700, as Amended, Otherwise Known as the Anti-Subversion Act,* Republic Act No. 7636, September 24, 1992.

45 **Years of internal purges:** Mark Thompson, "The Decline of Philippine Communism," *Southeast Asia Research* 6, no. 2 (1998): 105–29.

45 **foreign terrorist organization:** Defense Secretary Colin L. Powell, statement, "On the Designation of a Foreign Terrorist Organization," August 9, 2002.

48 **the 1970s the Spanish word** *desaparecer:* Gail Holst-Warhaft, *The Cue for Passion: Grief and Its Political Uses* (Cambridge, Mass.: Harvard University Press, 2000), 104–5.

48 **dissidents vanished during the military junta:** Emilio Crenzel, "Toward a History of the Memory of Political Violence and the Disappeared in Argentina," in *The Struggle for Memory in Latin America: Recent History and Political Violence,* ed. Eugenia Allier-Montaño and Emilio Crenzel (New York: Palgrave Macmillan, 2015).

48 **systematic kidnapping of children:** Francisco Peregil, "Videla Convicted for Baby Stealing," *El País,* July 12, 2012.

48 **the disappeared:** Amnesty International, *Philippines: Not Forgotten, the Fate of the "Disappeared"* (Amnesty International, 1996).

48 **"To disappear, transitive":** *Oxford English Dictionary* (Oxford: Oxford University Press, 2023), continually updated at http://www.oed.com/.

48–49 **Sherlyn Cadapan . . . teenage boy . . . escaped detainee . . . bound and blindfolded . . . pregnant . . . pieces of wood . . . drink their own piss:** This account of the disappearance of Sherlyn Cadapan and Karen Empeño is drawn from the author's reporting on human rights violations alleged against Maj. Gen. Jovito Palparan. Palparan was convicted in 2018 for kidnapping and serious illegal detention. See Patricia Evangelista, "Rage," *Philippine Daily Inquirer,* November 23, 2008; Patricia Evangelista, "The Rape of Raymond Manalo," *UNO Magazine,* September 2008; and Patricia Evangelista, "The Darkness of Fear," *Esquire Philippines,* May 2012. See also Kiri Dalena and Patricia Evangelista, "People of the Philippines vs. Jovito Palparan," Rappler, March 29, 2012; and Paolo Villaluna and Patricia Evangelista, "Storyline: Stolen," ABS-CBN News Channel, June 27, 2008.

49 **farmers demanding land reform were massacred:** Lisandro E. Claudio, *Taming People's Power: The EDSA Revolutions and Their Contradictions* (Quezon City: Ateneo de Manila University Press, 2013).

50 **last regions to fall to colonial rule:** Donna Amoroso, "Inheriting the 'Moro Problem': Muslim Authority and Colonial Rule in British Malaya and the Philippines" in *The American Colonial State in the Philippines: Global Perspectives*, ed. Julian Go and Anne L. Foster (Durham, N.C.: Duke University Press, 2003).

50 **"people of the flood plain":** Gwyn Campbell, *Bondage and the Environment in the Indian Ocean World* (Switzerland: Springer, 2018).

51 **the Ampatuan stronghold:** Jocelyn R. Uy, "Ampatuan Aide Says Arroyo Ordered Governor to Rig 2007 Senatorial Polls," *Philippine Daily Inquirer*, October 4, 2011.

51 **On November 23:** *People of the Philippines v. Ampatuan et al.*, Criminal Case Nos. Q-09-162148-72/Q-09-162216-31/Q-10-162652-66/Q-10-163766/GL-Q-12-178638; Human Rights Watch, *"They Own the People": The Ampatuans, State-Backed Militias, and Killings in the Southern Philippines* (Human Rights Watch, November 16, 2020); Center for Media Freedom and Responsibility, "The Ampatuan Massacre: Summary of Case Trial," Philippine Center for Investigative Journalism, December 18, 2019; Patricia Evangelista, "Carnage," *Philippine Daily Inquirer*, November 29, 2009; Patricia Evangelista, "Killing Bebot Momay," *Philippine Daily Inquirer*, September 29, 2012; Patricia Evangelista, "These Are Their Names," *UNO Magazine*, December 2010; and Kiri Dalena and Patricia Evangelista, "58," ABS-CBN News Channel, November 23, 2010.

54 **"to face my parents":** Benigno S. Aquino III, "Inaugural Address of President Benigno S. Aquino III," delivered at the Quirino Grandstand, Manila, June 30, 2010; English translation in *Official Gazette*, June 30, 2010.

54 **A dismissed police officer:** On the hostage siege in Manila and Benigno Aquino, Jr.'s, subsequent reaction, see "Hong Kong Hostages Killed in Manila Bus Siege," BBC, August 23, 2010; Raissa Robles, " 'I Smile When I'm Fed Up': Benigno Aquino III Defends 'Inappropriate' Grins That Sparked International Outrage," *South China Morning Post*, April 21, 2015; Cris Larano, "Philippine President: No Apology over Hong Kong Hostages," *Wall Street Journal*, October 23, 2013; and Samuel Chan, "Smiling Aquino 'Ridiculous' and 'Lacking Empathy,' Manila Hostage Crisis Survivors Say," *South China Morning Post*, April 21, 2015.

56 **human shields . . . rained blood . . . Thirteen of the dead:** On the siege of Zamboanga City, see "Philippine Rebels Use 'Human Shields'

in Standoff with Troops," Agence France-Presse, September 10, 2013; Richard Falcatan, "Zamboanga City Remembers Infamous 2013 Siege, Honors 38 Heroes," Rappler, September 9, 2022; "What Went Before: The MNLF siege of Zamboanga City," *Philippine Daily Inquirer,* September 8, 2014; Patricia Evangelista, "Blood from the Sky," Rappler, October 7, 2013; Patricia Evangelista, "Zamboanga Still Under Siege," Rappler, January 17, 2015; Paolo Villaluna and Patricia Evangelista, "The Children of Sta. Barbara," Rappler September 26, 2013; and "Santa Catalina," Rappler, October 12, 2013.

56 **"Was that not the skill demonstrated"**: Benigno Aquino III, speech at the Agenda-Setting Dialogue with Partners in Malacañang, September 12, 2014.

56 **"How should I have reacted?"**: Katerina Francisco, "Aquino Turns Defensive over Criticism He Lacks Empathy," Rappler, May 26, 2016.

57 **Super Typhoon Haiyan:** On the devastation left by Super Typhoon Haiyan, see UN Office for the Coordination of Humanitarian Affairs, "Philippines: Concern growing for people cut off by Super Typhoon Haiyan," UNOCHA.org, November 10, 2013; "Philippines: Typhoon Haiyan Emergency Appeal Final Report," ReliefWeb, October 5, 2017; Patricia Evangelista, "Land of the Mourning," *Esquire Philippines,* December–January 2014; and Patricia Evangelista, "Are You Still Alive? The Rhetoric of Benigno Aquino III," Rappler, June 25, 2016. See also *The Men of Village 88* (video), directed by Gym Lumbera and written by Patricia Evangelista, YouTube.

59 **A resident raised his hand:** Lalaine Jimenea, "Man Who Did Not Abandon Tacloban Passes Away," *Philippine Star,* August 4, 2015.

59 **"You're still alive"**: Willard Cheng, "PNP Didn't Rebuff Businessman: Palace," ABS-CBN News Digital, August 6, 2015.

59 **"I am not play-acting"**: "Me, Lack Empathy? Pnoy Reacts," ABS-CBN News Digital, May 27, 2016.

59 **"I don't attend wakes"**: Aries Joseph Hegina, "Aquino on Attending Laude Wake: 'I Don't Attend Wakes of People I Don't Know,'" Inquirer.net, October 22, 2014.

59 **praising Mitsubishi Philippines:** "PNoy Goes to Car Plant Opening as Fallen SAF Men Arrive," ABS-CBN News Digital, February 4, 2015.

59 **"My father also died"**: Anthony Taberna, "PNoy Leaves Some Families Hurt," ABS-CBN, February 21, 2015.

60 **the straight path:** The second Aquino administration used this language, first in his State of the Nation address on July 26, 2010. The "straight path," or "Tuwid na Daan," refers to Aquino's social contract with the Filipino people, promising to champion transparent, accountable, and participatory governance.

60 **President Aquino's six years . . . His approach to foreign policy . . . The economy was a billion dollars larger . . . The long-fought-for Reproductive Health Law . . . The education budget doubled . . . massive social welfare program:** On the legacy of Benigno Aquino III, see Camille Elemia, "Did Aquino Deliver on His Promises?" Rappler, part 1, July 22, 2015, and part 2, July 24, 2015; Antonio T. Carpio, "Aquino and the Arbitration Against China," Inquirer.net, July 1, 2021; Patricia Mirasol, "A Look Back at the PNoy Administration," *BusinessWorld,* June 24, 2021; "President Aquino Signs RH Bill into Law," Rappler, December 28, 2012; Ding Cervantes, "P271.6B 2011 Education Budget Biggest in Phl History—P-Noy," *Philippine Star,* December 9, 2010; Tricia Aquino, "PNoy: 7.7 Million Filipinos Lifted from Poverty Through Conditional Cash Transfer Program," Philippine Institute for Development Studies, January 15, 2016.

60 **"You are my bosses":** "Speeches of Benigno 'Noynoy' Aquino During His Presidency," ABS-CBN News Channel, June 24, 2021.

Chapter 4: The Rise of the Punisher

61 **Soling, was a Spanish mestiza . . . father was of Chinese descent:** Rodrigo Duterte, drawn from speech at Proclamation Rally, Tondo, Manila, February 10, 2016.

61 **grandmother was of the southern Maranao:** Rodrigo Duterte, drawn from speech at Campaign Rally, Lipa City, April 14, 2016.

61 **"son of a migrant to Mindanao":** Rodrigo Duterte, quoted from speech at a meeting with Troops of the 4th Infantry Division—Philippine Army, Camp Edilberto Evangelista, Barangay Patag, Cagayan de Oro City, August 9, 2016.

61 **"born to a poor family":** Rodrigo Duterte, quoted from speech at the launching of the Pilipinong May Puso Foundation, Davao City, November 11, 2016. See also "Duterte Flip-Flops on Family's Wealth," *VERA Files,* February 18, 2017.

61 **scoffing at the Latin honors:** Germelina Lacorte, "Duterte Hits Back at Roxas, Says Wharton Red Is a Myth," Inquirer.net, December 13, 2015.

61 **"I am a small-town boy":** Rodrigo Duterte, quoted from speech at the Parish Pastoral Council for Responsible Voting's Board of Trustees, Officers, and Delegates, Malacañang, August 3, 2016.

62 **"I am an ordinary Filipino":** Rodrigo Duterte, quoted from speech at the Plenary of the 42nd Philippine Business Conference and Exposition of the Philippine Chamber of Commerce and Industry, Manila Marriott Hotel, Pasay City, October 13, 2016.

62 **"sentiment of the ordinary people"**: Rodrigo Duterte, quoted from speech at the MAD for Change Concert, Taguig City, November 29, 2015.

62–71 **He was a wild child . . . order paninis . . . beerhouses . . . joined a gang . . . bought guns . . . was stabbed . . . transferred, was expelled . . . born one of six . . . son of a two-term governor . . . land-rich Mindanao . . . "skinny and short and not handsome" . . . "awkward and unattractive" . . . "an ordinary and unspectacular student" . . . eighteen when his father was reelected . . . losing a congressional election . . . home for the funeral . . . wept at the casket . . . frequented target ranges . . . Octavio as something of a bully . . . playing with guns in the school . . . pushing, and shoving . . . challenged him to a shoot-out . . . Octavio had a homemade revolver . . . Octavio's gun failed . . . Octavio Goco survived . . . Lex Talionis fraternity brothers rallied . . . school prefect wanted him expelled . . . rewarded with a blue Volkswagen Beetle . . . "Soling Duterte knew that Rody" . . . people called her Soling . . . Yellow Friday Movement . . . "Nanay Soling declined the post" . . . Aquino approved of the substitution . . . Forty-one-year-old assistant city prosecutor . . . "of truth and justice" . . . murders of petty thieves, criminals**: On Duterte's childhood and early political career, see Earl G. Parreño, *Beyond Will and Power: A Biography of President Rodrigo Roa Duterte* (Lapulapu City: Optima Typographics, 2019); and Jonathan Miller, *Duterte Harry: Fire and Fury in the Philippines* (Australia: Scribe, 2018). The author has also sought and received written permission from Parreño to except several paragraphs for use in this book. See also Sheila Coronel, "The Vigilante President," *Foreign Affairs,* August 12, 2019.

62–64 **whipped by his mother . . . troubled son of privilege . . . affiliation to powerful political clans . . . a cook and a driver . . . skipped school for months . . . a heart attack . . . Octavio had taunted Rody . . . Octavio instigated a scuffle . . . Rody howled . . . He was hit in the nose . . . Rody jumped onto a boat . . . Rody had pulled the trigger**: Details and characterizations of Rodrigo Duterte's life are drawn from Miller, *Duterte Harry.*

63 **secretary of the Department of General Services**: Miguel Paolo P. Reyes, "The Duterte–Marcos Connection," *VERA Files,* September 29, 2019.

63 **jail and violence did not trouble**: Rodrigo Duterte, drawn from speech at the Urban Poor Solidarity Week, Hardin ng Pag-Asa, Barangay Addition Hills, Mandaluyong City, December 7, 2016.

63–65 "used to shooting" . . . shooting *people* . . . "graduate from San Beda when I shot a man" . . . "put him in his place . . . bang": Rodrigo Duterte, drawn from campaign speech at La Paz Plaza, Iloilo City, April 21, 2016.

64 Octavio Goco was shot: Fe Zamora, "Law Student Duterte Shot Frat Brod on Campus in '72," *Philippine Daily Inquirer,* April 22, 2016.

65–66 led by another widow in yellow . . . Rodrigo Duterte woke his own children . . . "Do not ever forget" . . . Davao City was offered to Soling . . . seventy years old: Pia Ranada, "Meet Davao's Foremost 'Yellow' Activist: Soledad Duterte," Rappler, March 4, 2017; Allan Nawal and Nico Alconaba, "Sara Duterte Fires Back: My Father Understood Spirit of Edsa," *Philippine Daily Inquirer,* February 25, 2017.

66 appointment of caretaker administrators: Ninoy and Cory Aquino Foundation, "Essential Cory Aquino: The Unpaved Road to the Presidency," CoryAquino.ph, 2010.

66 a total of twenty-two years: "Fact Check: How Long Did Duterte Serve as Davao City Mayor?" *VERA Files,* December 10, 2016.

66 "I am a child of destiny" . . . "I never wanted to be a mayor" . . . "I was with the people": Carolyn O. Arguillas, "People Power 1986 and Duterte's Destiny," MindaNews, February 26, 2017.

67 "urban slums racked by poverty, violence": Louise Williams, Paul Grigson, and agencies, "In Rambo Town, Jackie Didn't Have a Chance," *Sydney Morning Herald,* August 17, 1989.

67 "murder city" . . . "crime capital": Several publications described Davao City as "murder capital" or "murder city." See *Asiaweek* 2, no. 37 (September 13, 1985): 6–18 found in Barbara LePoer and William Shaw, "A Selective, Annotated Bibliography on Philippine Insurgencies," Federal Research Division, Library of Congress; William Branigin, "Davao Known as Philippines' 'Murder Capital,'" *Washington Post,* August 8, 1985; and Michael Peel, "Drugs and Death in Davao: The Making of Rodrigo Duterte," *Financial Times,* February 1, 2017.

67–70 "concentrates every Philippine problem" . . . gathered together a paramilitary group . . . nine thousand in Davao City alone . . . "liquidations of suspected rebels" . . . at least two hundred vigilante groups . . . Davao group named Tadtad . . . head of a Communist guerrilla . . . died down in the late 1980s: Richard Hastings of the *Sydney Morning Herald* quoted in Ronald J. May, "Vigilantes in the Philippines: From Fanatical Cults to Citizens' Organizations," Philippine Studies Occasional Paper No. 12 (Center for Philippine Studies, School of Hawaiian, Asian and Pacific Studies, University of Hawaii at Manoa, 1992).

67 **more visible than in Agdao:** Col. Franco Calida, testimony, January 13, 1988, quoted in *Report on Vigilantes,* Senate of the Philippines, Committee on Justice and Human Rights, 8th Congress, 1988.

67 **"the Communist Party, not the government":** Paul Quinn-Judge, "In Agdao, Not Even 'Baby' Aquino Can Keep the Communists at Bay," *Christian Science Monitor,* March 26, 1985.

68 **politician was murdered in cold blood . . . gunned down a suspected Communist . . . "*Mag-alsa na ta*":** Enriquez Delacruz, Arda Jordan, and Jorge Emmanuel, *Death Squads in the Philippines* (San Francisco: Alliance for Philippine Concerns, 1987).

68 **became known as the Alsa Masa:** On the group's founding, see Brennan Weiss, "Duterte's Death Squads Were Born in America's Cold War," *Foreign Policy,* July 10, 2017.

68 **Metropolitan District Command (Metrodiscom):** The Metrodiscom was a unit of the Philippine Constabulary (PC), a predecessor of the PNP. During the martial law years, the PC integrated the country's municipal and city police, fire, and penitentiary services as a branch of the Armed Forces of the Philippines (AFP). In 1991 the PC was replaced by the newly created civilian PNP.

68 **"fight between democracy and Communism" . . . "system of checkpoints, armed patrols, taxation":** Seth Mydans, "Right-wing Vigilantes Spreading in Philippines," *New York Times,* April 4, 1987.

68–70 **Cagay drew up lists . . . "tomorrow they will die" . . . "I am overjoyed to join you here" . . . "They aren't sort of free-floating vigilante groups" . . . death squads wore yellow:** Details on Alsa Masa and recorded statements of former president Corazon Aquino and then-U.S. secretary of state George Schultz are drawn from *A Rustling of Leaves: Inside the Philippine Revolution* (documentary), dir. Nettie Wild (Vancouver: Canada Wild Productions, 1988).

69 **"strong evidence" that members of Alsa Masa:** Amnesty International, *Philippines: Unlawful Killings by Military and Paramilitary Forces* (Amnesty International, 1988).

69–73 **murder, harassment, forced enlistment, and threats . . . "No one involved covers his face":** Philippine Alliance of Human Rights Advocates, *Right Wing Vigilantes and U.S. Involvement: Report of a U.S.-Philippine Fact-Finding Mission to the Philippines* (Quezon City: Philippine Alliance of Human Rights Advocates, May 20–30, 1987).

69 **"discussing the peace initiatives" . . . "answer to terrorism":** Peter Tarr, "Philippine Vigilantes Reflect U.S. Strategy for 'Low Intensity Conflict,'" *Los Angeles Times,* October 11, 1987.

70 **"A letter to the Institute" . . . some abuses, but they were "isolated happenings" . . . "Without the support of the government" . . .**

"the Alsa Masa would collapse": Erik Guyot was a fellow at the Institute of Current World Affairs from 1987 to 1989, and filed dispatches from Thailand and the Philippines. This letter has been quoted in various publications, and is available on the Institute of Current World Affairs' website: Erik Guyot, "Alsa Masa: 'Freedom Fighters' or 'Death Squads'?" icwa.org, August 6, 1988.

71–81 brutal purges within the Communist Party . . . alleged drug dealers, petty criminals . . . "Christopher had been stabbed, I was startled" . . . They killed Richard Alia first . . . Bobby's turn came three years later . . . The last was Fernando . . . "DDS [Davao Death Squad] fall into two main groups" . . . young men . . . "If you are doing an illegal activity": Human Rights Watch, *"You Can Die Any Time": Death Squad Killings in Mindanao* (Human Rights Watch, 2009).

71–72 "targeted and killed drug addicts" . . . target was a known drug dealer . . . kill to the New People's Army . . . "Do not be like the scum of society" . . . The mayor, deep in talks with the NPA . . . note was scrapped . . . It was the squad leader and the chief . . . Nobody shot back . . . No guns were recovered . . . No drugs were confiscated . . . corpse they found was of a housemaid . . . It was signed Davao Death Squad: Arturo "Arthur" Lascañas (retired Davao police officer and Davao Death Squad member), signed and notarized affidavit, February 19, 2017.

72 "former New People's Army partisans": Carlos Conde, "A Season of Death," *Newsbreak,* ABS-CBN News Digital, December 5, 2001.

72–85 "repertoire of warfare" . . . "revealed a lull in the killings": Sheila Coronel, "The Forever War," in *The Marcos Era: A Reader,* ed. Leia Castañeda Anastacio and Patricio N. Abinales (Quezon City: Bughaw / Ateneo de Manila University Press, 2022).

72 eighty-four vigilante killings: Based on research from the archives of the *Mindanao Daily Mirror*'s reporting in the first three months of 2005. See the report "Gunmen Kill Victims 82, 83, 84," *Mindanao Daily Mirror,* April 13, 2005.

72 "vigilante group linked with Davao Mayor": Details are based on an alleged U.S. Mission document by Andrew McClearn (political officer), "More Vigilante-Style Killings Reported in Davao City," January 20, 2005, made available through WikiLeaks. The authenticity of this document, marked confidential, is uncertain. Its content was cited in "Philippines: Probe Mayor's Alleged 'Death Squad' Links" (press release), Human Rights Watch, May 19, 2015; and in Karlos Manlupig, "Duterte Calls U.S. Rights Groups Hypocrite," *Inquirer Mindanao,* May 20, 2015.

72 up to five hundred deaths . . . "publicly and with methodical indif-

ference" . . . "deny the existence of a death squad" . . . "consumption and would have no effect": UN Human Rights Council, *Report of the Special Rapporteur on Extrajudicial, Summary or Arbitrary Executions, Philip Alston, on his Mission to Philippines (12–21 February 2007)* (Geneva: UN Human Rights Council, April 16, 2008).

73 **"don't mind us being called the murder capital"** . . . **"very, very dangerous for criminals"** . . . **"a place where you can die any time":** Rodrigo Duterte quoted in Alan Sipress, "In Philippine City, Public Safety Has a Dark Side," *Washington Post,* November 27, 2003.

74 **leave the city, or they would die:** Rodrigo Duterte quoted ibid.

75 **"DDS is non-existent":** Rodrigo Duterte, interview by Erwin Romulo, for Atom Araullo, "How to Be a Man: The Passions of Rodrigo Duterte," *Esquire Philippines,* March 2015.

75 **announced a public inquiry:** Commission on Human Rights (CHR) (IV), Resolution No. A 2009-015, February 12, 2009.

75 **The CHR, an independent government body:** Executive Order No. 163, s. 1987, May 5, 1987, Presidential Management Staff Library, Malacañang.

76 **"make Davao City the most dangerous place"** . . . **"I am responsible for the uplift of this community"** . . . **"rioting and retaliation"** . . . **"I do not go for small crimes"** . . . **"they are doing it on their own"** . . . **he believed in due process** . . . **shot only in self-defense** . . . **"No ma'am, there is none"** . . . **"unexplained, unresolved" killings** . . . **"there is none because I have not seen one"** . . . **"I said I was not there"** . . . **"Outside of the purview of the law"** . . . **"Name, I really would not know. It could be a revenge":** Rodrigo Duterte, testimony under questioning by CHR chair Leila de Lima, *Hearing on Extrajudicial Killings Attributed or Attributable to the Davao Death Squad, Before the CHR,* Davao City, March 30–31, 2009.

77 **Duterte claimed he had asked CHR regional director Alberto Sipaco, Jr. . . . His co-founder was Rodrigo Duterte:** Ibid.

77 **"the law of retribution":** Merriam-Webster.com Dictionary, s.v. "lex talionis," accessed June 9, 2023; A Dictionary of Law, 7th ed. (Oxford: Oxford University Press: 2009); Fe Zamora, "Bond of Brothers: Lex Talionis Frat Members Get Key Gov't Posts," Inquirer.net, May 21, 2017.

77 **one of the founders of the fraternity's chapter:** Alberto Sipaco, Curriculum Vitae, Philippine Mining Development Corporation (PMDC) official website, accessed on April 17, 2023. Sipaco holds the position of president, chairman, and CEO at PMDC.

77 **"Alberto Sipaco (strictly protect)":** Kristie Kenney (former U.S. ambassador to the Philippines), confidential cable to the secretary of state,

May 8, 2009, made available through Wikileaks. In September 2016, asked by Rappler for comment, the U.S. embassy in the Philippines refused to confirm the authenticity of the document. Molly Koscina, press attaché at the embassy, said, "We do not comment on the substance or authenticity of materials, including allegedly classified documents, which may have been leaked." For more details, see Paterno Esmaquel II, "Duterte 'Admitted Complicity' in Davao Killings—WikiLeaks," Rappler, September 25, 2016. On May 12, 2023, before the publication of this book, the author sought comment from Sipaco through a letter of request sent via messenger to Sipaco's office at the Philippine Mining Development Corporation (PMDC) in Pasig City, by direct courier to the PMDC's Davao City Office, and through Sipaco's personal email address. Sipaco, who at the time of publication was the chairman, president, and CEO of the PMDC, has not responded.

78–79 **"killed in your presence and buried by you"** . . . **"blindfolded before they were killed"** . . . Jose worked in an office . . . office belonged to the Davao City Police . . . mission was peace and order . . . Isuzu Fuego that had once belonged to Mayor Rodrigo Duterte . . . member of the Police Anti-Crime Unit . . . his job was to bury the bodies . . . he never held the knife . . . snatched Jovani outside the market . . . blindfolded Jovani . . . One cop stabbed Jovani . . . pick up the body and go . . . went into homes and killed . . . that meant murdering witnesses too . . . There were thirteen, and Jose watched . . . There was Jovani . . . Alex and Dondon . . . Tony and Bobong and Toto and Peping and Alvin, and then Jay . . . didn't know very much about them . . . he couldn't sleep for many nights . . . someone would make him go quiet: "Jose Basilio" (witness using a pseudonym), deposition, and "Jose Basilio," affidavit signed but not notarized, June 2009. Basilio affixed his thumbmark instead of a signature to the affidavit. While there are indications this was subscribed to at the CHR main office in Quezon City on May 30, 2009, pertinent details have been redacted. Both the affidavit and the deposition are part of a collection of documents obtained by Rappler from the CHR. Rappler has consented to the use of these documents for this book.

79 **Bienvenido Laud:** *Laud v. People of the Philippines,* G.R. No. 199032, November 19, 2014; Rappler Investigative Team, "Why the Laud Quarry, 'Mass Grave' for DDS Victims, Haunts Lascañas," Rappler, November 13, 2021.

80–81 **"I sat beside the target"** . . . **"Kulot stabbed him from the front"** . . . Ramon was a paid informant . . . Most of them were drug addicts and thieves . . . a thief named Marlon . . . It was "sad," said Ramon: "Ramon Evangelista" (witness using a pseudonym), notarized affidavit, Davao City, July 4, 2009, included in documents obtained by Rappler from the CHR.

81 "you are a legitimate target of assassination": Rodrigo Duterte, quoted in Human Rights Watch, *"You Can Die Any Time."*

81–82 "I started my new job" . . . "a list of the wanted men I was supposed to kill" . . . Crispin, a former NPA rebel, arrived at the mayor's home . . . asked the mayor, be inclined toward killing . . . sometimes by Mayor Duterte himself . . . mayor gave Crispin a .375 revolver . . . first kill was a nineteen-year-old boy . . . Every kill was worth ₱15,000 . . . mayor's name in front and his signature on the back . . . a total of forty kills . . . The mayor ran down the target himself . . . cops learned to be afraid of the mayor: "Crispin Salazar" (witness using a pseudonym), affidavit affixed with a thumbmark, June 24, 2009. While there are indications it was subscribed to at the CHR main office in Quezon City on May 30, 2009, pertinent details have been redacted. The affidavit is part of a collection of documents obtained by Rappler from the CHR.

83 "I helped carry the bodies, sir" . . . Ernesto was a hired hand . . . helped bury six bodies . . . One was Pedro . . . Stabbed, not shot . . . two bodies to a cavern . . . He wanted to tell them what he had seen . . . a single bone protruded from the dirt: "Ernesto Avasola" (witness using a pseudonym), signed and notarized affidavit, July 10, 2005; and hearing before Judge William Simon P. Peralta (stenographic transcript), Branch 40, Manila Regional Trial Court, July 10, 2009. Both are among the documents obtained by Rappler from the CHR.

83 Manila court issued a second warrant: "More Human Bones Found at the Site Covered by the Search Warrants: New Video Clips and Photos Released," CHR, July 14, 2009.

83 Investigators found human remains: PNP Medico-Legal Report No. A09-506, signed by Police Lt. Col. Ruby Grace D. Sabino Diangson, M.D., L.L.B. (chief of Medico-Legal Division), Police Col. Salome Delos Reyes Jose, MPA (chief of Directorial Staff), Police Maj. Joseph C. Palermo, M.D. (medico-legal officer), Crime Laboratory, PNP National Headquarters, July 27, 2009.

84 Laud's lawyers contested the search: Progress Report on Reimplementation of Search Warrant at Gold Cup Firing Range in Davao City by CHR Multi-Agency Task Force, signed by Police Col. Roberto B. Fajardo, July 23, 2019.

84–85 The Manila judge withdrew the warrant . . . circuitous way from judge to judge . . . probable cause to search the area: Malou Mangahas, "SC on Davao Death Squad Case: PNP Can Search Quarry for Bodies," Philippine Center for Investigative Journalism, September 23, 2016.

84 **"dearth of evidence to support a finding of direct complicity"** . . . **"could be construed as tolerance"** . . . **"Davao Death Squad and its responsibility for the killings"** . . . **"There was a systematic practice of extrajudicial killings":** CHR Resolution Re: Extra-Judicial Killings Attributed or Attributable to the So-Called Davao Death Squad, Davao City, June 28, 2012.

84–85 **closed in 2014 with no categorical results** . . . **Sipaco, his office had no proof** . . . **"rumor and other gossips":** Office of the Ombudsman Field Investigation Office disposition form, January 15, 2016; transmittal letter from the assistant ombudsman to CHR, October 3, 2016; Ombudsman Field Investigation Office, *Fact-Finding Report,* May 5, 2014.

85 **unclear if the PNP conducted a search:** In an October 3, 2016, hearing, then-senator De Lima said she had no information about the 2014 SC ruling and had not been able to monitor it during her stint as justice secretary. De Lima said, "I have no knowledge, and I guess this is just a speculation. It was never done." *Hearing to Investigate the Recent Rampant Extrajudicial Killings and Summary Executions of Suspected Criminals, Before the Senate Committee on Justice and Human Rights and Committee on Public Order and Dangerous Drugs* (video recording and transcript), Senate of the Philippines, 17th Congress.

85 **deaths attributable to the Davao Death Squad at 1,424:** Carolyn Arguillas, "2011 to 2016 Killings in Davao City Among Those to Be Probed by International Criminal Court," MindaNews, September 16, 2021.

85–89 **"Davao Death Squad, sir"** . . . **"Mayor Duterte created the DDS"** . . . the witness sat, graying and unremarkable . . . born on the outskirts of Davao . . . "drug pushers, rapists, snatchers" . . . member of the city's Civil Security Unit . . . Mayor Duterte would occasionally drop by . . . small group, until 1993 . . . didn't particularly like killing people . . . orders came from cops . . . stripped, dismembered, and buried . . . no courts or judges . . . investigations were for show . . . dealt with the small fry . . . Matobato was a veteran . . . targets were the bigger fish . . . operated in the open . . . black van ready for abductions . . . strafed mosques . . . snatch a man . . . Every death squad cop carried two guns . . . first would be for killing . . . second for evidence . . . "Someone gets killed—he gets a gun" . . . left the business of planting evidence to the cops . . . raise his gun to shoot . . . chopped to pieces for

burial . . . shove a bleeding man into a swamp . . . at least a thousand in Davao City alone . . . "I remember how many since I
started killing" . . . Charlie Mike sent orders . . . approved of the
targets . . . Charlie Mike treated him like a brother . . . death
squad's field boss . . . Matobato was Lascañas's . . . Lascañas who
strangled . . . watch was a gift . . . "Everyone reported to him" . . .
"generals bow to Arturo Lascañas" . . . "If you weren't around,
Tur" . . . Charlie Mike was a code name . . . "It was Mayor
Duterte": *Hearing to Investigate the Recent Rampant Extrajudicial Killings
and Summary Executions of Suspected Criminals, Before the Senate Committee
on Justice and Human Rights and Committee on Public Order and Dangerous
Drugs* (video recording and transcript), Senate of the Philippines, 17th
Congress, September 15, 2016; Edgardo Matobato, signed but unnotarized and undated affidavit; Edgardo Matobato, signed and notarized
affidavit with his thumbmark affixed, September 4, 2014.

86 **"we can link what is happening now"**: Leila de Lima, a detained
former senator, served as justice secretary under the Arroyo and second
Aquino administrations and as CHR chair. In the latter role, she led the
2009 investigation of the Davao Death Squad. After winning a senatorial seat in 2016, she probed allegations of extrajudicial killings under the
Duterte administration. She was jailed in 2017 on three drug-related
charges, filed in the aftermath of a public denunciation by President
Rodrigo Duterte. She was acquitted in one case and sought bail for two
others after key witnesses recanted their testimonies. De Lima marked
her sixth year in detention in February 2023. See Carmela Fonbuena,
"CHR to Probe 'Davao Death Squad,'" *Newsbreak,* ABS-CBN News
Digital, February 14, 2009; Julie McCarthy, "Jailed Under Duterte,
Philippine Politician Sends Dire Warnings on Democracy," NPR, Oc-
tober 5, 2022; and Amnesty International, *Philippines: Six Years On,
Arbitrary Detention of Former Senator Leila de Lima Continues* (Amnesty
International, February 23, 2023). See also *Hearing to Investigate the Re-
cent Rampant Extrajudicial Killings and Summary Executions of Suspected
Criminals, Before the Senate Committee on Justice and Human Rights and
Committee on Public Order and Dangerous Drugs,* Senate of the Philippines,
17th Congress, September 15, 2016.

88 **Police Chief Master Sergeant:** In February 2019, a new law, Republic
Act 11200, amended Republic Act 6975 or the Department of the Interior and Local Government Act of 1990, which changed the ranking
of Philippine National Police officials. A police officer I is now referred
to as patrolman or patrolwoman; a police officer II to police corporal;
police officer III to police staff sergeant; senior police officer I to police

master sergeant; senior police officer II to police senior master sergeant; senior police officer III to police chief master sergeant; senior police officer IV to police executive master sergeant; inspector to police lieutenant; senior inspector to police captain; chief inspector to police major; superintendent to police lieutenant colonel; senior superintendent to police colonel; chief superintendent to police brigadier general; director to police major general; deputy director-general to police lieutenant general; and director-general to police general. To avoid confusion, all references to police ranks in this book have been updated to conform to the 2019 law.

89–90 "Usually, Your Honor, it's CM" . . . "Mayor Rody is what he's usually called" . . . Edgar Matobato was a liar . . . "There is no Davao Death Squad" . . . occasionally worked with Matobato . . . slept in Lascañas's home . . . Lascañas's watch . . . good man he once called his mayor: Arturo Lascañas (former police chief master sergeant), in *Hearing to Investigate the Recent Rampant Extrajudicial Killings and Summary Executions of Suspected Criminals, Before the Senate Committee on Justice and Human Rights and Committee on Public Order and Dangerous Drugs* (transcript), Senate of the Philippines, 17th Congress, October 3, 2016.

90–93 "The Davao Death Squad is real" . . . It started with his failing kidney . . . "like zombies" . . . It was a bad dream . . . "I embraced the name of Jesus Christ" . . . listed murder after murder . . . named the killers . . . It was the city mayor, Lascañas said . . . ordered the bombing of mosques . . . ordered the murder of a journalist . . . ordered the murder of Chinese drug dealers . . . entire family should be "erased" . . . "Go ahead, just make it clean" . . . exception for the four-year-old boy . . . six people were shot . . . grave deep in the Laud quarry . . . bounty was split . . . pour oil over the fresh soil . . . "In my absolute loyalty" . . . "had my own two brothers killed" . . . "submit myself to God": Arturo Lascañas in *Hearing conducted by the Senate Committee on Public Order and Dangerous Drugs* (transcript), Senate of the Philippines, Pasay City, March 17, 2017; Arturo Lascañas, handwritten confession, July 10, 2005; Arturo Lascañas, filed affidavit, February 19, 2017; press conference organized by then Senator Antonio Trillanes IV and the Free Legal Assistance Group at the Senate of the Philippines, Pasay City, February 20, 2017.

92 "I will not create a DDS": Rodrigo Duterte, press conference, Rizal Hall, Malacañang, March 7, 2017.

93 "Am I the death squad?": Rodrigo Duterte, on television show *Gikan sa Masa, Para sa Masa*, ABS-CBN News, May 24, 2015. According to

Carolyn Arguillas of MindaNews, *Gikan sa Masa, Para sa Masa* was launched in 1998 when Duterte was a Davao City representative. It has followed his career ever since, going off air when he is not in office or unavailable to commit to regular airings. When he became president, the show was rebranded as *Mula sa Masa, Para sa Masa* (a Tagalog translation of the original Cebuano) and was carried by the government-owned People's Television Network.

Chapter 5: Defend the Mayor

94–123 **"most of the people were Duterte"** . . . **to be Duterte was to belong** . . . **read about the mayor** . . . **old bed draped with mosquito netting** . . . **easy to campaign for Duterte** . . . **She called him Father** . . . **Diehard Duterte Supporter** . . . **turn everyone she knew** . . . **the man she called Father** . . . **Thirty pesos, for Du30:** Ann Valdez (Duterte supporter), interview by the author, August 1, 2021.

95 **death squad investigations:** Human Rights Watch, *"You Can Die Any Time": Death Squad Killings in Mindanao* (Human Rights Watch, April 6, 2009).

96–98 **elected mayor punching a sheriff** . . . **began with a riot** . . . **sheriff appeared; shoulders hunched** . . . **"Come here, sir"** . . . **The first punch caught** . . . **live on the phone** . . . **raised a middle finger** . . . **"I'll shoot you"** . . . **consternation from human rights groups:** "Duterte Punches Court Sheriff amid Demolition Ops in Davao City," ABS-CBN News Channel, July 1, 2011; Jeffrey M. Tupas, "Davao Mayor Duterte Punches Sheriff Over Demolition of Shanties," *Philippine Daily Inquirer,* July 1, 2011; Juan L. Mercado, "Dirty Finger Drill," *Philippine Daily Inquirer,* July 15, 2011; David Dizon, "Rudy Duterte: Punch Me and I'll Shoot You," ABS-CBN News, July 5, 2011; David Dizon, "CHR: Duterte Abuse of Sheriff Inexcusable," ABS-CBN News, July 4, 2011; Sara Duterte, interview by the author in "The Mayors Duterte" (documentary), by Kiri Dalena, Patricia Evangelista, and Karlos Manlupig, Rappler, April 4, 2012.

96 **three consecutive electoral terms:** 1987 Constitution, Article VI, Section 5 (2).

96 **same surnames in the next:** Steven Rood, "Families, Not Political Parties, Still Reign in the Philippines," Asia Foundation, May 22, 2013.

96–97 **in his mother Soledad Duterte's** . . . **chambers were so tedious** . . . **campaign again as mayor** . . . **mayor called himself vice-mayor:** Miguel Paolo P. Reyes, "The Duterte-Marcos Connection," *VERA Files,* September 29, 2019; K. D. Suarez, "How Did Rodrigo Duterte

Fare as Congressman?" Rappler, May 28, 2016; "Duterte–De Guzman Battle Looms in Davao City in 2001 Elections," *Philippine Star,* November 21, 2000; and Cheryll D. Fiel, "2010 Elections: Dutertes Proclaimed as Winners in Davao Polls," Bulatlat.com, May 13, 2010.

97 **"I've been a prosecutor":** Rodrigo Duterte, quoted from speech at the Integrated Bar of the Philippines' Regional Convention, Manila Hotel, November 4, 2016.

99 **"defend our mayor":** Duterte Defense Squad, "We Defend Our Mayor Because They Defend Us," Facebook, July 5, 2011.

100 **Diehard Duterte Supporters:** The author verified the existence and content of each of the sampled Facebook groups in 2020. See also Allan Nawal, "Facebook Groups Add Meaning to DDS," *Philippine Daily Inquirer,* May 27, 2015.

100–122 **At fifteen minutes . . . "Sir Rody Duterte" . . . "finger lickin' good" . . . "Has he declared" . . . "if he doesn't run" . . . "Everybody is praying" . . . "The mayor is smart" . . . Morocco and Tanzania . . . not fanatical in his patriotism . . . Pope Francis at Luneta Park . . . mayor was a fresh face . . . evils of martial law . . . "whether he lived or died" . . . did not contradict . . . never used drugs . . . necessary to his preservation . . . eliminate a drain on resources . . . the country will be like Davao . . . never been to Davao:** Dondon Chan, Facebook posts and interactions; Dondon Chan, interviews by the author, July 23, 2021, August 8, 2021, and March 11, 2023.

101 **"Run Duterte Run":** "Libo-libo, Sumali sa 'Run, Duterte, Run,'" ABS-CBN News, May 23, 2015.

102 **"It's going to be bloody":** Maria Ressa, "Duterte, His 6 Contradictions and Planned Dictatorship," Rappler, October 6, 2015.

102 **did not want to be president:** Rodrigo Duterte, "Open Letter to the Public," October 12, 2015.

102 **he was too old . . . country had no need for him:** Rodrigo Duterte, drawn from speech at the 37th Masskara Festival, Bacolod City, October 2, 2016.

102 **no money, no machinery . . . no ambition beyond retirement:** Rodrigo Duterte, drawn from interview by Jessica Soho (broadcast journalist), *State of the Nation,* GMA Integrated News, May 26, 2015.

102–3 **naked ambition . . . end to the posters . . . did not want to be a hypocrite . . . "jamming" with the people:** Rodrigo Duterte, drawn from press conference, Davao City, November 11, 2014.

102 **abolish Congress:** "How to Be a Man: The Passions of Rodrigo Duterte," *Esquire Philippines,* March 2015.

102–3 **country like a dictator . . . unless it was God's will:** Rodrigo Duterte, drawn from speech at the Rappler "#TheLeaderIWant" Presidential Forum, De La Salle University, Manila, January 20, 2016.

102 **reinstitute the death penalty:** Rodrigo Duterte, interview by Martin Andanar (secretary of the Presidential Communications Office of the Philippines), March 15, 2015.

102 **more funeral parlors:** Rodrigo Duterte, drawn from speech at Federalism Summit, Baguio City, February 19, 2015.

103 **listening tour:** Rodrigo Duterte, drawn from speech at Federalism Summit, Butuan City, January 22, 2015.

103 **no, once, twice, thirteen times:** Rodrigo Duterte, drawn from press conference, Davao City, December 1, 2014.

103 **each refusal reported by the dailies:** "Duterte: I Won't Run for National Post in 2016," ABS-CBN News Digital, May 23, 2015; Yuji Vincent Gonzalez, "Duterte's Final Answer: I Won't Run for President," Inquirer.net, September 7, 2015; "Duterte Insists: I'm Not Running," *Philippine Star,* October 12, 2015; "Duterte: I'm Not Running but if I Were the President . . . ," *Philippine Daily Inquirer,* July 4, 2015.

103 **deputy secretary general, Martin Diño:** "VACC Chair Martin Diño Files COC for President," GMA News Online, October 16, 2015; Allan Nawal and Tina Santos, "Door Still Open for Duterte Run," *Philippine Daily Inquirer,* October 30, 2015; Paterno Esmaquel II, "Duterte Placeholder Diño Withdraws Presidential Bid," Rappler, October 29, 2015; and Pia Ranada, "Explainer: Can Rodrigo Duterte Run for President?," Rappler, November 24, 2015.

103 **"Ignacio for President":** "Ignacio Files CoC for President," Rappler, October 12, 2015; "Archangel Lucifer, Other 'Nuisance' Candidates Soar on Twitter," Rappler, October 13, 2015; Michael Sullivan, "In Philippines' Presidential Race, a Chaotic Cast of Characters," NPR, November 7, 2015; "Man Who 'Talks to Aliens' Wants to Be President," ABS-CBN News Digital, October 14, 2015.

104–5 **The American in question . . . married a Filipino American . . . ensconced in Virginia . . . filed for dual citizenship . . . "Who would've thought" . . . courted by the ruling party . . . candidate of choice . . . loudspeakers boomed . . . leading a field of three . . . petition for disqualification . . . "They say I am not a Filipino because I am a foundling" . . . 5-4 in her favor:** "Timeline: Grace Poe's Citizenship, Residency," Rappler, September 4, 2015; Miriam Grace A. Go, "What We Know About Grace Poe's Former House in Virginia," Rappler, March 8, 2016; Patricia Evangelista, "The Independence of Grace Poe," Rappler, November 15, 2012; "State Media:

Philippines Charges Arroyo with Election Fraud," *CNN World,* November 18, 2011; "Fernando Poe Jr., 65, Philippine Actor-Politician, Dies," Associated Press, December 14, 2004; Ramon Farolan, "Amazing Grace," *Philippine Daily Inquirer,* December 8, 2014; "When Grace Poe Found Out She Was Number One," Rappler, May 17, 2013; Camille Elemia, "Grace Poe: I Offer Myself as Your President," Rappler, September 16, 2015; K. D. Suarez, "Grace Poe Could Propel NPC as PH's Biggest Political Party," Rappler, August 10, 2015; Miriam Grace A. Go, "Grace Poe Overtakes Binay in Latest Presidential Survey," Rappler, June 18, 2015; "A Second Chance: Grace Poe Urges Comelec to Reconsider DQ Case," *Politiko,* December 7, 2015; "New Philippine Senator Poe Widens Lead in Presidential Opinion Polls," Reuters, September 21, 2015; Tina G. Santos, "Comelec Disqualifies Grace Poe," *Philippine Daily Inquirer,* December 2, 2015; "SET Votes 5-4 in Favor of Grace Poe," ABS-CBN News Digital, November 17, 2015; and Grace Poe, speech to Filipino migrant workers, Hong Kong, December 26, 2015.

105 **"not about politics"** . . . **"the option to run":** Rodrigo Duterte, quoted from speech to Doctors' Forum, Iloilo City, November 21, 2015.

105 **"an American president"** . . . **fill the slot** . . . **"I Am Running":** Pia Ranada, "Rodrigo Duterte: I Am Running for President," Rappler, November 21, 2015.

105 **"The die is cast":** Rodrigo Duterte, quoted from press conference, San Juan City, November 23, 2015.

106–7 **the fucking government** . . . **the fucking airport** . . . **the fucking drunks** . . . **fucking his two girlfriends** . . . not admit to killing men . . . really hasn't killed too many . . . Drugs have screwed . . . Fair warning . . . you will have to die . . . Let the human rights activists come . . . He'll accept responsibility . . . kill every drug addict in the country . . . will have to kill himself . . . Let the activists hunt him down . . . Let Congress investigate . . . send in the war tanks . . . shoot those idiots . . . Try him . . . happy to rot in jail . . . He's killed two cops . . . can't protect people without killing people . . . hunt down those bastards . . . won't accept surrender . . . have his cops shoot . . . plant guns on each hand . . . bastards fought back . . . Davao is safe . . . tits or their panties or their wallets . . . Stay in jail . . . Nothing to fear for everyone. . . . **no reason to be afraid:** Rodrigo Duterte, drawn from speech at MAD for Change Concert, Taguig City, November 29, 2015.

107 **Butcher and the Punisher:** "Duterte on Drug War: 'I Might Go Down

in History as the Butcher,'" *Sunstar,* January 9, 2017; see also Charlie Campbell, "The Next President of the Philippines Could Be 'The Punisher,'" *Time,* April 7, 2016.

108 **worried one former governor, Manny Piñol . . . "unstable, disrespectful, irreverent" . . . "'Dutertards'" . . . "still vacillating in their choice":** Piñol (former secretary of agriculture), "To Duterte's Supporters Let's Promote Our Candidate Not Intimidate Non-Believers," Facebook, January 2, 2016.

108–22 **Jason Quizon was born in Pampanga . . . at dawn to hunt frogs . . . a massive volcanic eruption . . . the best man Jason knew . . . "I followed the money" . . . "libtard though" . . . drug addiction was a disease . . . reduced to a bullet . . . "You go to NAIA" . . . "'miss your flight'" . . . wrapping his suitcases . . . "problem with Aquino and his public relations" . . . "it was a big deal" . . . man of action . . . Filipinos as gullible folk . . . Idiots all . . . cater to the simple-minded . . . mayor was joking . . . booked a flight from Abu Dhabi to Doha . . . "politically benign":** Jason Quizon (overseas Filipino worker), Facebook posts and online interactions; Jason Quizon, interviews by the author, July 30, 2021, and March 11, 2023.

110–12 **Lane Michael White . . . ammunition a crime . . . scam was called** *laglag-bala* **. . . "he was holding bullets" . . . disappearance amounted to ₱500 . . . A teenager flying to Seoul . . . bullet wrapped in a red cloth . . . bailed out for ₱80,000 . . . padlocked her luggage . . . only seven victims named . . . dismissed the issue as largely sensationalized . . . Mayor, please be our lawyer . . . "matter of extortion" . . . "five days to do" . . . "do something drastic":** "After Long Ordeal, U.S. Missionary 'Tanim-Bala' Victim Leaves PH," ABS-CBN News Digital, December 15, 2015; *An Act Providing for a Comprehensive Law on Firearms and Ammunition and Providing Penalties for Violations Thereof,* Republic Act No. 10591, 15th Congress; Resolution No. 1644, Senate of the Philippines, 16th Congress, November 3, 2015; Rhed Austria de Guzman, "Nakakaloka Talaga ang NAIA!!! I Just Got Off a Flight from Manila to LAX at Talaga Namang ang Pangongotong sa Pilipinas e Hindi Natatapos!!!" Facebook, September 19, 2015; "'Tanim-Bala' Victim Files Raps vs 4 OTS Men," ABS-CBN News, November 24, 2015; "Timeline: Recent Cases of Alleged Bullet Scam at NAIA," Rappler, November 2, 2015; Jeannette I. Andrade, "Japanese Carrying 2 Bullets in Bag Arrested at NAIA," *Philippine Daily Inquirer,* October 27, 2015; "Tanim-Bala? 68-Yr-Old Woman in Trouble for Bullet in Bag," ABS-CBN News, November 1, 2015; Aie Balagtas et al., "PAO Gets 12 'Tanim-Bala'

Suspects Freed," *Philippine Daily Inquirer,* November 10, 2015; Patricia Lourdes Viray, "PNoy Says 'Laglag-Bala' Issue Sensationalized," Philstar.com, November 23, 2015; Editha Caluya, "Duterte Vows to Lawyer for Laglag-Bala Victims," Rappler, November 2, 2015; Germelina Lacorte, "Duterte Urges Aquino to 'Take Drastic Step' in Stopping 'Tanim-Bala,'" *Philippine Daily Inquirer,* November 3, 2015.

113 **a mayor should be the first to rape:** Rodrigo Duterte, drawn from speech at a campaign rally, Amoranto Sports Complex, Quezon City, April 12, 2016; "Duterte Says Sorry to Filipinos; 'Rape Remarks Not a Joke,'" ABS-CBN News, April 17, 2016.

113–14 **"I'm telling you a story"** . . . **"Australian embassy kept calling"** . . . **"That she was raped?"** . . . **"The mayor should have been first"** . . . **"What a waste":** Rodrigo Duterte, quoted in speech at a campaign rally, Amoranto Sports Complex, Quezon City, April 12, 2016. This is not the only time Duterte told Jacquiline Hamill's story during his candidacy and presidency. See Lindsay Murdoch, "Philippines: Rodrigo Duterte Condemned for Comments on Rape of Australian Missionary," *Sydney Morning Herald,* April 17, 2016; Patricia Lourdes Viray, "Australia: Rape Should Never Be Joked About," Philstar.com, April 17, 2016; Charlie Campbell, "Philippine Presidential Candidate Defends Remarks on Rape: 'This Is How Men Talk,'" *Time,* April 18, 2016.

114–22 **Joy Tan believed in God** . . . **did not believe in rape and murder** . . . **the mayor could kill** . . . **traveled the two hours to Davao** . . . **He smoked pot** . . . **occasional armed robbery** . . . **"Here's the thing, pal"** . . . **it was her cousin's fault** . . . **found a ride home** . . . **terrified enough to practice restraint** . . . **punctuated with cannon blasts** . . . **It was the MNLF** . . . **lost everything, but they lived** . . . **angry at the Aquino government's neglect** . . . **began writing letters** . . . **arrest the boys** . . . **like seeing Jesus** . . . **what the second D** . . . **Asus K424 laptop** . . . **hocked it for ₱5,000:** Joy Tan (wife and mother from North Cotabato), online interactions; Joy Tan, interviews by the author, July 29, 2021, and March 11, 2023.

117 **cut America out of military agreements:** Rodrigo Duterte, drawn from speech at 37th Masskara Festival, Bacolod City, Negros Occidental, October 2, 2016.

117 **Barack Obama was a son of a bitch:** Rodrigo Duterte, drawn from interview by media on his departure to Indonesia and Laos for 28th and 29th ASEAN Summits, Davao City, September 5, 2016.

118 **willing to ride a Jet Ski out into the open sea:** Rodrigo Duterte, drawn from speech at PiliPinas Debates 2016, Lingayen, Pangasinan, April 24, 2016.

118 **he was a killer:** Rodrigo Duterte, drawn from speech at Wallace Business Forum Dinner, Malacañang, December 12, 2016.

118 **joking when he said he was a killer:** Rodrigo Duterte, drawn from speech at Talk to the People on COVID-19, Malacañang, October 5, 2016.

118 **specter of a narco state:** Rodrigo Duterte, drawn from speech during visit to Ozamiz City Police Station, Ozamiz City, Misamis Occidental, August 17, 2017.

118 **only playing to the crowd:** Rodrigo Duterte, drawn from speech at Talk to the People on COVID-19, Davao City, May 10, 2021.

118 **drug addiction is criminal:** Rodrigo Duterte, drawn from speech at oath taking of New Officers of the League of Cities of the Philippines and League of Provinces of the Philippines, Malacañang, July 27, 2016.

118 **drug addicts are not human:** Rodrigo Duterte, drawn from speech at the tenth anniversary of the Eastern Mindanao Command, Davao City, August 26, 2016.

118 **massacre can be considered acceptable public policy:** Rodrigo Duterte, drawn from speech to Joint Meeting of the National Task Force—Regional Task Force to End Local Communist Armed Conflict in Region IV-A, Lucena City, Quezon, October 21, 2021.

118 **disappear in three to six months:** Rodrigo Duterte, drawn from speech to PiliPinas Debates 2016, Cagayan de Oro City, February 21, 2016.

118 **ordering undesirables out of his city:** Rodrigo Duterte, drawn from speech at dinner with V. Luna and Cotabato wounded-in-action soldiers, Malacañang, August 29, 2016.

118–22 **snipers a target . . . Best to kill him here . . . kisses the flag . . . no claim to greatness . . . specialist in nothing except death . . . given it to her good . . . Someone should answer . . . no single ship . . . commuters wait daily . . . none of the promises kept . . . hungry, sad, on bended knee . . . son-of-a-bitch government . . . Watch him . . . slap a man, kill a man . . . poor man, vote for him . . . looking to be fed . . . protect you from the landowners . . . men are afraid now . . . corrupt sons of bitches . . . Latin honors in school . . . There are many of us . . . eternal justice of God . . . in the vastness of the sky . . . cook up crystal meth . . . an eighteen-month-old . . . pull on Satan's fucking tail . . . start the day he steps . . . he will kill you . . . kill him, or he'll kill you . . . protect idiot criminals . . . can kill the criminals . . . he will do it . . . Mark it on your ass or on your balls:** Rodrigo Duterte, drawn from speech at Miting de Avance, May 7, 2016, supplemented by the author's field reporting.

123–24 **The Imagined President . . . "If Rodrigo Duterte wins" . . . "streets will run red" . . . "know you could be next":** Nicole Curato and Patricia Evangelista, "The Rapture of Rodrigo Duterte," Rappler, May 2, 2016.

Chapter 6: Salvation

127 **five-way race . . . sixteen million votes . . . Aquino ally Leni Robredo:** "Rodrigo Duterte Officially Wins Philippines Presidency," *Al Jazeera,* May 27, 2016.

127 **appealed for a recount . . . lost in court:** "Supreme Court Unanimously Junks Marcos' VP Poll Protest vs Robredo," CNN Philippines, February 16, 2021.

127–28 **He thanked former presidents . . . quoted Abraham Lincoln . . . "mere symptoms":** Rodrigo Duterte, speech on his inauguration as 16th President of the Republic of the Philippines, Malacañang, June 30, 2016.

128 SOLIDARITY DINNER WITH THE POOR **. . . orange-walled gymnasium:** PTV, "Heads Up: President Rody Duterte to Hold Solidarity Dinner with the Poor at Del Pan Sports Complex, Tondo, Manila Tonight," Facebook, June 30, 2016; "Duterte Holds Solidarity Dinner in Tondo," ABS-CBN News, July 1, 2016.

128 **Tondo, population 630,363:** City of Manila Statistical Tables, Philippine Statistics Authority, 2015.

128 **Slum Tour:** "Smokey Tours," TripAdvisor.com.

129 **The sons of bitches would die . . . he will kill you . . . "there's been enough warning" . . . "they asked for it" . . . "kill them yourselves":** Rodrigo Duterte, drawn from speech at Solidarity Dinner with the Poor, Delpan Sports Complex, Tondo, Manila, June 30, 2016.

129 **first of the dead men . . .** I AM A CHINESE DRUG LORD **. . . "male person alleged victim":** Spot Report Re: Murder (by Gun Shooting), signed by Police Cpl. Dennis N. Turla (investigator-on-case), Crimes Against Person Investigation Section (CAPIS), Manila Police District, July 1, 2016.

129 **Extrajudicial killing:** The United Nations defines *extrajudicial killings* as "killings committed, e.g., by vigilante groups or secret government agents, outside judicial or legal process, that is in contravention of, or simply without, due processes of law." For a more detailed discussion on the similarity of terms used in the Philippine context, see Peter Bouckaert, "License to Kill," Human Rights Watch, March 2, 2017; Solita Collas-Monsod, "Amnesty International Received Nobel Peace Prize in '77," *Philippine Daily Inquirer,* February 4, 2017.

130–32 **The entry for the verb** *salvage* **. . . introduced by the conquista-**

dors . . . "used in Filipino is different" . . . *Salbahe* was anglicized . . . "visual similarity" . . . "due process for common
criminals" . . . "did not 'kill,' they 'salvaged'" . . . "Another 303
political activists": On the word *salvage,* see *Oxford English Dictionary*
(Oxford: Oxford University Press, 2023), continually updated at http://
www.oed.com/. On the historical evolution of the word, see Ambeth
Ocampo (historian), discussion with the author, September 23, 2021;
Jose F. Lacaba, "Carabeef Lengua," *Manila Times,* August 3, 1995. In-
ternational publications subscribe to the same definition; see William
Branigin, "Graft, Abuse of Power Corroding Philippine Institutions,"
Washington Post, January 30, 1994; Iain Guest, *Behind the Disappearances:
Argentina's Dirty War Against Human Rights and the United Nations* (Phil-
adelphia: University of Pennsylvania Press, 1990); *Globe and Mail,*
July 2, 1980, as cited in the OED.

131 **"execution committed by government agent(s)"** . . . **1,217 salvag-
ings** . . . **put the number at 3,240** . . . **McCoy counted 3,257** . . .
International Committee of Jurists: Nathan Ela, "On Salvaging,"
Task Force Detainees of the Philippines (2016); Task Force Detainees of the
Philippines, *Task Force Detainees' Glossary of Human Rights Terms* (1991);
ABS-CBN Investigative & Research Group, "By the Numbers: Human
Rights Violations During Marcos' Rule," ABS-CBN News Digital,
September 21, 2018; Thomas Maresca, "Marcos Victory Opens Old
Wounds for Martial Law Victims in Philippines," UPI, May 13, 2022;
Alfred W. McCoy, "Dark Legacy: Human Rights Under the Marcos
Regime," in *Memory, Truth-telling and the Pursuit of Justice: A Conference
on the Legacy of the Marcos Dictatorship* (Quezon City: Ateneo de Manila
University, 1999); Virginia Leary, A. A. Ellis, and Kurt Madlener, *The
Philippines: Human Rights After Martial Law* (Geneva: International
Commission of Jurists, 1984).

132 **does not exist in most Filipino dictionaries:** Local dictionaries do not
offer a definition of *salvage* as murder: *Vicassan's Pilipino-English Dictio-
nary,* abridged ed. (Pasig City: Anvil, 2006); *Filipino-English English-
Filipino Dictionary,* consulting ed. Luis S. Santos (Manila: Merriam &
Webster Bookstore, 2020); *Diksyunaryong Filipino,* ed. Aurea Jimenez
Santiago and Manuel Franco (Manila: Merriam & Webster Bookstore,
2008); *The Official Webster's English-Filipino Dictionary with Thesaurus*
(Manila: W.S. Pacific Publications, 2017). An exception is the *UP
Diksyonaryong Pilipino,* 2nd ed. (Manila: Sentro ng Wikang Filipino,
2010), which defines *salvage* in the Philippines as "killing conducted by
agents of the state in violation of proper processes required by law in the
treatment of criminals or prisoners," comparative to summary executions.

132–33 "Nightcrawlers of Manila" . . . "night on the front lines" . . . "rain-slicked slum" . . . "it's gory" . . . "The Shot": Jonathan Kaiman, "Meet the Nightcrawlers of Manila," *Los Angeles Times,* August 26, 2016.

133–44 "kind of label" . . . "unethical photographer" . . . "completely opposite" . . . night shift in 2007 . . . took his camera to the MPD . . . "That was it" . . . *"you sons of bitches"* . . . crackled out a flash . . . YOU WILL BE NEXT . . . " 'Don't you have hearts?' ": Raffy Lerma (photojournalist), interview by the author, November 23, 2020.

133 "cut-throat, dangerous realm": *Nightcrawler* synopsis (Open Road Films, 2014).

133–35 "That's just nonsense" . . . began at 5:03 . . . battered 1997 Mitsubishi . . . Bureau chiefs . . . Chinese immigrant . . . butt of a gun . . . there was no body: Vincent Go (photojournalist), interview by the author, August 27, 2022.

135 "Manila, July 6, 2016": Vincent Go, "Manila July 6, 2016, A Body Bound with Duct Tape Was Dumped at Dawn on Top of Delpan Bridge," Facebook, July 6, 2016.

136 "Voice shows": *Chicago Manual of Style,* 17th ed. (Chicago: University of Chicago Press, 2017).

136 "Never use the passive": George Orwell, *Politics and the English Language* (1946; reprint London: Penguin Modern Classics, 2013).

136 "forcible writing" . . . "Use the active": William Strunk, *The Elements of Style,* 4th ed. (New Jersey: Pearson, 1999).

136 "Passive voice": John Bremner, *Words on Words: A Dictionary for Writers and Others Who Care About Words* (New York: Columbia University Press, 1980).

137 eighteen drug suspects . . . district of Tondo alone . . . Four had been shot . . . Fourteen were killed: "The Kill List," *Philippine Daily Inquirer,* July 7, 2016.

137–39 four-lane MICT Access Road . . . Jerome Roa, twenty-seven . . . Parola Gate 64 . . . One bare foot . . . camouflage-print cargo pants . . . ribbon of yellow tape . . . Her name was Josephine . . . lived on the street . . . enough for a fix . . . *pray for us* . . . "Is it dangerous to live here?" . . . "as long as you behave": Josephine (Jerome's grandmother) and bystanders at the crime scene, interviews by the author, August 20, 2016; Spot Report Re: Murder (by gun shooting), signed by Police Cpl. Dennis N. Turla (investigator on case), CAPIS, Manila Police District, August 20, 2016.

139–41 began with five bodies . . . carrying beribboned shovels . . . trailed the night shift . . . "victim was a drug dealer" . . . naked, bloodied . . . "He denied everything" . . . "I wanted him to die

too": Eloisa Lopez (photojournalist), interview by the author, February 26, 2022.

141 **Salvadoran Civil War . . . Chilean Socialists . . . lynchings of emancipated African Americans:** See Amnesty International, *El Salvador: The Spectre of Death Squads* (Amnesty International, December 1, 1996); Human Rights Watch, *When Tyrants Tremble* (Human Rights Watch, 1999); and Equal Justice Initiative, "Lynching in America: Confronting the Legacy of Racial Terror" (Equal Justice Initiative, 2017).

141 **"carefully selected and intentionally targeted":** UN Human Rights Council, *Report of the Special Rapporteur on Extrajudicial, Summary or Arbitrary Executions, Philip Alston: Addendum: Mission to Philippines* (UN Human Rights Council, April 16, 2008).

142 **"current wave of extrajudicial killings":** "UN Experts Urge the Philippines to Stop Unlawful Killings of People Suspected of Drug-Related Offences," Office of the High Commissioner, August 18, 2016.

142 **899 people were killed . . . "floating along canals":** Bea Cupin, "Dela Rosa: PNP Investigating 899 Drug-Related Deaths," Rappler, August 18, 2016.

142 **"deaths under investigation":** Maila Ager, "Deaths 'Under Investigation' Now at 899—Dela Rosa," Inquirer.net, August 18, 2016.

142 **"homicides under investigation":** Bianca Dava, "PNP-IAS: Call Them 'Homicides Under Investigation,' Not EJKs," ABS-CBN News Digital, October 9, 2017.

142 **"term it as plain homicide":** Cecile Suerte Felipe, "Bato: Drug Deaths Homicide, Not EJK," *Philippine Star,* March 27, 2017.

142 **Deputy Speaker Gwendolyn Garcia:** Yuji Gonzales, "House Body Drops Use of 'Extrajudicial Killing,'" Inquirer.net, September 18, 2016.

143 **There were three victims:** Kevin Manalo, "3 Patay sa Buy-Bust Operation sa Pandacan," ABS-CBN News Digital, July 16, 2016.

Chapter 7: How to Identify an Addict

145 **did not call for murder:** Rodrigo Duterte did not explicitly call for the murder of criminals. He did, however, ask for time to commit murder himself. "If I cannot control drugs, if I cannot defeat terrorism, you will have my resignation," he said in 2017. "Believe me. I'll tell you straight. But give me a chance to kill them one at a time. It is not easy to commit murder." Duterte, speech to the Philippine Development Forum: Sulong Pilipinas 2017, DSA Shangri-La Hotel, Mandaluyong City, August 9, 2017.

145 **"have to perish":** Rodrigo Duterte, quoted from speech at Inauguration of the Governor Miranda Bridge II, Davao del Norte, May 18, 2017.

145 **"wiped out"**: Rodrigo Duterte, quoted from speech at the 116th Police Service anniversary of the PNP, Quezon City, August 9, 2017.

145–55 **"slaughter those idiots"** . . . **"Give it a liberal addition"**: Rodrigo Duterte, quoted from State of the Nation Address, Batasang Pambansa, Quezon City, July 25, 2016.

145 **boat in the Pacific**: Rodrigo Duterte, drawn from interview on *ANC Headstart,* ABS-CBN, June 24, 2015.

145 **Push them out of helicopters**: Rodrigo Duterte, drawn from speech at Kaamulan Festival, Malaybalay City, March 25, 2017.

145 **"not with rope"**: Rodrigo Duterte, quoted from interview by Martin Andanar (anchor), TV5, April 7, 2015.

145 **bound man begging for his life**: Rodrigo Duterte, drawn from speech at Dialogue with Partner Communities of the National Housing Authority, Quezon City, February 9, 2017.

145–47 **"I declared war"** . . . **"is there a crime?"** . . . **"never said do it from behind"** . . . **"I am the president now"**: Rodrigo Duterte, quoted from interview by media, Cagayan de Oro City, March 3, 2017.

146 **called himself a killer**: Rodrigo Duterte, drawn from interview by Maria Ressa (Rappler CEO and journalist) for "#TheLeaderIWant," Davao City, October 29, 2015.

146 **"just an ordinary killer"**: Rodrigo Duterte, quoted from speech to the Federalism Summit, Baguio City, February 19, 2015.

146–47 **He was only kidding** . . . **sent to purgatory**: Rodrigo Duterte, drawn from speech at Solidarity Dinner with the Poor, Tondo, Manila, June 30, 2016.

146 **He would pardon himself**: Rodrigo Duterte, drawn from speech at Makati Business Club, Makati City, April 27, 2016.

146 **"Charge me when I step down"**: Rodrigo Duterte, quoted from speech at dinner with Philippine Military Association Alumni, Malacañang, October 4, 2018.

146 **Article 248 of the Philippine Revised**: Revised Penal Code, Article 248.

146 **reduced to homicide** . . . **term of twelve to twenty years**: Revised Penal Code, Article 249.

146 **not a license to murder**: Rodrigo Duterte, speech during the destruction of dangerous drugs in Trece Martires City, December 3, 2020. This speech is illustrative of how Duterte distinguishes between murder and homicide. He advised cops not to "kill intentionally or killing, that's murder. But if he has a gun or manages to pull it out or if it's at his waist, shoot him because he'll really pull it out and then you'll die."

146 **single day behind bars**: Rodrigo Duterte, drawn from speech at the

oath-taking of newly elected Punong Barangays of Region IX, Zamboanga del Sur, June 26, 2018.

146 **"duty to kill"**: Rodrigo Duterte, quoted from speech at 115th anniversary of the Bureau of Customs, BOC Gymnasium, Port Area, Manila, February 8, 2017.

147 **Article 11 of the Penal Code . . . "anyone who acts in defense" . . . "lawful exercise of a right" . . . "acts in obedience to an order"**: Revised Penal Code, Articles 11, 11.1, 11.5, 11.6.

147–57 **The president would provide bounties . . . "you have my support" . . . "no longer a viable option" . . . Shoot if they fight back**: Rodrigo Duterte, drawn from speech at Thanksgiving Party, Davao City, June 4, 2016.

147–50 **"to hunt them, and then to kill them" . . . 77,000 victims had been killed . . . "robbery with rape and homicide" . . . dead in three to four years**: Rodrigo Duterte, drawn from speech at Inauguration of the Metro Manila Crisis Monitoring and Management Center, Makati City, April 5, 2017.

147 **They would be drowned . . . dropped into Manila Bay, fed to fishes**: Rodrigo Duterte, drawn from speech at Golden Topper Corporate Launch, Parañaque City, September 25, 2019.

147 **stabbed, shot**: Rodrigo Duterte, drawn from speech at Peace and Order Summit for Barangay Officials, Legazpi City, Albay, February 8, 2019.

147 **buried**: Rodrigo Duterte, drawn from speech at Thanksgiving Dinner for Senator Bong Go, Davao City, May 27, 2019.

147 **"Simple justice," he said. "Not murder-murder"**: Rodrigo Duterte, quoted from speech to victims of the Jolo Cathedral Bombing in Sulu (official transcript), January 29, 2019. The transcript was uploaded by the Presidential Communications Operations Office and accessed by researcher Jodesz Gavilan in 2019. The transcript is no longer accessible as of March 2023, but it can be found in an archived webpage on Archive.org. The author's copy reads, in translation, "Now in Davao, when I was mayor, I said, 'Get out of Davao. Don't destroy my city or I will kill you all. Look at Davao now. I told them don't feed drugs to my children. If you destroy my children, I will kill you. Simple justice. Not murder-murder. I ordered you to destroy the organization." A thirty-minute video uploaded to the official Radio Television Malacañang (RTVM) YouTube channel does not include portions of this line. Roughly a quarter of the official transcript is omitted from the footage, including "Simple justice. Not murder-murder." See also Duterte's thoughts on death as retribution: "It's not a deterrent, actually. In my book, it's pay for the crime. I do not really care if you're deterred or not.

But if you're caught, that's the retribution. That would assuage society's conscience, actually." "How to Be a Man: The Passions of Rodrigo Duterte," *Esquire Philippines,* March 2015.

147–48 "I'll give it to you raw" . . . "this addict also came" . . . "this is my niece" . . . Dead, with her belly torn open: Rodrigo Duterte, drawn from speech at Parish Pastoral Council for Responsible Voting's Board of Trustees, Officers and Delegates, Malacañang, August 3, 2016. The president has told a version of this story at least six times, with varying details.

148–49 "So people got together" . . . snub-nosed Ruger revolver . . . "right there at the station": Rodrigo Duterte, drawn from speech to Agila Troopers, Camp General Manuel T. Yan, Sr., 10th Infantry Division, Philippine Army, Barangay Tuboran, Mawab, Compostela Valley, September 20, 2016.

148–49 The niece was eighteen months old . . . "You, if you were the mayor": Rodrigo Duterte, drawn from speech at 120th anniversary celebration of the Department of Justice, Philippine International Convention Center, Pasay City, September 26, 2017.

148–49 The police caught the uncle . . . "'end up fucking the goats'" . . . "If that's the answer you get" . . . "I did do something" . . . "because the media is here": Rodrigo Duterte, drawn from speech to 29th Annual National Convention of the Prosecutors' League of the Philippines, Angeles City, Pampanga, April 6, 2017.

148 the journalists who were there never forgot: This account was sourced by a Davao-based fact-checker from a number of journalists who had covered the rape of a baby in Mandug. The journalists recalled the event from memory and refuse to be named.

149 "Guess what I did" . . . "not one, two, three" . . . "every day, in the whole country": Rodrigo Duterte, drawn from speech at Proclamation Rally, Tondo, Manila, February 10, 2016.

149 "if I am driven also to insanity": Rodrigo Duterte, quoted from speech at State of the Mindanao Environment Day, Ateneo de Davao University, Davao City, August 4, 2016.

150 "He's smelly": Rodrigo Duterte, quoted from speech at 43rd Philippine Business Conference and Exposition of the Philippine Chamber of Commerce and Industry, Manila, October 19, 2017.

150 "problem drug user": "Drug Statistics and Trends," United Nations Office on Drugs and Crime Prevention, 2010.

150 They were criminals, all of them . . . rehabilitation for a meth addict: Rodrigo Duterte, drawn from speech at Inauguration of the First Kapampangan Food Festival, Pampanga, December 7, 2017.

150 a dozen hits of meth: Rodrigo Duterte, drawn from speech at Su-

long Pilipinas: Local Governance Series, Davao City, September 20, 2016.

150 **human brain would be gone:** Rodrigo Duterte, drawn from speech at San Beda Law Alumni Association Testimonial Reception, San Juan City, July 14, 2016.

150 **"are raping children":** Rodrigo Duterte, quoted from speech at the oath-taking of the League of Cities of the Philippines and the League of Provinces of the Philippines Officers, Malacañang, July 27, 2016.

150 **It was a "pandemic":** Rodrigo Duterte, drawn from press conference at Presidential Guest House, Department of Public Works and Highways Depot, Panacan, Davao City, August 21, 2016.

150 **an epidemic responsible for the deaths:** Rodrigo Duterte, drawn from speech for Jewish New Year at Beit Yaacov Synagogue, Makati City, October 4, 2016.

150 **77,000 . . . dictated across eleven speeches:** Rodrigo Duterte gave the figure of 77,000 killed by drug addicts at least thirteen times between March and July 2017: on March 23, on March 24, an undated day in March, March 30, April 4, April 5, April 6, April 12, April 19, April 23, May 18, May 19, and July 24. This count is based only on speeches collated by the author. The true number may be higher.

150 **"in the wake of the drug contamination":** Rodrigo Duterte, quoted from speech to the 29th Annual National Convention of the Prosecutors' League of the Philippines, Angeles City, Pampanga, April 6, 2017.

151 **37,039 murders:** The total number of murders and homicides between 2012 and 2015 is derived from adding annual totals of all murders and all homicides publicly issued in Philippine Statistics Authority, *Philippine Statistical Yearbook* (Quezon City: Philippines Statistics Authority, 2012, 2013, 2014, 2015).

151 **"really crazy" . . . "out of their senses" . . . "no cognitive value" . . . "no longer viable as human beings":** Rodrigo Duterte, drawn from speech at 115th Police Service anniversary celebration, Quezon City, August 17, 2016.

151 **"beyond redemption":** Rodrigo Duterte, quoted from speech at meeting with Filipino Community, Laos and Vietnam, September 5, 2016.

151 **suitable for suicide than for sympathy:** Rodrigo Duterte, drawn from speech at Press Statement on Philippine Illegal Drug Trade Hierarchy, President's Hall, Malacañang, July 7, 2016.

151 **They assault the sons and daughters:** Rodrigo Duterte, drawn from speech to members of Fourth Infantry Division of the Philippine Army, Camp Edilberto Evangelista, Cagayan de Oro City, August 9, 2016.

151 **pedophiles and madmen:** This is a constant claim from the president,

who often refers to drug addicts as rapists with no "viable brain" who rape children.

151 **bestial and bizarre:** Rodrigo Duterte, drawn from speech at 18th anniversary of the Volunteers Against Crime and Corruption, Malacañang, August 29, 2016.

151 **when the monkey rides their backs . . . no questions asked:** Rodrigo Duterte, drawn from speech at 80th founding anniversary of the National Bureau of Investigation (NBI), NBI Gymnasium, Manila, November 14, 2016.

152 **"My God, I hate drugs":** Rodrigo Duterte, quoted from statement at Rappler's "#TheLeaderIWant" Presidential Forum, De La Salle University, Manila, January 20, 2016.

152–53 **classified a "current drug user" . . . estimated number of illegal drug users . . . 1.7 million . . . 1.3 million . . . 1.8 million . . . Less than half were meth users:** This definition of a drug user and corresponding government estimates are sourced from the Dangerous Drugs Board's *Nationwide Survey on the Nature and Extent of Drug Abuse in the Philippines* for the years 2008, 2012, and 2015.

152 **The 2015 study was completed . . . three months into the new administration:** Jodesz Gavilan, "DDB: Philippines Has 1.8 Million Current Drug Users," Rappler, September 19, 2016.

152 **career bureaucrat:** For Benjamin Reyes's career in government, see "His Excellency Dr. Benjamin P. Reyes, Secretary-General of the Colombo Plan," Colombo Plan.

153 **"Personally, I don't know":** Benjamin Reyes, statement at the forum "Drug Issues, Different Perspectives: The Philippine Drug Situation," University of the Philippines, Quezon City, May 6, 2017.

153 **Reyes, caught between principles . . . Reyes was fired:** Benjamin Reyes, interview by Christian Esguerra (broadcast journalist), *Early Edition,* ABS-CBN News Channel, May 24, 2017.

153–54 **"do not contradict your own government" . . . The DDB was wrong:** Rodrigo Duterte, drawn from press conference after arriving from Russia, Ninoy Aquino International Airport, Pasay City, May 24, 2017.

154 **Santiago had run for a Senate seat:** Pia Ranada, "Duterte 'Offended' by Santiago's Criticism of Drug Rehab Approach," Rappler, November 8, 2017.

154 **point to Santiago for confirmation:** Pia Ranada, "Is Duterte's '4 Million Drug Addicts' a Real Number?" Rappler, May 6, 2017.

154 **"guesstimate":** Regine Cabato, "Dangerous Drugs Board: 3 Million Figure for Drug Users 'a Guesstimate'," CNN Philippines, July 13, 2017.

154 **estimate was derived from a statistic:** Jonathan de Santos, "Duterte Fires Drug Board Chair for 'Contradicting Government,'" Philstar. com, May 24, 2017.

154 **"65.1 million multiplied":** Camille Diola, "Duterte Hikes Drug Use Figure Anew Despite Little Evidence," Philstar.com, September 23, 2016.

155 **three-to-eight-million-strong:** Daryl John Esguerra, "Palace: Duterte's 7–8 Million Drug Users Estimate Refers to 'National Figure,'" Inquirer .net, March 1, 2019.

155 **"world's estimate of drug prevalence":** Jose Ramon Albert (former chief statistician of the Philippines), interviews by Lian Buan (journalist), October 2022 and February 2023.

155 **conservative estimates:** Rodrigo Duterte, drawn from speeches at the reunion and fellowship of Bedans Batches '71 and '72 with nationwide legal coordinators, Heroes Hall, Malacañang, July 17, 2016; groundbreaking ceremony of a drug treatment and rehabilitation center, Malaybalay City, Bukidnon, March 25, 2017; Partido Demokratiko Pilipino-Lakas ng Bayan Zamboanga campaign rally, Mayor Vitaliano D. Agan Coliseum, Don Alfaro St. Tetuan, Zamboanga City, March 3, 2019.

155 **"three million plus one million":** Rodrigo Duterte, quoted from speech to the PNP-Police Regional Office X (PNP-PRO X), Camp 1 Lt. Vicente G. Alagar, Cagayan de Oro City, September 22, 2016.

155–56 **A Reuters investigation concluded . . . the president "just exaggerates it":** Clare Baldwin and Andrew R. C. Marshall, "As Death Toll Rises, Duterte Deploys Dubious Data in 'War on Drugs,'" Reuters, October 18, 2016.

156 **11,321 of the country's 42,065 . . . "victimized mostly the underprivileged" . . . "a proven existence of drug user" . . . *proven* was also undefined . . . "during the first six months":** Command Memorandum Circular No. 16-2016, PNP, Metro Manila, July 1, 2016. This is the official police document marking the launch of Operation Double Barrel under the Duterte government's drug war.

156 **"loyal soldier":** Ronald "Bato" dela Rosa (Bureau of Corrections director general), interview by the author, at the Bureau of Corrections (BuCor) in the New Bilibid Prison Reservation, Muntinlupa City, September 3, 2018. From 2012 to 2013, Dela Rosa held the position of Davao City police chief under then-mayor Rodrigo Duterte. After winning the 2016 election, Duterte appointed Dela Rosa as chief of the PNP. In 2018, Duterte appointed Dela Rosa to head the BuCor. He was elected a senator in 2019, during the midterm election. For

more on Ronald "Bato" dela Rosa's career in government, see Senator Ronald "Bato" dela Rosa, Senate of the Philippines, 19th Congress.

156 **"One touch of the barrel":** Bea Cupin, "Warning to Drug Dealers: PNP Has 'Double Barrel' Plan," Rappler, June 29, 2016.

157 **Tokhang did not exist:** "The True Spirit of TokHang," *Philippine Daily Inquirer,* January 24, 2018.

157 **Tokhang was Dela Rosa's own brainchild:** Hana Bordey, "Bato to Continue 'Oplan Tokhang' If Elected as President in Eleksyon 2022," GMA News Online, October 11, 2021.

157 **eradicated in three to six months:** Rodrigo Duterte, statement, PiliPinas Debates 2016, presidential debate hosted by the *Philippine Daily Inquirer* and GMA Integrated News, Capitol University, Cagayan de Oro City, February 21, 2016.

157 **resign or die if he failed . . . "bleeding-heart human rights people":** Rodrigo Duterte, drawn from speech at 67th founding anniversary of the First Scout Ranger Regiment (FSRR), Bulacan, November 24, 2017.

157 **Kill them if they resist violently:** Rodrigo Duterte, speech at PDP-Laban Campaign Rally, Isabela, March 13, 2019.

157 **Get them before they get you:** Rodrigo Duterte, drawn from interview by Erwin Tulfo (broadcaster) on *Sa Totoo Lang,* People's Television Network, September 29, 2017.

158 **Marcos government held the first parliamentary . . . "But fight we will":** "The Fall of the Dictatorship," *Official Gazette,* February 25, 2016. See also "From Senator to Prisoner: The Story of Ninoy Aquino," Martial Law Museum, project by the Ateneo de Manila University, Quezon City.

158 **Laban party lost nearly every seat:** *The Philippine Electoral Almanac, Revised and Expanded Edition* (Manila: Presidential Communications Development and Strategic Planning Office, 2015).

Chapter 8: How to Kill an Addict

163 *Blood thick . . . Tape over mouth . . . Cop uses own shirt . . . Bond paper inside wallet . . . Shorts, Hawaiian print:* Author's notes while on field coverage, October 26, November 21, and December 1, 2016.

164 **"After the consummated transaction":** PNP Spot Report on the Killing of "Alias Macoy," signed by Police Lt. Col. Raniel M. Valones, Santa Maria Police Station, August 15, 2017.

165 **twenty-four hours to bag thirty more corpses:** PNP Spot Reports on the Deaths of Jimmy Gongon and Bartolome Mari, Marilao Police Station; "a certain Alvin," signed by Police Maj. Napoleon D. Cruz (chief

of police), Balagtas Police Station; Cristopher Tecson, signed by Police Lt. Col. Isagani V. Enriquez, San Miguel Police Station; Wilfredo Alapide, signed by Police Lt. Col. Heryl L. Bruno, Malolos City Police Station; Jessie Andales, signed by Police Lt. Col. Fitz A. Macariola, San Juan Del Monte Police Station; Jefry Miranda, signed by Police Lt. Col. Heryl Liwanag Bruno, Malolos City Police Station; "Alias Macoy," signed by Police Lt. Col. Raniel M. Valones, Santa Maria Police Station. All Spot Reports sampled in this account of the Bulacan slaughter were filed on August 15, 2017, with the exception of an August 17 Development Report filed by the Obando Police Station, identifying Bernard Lizardo and Justine Bucacao as the men previously referred to only as "Enan" and "Justine" in a Spot Report signed by Police Maj. Arnulfo S. Tanggol.

166 **thirty-two who died . . . sixty-seven operations:** Andrew R. C. Marshall and Manuel Mogato, "Duterte's War on Drugs: Death of a Schoolboy," Reuters, August 25, 2017.

166–67 **"drug dealers killed" . . . "no longer in their right minds" . . . a hundred suspects "who yielded":** Emil Gamos, "11 Drug Dealers Killed, 45 Others Nabbed in Bulacan," Philippine News Agency, August 16, 2017.

167 **Police Colonel Romeo Caramat, Jr. . . . twenty-five separate gunfights:** Rambo Talabong, "32 Dead, 107 Arrested in Bulacan 'One-Time, Big-Time Operation,'" Rappler, August 16, 2017.

167 **97 percent:** Clare Baldwin, Andrew R. C. Marshall, and Damir Sagolj, "Police Rack Up an Almost Perfectly Deadly Record in Philippine Drug War," Reuters, December 5, 2016.

167 **police shootings in Rio de Janeiro:** Human Rights Watch, *"Good Cops Are Afraid": The Toll of Unchecked Police Violence in Rio de Janeiro* (Human Rights Watch, July 7, 2016).

167 **"no casualties on the PNP":** PNP Spot Report on the killing of "Alias Macoy," signed by Police Lt. Col. Raniel M. Valones, Santa Maria Police Station, August 15, 2017.

167–72 **Good, said the president . . . hope that more would die . . . The carpet was red . . . *"Maganda 'yun"* . . . "If we can kill another thirty-two" . . . Disciplined citizens . . . too much unlike the city of Davao . . . agencies were corrupt . . . had no unity . . . mayors had been bought by drug lords . . . "beating up on me" . . . "make so much noise" . . . had failed to solve the problem of drugs . . . "I think there will be an outcry again" . . . "a death certificate someday":** Rodrigo Duterte, drawn from speech at 19th founding anniversary of the Volunteers Against Crime and Corruption, Malacañang, August 16, 2017.

168 *maganda* means "beautiful": *Vicassan's Pilipino-English Dictionary,* abridged ed. (Pasig City: Anvil, 2006).

169 "seriously, not literally": "Understanding Duterte 101? 'Take Him Seriously but Not Literally,'" Rappler, December 17, 2016.

169 "creative imagination": Patricia Lourdes Viray, "Palace: Use 'Creative Imagination' to Interpret Duterte Remarks," Philstar.com, October 5, 2016.

169 "heightened bravado": D. J. Yap, "Duterte 'Rape Joke' Just 'Heightened Bravado'—Palace," *Philippine Daily Inquirer,* May 27, 2017.

169 A reader left a comment: "For the record, he did not say 32 dead was a good thing." Comment posted on the author's public page, Facebook, August 19, 2017.

169 Pajamas were beautiful . . . The president's girlfriend . . . So were the daughters of Davao City: Rodrigo Duterte, drawn from speech at MAD for Change Concert, Taguig City, November 29, 2015.

169–70 Roads were beautiful . . . The Miranda Bridge: Rodrigo Duterte, drawn from speech at Inauguration of the Governor Miranda Bridge, Tagum City, Davao del Norte, May 18, 2017.

169 Federalism: Rodrigo Duterte, drawn from speech at oath-taking of newly appointed government officials, Malacañang, October 28, 2019.

169 Scout Rangers' houses: Rodrigo Duterte, drawn from speech at the Inauguration of the Candon City Bypass Road, Candon City, Ilocos Sur, July 25, 2019.

169 King of Cambodia's mother: Rodrigo Duterte, drawn from speech on his departure for Cambodia, Ninoy Aquino International Airport, Pasay City, December 13, 2016.

169 An actress who was raped: Rodrigo Duterte, drawn from speech at PDP-Laban Campaign Rally, Don Faustino L. Dy Memorial Coliseum, Cauayan City, Isabela, March 13, 2019.

169 A white missionary who was murdered: Rodrigo Duterte, drawn from speech at *Manila Times* Fifth Business Forum, Davao City, February 10, 2017.

169–70 island of Mindanao . . . his own daughters . . . song written about him: Rodrigo Duterte, drawn from speech at Miting de Avance, Manila, on May 7, 2016.

169–170 "even if everyone is dead": Rodrigo Duterte, drawn from speech at dinner with V. Luna and Cotabato wounded-in-action soldiers, Malacañang, August 29, 2016.

170 the International Narcotics Control Board brochure: Rodrigo Duterte, drawn from speech at Kapampangan Food Festival, ASEAN Convention Center, Clark Freeport Zone, Pampanga, December 7, 2017.

170 **German ex-wife:** Rodrigo Duterte, drawn from speech at PCL 2nd Quarterly National Executive Officers and Board Meeting and Fifth Continuing Local Legislative Education Program, Mandurriao, Iloilo City, June 20, 2018.

170 **being called mayor instead of president:** Rodrigo Duterte, drawn from speech at oath-taking of the League of Cities of the Philippines and the League of Provinces of the Philippines Officers, Malacañang, July 27, 2016.

170 **rapport with the military and police:** Rodrigo Duterte, drawn from speech at Thanksgiving Dinner for the Presidential Security Group, Malacañang, July 31, 2016.

170 **Filipino women were beautiful:** Rodrigo Duterte, drawn from speech at a meeting with the Families of the Slain Special Action Force 44, Heroes Hall, Malacañang, January 24, 2017.

170 **His sidearm was beautiful:** Rodrigo Duterte, drawn from speech to Second Marine Brigade, Jolo, Sulu, August 12, 2016.

170 **Church of Duterte:** Rodrigo Duterte, drawn from speech at a meeting with Filipino Community, Vientiane, Laos, September 5, 2016.

170 **eliminated corruption, criminality, and drugs:** Rodrigo Duterte, drawn from press conference, Grand Hyatt Hotel, Beijing, China, October 9, 2016.

170 **U.S. president Barack Obama:** Rodrigo Duterte, drawn from speech at 42nd Philippines Business Conference and Expo, Marriott Grand Ballroom, Newport City Complex, Pasay City, October 13, 2016.

170 **female mayor of Taguig City:** Rodrigo Duterte, drawn from speech at a meeting with Filipino Community, Indoor Stadium, Hassanal Bolkiah National Sports Complex, Brunei Darussalam, October 16, 2016.

170 **Melania Trump was beautiful:** Rodrigo Duterte, drawn from speech at League of Municipalities of the Philippines-Visayas Cluster Conference, Radisson Blu Hotel, Cebu City, August 21, 2018.

170 **So were motorcycles . . . 750 Harley Davidson Sportster:** Rodrigo Duterte, drawn from speech at Graduation Ceremony of Motorcycle Riding Course Class 06-2016, Feliz Beach Resort, Matina Aplaya, Davao, December 2, 2016.

170 **And the economy:** Rodrigo Duterte, drawn from speech at the 2016 Search for Outstanding Government Workers, Heroes Hall, Malacañang, December 19, 2016.

170 **"only had one bullet hole":** Rodrigo Duterte, drawn from speech at Convergence of Nanay Volunteers as Community Drugwatch, Parade Grounds, Clarkfield, Angeles City, Pampanga, December 22, 2016.

170 **Beaches in the Visayas:** Rodrigo Duterte, drawn from speech at the 69th Araw ng Ipil, Zamboanga Sibugay, July 26, 2018.

170 **auditoriums in Iloilo:** Rodrigo Duterte, drawn from speech at Gift-Giving Activity for Barangay Officials, Davao City, December 27, 2016.

170 **The candidates of the 65th Miss Universe Competition:** Rodrigo Duterte, drawn from speech at Presentation of the 65th Miss Universe Competition Contestants and Miss Universe Organization, Malacañang, January 23, 2017.

170 **His circumcised penis:** Rodrigo Duterte, drawn from speech at National Housing Authority Summit: Dialogue with Partner Communities, NHA Multi-Purpose Covered Court, Elliptical Road, Diliman, Quezon City, February 8, 2017.

170 **Filipino women who marry Russians:** Rodrigo Duterte, drawn from speech at a meeting with Filipino Community, Moscow, Russia, October 5, 2019.

170 **"women of Cagayan de Oro":** Rodrigo Duterte, drawn from speech at the Closing Plenary of the 26th Mindanao Business Conference, Convention Hall, Xavier Sports and Country Club Xavier Estates, Masterson's Road, Uptown, Cagayan de Oro City, September 9, 2017.

170 **The sky at dusk:** Rodrigo Duterte, drawn from speech at inspection of newly delivered air assets and Talk to Troops, Clark Air Base, Air Force City, Clark Field in Pampanga, February 12, 2021.

170 **The defense secretary's hair:** Rodrigo Duterte, drawn from speech at Exchange of Signed Business Agreements, Grand Hyatt Beijing, China, April 26, 2019.

170 **His nurse:** Rodrigo Duterte, drawn from speech at a meeting with Filipino Community, Royal Thai Navy Hall Headquarters, Bangkok, Thailand, May 22, 2017.

170 **His relationship with China:** Rodrigo Duterte, drawn from press conference on his departure for the Boao Forum for Asia Annual Conference 2018 in China, Davao International Airport, Davao City, April 9, 2018.

170 **The Nighthawk .45 pistol:** Rodrigo Duterte, drawn from press conference, Pasay City, March 23, 2017.

170 **Linens at the Peninsula Hotel:** Rodrigo Duterte, drawn from speech at 16th National Convention of Lawyers of the Integrated Bar of the Philippines, Marriott Hotel, Pasay City, March 23, 2017.

170 **The vice president, whose knees:** Rodrigo Duterte, drawn from speech at Third Year Commemoration of Super Typhoon Yolanda, Tacloban Mass Grave, Barangay Basper, Tacloban City, November 8, 2016.

170 **red shoes worn by a reporter:** Rodrigo Duterte, drawn from speech on his arrival from Cambodia, Hong Kong, China, F. Bangoy International Airport, Davao City, May 16, 2017.

170 **The City of Marawi:** Rodrigo Duterte, drawn from speech at a visit to the First Mechanized Infantry (Maasahan) Brigade Mechanized Infantry Division Philippine Army, Camp Leono, Barangay Kalandagan, Tacurong City, June 7, 2017.

170 **Middle Easterners . . . "beautiful race of Muslims":** Rodrigo Duterte, drawn from speech at Eid'l Fitr celebration, Rizal Hall, Malacañang, June 27, 2017.

170 **Chinese-made sniper rifles . . . American-made Barretts:** Rodrigo Duterte, drawn from speech at a visit to the PNP—Police Regional Office XI, Camp Quintin M. Merecido, Catitipan, Buhangin, Davao City, June 29, 2017.

170 **Jericho handguns:** Rodrigo Duterte, drawn from speech to 103rd Infantry (Haribon) Brigade, First Infantry Division of the Philippine Army, Kampo Ranao, Marawi City, July 20, 2017.

170 **The Glock:** Rodrigo Duterte, drawn from speech at 26th anniversary of the Bureau of Fire Protection, AFP Theater, Camp Aguinaldo, Quezon City, August 2, 2017.

170 **A woman named Lia:** Rodrigo Duterte, drawn from speech at 50th founding anniversary of Davao del Norte, Davao del Sur Coliseum, Barangay Matti, Digos City, Davao del Sur, July 1, 2017.

171 **"not expensive to be beautiful":** *Imelda* (documentary), dir. Ramona Diaz (Maryland: CineDiaz Inc., 2003).

171 **"No excuses":** Rodrigo Duterte, quoted from speech at Awarding Ceremonies of the Ten Outstanding Young Men and Women, Rizal Hall, Malacañang, December 12, 2016.

172 **To kill a drug addict . . . shoves a hand into his pocket . . . you can't help where the bullets go:** Rodrigo Duterte, drawn from speech at a visit to the Philippine National Police Regional Office 12, Brgy. Tambler, General Santos City, September 23, 2016.

172 **You have to have a warrant . . . announce your authority . . . Announce you're there for an arrest . . . Demand that the addict give up . . . follow you to the station . . . duty is to overcome . . . no intent beyond survival:** Rodrigo Duterte, drawn from speech at 17th Araw ng Digos, City Gymnasium, Digos City, Davao del Sur, September 8, 2017.

172–74 **watch crystal meth exchange hands . . . "and if he resists arrest violently":** Rodrigo Duterte, drawn from speech at Office of the President Christmas Tree Lighting Ceremony, Kalayaan Grounds, Malacañang, December 3, 2018.

172 **you have to reach for your gun . . . dregs of an afternoon's drunk:** Rodrigo Duterte, drawn from speech at a visit to wake of killed-in-action soldiers, Naval Forces Eastern Mindanao, Panacan, Davao City, August 7, 2016.

172–73 **If the addict's weapon is lethal . . . "If you kill the five people behind him" . . . "if you squeeze [the trigger of your] M-16":** Rodrigo Duterte, drawn from speech at Ninth National Biennial Summit on Women in Community Policing, Apo View Hotel, Davao City, September 30, 2016.

172 **all addicts are armed:** Rodrigo Duterte, drawn from press conference, Unveiling of the Grand Hyatt Manila Marker, Grand Hyatt Manila, BGC, Taguig City, September 5, 2017.

172 **it is necessary to be afraid:** Rodrigo Duterte, drawn from speech at Talk to the Nation on COVID-19, Malacañang, April 3, 2020.

172 **You do not operate in anger:** Rodrigo Duterte, drawn from speech at a dinner with V. Luna and Cotabato wounded-in-action soldiers, Malacañang, August 29, 2016.

172 **widow your wife . . . orphan your children:** Rodrigo Duterte, drawn from speech at Talk to the Nation on COVID-19, Malacañang, April 3, 2020.

172 **a machine gun instead of a revolver:** Rodrigo Duterte, drawn from speech at the Awarding of Madayaw Residences Units, Kadayawan Homes, Davao City, June 2, 2022.

172 **You hit the addict . . . five people behind him . . . five others die . . . Ten people, a hundred die:** Rodrigo Duterte, drawn from speech at Talk to the Troops, Barangay Kilala, Marawi City, August 24, 2017.

172 **The bullets ricochet:** Rodrigo Duterte, drawn from speech at a meeting with SP02 George Canete Rupinta, a former prisoner of war of the New People's Army, Matina Enclaves, Davao City, September 16, 2017.

173 **"your duty to kill":** Rodrigo Duterte, quoted from speech at 115th anniversary of the Bureau of Customs, BOC Gymnasium, Port Area, Manila, February 8, 2017.

173 **This was legal:** Rodrigo Duterte, drawn from speech at a meeting with the Filipino Community, Intercontinental Hotel, Vietnam, September 28, 2016.

173 **"The presumption of regularity":** Rambo Talabong, "PNP to SC: Presumption of Regularity Is on Our Side," Rappler, April 12, 2018.

173–78 **"what really happened on the field" . . . fatal encounters comprised only 6 percent:** Guillermo Eleazar (Quezon City Police chief), interview by the author, November 7, 2017.

173 **"satisfactory if uncontradicted"**: Rules of Court, Section 3, Rule 131.

174 **"in the fulfillment of a duty"**: Revised Penal Code, Article 11, Section 5.

174 **very few of the thousands**: Lian Buan, "In Nearly 2,000 Deaths in Police Drug Operations, Only 10 Reached Courts," Rappler, January 16, 2021.

174 **"I told the police"**: Rodrigo Duterte, quoted from speech at Lighting Ceremony of the Office of the President Christmas Tree, Malacañang, December 4, 2018.

174 **at least 6,252 times**: Zacarian Sarao, "6,252 Drug Suspects Killed as of May 31—PDEA," Inquirer.net, June 22, 2022.

175 **in front of his seventeen-year-old cousin**: Patricia Evangelista with research by Kimberly dela Cruz, "Where the Drug War Began," Rappler, April 24, 2017.

175 **thirty-one police officers**: Patricia Evangelista et al., "This Is Where They Do Not Die," Rappler, November 25, 2017.

175–79 **seventeen-year veteran . . . "That's how addicts are"**: Allan Formilleza (police staff sergeant, PS-6, Quezon City, PNP), interview by the author, October 10, 2017. The complaint filed by Efren Morillo was not Formilleza's first brush with criminal allegations. In 2013, Formilleza and another police officer were accused of killing a thirty-four-year-old street vendor who had earlier filed complaints against them of robbery, illegal arrest, grave threats, and physical injury. Formilleza was later assigned to PS-6, where he was stationed during the fatal Tokhang operation that killed four and injured Efren Morillo. Formilleza was reassigned to the National Capital Region Police Office's Regional Police Holding and Administrative Unit. He was again accused of murder in 2017, this time of a thirty-nine-year-old security guard from Payatas in Quezon City. Quezon City Police Director Guillermo Eleazar told reporters that Formilleza was "nowhere to be found" and was considered absent without leave. Despite this, Formilleza appeared three times in court. He was in the uniform of the Eastern Police District when he spoke to the author after one of the hearings. Asked about his disappearance, he said, "It is normal to a human being to take any vacation, leave, like any normal person, even a civilian." It is unclear when Formilleza was dismissed from service. He was arrested in 2020 for an altogether different case, the kidnapping and robbery of officials from the Bureau of Internal Revenue. The PNP described Formilleza as a known hitman and member of a criminal gang. See "2 Cops Charged with Vendor's Killing Relieved," *Philippine Daily Inquirer*, September 15, 2013; Reiner Padua, "2 Cops Charged with Vendor's Murder," *Philippine Star*, September 15, 2023; Jhesset Ennano,

"QC Cop in 'Tokhang' Case Faces New Murder Charge," *Philippine Daily Inquirer,* July 11, 2017; Daphne Galvez, "Ex-Cop Linked to Kidnap Gang Nabbed in Bulacan," Inquirer.net, June 16, 2020; and Doris Franche-Borja, "Ex-Police Dawit sa Kidnapping ng BIR Officials, Timbog," *Pilipino Star Ngayon,* June 17, 2020.

175–76 **Formilleza was not alone . . . All** *nanlaban* **. . . five pistols . . . "For awards and commendation":** PNP Spot Report: Re-Encounter Between Operatives of Batasan Police Station PS-6, QCPD Resulting in the Death of Four (4) Male Drug Personalities and One (1) Male Injured, signed by Police Lt. Col. Rodelio B. Marcelo, Criminal Investigation Detection Unit, Quezon City Police District, August 22, 2016; Joint Affidavit of Arrest, signed by Police Capt. Emil de Los Santos Garcia, Police Staff Sgt. Allan Formilleza, Patrolman James Aggarao, Patrolman Melchor Navisaga, Quezon City, August 28, 2016; Spot Report, Re-encounter Between Elements of this Station Resulted to the Death of Four (4) Male Suspects for Violation of R.A. 9165 (Re-Oplan Tokhang) and Direct Assault, signed by Police Lt. Col. Lito Engkig Patay, Batasan Police Station 6, Quezon City Police District, August 21, 2016; After Operation Report Re: Encounter between PCP 4 Personnel of Batasan Police PS-6, QCPD and Five (5) Male Persons Resulting to the Death of Four (4) Male Persons and One (1) Injured, signed by Police Lt. Col. Lito Engkig Patay, Station Anti-Illegal Drugs Special Operations Task Group, Batasan Police Station 6, Quezon City Police District, August 23, 2016.

176 **Emil Garcia, interviewed . . . "suddenly, they fired at us":** Kevin Manalo, TV news report on *Umagang Kay Ganda,* ABS-CBN News, August 22, 2016; Tek Ocampo, TV news report on *Balita Pilipinas,* GMA Integrated News, August 22, 2016.

176–77 **The theory of regularity . . . requires a regular connection:** Helen Beebee, Christopher Hitchcock, and Peter Menzies, eds., *Stathis Psillos: The Oxford Handbook of Causation* (Oxford: Oxford University Press, 2009).

177 **"Now if you pull out your gun" . . . "resistance by whatever means":** Rodrigo Duterte, quoted from interview by Erwin Tulfo for TV show *Sa Totoo Lang,* People's Television Network, September 15, 2017.

177 **"sick with paranoia" . . . "standard behavior":** Rodrigo Duterte, quoted from press conference, Davao City, August 21, 2016.

177 **"They really fight back":** Rodrigo Duterte, quoted from statement, Rappler "#TheLeaderIWant" Presidential Forum, De La Salle University, Manila, January 20, 2016.

178 **Millions who could have died . . . "logically rule out EJK":** Jho-

anna Ballaran, "PNP Dispels Insinuations That Drug Deaths Are Gov't-Sanctioned," Inquirer.net, April 12, 2018.

179–87 There were five of them that day . . . Marcelo and Jessie and Efren played pool . . . Seven people stood outside . . . None of them wore their uniform . . . "Nobody runs" . . . five young men raised their arms . . . bound, cuffed, and beaten . . . police didn't carry enough handcuffs . . . electric wire from the shed roof . . . cops ransacked . . . cell phone, a tablet, a lighter . . . led into the backyard . . . into the makeshift tarpaulin shanty . . . gun and aimed the barrel . . . He said he knew nothing . . . he was clean . . . a vendor, sold fruits . . . nothing to do with anything . . . "Really?" asked Formilleza . . . Efren's chest, just under his heart . . . twice, thrice, in quick succession . . . more shooting from the backyard . . . "Say they all fought back" . . . The man who sat across from me . . . never touched illegal drugs . . . fruit vendor, father of two . . . Efren wanted to get it back . . . blood soaking his underwear . . . lay limp and still . . . prayed through the gunshots . . . through the screaming . . . two small children . . . Efren waited . . . staggered to his feet . . . *Help me* . . . threw himself down a ravine . . . occur to him he could die . . . to get away . . . from the hills onto the highway . . . found the highway past four . . . dare go to any Quezon City . . . find him and finish him . . . found an old friend . . . ride to a clinic . . . back of a jeep . . . no doctor present . . . bind his wounds . . . Efren stayed conscious . . . get his mother . . . half past ten in the evening . . . was told he was dead . . . Rizal cops were inside . . . promised Efren they would help . . . The ambulance left . . . "kicked up the drama" . . . "he's still alive" . . . ambulance sat parked . . . midnight when Efren was carried . . . Quezon City police cuffed him . . . charged with assault . . . wrist locked to the hospital bed . . . Morillos sold their house . . . bail was paid: Efren Morillo (shooting survivor), complaint-affidavit submitted to the Office of the Ombudsman, March 2, 2017; Efren Morillo, Sinumpaang Salaysay, August 26, 2016; Joint Petition for Issuance of the Writ of Amparo submitted to the Supreme Court, January 26, 2017; Efren Morillo, statement to the Tom Lantos Human Rights Commission, U.S. Congress, May 5, 2017; Efren Morillo, interview by the author, August, 1, 2017.

179–82 truck driver's assistant . . . where his mother had given birth . . . Marcelo's mother had found her husband . . . her son was in trouble . . . planted in the year he was born . . . right leg crossed over his left . . . bullet hole was a black star . . . Blood streamed out of his mouth . . . "Why would we leave?": Maria Belen Daa (mother of Marcelo Daa), interview by the author, August 21, 2017.

179–80 watched television . . . children chased spiders . . . "They took my hearing aid" . . . "We didn't find anything": Francesca Cordero (aunt of Marcelo Daa), interview by the author, August 21, 2017.

180–82 Marcelo's father, sixty-nine . . . The yard was crowded . . . shoved Marcelo's father . . . called Marcelo's father a criminal . . . "told me they were cops" . . . "I'll take care of this" . . . He wished he hadn't . . . parents slept at home: Marcelo Daa, Sr. (father of Marcelo Daa), interview by the author, August 21, 2017.

180–89 witnesses named Allan Formilleza . . . "cinematic, thespian, histrionic" . . . retracted all claims . . . seven suspects, not five . . . Three, not one . . . Garcia had not been present: Police Lt. Col. Emil Garcia, position paper submitted to the Office of the Ombudsman, September 14, 2017.

181–82 women were kept inside the house . . . commotion and made for the trees . . . Rhaffy and Anthony sprawled . . . Jessie Cule, on his knees . . . who might have been a cop . . . shouting, screaming, until the man . . . recycled wire mesh . . . "one of them is still breathing" . . . There were two more gunshots: Rowena Cordero, affidavit, January 13, 2017, submitted as an annex to Efren Morillo's complaint-affidavit, Office of the Ombudsman, March 2, 2017.

182 saw the shooting from above . . . Jessie was the last to die . . . Jessie had thrown his arms . . . "That's what I can't accept" . . . "He was begging": Marilyn Malimban (girlfriend of Jessie Cule), interview by the author, August 21, 2017.

182 Marcelo's partner ran out: Maribeth Bartolay (Marcelo Daa's wife), affidavit, January 13, 2017, submitted as an annex to Efren Morillo's complaint-affidavit, Office of the Ombudsman, March 2, 2017.

183 Rule 7 begins . . . "lives and properties during armed confrontation" . . . *reasonable* is used so often . . . officer must exercise "sound discretion" . . . officer's goal is merely to "subdue" . . . "actual, imminent and real" . . . prevent, repel, and immobilize . . . "first possible opportunity": PNP, *Revised Philippine National Police Handbook* (PNP Directorate for Operations, 2013).

184–86 "Shoot him" . . . "well, that's too bad" . . . Kill them if they make a move: Rodrigo Duterte, speech at wake of fallen soldiers, Naval Forces Eastern Mindanao, Panacan, Davao City, August 7, 2016.

184–86 "If there is a weapon" . . . "you just have to kill him" . . . Kill if they refuse to surrender: Rodrigo Duterte, drawn from speech at Ninth National Biennial Summit on Women in Community Policing, Apo View Hotel, Davao City, September 30, 2016.

184 "If you are confronted" . . . "That is my order": Rodrigo Duterte, quoted from speech at 29th Annual National Convention of the Pros-

ecutors' League of the Philippines, Royce Hotel and Casino, Clark Freeport Zone, Angeles City, Pampanga, April 5, 2017.

184 **"You have no obligation" . . . "they will die"**: Rodrigo Duterte, quoted from speech at a meeting with soldiers, Battleground Command Post, Barangay Kilala, Marawi City, August 24, 2017.

184 **"Now if he fights back" . . . "as they say"**: Rodrigo Duterte, quoted from speech at 11th founding anniversary celebration of the Eastern Mindanao Command, Naval Forces Eastern Mindanao Command Covered Court, Naval Station, Felix Apolinario, Panacan, Davao City, September 1, 2017.

184 **He would believe them:** Rodrigo Duterte, drawn from speech at Change of Command Ceremony and Testimonial Review in Honor of Outgoing AFP Chief of Staff Ricardo Visaya, Camp Gen. Emilio Aguinaldo, Quezon City, December 7, 2016.

185 **"Don't be afraid" . . . "Psst, police"**: Rodrigo Duterte, quoted from speech at mass oath-taking of newly elected officers of the League of Cities of the Philippines and Liga ng mga Barangay, Malacañang, August 6, 2019.

185 **scars on his narrow chest:** Patricia Evangelista, with additional reporting by Lian Buan, Kimberly dela Cruz, and Alex Evangelista, "The Fifth Man," Rappler, December 5, 2017.

186–94 **Shoot them in the head: . . . "But I've always told you" . . . "have the best lawyers"** Rodrigo Duterte, drawn from speech at 116th Police Service anniversary, PNP Headquarters, Camp Crame, Quezon City, August 9, 2017.

187 **He filed administrative charges . . . criminal charges . . . list was long . . . Center for International Law:** Efren Morillo, complaint-affidavit filed before the Military and Other Law Enforcement Offices, Office of the Ombudsman, March 2, 2017. In 2023, the Office of the Ombudsman, the body responsible for investigating and prosecuting crimes committed by public officials, released a resolution dismissing every complaint Morillo filed against the Payatas cops. The ombudsman claimed that while the deaths were "unfortunate," the police were acting in the fulfillment of duty, a justifying circumstance during the enforcement of a "legitimate police operation." They further noted that the statements of Morillo, the sole eyewitness, "are suspect considering he was one of the subjects of the very police operation which preceded the incident." For the joint resolution see Morillo, et al. v. P/SInsp. Garcia, et al., Office of the Ombudsman, November 28, 2022, approved by Ombudsman Samuel R. Martires on June 5, 2023.

188 **Physicians for Human Rights . . . more than a hundred assessments:** Dr. Homer Venters (director for programs, Physicians for

Human Rights) to Gil Anthony Aquino (attorney at CenterLaw), November 8, 2017.

188 **PHR, which won:** Details are based on information on the official website of Physicians for Human Rights. See also Office of the High Commissioner for Human Rights, *Istanbul Protocol: Manual on the Effective Investigation and Documentation of Torture and Other Cruel, Inhuman or Degrading Treatment or Punishment* (New York and Geneva: Office of the United Nations High Commissioner for Human Rights, June 29, 2022).

188 **QCPD "failed to provide empirical evidence" . . . PHR report pointed out mistakes . . . "highly unusual" failure to perform . . . paths of a number of bullets . . . "autopsy findings support the eyewitness narrative":** Dr. Nizam Peerwani (PHR forensic consultant) to Dr. Homer Venters, October 31, 2017.

189 **three policemen on the scene:** Allan Formilleza, testimony in Branch 42, Quezon City Metropolitan Trial Court, National Capital Judicial Region, October 10, 2017; Allan Formilleza, James Aggarao, and Melchor Navisaga, joint position paper submitted to the Office of the Ombudsman, September 14, 2017. On May 12, 2023, before this book's publication, the author sought comment from Garcia through a letter of request sent via fast courier to Garcia's office at the Pasig City Police Station, where Garcia held the position of chief of the Mobile Patrol Team. The letter was copy furnished to the Pasig City Police Headquarters. The author holds an affidavit of service, notarized on the same day in Pasig City, noting that recipients at both addresses refused service. The author reached out through email. Garcia responded and refused to comment, saying he was only willing to speak "at the proper forum to observe due process." He offered a copy of his complaint file against Efren Morillo for reference. The author accepted the offer. No complaint file was sent.

189 **misreported his presence:** Police Lt. Col. Emil Garcia, interview by the author, October 10, 2017.

189 **There had been no stealing . . . asked one of his men . . . glass owned by the Daa family . . . never touched their spoons or forks:** Allan Formilleza, judicial affidavit submitted to the Court of Appeals, February 7, 2017.

189 **Daa family's food . . . Formilleza hadn't had time for lunch:** Melchor Navisaga, judicial affidavit submitted to the Court of Appeals, February 7, 2017.

189–90 **only a single shooter . . . rookies had not drawn . . . Only Allan Formilleza:** Allan Formilleza, James Aggarao, and Melchor Navisaga, joint position paper submitted to the Office of the Ombudsman, September 14, 2017.

190 **fourteen bullets . . . in the head and torso:** Dr. Nizam Peerwani (senior consultant, Physicians for Human Rights) listed thirteen sets of
gunshot wounds for the four men who died. Dr. Nizam Peerwani to
Dr. Homer Venters, October 31, 2017. Twelve bullets were through-
and-through, each with an entry and exit wound. A single bullet was
recovered from the left lower pulmonary lobe of Anthony Comendo's
scapular region. Peerwani also enumerated the locations of entry and
exit wounds. Eleven penetrated heads and torsos. Two penetrated
Rhaffy Gabo in the left upper extremity—the proximal left arm and the
distal third of the left forearm. The total number of penetrating bullets
was confirmed to the author by Colene Arcaina (lawyer, CenterLaw),
who also confirmed to the author the location of the bullet that Efren
Morillo sustained in the chest, amounting to a total of fourteen penetrating bullets, twelve fired into heads and torsos. Colene Arcaina to the
author and fact-checker Mike Navallo, email, March 4, 2023.

190–92 **prosecutor asked Formilleza . . . "Correct?" . . . "Yes, sir" . . .
Morillo had a companion . . . "What happened to his companion?":** Allan Formilleza, court testimony (recording), Branch 42, Quezon City Metropolitan Trial Court, National Capital Judicial Region,
October 10, 2017.

191 **Project Double Barrel:** Command Memorandum Circular No. 16-
2016, PNP, Metro Manila, July 1, 2016.

191 *neutralize* **meant only "to overcome resistance":** Details on individuals who were "neutralized" are drawn from official police reports. See
Spot Reports on the deaths of Raymond Yumul, signed by Police Lt.
Col. Ariel Rebancos Red, Capas Police Station, October 22, 2016; Jef-
frey Cruz, signed by Det. Jonathan L. Bautista (investigator on case) and
Police Capt. Rommel S. Anicete, Manila Police District, November 26,
2016; Wilfredo Chavenia, signed by Police Lt. Col. Rodelio B. Marcelo and Police Lt. Rene T. Balmaceda, Quezon City Police District,
June 14, 2017; John Ryan Baluyot, Olongapo City Police Office,
July 14, 2016; two unidentified male suspects wearing white and gray
shirts, signed by Police Lt. Col. Rodelio B. Marcelo and Police Lt.
Rene T. Balmaceda, Quezon City Police District, August 2, 2017; Fer-
nando Gunio, signed by Police Lt. Col. Rodelio B. Marcelo, Quezon
City Police District, November 14, 2016; Arnel Cruz and Oliver Rega-
nit, signed by Police Lt. Col. Franklin Palaci Estoro, Gerona Police
Station, July 27, 2017; Renato dela Rosa, signed by Police Lt. Col.
Rodelio B. Marcelo, Quezon City Police District, September 2, 2016;
Justine Bucacao and Bernard Lizardo, Obando PS, August 17, 2017.

191 **"sensed the presence":** For a sampling of the phrase, see "sensed the
presence of operatives" in Jimmy Gongon and Bartolome Mari, Marilao

Police Station, August 15, 2017; "sensed the presence of policemen" in Report on Anti-Illegal Drugs Operation that Resulted in the Death of Gerardo Tumang y Lugo, Zambales Police Provincial Office, September 16, 2016; and "sensed the presence of policemen" in Spot Report on Violation of RA 91655 (Death of the Suspect Artemas Baylon Jr y Reyes and unidentified male person), unsigned in the name of Police Maj. Generico M. Binan, Botolan Municipal Police Station, March 28, 2017.

192 **"no hand in extrajudicial killings"** . . . **"You can see who is dead"** . . . **"neutralized—those are dead":** Rodrigo Duterte, quoted from press conference, Malacañang, November 19, 2019.

193 **Branch 133 acquitted Efren Morillo . . . innocence trumped the presumption of regularity . . . single irregularity in the daily circumstances:** *People of the Philippines v. Efren Morillo,* Branch 133, Quezon City Metropolitan Trial Court, National Capital Judicial Region, March 3, 2023.

Chapter 9: My Friend Domingo

195–212 **He was short and square . . . "zero tolerance" . . . "first line of defense" . . . The golden age . . . All involved in illegal drugs . . . There were many informants . . . operated with a quota: . . . Colonel Domingo came striding out . . . "It's cute, right?"** Unless stated otherwise, this account of Police Lt. Col. Robert Domingo (station commander, PS 6 Santa Ana, Manila) draws from interviews, conversations, and encounters with the author from 2016 to 2018. They include recorded interviews conducted at PS-6 Santa Ana on September 6 and October 4, 2016; an encounter at PS-1, Raxabago Street, on November 23, 2016; a recorded discussion, also at PS-1, on January 26, 2017; and a series of text message conversations in 2018. Portions of those accounts were previously reported in Patricia Evangelista, "Legendary," Rappler, October 10, 2016; Patricia Evangelista, "Welcome to the End of the War," Rappler, February 7, 2017; Patricia Evangelista, "Murder in Manila," Rappler, October 5, 2018. On May 12, 2023, before this book's publication, the author sought comment from Domingo through a letter of request sent via messenger to Domingo's office at the Eastern Police District in Pasig City, where he held the position of chief of the District Investigation and Detective Management Division. The letter was acknowledged and received by his office. The author also sent the letter via email, and reached out via text message to Domingo's number. Domingo responded. He apologized for his refusal to comment—"I'm sorry my dear friend"—citing ongoing court cases. The author informed Domingo that he would be featured in multiple chapters and encouraged him to comment. The offer was again refused, with kind regrets. The conversation ended with good wishes from the colonel. "Friends for keeps," Domingo signed off. "God bless your heart always and stay safe always ok?"

195 **Manila is divided into fourteen:** In 2016, during Domingo's term as commander of PS-6 Santa Ana, the city of Manila was divided into eleven police districts. In 2019 and 2020 three precincts were converted into stations.

195 **Each police station:** The command hierarchy of police stations is laid out in the National Police Commission (Napolcom) Memorandum Circular (MC) No. 2004-2007, Metro Manila, September 3, 2004.

195 **population roughly 195,000 . . . established by Franciscan priests . . . under the stone shadow . . . whose bells rang:** This description of PS-6 Santa Ana and its environs is drawn from the author's coverage in 2016, when Domingo estimated Santa Ana's population at 185,000. The PSA Census of Population and Housing, however, noted a population of 195,155. In 2021 the station transferred to a new location by the Santa Ana River Ferry Bus Station. See *Built Heritage Tradition of the Sta. Ana Church,* National Museum of the Philippines, accessed March 6, 2023. https://www.nationalmuseum.gov.ph; Jaime C. Laya, *Santa Ana Church of Manila: Parish of Our Lady of the Abandoned: A Historical Guide* (Manila: Cofradía de la Inmaculada Concepción Foundation, 2008).

196–99 **Buwaya, so the story went . . . "We encountered him" . . . On the morning of August 28 . . . Supreme Court petition filed by CenterLaw . . . One of them was Valerie:** The public narrative of Ryan Eder, alias Buwaya, is based on recorded interviews by a number of police and local village officials. To the author, Robert Domingo first referred to Eder's case as an example of effective community policing. Subsequently Police Capt. Dave Abarra, Village Capt. Aly Pitaylan, and sources who chose to remain unnamed expanded the narrative in interviews by the author on October 4, 2016, during a night tour of Santa Ana. See also Spot Report, Re Buy Bust Operation with Shooting Incident, authenticated by Police Capt. Apolonio N. Balubal (chief administrator), Santa Ana Police Station (PS-6), Manila Police District, August 28, 2016. Valerie Aguilan's opposing narrative of Eder's death is drawn from Annex-T of *CenterLaw v. PNP,* Supreme Court of the Philippines, Manila, October 18, 2017.

196 *Buwaya* **was an alias:** The word *buwaya* can also mean "excessively covetous person." *Vicassan's Pilipino-English Dictionary,* abridged ed. (Pasig City: Anvil, 2006).

197 **The word** *encounter:* *Oxford English Dictionary* (Oxford: Oxford University Press, 2023), continually updated at http://www.oed.com/.

201 **He was promoted to spokesperson . . . bans on the wearing of baseball caps:** Jaymee T. Gamil, "9,000 New Metro Cops Wanted," *Philippine Daily Inquirer,* May 22, 2014; Kristine Angeli Sabillo, "Caps, Cops in Uniform Banned in Metro Malls," *Philippine Daily Inquirer,* December 23, 2013.

201–10 **informed a German correspondent . . . freelanced for *National Geographic* . . . "We are very dead serious" . . . "we will go to apprehend him":** A number of impressions and statements by Domingo were drawn from a recorded interview by Carsten Stormer (foreign correspondent), PS-6 Santa Ana, Manila, July 28, 2016.

201 **The story had gone viral:** Kaibigan Ermita Outreach Foundation, "Kaibigan Foundation Condemns the Killing of Jefferson Bunuan, a 20-Year-Old Student Beneficiary," Facebook, July 19, 2016.

202–5 **in Domingo's squad car . . . footage went unreleased:** Raw video shot by Stormer was provided to the author and is the basis for the account of Domingo's July 28, 2016, Tokhang operation.

206 **I had seen a picture:** The crime scene photo depicting the aftermath of the killings of Jefferson Bunuan, Mark Anthony Bunuan, and Tutong Manaois was sent to the author by a photojournalist who has chosen to remain unnamed. A similar photo of the same incident was photographed by freelance photojournalist Ezra Acayan and was published by Paalam.org.

207 **The president had his own:** Rodrigo Duterte, drawn from speech at a visit to Philippine National Police—Police Regional Office 13, Camp Rafael C. Rodriguez Grandstand, Libertad, Butuan City, October 6, 2016; Rodrigo Duterte, speech at Awarding Ceremony of the Philippine National Police and Armed Forces of the Philippines Golf Tournament, AFP General Headquarters, Camp Emilio Aguinaldo, Quezon City, December 20, 2016.

207 **repent, resign, or die:** Rodrigo Duterte, drawn from speech at mass oath-taking of newly appointed government officials, Malacañang, January 9, 2017.

207 **he went on television and read their names . . . judges, police officials, congressmen, generals, mayors . . . involvement in the narcotics trade:** Rodrigo Duterte, drawn from speech at visit to wake of killed-in-action soldiers, Davao City, August 7, 2016.

207–8 **The president said he had "intel":** Rodrigo Duterte, drawn from speech at mass oath-taking.

208 **his own staff said they had no knowledge:** Bea Cupin, "PDEA, NBI, PNP Quizzed: Where Did Duterte Get Drug List Info?" Rappler, September 2, 2016.

208 **likely right, because he was the president:** Over the years, Rodrigo

Duterte's many spokesmen have defended the veracity of the president's accusations with regard to alleged drug dealers and alleged dissidents, as well as his characterization of the drug problem. "I don't have to verify what the President told me because he is the President. The President does not lie about those things," said Spokesperson Salvador Panelo, speaking on a matrix of alleged coup plotters allegedly provided to the Office of the President by foreign allies. "The President does not lie on anything, on serious matters. He's a very honest man." See Pia Ranada, "'The President Does Not Lie'—Panelo," Rappler, May 2, 2019; Salvador S. Panelo (president spokesperson and chief presidential legal counsel secretary), press briefing, March 29, 2019; Rambo Talabong, "Duterte Narco List Now 6,000 Names Long and Counting—Panelo," Rappler, December 13, 2017; Kyle Aristophere T. Atienza, "Duterte Claim vs Narco-Politician Based on Intel," BusinessWorld, November 19, 2021; and "Duterte Says He Deliberately Read Old List of 'Narco Officials,'" Philstar.com, August 10, 2016.

208 **Several of them did die:** Jodesz Gavilan, "Mayors, Vice Mayors Killed Under Duterte," Rappler, July 12, 2018.

208 **"You've been ambushed twice":** Rodrigo Duterte, quoted from speech at PDP-Laban Campaign Rally, Puerto Princesa Coliseum, Puerto Princesa City, April 4, 2019.

208 **"If your name is there":** Rodrigo Duterte, quoted from speech at mass oath-taking of newly appointed government officials, Rizal Hall, Malacañang, January 9, 2017.

209 **what was known as BADACs:** Department of the Interior and Local Government MC No. 2015-6, June 16, 2015. BADAC is short for "Barangay Anti-Drug Abuse Council."

209 **"I can tell from the eyes":** Payatas Barangay Capt. Juliet Peña, interview by the author. See Patricia Evangelista, "The Red Mark," Rappler, November 30, 2017.

210 **at least 144,202 names:** Police General Ronald Dela Rosa (chief of the PNP), statement, *Hearing to Investigate the Recent Rampant Extrajudicial Killings and Summary Executions of Suspected Criminals, Before the Senate Committee on Justice and Human Rights and Committee on Public Order and Dangerous Drugs,* Senate of the Philippines, 17th Congress, August 23, 2016.

214–24 **almost seven months . . . She had chosen the name Heart . . . She was put on a watchlist . . . On January 10, 2017 . . . held his gun with both hands . . . "dead male body" . . . Navotas denied responsibility . . . "She didn't make it here" . . . "Point it out on video too!" . . . called Heart a "suspicious" character . . . "she's dirt poor" . . . "didn't know anything about anyone":** This account of Heart de Chavez's death and circumstances is based on official police reports, interviews with police officers, members of the De Chavez family, and unnamed witnesses. See Spot Report Re—Found Dead Male Body, signed by Police Col. Dante Pesa Novicio (chief of police), Navotas City Police Station, January 11, 2017; Arriane de Chavez (sister of Heart de Chavez) and Elena de Chavez (mother of Heart de Chavez), interviews by the author, January 21 and 30, 2017; Police Col. Dante Novicio (chief of police, Navotas City), Navotas City PS, Metro Manila, interview by the author, January 26, 2017; Adonis Sugie (officer on duty, PS-1), PS-1, Tondo, Manila, interview by the author, January 26, 2017; Domingo and Police Capt. Edwin Fuggan (station commander of the Pritil Police Community Precinct), in a discussion with Elena, PS-1, Tondo, Manila, January 26, 2017. This discussion was conducted in the presence of the author and the filmmaker Paolo Villaluna. See also Police Capt. Edwin Fuggan, interview by the author, PS-1, Tondo, Manila, February 4, 2017. The full investigation of Heart de Chavez's death was previously published as "Impunity: Welcome to the End of the War," Rappler, February 7, 2017. On May 12, 2023, before the publication of this book, the author sought comment from Fuggan through a letter of request sent via messenger to his office to Police Station 6 in Santa Ana, Manila, where Fuggan held the position of chief of the Warrant and Subpoena Section. The letter was received by the office. A researcher working for the author also reached out to Fuggan in an attempt to secure Fuggan's official email for the sending of a formal invitation. The researcher, in notes to the author, reported that Fuggan had inquired as to the nature of the interview, and noted that he would refuse if the interview involved the drug war. "It's over," Fuggan said over the phone in Filipino. "I don't want to be interviewed about that. Because that case is in court, all the documents we passed are in court now." The author sent a text message to the major following up the letter of request. Fuggan is yet to respond.

224 **a series of executions:** The alleged executions are based on an investigation of Police Station 2 Moriones that was previously published. Patricia Evangelista, with research by Kimberly dela Cruz, "Where the Drug War Began," Rappler, April 24, 2017.

225 **Chito Gascon, a former student activist . . . Gascon was an Aquino appointee:** See Gavilan, "In Fight vs. Rights Abuses Under Duterte, Chair Chito Never Backed Down," Rappler, October 9, 2021; K. D. Suarez, "Aquino Names LP Official as New CHR Chair," Rappler, June 18, 2015.

225–27 **a secret detention facility was hidden . . . "don't leave us here" . . . sheet of galvanized iron . . . cops had held them hos-**

tage . . . as long as eight days . . . amounts as high as ₱100,000 . . .
bruises from a beating . . . "They said we would be killed" . . . jail
was newly constructed . . . TEMPORARY STAGING AREA . . . Domingo
was briefly relieved . . . Commission on Human Rights filed complaints . . . The complaints were dismissed: This account of the discovery of a secret jail cell in PS-1 draws from interviews with journalists
who were present for the search, including photojournalists Raffy
Lerma and Vincent Go. The narrative is supplemented by published
reports: "Secret Jail Nadiskubre sa Manila Police District," ABS-CBN
News, April 27, 2017; "Hidden 'Jail' Discovered in Manila," CNN
Philippines, April 28, 2017; Alyx Ayn Arumpac, *Aswang*, Cinemato-
grafica Films, 2019; Jenny Dongon, "12 Preso, Sisiksikan at Itinago
Daw sa Likod ng Aparador sa Isang Kulungan sa Maynila," TV5,
April 28, 2017; Eloisa Lopez, "CHR Team Finds Detainees in 'Secret'
Police Cell," Rappler, April 27, 2017; Dindo Flora, " 'Secret Jail'
Umano sa Manila Police District Station 1, Nadiskubre Sa Inspeksyon
ng CHR," TV5, April 28, 2017; Bea Cupin, "Police Station Chief Relieved over Secret Jail Cell," Rappler, April 28, 2017. For the verdict,
see *CHR v. PSupt. Domingo et al.,* Office of the Ombudsman, July 28,
2020.

Chapter 10: Some People Need Killing

228–31 **South Korean businessman . . . armed men had shoved . . . the
men involved were cops . . . police officers who dragged Jee Ick
Joo . . . South Korean embassy called . . . flushed the ashes . . .
"focus on internal cleansing" . . . preferred to kill the cops in-
volved . . . "melt in shame" . . . an embarrassment . . . refused
Dela Rosa's offer to resign . . . in his white dress uniform:** This
account of Jee Ick Joo's death draws from Tarra Quismundo, "Is Sokor
Businessman Victim of 'Tokhang for Ransom'?" *Philippine Daily In-
quirer,* January 8, 2017; AJ Bolando, "De Lima: CCTV Footage Fail to
Show Sta. Isabel in Jee Kidnapping," Philstar.com, January 26, 2017;
Maila Ager, "Maid Relates Last Moments She Saw Jee Ick-Joo Alive,"
Inquirer.net, January 26, 2017; "Kidnapped South Korean Was Killed
By Filipino Cops," ABS-CBN News Digital, January 18, 2017; Evelyn
Macairan, "Kidnapped Korean Killed at Crame," *Philippine Star,* Janu-
ary 20, 2017; Embassy of the Republic of Korea in the Philippines,
*Statement of the Embassy of the Republic of Korea to the Republic of the Philip-
pines on the Memorial Service of Korean Businessman Jee Ick-joo* (press re-
lease), Ministry of Foreign Affairs, Republic of Korea, February 6, 2017;
Nancy Carvajal and Davinci Maru, "Korean Cremated as 'Jose Ruamar
Salvador, Filipino,' " Philippine Center for Investigative Journalism,

January 24, 2017; Kristine Angeli Sabillo, "I Want to Melt in Shame—Bato," Inquirer.net, January 19, 2017; "A Slap on the Face: Panelo Admits Duterte Embarrassed by Jee's Killing," *Politiko,* February 2, 2017; Gerg Cahiles, "Duterte Turns Down Dela Rosa's Offer to Resign," CNN Philippines, January 23, 2017.

229 **suspended the same police institution:** Tricia Macas, "Duterte Slams PNP as 'Corrupt to the Core,' " GMA News Online, January 30, 2017.

229 **"corrupt, corrupt to the core":** Rodrigo Duterte, quoted from press conference, Malacañang, January 30, 2017.

230 **no new names were added:** Field observations by the author; Clarissa David et al., "Building a Dataset of Publicly Available Information on Killings Associated with the Antidrug Campaign," The Drug Archive Philippines, noted that December 25, 2016, and January 30, 2017, were the first two days free of media-reported drug war deaths during the Duterte administration.

230 **death toll stopped:** Human Rights Watch, *License to Kill: Philippine Police Killings in Duterte's "War on Drugs"* (Human Rights Watch, March 2, 2017).

231 **"to tell deliberate lies":** George Orwell, *Nineteen Eighty-four* (London: Penguin Classics, 1949).

231 *pseudo-event:* Daniel J. Boorstin, *The Image: A Guide to Pseudo-events in America* (New York: Harper Colophon, 1964).

231 **"they will suffer":** Rodrigo Duterte, quoted from speech at the ceremonial switch-on of Section 1 and Kick-Off Ceremony of Section 2 of the Sarangani Energy Corporation Power Plant Maasim, Sarangani, January 26, 2017.

231 **police had been fabricating evidence:** Amnesty International, *Philippines: "If You Are Poor You Are Killed": Extrajudicial Killings in the Philippines' "War on Drugs"* (Amnesty International, January 2017).

232–34 **top brass were on full display . . . "They did kill him" . . . CSG had threatened the Saladaga family . . . operatives confiscated several items . . . "This is their uniform" . . . "They said he was a thief" . . . "attributed to the police":** PNP, press conference, CNN Philippines, February 9, 2017.

233 **cell phone messages and tactical interrogation:** The PNP's claim that the arrested CSG members admitted their responsibility was confirmed by Police Maj. Rosalino Ibay, who was chief of the District Intelligence and Operation Unit of the Manila Police District. Police Major Ibay, in an interview with the author, said the suspects confessed. It was, however, only "for our own consumption," as there were no signed affidavits after the suspects were provided legal counsel. Ibay also confirmed that confiscated cell phones contained incriminating messages that

named targets—"including who else they were going to kill, and their next target." A portion of that confession is also documented in an exclusive video of the CSG raid, released by *The Philippine Star,* that showed one of the cuffed suspects confessing that they were vigilantes and that the group had killed "many, sir." For the full video, see *Philippine Star,* "Exclusive: Three Suspected Members of Vigilante Group Responsible for Conducting 'Tokhang' Operations in Tondo Were Arrested," Facebook, February 9, 2017.

234 **endorsed by the president himself:** Rodrigo Duterte, drawn from speech at the 120th celebration of Philippine Independence Day, Cavite, June 12, 2018.

235–49 **"they were showing off"** . . . **"our job was to clean out"** . . . **There was a meet** . . . **"we were going to kill"** . . . **"I wasn't ready"** . . . **estimated twenty to forty members** . . . **soldiers in Rodrigo Duterte's war** . . . **"the area gets hot"** . . . **two men in Payatas** . . . **one in Caloocan** . . . **last one was in Blumentritt** . . . **Commander Maning set the bounty** . . . **"paid if we killed"** . . . **"The police knew"** . . . **"If Maning says to kill someone"** . . . **"I finish the job"** . . . **"we'd all be dead"** . . . **"It was Domingo"** . . . **"get it from the chief"** . . . **"That meant money"** . . . **"Domingo was well known"** . . . **"The CSG were bragging"** . . . **"paid two, maybe three thousand pesos":** This account of vigilante operations was drawn from the author's interview with "Angel," a self-described vigilante and member of CSG Tondo Chapter 2 who admitted to executing targets in Manila, Caloocan, and Quezon City. The interview, conducted on July 24, 2018, was recorded under the condition all publication would withhold identifying details. The author is in possession of Angel's credentials and is satisfied as to their veracity. Many of the details Angel offered were corroborated by other sources, many of whom are not named. Portions of this interview, as well as further details about the CSG, were originally published in a seven-part series: Patricia Evangelista with additional reporting by Lian Buan and Rambo Talabong, "Murder in Manila," Rappler, October 4–11, 2018.

236 **The Confederate Sentinels Group Incorporated** . . . **"purview of social welfare and development":** Registration documents filed with the Securities and Exchange Commission in 2009 and 2014. The CSG's official Facebook group has since rebranded to "Confederate Sentinels of God."

236–37 **"protectors of the weak and needy"** . . . **"our offering to God"** . . . **"does not include vigilante killings":** Alvin Constantino (CSG national group founder), interview by the author, August 30, 2018.

237 **"ready for orientation"**: Constantino claimed no responsibility over the recruitment of the members of CSG Tondo Chapter 2. He named another cop, Police Lt. Jonar Cardozo, the former precinct commander of Smokey Mountain, as the man who had personally introduced and recruited Ricardo Villamonte, also known as Commander Maning, into the CSG. The Smokey Mountain Precinct oversees Village 105 and is under the area of responsibility of Domingo's PS-1. Cardozo refused an interview with the author but replied to a series of text messages on September 2, 2018. "Our role was to organize the different community sectors in forging a united front against crime, terrorism and other forms of lawlessness," that included forming "force multipliers through the empowerment of people toward community involvement." Cardozo did not deny recruiting the members of CSG Tondo Chapter 2. "All who are willing for community service and public safety are welcome and invited." He conceded problems may arise with force multipliers "when they're left on their own and they're not guided, especially if they're no longer active or there are no PNP members going there." Asked if he agreed with the PNP's characterization of CSG Tondo Chapter 2 as a vigilante group, Cardozo responded on October 3 with "no comment," and "God bless." Commander Maning, on his part, told the author he once considered Cardozo "a good friend."

237–38 **"They were the killing arm"** . . . **"They're the CSG"** . . . **"village watchmen were afraid of them"** . . . **"They shoot like cowboys"** . . . **"they were killing"**: At least five people with knowledge of CSG Tondo Chapter 2's activities were interviewed by the author during a four-month period in 2018. Identifying details of these sources have been withheld for their protection.

238 **a man named Ernesto Sabado**: "Sputnik Man Slain," *Tempo Online*, November 16, 2016; "Sputnik Member, Pinatay sa Harap ng Nagmamakaawang Ina," *Abante Tonite*, November 16, 2016.

239–51 **"I was scared"** . . . **"make people go crazy"** . . . **"we're what you call vigilantes"** . . . **"killing was automatic, one after another"** . . . **"I'm really not a bad guy"** . . . **"Some people need killing"** . . . **"We were confident"** . . . dealer the locals called "Mommy" . . . **"down, and no screwups"** . . . made mistakes along the way . . . **"That's how we got Sitoy"** . . . Sitoy was so dangerous . . . **"on the orders of the police"** . . . **"shot him in the ass"** . . . **"I felt bad for him"** . . . **"We were the ones killing"** . . . **"should have surrendered him first"** . . . **"because he was a troublemaker"** . . . **"We caught him again and again"** . . . **"dead who have to run"**: "Simon," a self-described vigilante and member of CSG Tondo Chapter 2, interview by the author, July 29, 2018. He confessed to participating in the execution of alleged drug suspects. The interview was recorded on the condition all publication would withhold identifying details. Many of the details cited here were corroborated with other sources. Portions of this interview, as well as further details about the CSG, were originally published in a seven-part investigative series: Patricia Evangelista, "Murder in Manila," Rappler, June 3, 2018.

243 **Sitoy, "who is determined to kill":** Spot Report Re: Follow-up Police Operation Resulting to Gun Shooting Incident (DOS), signed by Police Chief Master Sgt. Milbert Balinggan (investigator on case), CAPIS, Manila Police District, February 1, 2017.

245 **"the one with the grenade":** Robert Domingo (station commander of Manila PS-1 Raxabago), interview by Vonne Aquino, in "Umano'y Holdupper, Patay sa Operasyon ng Pulis," *Unang Balita,* GMA Integrated News, February 1, 2017.

245 **He acknowledged receipt:** The author sent a letter to Domingo on October 1, 2018, via an email address he provided, seeking "an interview to ask comments for a story we have been investigating regarding allegations of human rights violations committed during your term as station commander of Manila Police District Station 1 along Raxabago in Tondo." The author also sent messages to Domingo to a mobile number on the same day, where he acknowledged receipt of the email.

247–48 **"They really were" . . . "No comment":** Ricardo Villamonte (also known as "Kumander Maning"), interview by the author in Village 105, October 3, 2018.

249–50 **"It's why we thank the president" . . . "yes, there were killers" . . . "the mother, she's negligent":** Leny Reyes (Village 105 elected head), interview by the author, August 28, 2018.

251–54 **last time Cristina saw her son . . . "the ones who kill us" . . . And then they ran . . . she retracted her sworn statement . . . result of "a misunderstanding":** Cristina Saladaga, interviews by the author, August 15 and November 1, 2019. Cristina's daughter, Exmila was present during the interview. Cristina Saladaga's affidavit of desistance, dated February 15, 2017, was accessed by Lian Buan (Rappler justice reporter) at the Manila Office of the City Prosecutor in July 2018, during the course of investigation for Patricia Evangelista et al., "Some People Need Killing," Rappler, October 2018.

252 **He listened:** Police Maj. Rosalino Ibay confirmed assisting the Saladaga family. He affirmed to the author Cristina's claim that he spent his own money to provide support and allowed the family to sleep in his MPD office at the time they were under threat. He spoke in general of the need to support possible witnesses.

254 **"gotten them implicated"**: Dela Rosa (Bureau of Corrections director general), interview by the author, at the Bureau of Corrections (BuCor) in the New Bilibid Prison Reservation, Muntinlupa City, September 3, 2018.

Chapter 11: Djastin with a D

256–62 **"shoot him, then slap him"** . . . **"Three cops were taking turns"** . . . stood a few meters away . . . saw a young man running . . . saw the raised gun . . . did not realize it was his nephew who had fallen . . . someone did not scream . . . **"They shot him after they slapped him"** . . . shot Djastin again . . . kicked him, and shot him again: Nestor Lopez (Djastin's uncle), interview by the author in Tondo, Manila, May 28, 2017. The interview corroborates details in Nestor's signed, unnotarized, and undated affidavit, provided by the Lopezes' lawyers.

256–82 **JR first, then Djastin** . . . Lito began counting again . . . Djastin, she told him, was dead . . . irregularly shaped single-story room . . . a household of sixteen people . . . single prepaid power account . . . men scraping tin . . . twenty-eight members . . . **"so he got a silent D"** . . . first seizure at four . . . through a Manila flood . . . phenobarbital . . . dropped out of school . . . arrested once . . . weren't particularly afraid . . . he was no dealer . . . a day since the last convulsion . . . **"we're eating"** . . . **"It's nobody"** . . . yellow Nike T-shirt . . . girlfriend left the house . . . Gloria sent her son Nestor . . . wiped him down with a damp towelette . . . fish balls . . . twenty-five years old . . . phone was broken . . . **"Tirek is gone"** . . . He was wearing a yellow Nike T-shirt . . . **"You can't go there"** . . . **"Mama, it's him"** . . . **"you heartless bastards"** . . . **"I wish my brother had a gun"** . . . cost of burial . . . Archangel Funeral Homes . . . **"He was the sick one"** . . . **"Mama, they're coming to kill you"** . . . faces were pressed against the opening . . . **"I always start with the puzzles"** . . . **"news about an epileptic"** . . . trip to the North Cemetery . . . spoke at protests . . . Normita at a street protest . . . **"Geñalope was jailed"** . . . **"there was a warrant"** . . . **"no more settlement"** . . . **"There might have been"** . . . fifty grand as initial payment . . . **"not like I could do anything"** . . . understanding that the family would stop . . . The money helped . . . I shouldn't have done it: Normita "Normy" Lopez (Djastin's mother), interviews by the author, May 28, 2017; July 7, 15, and 22, 2019; August 13, 2019; April 7, 8, and 13, 2020; February 25 and 28, 2023.

257–70 Sometime in the 1980s . . . room rentals . . . Miss Universe herself . . . turn in the family fortunes . . . running errands for the tin business . . . followed Djastin on his mother's order . . . You can't have my boy . . . Shoved a hard elbow . . . "Even a buffalo wouldn't have survived that" . . . challenge the killer to a duel: Cornelio Lopez (Djastin's grandfather), interview by the author, May 28, 2017.

259–60 doctor taught Normy . . . father of two . . . did not vote for the mayor . . . basketball court nearby to threaten: Lito Lopez (Djastin's father), interview by the author, May 28, 2017.

261 aim a gun at Djastin . . . Please don't shoot: Mary Rose dela Cruz (witness), sworn statement, September 14, 2017.

262 size of a toddler's thumbnail . . . heavy slugs ripping open lung: Medico-Legal Report No. M-2017-243, signed by Police Maj. Mesalyn Milagros Ripa Probadora, M.D. (medico-legal officer), Crime Laboratory Office Headquarters, Manila Police District, May 19, 2017.

262 blotter entry: A copy of the blotter entry at 6:40 p.m., May 18, 2017, is attached to the counter-affidavit of Normita Lopez, December 15, 2017.

266–67 "armed encounter" . . . "spotted a male person acting suspiciously" . . . "to accost the suspect" . . . "shot the police officers twice but missed" . . . "[to] defend himself" . . . "Drugs Watchlist Personalities": Spot Report Re: Armed Encounter, signed by Police Lt. Col. Alex Daniel (station commander), Jose Abad Santos Police Station (PS-7), Manila Police District, May 18, 2017.

267–68 Michael Turla . . . "covered with his own blood" . . . "Anti-Criminality Operation and Follow-up" . . . "able to evade arrest" . . . "fired another shot" . . . "died on the spot" . . . "Justin Cacay Lopez" . . . report enumerated all the evidence: Spot Report Re: Police Operation (Anti-Criminality Campaign and Follow-up Operation) Resulting in the Neutralization of an Alleged Drug Suspect (DOS), signed by Police Staff Sgt. Aldeen Cruz Legaspi (case investigator), CAPIS, Manila Police District, May 18, 2017.

269–71 "alleged drug suspect" . . . drug buy-bust . . . "intent to rectify the name": Progress Report 1, signed by Police Staff Sgt. Aldeen Cruz Legaspi (case investigator), CAPIS, Manila Police District, June 9, 2017.

271 murder complaint: The complaint is dated September 27, 2017, a copy of which was received by the Office of the Ombudsman, September 28, 2017.

273 "I thought maybe I could save Mama": Luinor Lopez (Normy Lopez's youngest daughter), interview by the author, August 13, 2019.

273 "New Win vs. Tokhang": Lian Buan, "New Win vs. Tokhang: Ombudsman Orders Murder Charges vs. Manila Cop," Rappler, April 4, 2019.

273 "Grieving Poet-Mother": Inday Espina-Varona, "Grieving Poet-

Mother Gets Sliver of Victory as Ombudsman Orders Dismissal of 'Tokhang Cop,'" ABS-CBN News Digital, April 3, 2019.

273 **"Cop Axed for Killing Epileptic"** . . . **"We welcome it"**: "Cop Axed for Killing Epileptic in 'Drug Raid,'" *Philippine Daily Inquirer,* April 5, 2019.

274 **"information for Murder be FILED"** . . . **guilty of grave misconduct:** Ombudsman Joint Resolution, August 13, 2018.

275–80 **first attempt to offer a settlement** . . . **Absolutely not** . . . **"my son's life"** . . . **second settlement** . . . **Normy followed him** . . . **walked home together** . . . **"angry at Lito"** . . . **third and final offer** . . . **there would never be a settlement** . . . **"why did you say that?"** . . . **"I don't need money"** . . . **"So I messaged the lawyers"** . . . **"What she wants goes for me"** . . . **"I'm not changing my mind"** . . . **"if one of us is killed"** . . . **"I'm afraid now"** . . . **"We're up against cops"** . . . **"fucking money is tearing us apart"** . . . **"what other people are thinking"** . . . **"Not just three years"** . . . **"I just want to fight"**: Normita, Lito, and Eray Lopez (daughter), family discussion witnessed and recorded by the author, July 15, 2019.

282 **take the money:** While based on an interview with Normita Lopez, this account is verified through a letter shown to the author by Normita Lopez's counsel. The letter, from Geñalope's counsel, requests a meeting to discuss the settlement and confirms the Lopez family's acceptance of a cash advance.

282 **provisionally dismissed:** Manila Regional Trial Court Branch 7 Order, February 15, 2022.

283 **Both went without response . . . his wife, Edna, who spoke to me:** The author sent a letter to Gerry Geñalope's counsel Rolando B. Aquino on February 21, via an email address he listed as active as of January 7, 2021, seeking "an interview with your client, former Police Staff Sgt. Gerry Geñalope (or his representatives) to request comment on his dismissed murder case, as well as to inquire as to his version of the shooting incident that killed Djastin Lopez." The author also sent messages to Aquino through two mobile numbers on February 23, 2022. The author reached out directly to Geñalope's wife, Edna, who consented to a recorded phone interview by the author on February 24, 2023, and promised to extend the author's request to interview Geñalope himself. Neither Gerry nor Edna Geñalope has responded since.

Chapter 12: My Father Is a Policeman

285–92 **His name was Anton** . . . **lanky and shirtless** . . . **"if you didn't have that gun"** . . . **"I'm arresting you"** . . . **big man was dragging**

Anton . . . stop, please stop . . . small hand yanked at her hair . . . he pulled out a gun . . . clip that went viral . . . extended version . . . *"slaughtered like chickens"* . . . chorus of screaming voices . . . "We can talk this out" . . . "You be the cop so you can get a gun" . . . "Let my son go" . . . "Stop yanking" . . . "Let go of him!" . . . "You let go" . . . "My father is a police" . . . "I don't care-eh-eh-eh-eh-eh" . . . "you want me to end you now" . . . The gun barks . . . Every screaming voice goes silent . . . screaming begins again . . . the cop and his daughter walked away: This narrative of the Tarlac shooting draws from a total of four videos. They include two raw videos sourced by the author, the details of which are confirmed by two videos posted on Facebook; see *Daily Tribune,* "EXCLUSIVE: (WARNING: Graphic content) A Paranaque City police officer shot dead two unarmed victims at point-blank range," Facebook, December 20, 2020; Ronjie Daquigan, "Mother and son from Paniqui Tarlac," Facebook, December 21, 2020. These videos are confirmed to have been shot by a minor cousin of Frank Anthony Gregorio, TeleRadyo, ABS-CBN News, December 21, 2020.

287 **police report for one death:** Spot Report Re: Found Dead Body signed by Police Cpl. Leo C. Afable (Night Shift investigator), Moriones Tondo PS (PS-2), Manila Police District, November 22, 2016.

287 **Night Shift Messaging Group:** The conversation took place in a messaging group of drug war journalists on December 21, 2020. The author was granted permission to publish.

292 **"Why," bemoaned one celebrity . . . hashtags . . . "It happens every day" . . . "Your Father said" . . . "an outrage":** Online reactions to the Tarlac shooting draw from Maine Mendoza (@mainedcm), "BAKIT KAILANGANG UMABOT DOON? Hindi ko kaya, grabe," Twitter, December 21, 2020, 7:33 am; Ezra Acayan (photojournalist), "Ang tagal na nangyayari pero ngayon lang uli kayo galit dahil may video?," Facebook, December 1, 2020; Barnaby Lo (journalist), "Kung walang video, hinid mananagot yung pulis na mamamatay-tao," Facebook, December 21, 2020; Inday Espina Varona (@indayevarona), "A child calling for blood," Twitter, December 21, 2020, 8:15 am. A screenshot of Twitter hashtags that trended a day after the Tarlac shooting can be found in Iya Gozum, "Rage and Fury Over Cop's Killing of Mother and Son: 'No License to Kill,'" Rappler, December 1, 2020.

293–95 **surrendered to officers . . . Parañaque City Crime Laboratory . . . Nuezca's record . . . at least six administrative cases . . . Two other cases pertained to deaths . . . "who among the three policemen":** See Austria, "Cop in Viral Shooting Video Surrenders to Rosales Police," Philippine News Agency, December 21, 2020; JC

Gotinga, "Cop in Tarlac Shooting Faced Two Cases Involving Homicide in 2019," Rappler, December 21, 2020; Cathrine Gonzales, "Cop Who Shot Mother and Son in Tarlac Had Previous Administrative Cases," Inquirer.net, December 21, 2020; Jeannette Andrade, "How Killer Cop Got Cleared in 2 Earlier Homicide Cases," *Philippine Daily Inquirer,* December 26, 2020.

294–95 **"our police officers now have self-restraint"** . . . **secretary of the interior** . . . **two counts of murder** . . . **Senate called for a probe** . . . **"committed by one of our police"** . . . **"The president is angry"**: See Christopher Lloyd Caliwan, "No Need to Muzzle Cops' Gun for Holidays: Sinas," Philippines News Agency, December 15, 2020; Pia Ranada, "Año Condemns Tarlac Shooting but Calls It 'Isolated' Incident," Rappler, December 21, 2020; Lian Buan, "Cop in Tarlac Shooting Charged with 2 Counts of Murder," Rappler, December 21, 2020; P.S. Resolution No. 605, Senate of the Philippines, 18th Congress, January 7, 2021; and Christopher Lloyd Caliwan, "PNP Assures Justice for Victims of Cop in Tarlac Shooting," Philippine News Agency, December 21, 2020.

294 **heated argument:** Rosario Rufina Gundran (Sonya Gregorio's sister), interview by the author, December 23, 2020.

296–97 **"This cop is an isolated case"** . . . **"you've seen how much I love you"** . . . **if Nuezca were fried alive**: Rodrigo Duterte, drawn from speech at Talk to the People, Davao City, December 21, 2020.

296 **"We never tolerate"** . . . **"deep breathing"** . . . **"Sir, I admit, sir, my mistake"** . . . **he was to be removed from the service** . . . **"No one is on your side"**: Police Regional Office 3, "PRO3 RD PBGEN VAL T DE LEON to PSSg Nuezca," Facebook, December 23, 2020.

297 **"don't you dare yell"** . . . **old women owed respect to police** . . . **"heroic acts [of the police]"**: This account of police reactions to the Tarlac shooting draw from a deleted post by Tres Mj, "I I care eh eh eh! Malamang ganun din ginawa ko tao lang ako," Facebook, December 21, 2020, accessed through Ogie Diaz, "'Wag kang OA, I. Sinigawan lang ang anak mo, papatay ka na?," Facebook, December 22, 2020; a deleted post by Ariel Ruego Buraga, "My Father is a Policeeeee Mannnnn ha!!!," December 21, 2020, accessed by the author on January 10, 2021. See also Alexis Romero, "Duterte on 'Crazy' Killer Cop: Feed Him COVID-19," *Philippine Star,* December 23, 2020.

297 **"I thank President Duterte"**: Adrian Ayalin, "Gregorio Widower Thanks Duterte as Rights Groups Blame Him for Alleged Culture of 'Impunity,'" ABS-CBN News Digital, December 22, 2020.

298 **first-class municipality of Paniqui** . . . **one of the only holdouts against Duterte:** See Kallie Szczepanski, "Biography of Corazon

Aquino, First Female President of the Philippines," ThoughtCo.com, July 3, 2019; Camille Elemia, "Roxas, Robredo Win by Slim Margin in Aquino Hometown," Rappler, May 25, 2016.

298–302 **tenant farmer who was awarded land . . . met Florentino Gregorio . . . "pay me back with a date" . . . married in 1991 . . . drove dump trucks . . . prepare coffee—"always two cups" . . . "Pa, bring me home plants" . . . property dispute . . . Sonya had been shot too:** Rosario Rufino Gundra (Sonya Gregorio's sister) and Florentino Gregorio (Sonya Gregorio's husband), interviews by the author, December 23, 2020.

298–303 **raised seven children . . . did not feel safe surrounded by cops . . . "we can't blame it on everyone":** Mark Gregorio (Sonya Gregorio's son), interview by the author, December 23, 2020.

299–305 **Condolences from Police General Debold Sinas . . . coffins lined the unpainted walls . . . Political signage . . . "Please move back":** Impressions are based on the author's coverage of Sonya and Frank Gregorio's wake on December 23, 2020 and funeral on December 27, 2020.

302 **"rampant abuse of authority:"** Regine Cabato, "Philippine Police Office Fatally Shoots Mother and Son on Camera, Reigniting Nation's Debate over Police Impunity," *Washington Post,* December 21, 2020.

302 **"wave of outrage":** Jason Gutierrez, "A Brazen Police Shooting Caught on Video Sparks Anger in the Philippines," *New York Times,* December 21, 2020.

302 **"execution-style" slaying:** Office of Senator Leila de Lima, "De Lima Deplores Cop's Killing of 2 Unarmed Citizens" (press release), Senate of the Philippines, December 21, 2020.

302 **"enabling environment for police violence":** "Rights Watchdog on Tarlac Murder: Many PH Cops 'Simply Out of Control,'" Inquirer .net, December 21, 2020.

304–7 **"We don't really have a hotline" . . . "We partner with the police" . . . "Justice for Sonya and Frank Anthony" . . . "Justice!" . . . "Reporter of the Philippines" . . . peace and order, security, traffic assistance, monitoring, and rescue operations . . . "Justice for Nanay Sonya, Justice for Frank Anthony, and Justice for All" . . . "quick impulse by this cop" . . . "just this cop" . . . "none, none at all":** This characterization is drawn from Ronjie Daquigan's livestream, social media profile, and an interview with the author, December 27, 2020.

304–5 **"They look like idiots" . . . "they're just morons" . . . "folks who can't see the bigger picture":** Vincent Go (photojournalist), interview by the author, December 27, 2020.

308 applauding the work of the police . . . No cop should be afraid to kill in self-defense . . . "kill them so it's done" . . . "One less idiot in this world" . . . "Do your duty" . . . "be alert and be wise" . . . "They make one mistake, shoot them": Rodrigo Duterte, drawn from speech at the Destruction of Dangerous Drugs, Integrated Waste Management, Inc., Trece Martires City, Cavite, December 3, 2020.

310 Jonel Nuezca stood before a judge . . . pleaded not guilty . . . was convicted . . . "died of cardiac arrest": This account of Jonel Nuezca's conviction and subsequent death is drawn from Kristine Joy Patag, "Court Convicts Ex-Cop Nuezca of Murder in Killing of Mother, Son in Tarlac," Philstar.com, August 26, 2021; Lian Buan, "Killer Ex-Cop Jonel Nuezca Dies Inside Bilibid; Foul Play Probed," Rappler, December 1, 2021; and Benjamin Pulta, "Initial NBI Probe Shows Nuezca Died of Heart Attack: DOJ," Philippine News Agency, December 9, 2021.

311 put those deaths at 7,884: Rambo Talabong, "Unreal Numbers: Around 2,000 Drug War Deaths Missing in Duterte Gov't Tally," Rappler, September 11, 2020.

311 lowered the total to 6,252: Realnumbersph, "#RealNumbersPH Year 6 Toward a Drug-Cleared Philippines from July 1, 2016, to May 31, 2022," Facebook, June 21, 2022.

311 DUI numbers was released: Emmanuel Tupas, "29,000 Deaths Probed Since Drug War Launched," Philippine Star, March 6, 2019.

311 "gross underestimation": Sheila Coronel, Mariel Padilla, and David Mora, "The Uncounted Dead of Duterte's Drug War," The Atlantic, August 19, 2019.

311 "total of 20,322 deaths": Lian Buan, "Supreme Court Rules to Release Drug War Documents," Rappler, April 2, 2019.

311 "as high as 27,000": Davinci Maru, "CHR Chief: Drug War Deaths Could Be as High as 27,000," ABS-CBN News Digital, December 5, 2018.

311 "between 12,000 and at least 20,000": "Situation in the Republic of the Philippines Decision on the Prosecutor's request for authorization of an investigation pursuant to Article 15(3) of the Statute," International Criminal Court, ICC-01/21, September 15, 2021.

311 "Baseless and bloated": Department of the Interior and Local Government, "DILG: Crime Down by 46.66% Amid COVID-19 Pandemic, Urges Leftists and Critics to Stop Spreading Fake News" (press release), September 22, 2020.

311 "Propaganda attempts": Former PNP Spokesperson Benigno Durana, Real Numbers press briefing, November 27, 2018.

311 "clarify the confusing" . . . "narrative is being pushed": "PH Gov't

Moves to Counter 'False' Narrative on Drug War," Rappler, May 4, 2017.

311 **"Just don't bloat":** Julliane Love de Jesus, "'Bato' Urges Media: Be Fair in Reporting Drug War," Inquirer.net, March 23, 2017.

311–12 **Upon Dela Rosa's retirement . . . gratitude of the people . . . thank him, he said, and hug him . . . "love, trust, and respect their police":** Dela Rosa, interview by the author, at the Bureau of Corrections in the New Bilibid Prison Reservation, Muntinlupa City, September 3, 2018. On May 12, 2023, before the publication of this book, the author sought comment from Senator dela Rosa through a letter of request sent via fast courier to his office and over email through both his secretariat and media relations addresses. There has been no response.

312 **"smoke of gunfire subsides" . . . "after the smoke of gun battle subsided" . . . "lay in the cemented pavement" . . . "the smoke of gunfire subsided" . . . another cemented pavement:** This analysis is drawn from a review of ten police reports filed in Manila using variations of the phrase "smoke of gunfire subsides." See, in particular, Spot Report Re: Buy-Bust Operation Resulting in a Gun Shooting Incident signed by Police Staff Sgt. Ryan Jay D. Balagtas (Investigator-on-case), CAPIS, January 8, 2017; Spot Report Re: Police Operation (Follow-up Operation) signed by Police Staff Sgt. Jorlan O. Taluban (Investigator), CAPIS, October 1, 2016; Spot Report Re: Gun Shooting Incident signed by Police Chief Master Sgt. Milbert Balinggan (Investigator-on-case), CAPIS, August 16, 2016; Spot Report Re: Follow-up Operation Resulting to a Gun Shooting Incident, prepared by Police Chief Master Sgt. Balinggan, CAPIS, December 14, 2016; and Spot Report Re: Gun Shooting Incident signed by Police Chief Master Sgt. Balinggan, CAPIS, September 19, 2016.

313 **average of six suspects killed . . . "drug-crazed heavily armed" . . . "lay down their lives" . . . "we are very sensitive" . . . killed a week went down [to] 69 . . . "only twenty-three deaths on the average":** Durana, Real Numbers press briefing, August 17, 2018.

313–14 **On September 15, 2021 . . . "crime against humanity of murder" . . . "publicly encouraged extrajudicial killings":** Situation in the Republic of the Philippines, Case No. ICC-01/21, Public Decision on the Prosecutor's request for authorization of an investigation pursuant to Article 15(3) of the Statute, September 15, 2021.

314 **"sons of bitches in the ICC":** Rodrigo Duterte, drawn from speech at the 32nd National Convention of the Prosecutors' League of the Philippines, Davao City, March 29, 2023.

Chapter 13: Acts of Contrition

317–19 Jason Quizon had booked a flight . . . did not regret his vote . . . "These kinds of people" . . . "he's a young kid" . . . "like the *Pietà*" . . . Filipinos are classists . . . "in a sloppy shirt" . . . "the most cowardly person" . . . Filipinos are still fucking morons: Jason Quizon (engineer, overseas worker), interview by the author, July 30, 2021.

318 "Olaires hugs partner Michael": Raffy Lerma, "Lamentation," *Philippine Daily Inquirer,* July 24, 2016.

318 Kian was killed in a spontaneous shoot-out . . . officers handed Kian a gun . . . *I have an exam:* Rambo Talabong, "How Kian delos Santos Was Killed, According to Police," Rappler, August 20, 2017; Dominic Almelor, "Binatilyo, Patay Nang 'Manlaban' sa Pulis; Pero Iba Ang Kuha sa CCTV," *TV Patrol,* ABS-CBN News, August 17, 2017; and Marc Jayson Cayabyab, "Witness Bares Kian's Ordeal Before Court," *Philippine Star,* March 20, 2018.

319–20 Dondon Chan voted for Rodrigo . . . He is regretful . . . Kwentong Ex-DDS . . . "You wouldn't think of doing this": Dondon Chan, interview by the author, July 23, 2021.

319 burial of Ferdinand Marcos: "Duterte Firm on Marcos Burial: 'The Law Is the Law,'" *Philippine Daily Inquirer,* November 13, 2016.

320 continued isolation of the opposition: Ina Andolong and Xave Gregorio, "Duterte Fires Robredo from Anti-Drug Czar Post," CNN, November 24, 2019.

320 shut down the ABS-CBN: "Duterte Admits Using Presidential Powers vs ABS-CBN," CNN Philippines, June 27, 2022.

320 more than seventy thousand: As of February 17, 2022, ahead of the May general elections, the Facebook group rebranded to "Kwentong Ex-DDS (Ex BBM na rin)," in reference to Ferdinand "Bongbong" Marcos.

320 padlocked under the Marcos dictatorship: Millard Lim, "ABS-CBN Shutdown: 1972 and 2020," *BusinessWorld,* July 13, 2020.

320 manage the Covid-19 pandemic: Zy-sa Suzara et al, "In This Pandemic, Duterte Has His Priorities All Wrong," *Al Jazeera,* June 6, 2021.

320 called God stupid: Rodrigo Duterte, speech at the National Information and Communications Technology Summit 2018, SMX Convention Center, Davao City, June 22, 2018.

321–23 Ann Valdez voted for Rodrigo . . . Father Digong . . . doctors ignored her . . . "I bashed them" . . . *You idiots. You dumbasses* . . . paid to be antagonistic . . . people she had harassed . . . "They can make up anything" . . . "I loved Duterte" . . . " 'Raze it to the ground' ": Ann Valdez, interview by the author, August 1, 2021.

323–26 **Joy Tan voted for Rodrigo . . . born and raised in Mindanao . . . sake of ordinary people . . .** *burying the traitor* **. . . Her relatives unfriended her . . . called her a Communist . . . skin you alive . . . bullet in your skull . . . finger up your vagina . . . "I'm just a typical housewife" . . . " 'at least I won't die DDS' " . . . "He is a demon":** Joy Tan, interview by the author, July 29, 2021.

324 **"That fucking idiot corona":** Rodrigo Duterte, speech at a meeting with local chief executives, SMX Convention Center, Pasay City, February 10, 2020.

324 **instituting lockdowns across the country so stringent:** Aie Balagtas See, "Inside One of the World's Strictest Lockdowns," *Time,* March 15, 2021.

Epilogue: We Are Duterte

327–28 **four minutes past eight . . . government calls a commemoration . . . papers call a celebration . . . Antonio Sotelo . . . "Edsa remained strong and alive" . . . over in under seven minutes . . . smallest of the four:** All impressions and details are from the author's coverage of the 36th anniversary of the 1986 Edsa People Power Revolution at the Edsa People Power Monument, Quezon City, February 25, 2022. See also "Celebrating the 36th Anniversary of the 1986 Edsa People Power Revolution," National Historical Commission of the Philippines, February 24, 2022; Dempsey Reyes and Jeannette I. Andrare, "Low-key Official Celebration and Dancing to Mark 36 Years After Edsa Revolt," *Philippine Daily Inquirer,* February 25, 2022; Ben Cal, "Turning Point of Historic 1986 People Power Revolution Recalled," Philippine News Agency, February 24, 2019.

328 **allowed the burial of the dictator Ferdinand Marcos . . . twenty-one-gun salute:** Details of Ferdinand E. Marcos's burial are drawn from the author's own coverage as well as from Pia Ranada, "Duterte Gives Go Signal for Marcos Hero's Burial," Rappler, November 9, 2016; and "Outrage as Marcos Gets Hero Burial in the Philippines," *Al Jazeera,* November 18, 2016.

329 **Congressman Ferdinand the Third:** During the 2022 elections, Ferdinand Alexander A. Marcos won the congressional seat for the first district of Ilocos Norte, defeating the incumbent, Ria Fariñas. See John Michael Mugas, "Neophyte Sandro Marcos Defeats Fariñas in Ilocos Norte 1st District," Rappler, May 10, 2022.

329 **jubilant crowds have poured into . . . A campaign volunteer weeps . . . "Edsa is ours":** Author's coverage of the aftermath of Fer-

dinand Marcos, Jr.'s, victory at the Edsa People Power Monument, Quezon City, May 9, 2022.

329 **I am a product of him . . . I am the same name:** Bongbong Marcos, "BBM vlog #9: Marcos Back in Malacañan," YouTube, April 7, 2018.

330 **Tell the police precincts:** Rodrigo Duterte, drawn from speech at the Cebu-Cordova Link Expressway groundbreaking ceremony, Virlo Public Market, Barangay Dapitan, Cordova, Cebu, March 2, 2017.

330 **deal with you himself . . . a barge down the Pasig River . . . "monopoly of evil":** Rodrigo Duterte, drawn from speech at the 55th birthday celebration of PNP Director General Ronald M. "Bato" Dela Rosa, PNP Headquarters, Camp Crame, Quezon City, January 22, 2017.

330–31 **There is no blood on the scene . . . red basketball shorts . . . Someone had scrawled . . . He takes out a cutter:** Author's coverage of the Desierto crime scene, November 22, 2016; Ivy Desierto, interview by the author, October 22, 2018. See also Blotter Entry No. 16-23089 3:35 am, signed by Police Capt. Edison Ouano (chief of SIB), November 22, 2016; Medico-Legal Report No. 2016-631, signed by Police Maj. Jesille Cui Baluyot, M.D. (medico-legal officer), Crime Laboratory Office Headquarters, Manila Police District; Spot Report Re: Found Dead Body, signed by Police Cpl. Leo C. Afable (night shift investigator), Moriones Tondo Police Station (PS-2), Manila Police District, November 22, 2016.

331 **A greeting . . . Filipino aloha . . . restaurateur launched a campaign:** On the use of the word *mabuhay,* see *Vicassan's Pilipino-English Dictionary,* abridged ed. (Pasig City: Anvil, 2006); *Southeast Asian Diaspora in the United States: Memories and Visions Yesterday, Today, and Tomorrow,* ed. Jonathan H. X. Lee (U.K.: Cambridge Scholars, 2015); and Luis Luna, "Welcome Rotonda to Have New Name," *Manila Standard,* May 5, 1995.

332 **back of the head . . . Died fourteen minutes past one in the afternoon:** Gerard N. Hill and Kathleen Thompson Hill, *The True Story and Analysis of the Aquino Assassination* (Sonoma, Calif.: Hilltop, 1983).

332 **What a queer coincidence:** Rodrigo Duterte, drawn from speech at the oath-taking ceremony of Davao City mayor-elect Sebastian "Baste" Z. Duterte, City Hall, Davao City, June 27, 2022.

333 **gasping out Mama:** Normita Lopez, drawn from interview by the author, March 1, 2023. In this fact-check interview, Lopez spoke of an unnamed witness who claimed to have seen the final moments of Djastin Lopez's life, describing Djastin's gasping attempt to mouth "Mama," in spite of the blood spilling out of his mouth.

333–35 **killed on the last Sunday . . . same railroad tracks . . . third of his** brothers . . . jailed on drug charges . . . in the gut . . . shot six times . . . down the street from his grandmother's . . . equipped for gunshot wounds . . . push when the police refused . . . knew to double down . . . same as for JR . . . salvaged with his fingernails ripped out . . . five dollars for ten . . . suit for sale . . . volunteer to carry the coffin . . . wilting white mums . . . white to the funeral . . . hundred dollars would cover the fee . . . Cristina sometimes forgot . . . how many the government has killed: All details on the killing of Mark Andy Ocdin and his brothers are drawn from the author's coverage of Mark Andy Ocdin's wake and author's interviews with Cristina Omolan (Mark Andy's mother), Criselda (Mark Andy's sister), and Hazel Nabua (Mark Andy's cousin) on June 30 and July 10, 2022.

335 Vincent had stayed to document the dead . . . yellow star for every corpse . . . might have voted for Duterte: Vincent Go (photojournalist), interview by the author, March 31, 2023.

336 Ask Normy Lopez: Normita Lopez, interview by the author, April 23, 2020.

337 "I have asked myself many times" . . . "he is worth dying for" . . . "nation's greatest untapped resource": Benigno Aquino, Jr., quoted from speech at the Asia Society, New York, August 4, 1980. The full speech is available at "The Filipino Is Worth Dying For," *Manila Times,* August 22, 2010.

338–39 Ivy lost her job . . . run up the bridge faster . . . might have let him live . . . "You wanted Daddy to die": Ivy Desierto (widow of Rene Desierto), interviews by the author, 2016, 2018, and 2020.

© MARK NICDAO

PATRICIA EVANGELISTA is a trauma journalist and former investigative reporter for the Philippine news company Rappler. Her reporting on armed conflict and the aftermath of Super Typhoon Haiyan was awarded the Kate Webb Prize for exceptional journalism in dangerous conditions. She was a Headlands Artist in Residence, a recipient of the Whiting Creative Nonfiction Grant, an ASU Future Security Fellow at New America, and a fellow of the Logan Nonfiction Program, the Marshall McLuhan Fellowship, the De La Salle University Democracy Discourse Series, and the Dart Center for Journalism and Trauma. Her work investigating President Rodrigo Duterte's drug war has earned a number of local and international accolades. She lives in Manila.

Twitter and Instagram: @patevangelista